TEEN TITANS

VOL.3 THE RETURN OF KID FLASH

BENJAMIN PERCY * **MARV WOLFMAN** * **SHEA FONTANA**
writers

SCOT EATON * **KHOI PHAM**
TOM DERENICK * **OTTO SCHMIDT**
pencillers

TREVOR SCOTT * **VICENTE CIFUENTES** * **NORM RAPMUND**
WAYNE FAUCHER * **OTTO SCHMIDT**
inkers

JIM CHARALAMPIDIS * **BLOND** * **OTTO SCHMIDT**
colorists

COREY BREEN * **CARLOS M. MANGUAL**
letterers

DAN MORA
collection cover artist

STARFIRE created by **MARV WOLFMAN** and **GEORGE PÉREZ**
BEAST BOY created by **ARNOLD DRAKE**

ALEX ANTONE **DAVE WIELGOSZ** Editors - Original Series
BRITTANY HOLZHERR **REBECCA TAYLOR** Associate Editors - Original Series
JEB WOODARD Group Editor - Collected Editions ✳ **ROBIN WILDMAN** Editor - Collected Edition
STEVE COOK Design Director - Books ✳ **MONIQUE NARBONETA** Publication Design

BOB HARRAS Senior VP - Editor-in-Chief, DC Comics
PAT McCALLUM Executive Editor, DC Comics

DAN DiDIO Publisher ✳ **JIM LEE** Publisher & Chief Creative Officer
AMIT DESAI Executive VP - Business & Marketing Strategy, Direct to Consumer & Global Franchise Management
BOBBIE CHASE VP & Executive Editor, Young Reader & Talent Development ✳ **MARK CHIARELLO** Senior VP - Art, Design & Collected Editions
JOHN CUNNINGHAM Senior VP - Sales & Trade Marketing ✳ **BRIAR DARDEN** VP - Business Affairs
ANNE DePIES Senior VP - Business Strategy, Finance & Administration ✳ **DON FALLETTI** VP - Manufacturing Operations
LAWRENCE GANEM VP - Editorial Administration & Talent Relations ✳ **ALISON GILL** Senior VP - Manufacturing & Operations
JASON GREENBERG VP - Business Strategy & Finance ✳ **HANK KANALZ** Senior VP - Editorial Strategy & Administration
JAY KOGAN Senior VP - Legal Affairs ✳ **NICK J. NAPOLITANO** VP - Manufacturing Administration
LISETTE OSTERLOH VP - Digital Marketing & Events ✳ **EDDIE SCANNELL** VP - Consumer Marketing
COURTNEY SIMMONS Senior VP - Publicity & Communications ✳ **JIM (SKI) SOKOLOWSKI** VP - Comic Book Specialty Sales & Trade Marketing
NANCY SPEARS VP - Mass, Book, Digital Sales & Trade Marketing ✳ **MICHELE R. WELLS** VP - Content Strategy

TEEN TITANS VOL. 3: THE RETURN OF KID FLASH

Published by DC Comics. Compilation and all new material Copyright © 2018 DC Comics. All Rights Reserved.
Originally published in single magazine form in TEEN TITANS 13-14, 16-19, DC HOLIDAY SPECIAL 2017 1. Copyright © 2017, 2018 DC Comics.
All Rights Reserved. All characters, their distinctive likenesses and related elements featured in this publication are trademarks of DC Comics.
The stories, characters and incidents featured in this publication are entirely fictional.
DC Comics does not read or accept unsolicited submissions of ideas, stories or artwork.

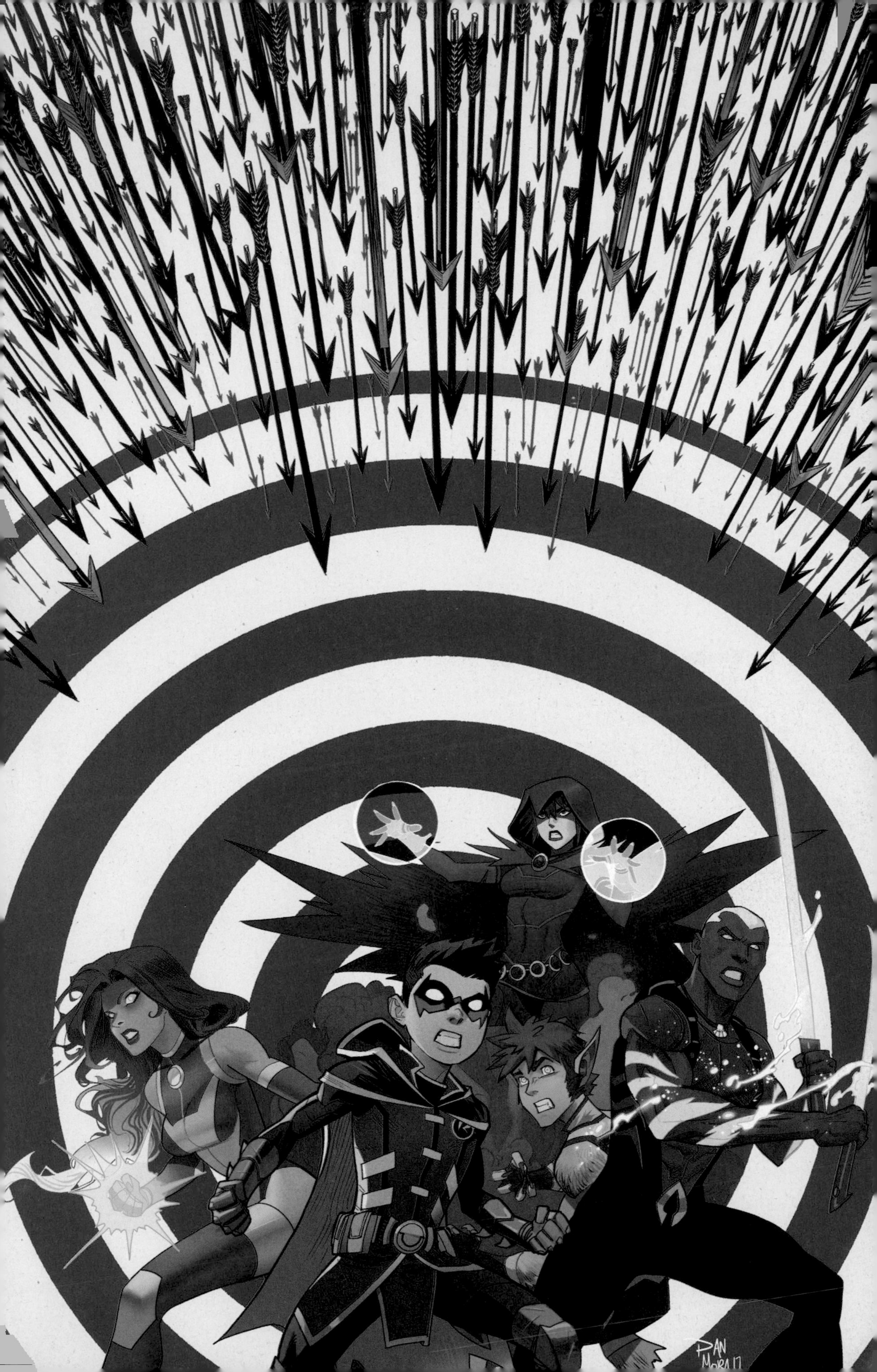
DAN MORA 17

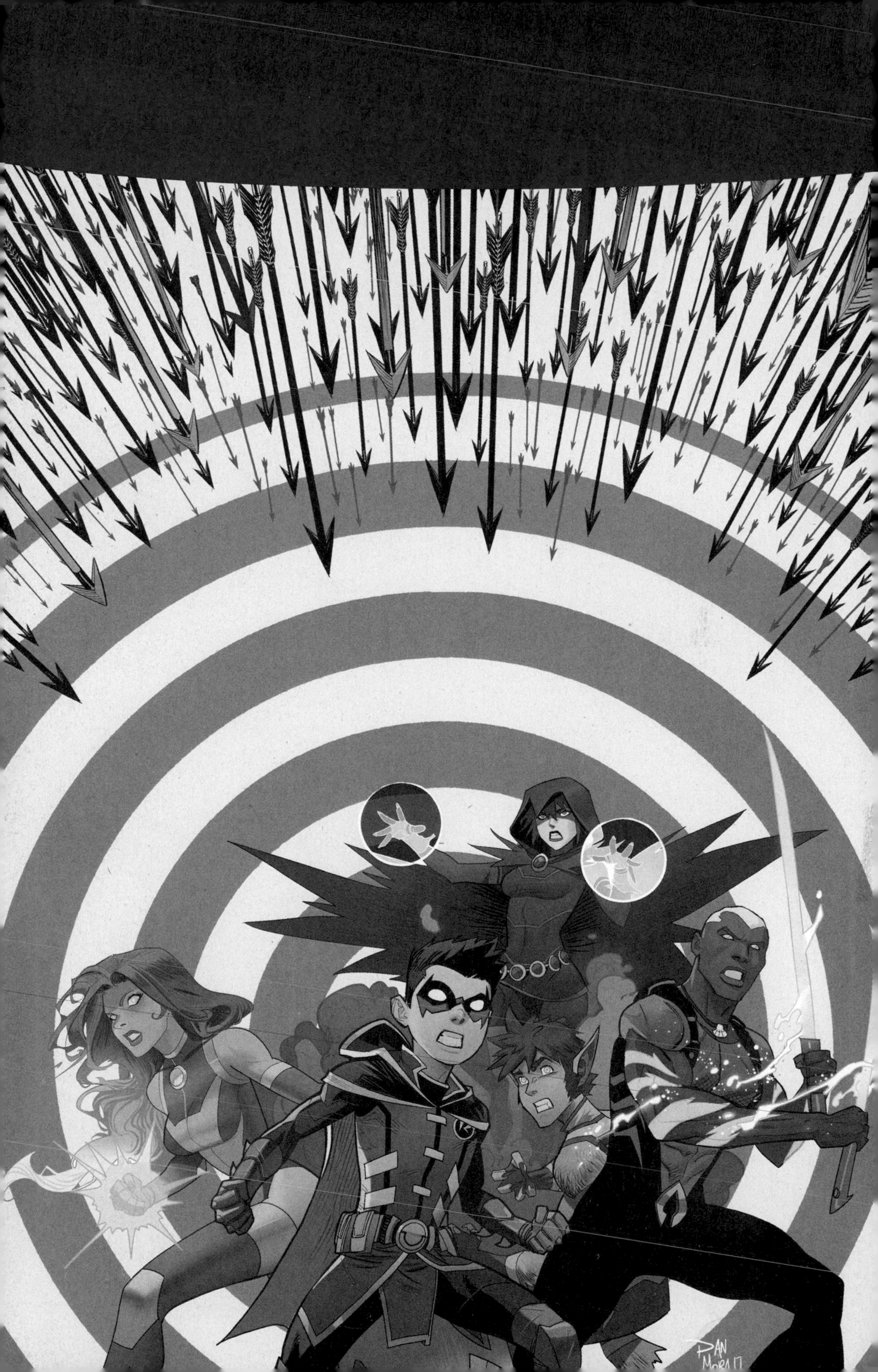
DAN MORA 17

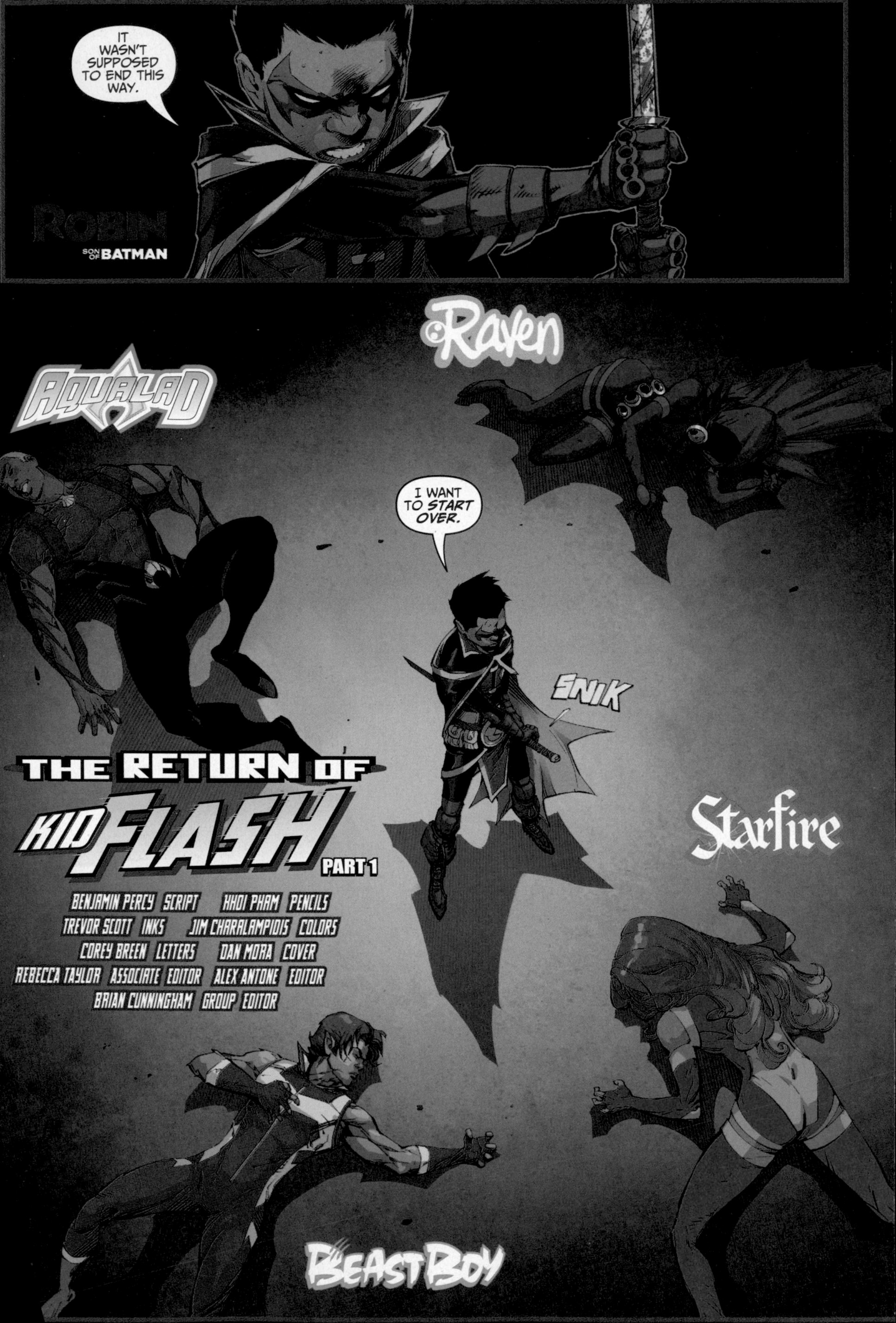
IT WASN'T SUPPOSED TO END THIS WAY.
ROBIN
SON OF BATMAN
Raven
AQUALAD
I WANT TO START OVER.
SNIK
THE RETURN OF
KID FLASH
PART 1
BENJAMIN PERCY SCRIPT KHOI PHAM PENCILS
TREVOR SCOTT INKS JIM CHARALAMPIDIS COLORS
COREY BREEN LETTERS DAN MORA COVER
REBECCA TAYLOR ASSOCIATE EDITOR ALEX ANTONE EDITOR
BRIAN CUNNINGHAM GROUP EDITOR
Starfire
BEAST BOY

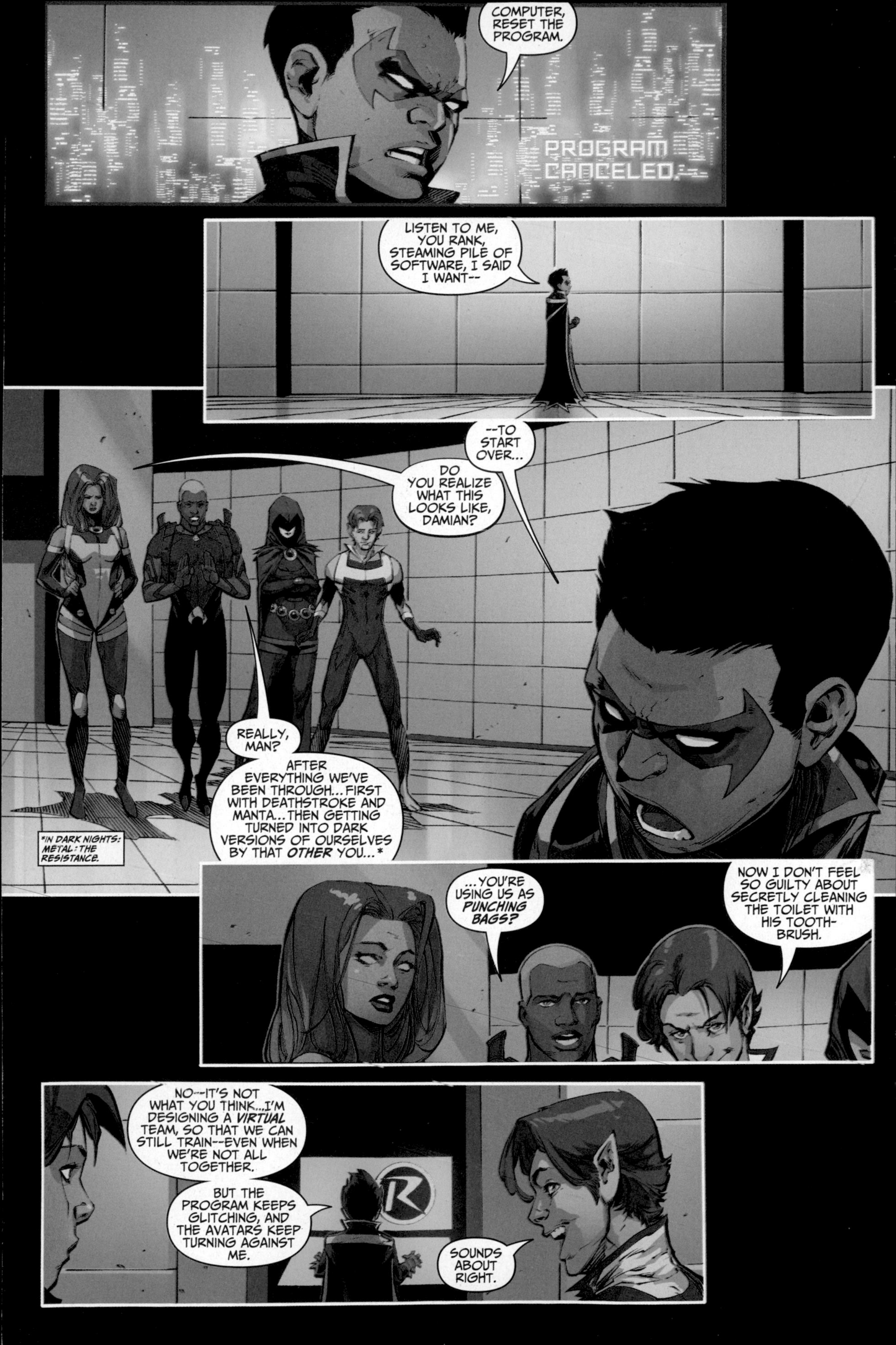
COMPUTER, RESET THE PROGRAM.
PROGRAM CANCELED.
LISTEN TO ME, YOU RANK, STEAMING PILE OF SOFTWARE, I SAID I WANT--
--TO START OVER...
DO YOU REALIZE WHAT THIS LOOKS LIKE, DAMIAN?
REALLY, MAN?
AFTER EVERYTHING WE'VE BEEN THROUGH... FIRST WITH DEATHSTROKE AND MANTA... THEN GETTING TURNED INTO DARK VERSIONS OF OURSELVES BY THAT OTHER YOU...*
*IN DARK NIGHTS: METAL: THE RESISTANCE.
...YOU'RE USING US AS PUNCHING BAGS?
NOW I DON'T FEEL SO GUILTY ABOUT SECRETLY CLEANING THE TOILET WITH HIS TOOTH-BRUSH.
NO--IT'S NOT WHAT YOU THINK...I'M DESIGNING A VIRTUAL TEAM, SO THAT WE CAN STILL TRAIN--EVEN WHEN WE'RE NOT ALL TOGETHER.
BUT THE PROGRAM KEEPS GLITCHING, AND THE AVATARS KEEP TURNING AGAINST ME.
SOUNDS ABOUT RIGHT.

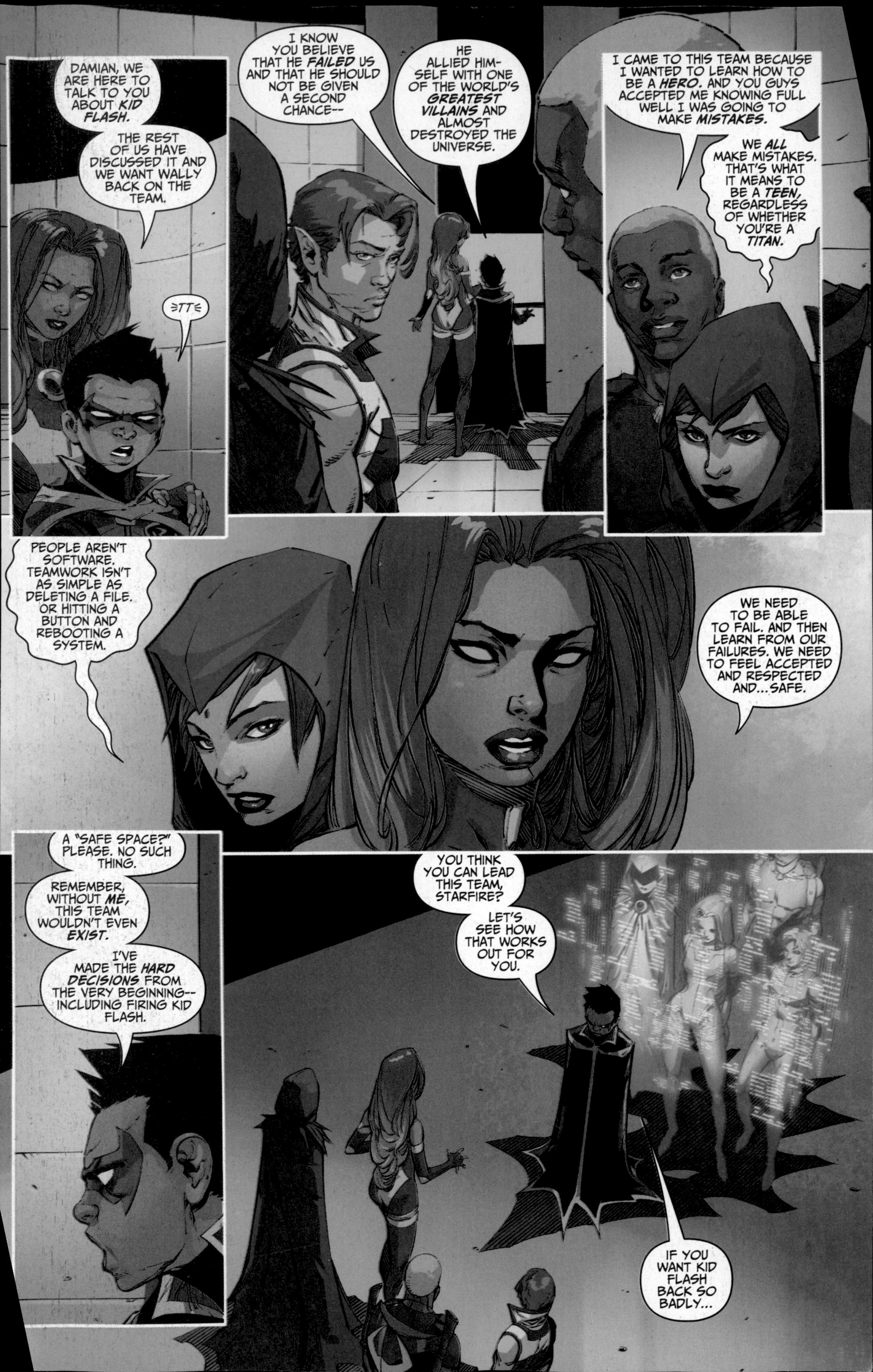
DAMIAN, WE ARE HERE TO TALK TO YOU ABOUT KID FLASH.
THE REST OF US HAVE DISCUSSED IT AND WE WANT WALLY BACK ON THE TEAM.
TT
I KNOW YOU BELIEVE THAT HE FAILED US AND THAT HE SHOULD NOT BE GIVEN A SECOND CHANCE--
HE ALLIED HIMSELF WITH ONE OF THE WORLD'S GREATEST VILLAINS AND ALMOST DESTROYED THE UNIVERSE.
I CAME TO THIS TEAM BECAUSE I WANTED TO LEARN HOW TO BE A HERO. AND YOU GUYS ACCEPTED ME KNOWING FULL WELL I WAS GOING TO MAKE MISTAKES.
WE ALL MAKE MISTAKES. THAT'S WHAT IT MEANS TO BE A TEEN, REGARDLESS OF WHETHER YOU'RE A TITAN.
PEOPLE AREN'T SOFTWARE. TEAMWORK ISN'T AS SIMPLE AS DELETING A FILE. OR HITTING A BUTTON AND REBOOTING A SYSTEM.
WE NEED TO BE ABLE TO FAIL. AND THEN LEARN FROM OUR FAILURES. WE NEED TO FEEL ACCEPTED AND RESPECTED AND...SAFE.
A "SAFE SPACE?" PLEASE. NO SUCH THING.
REMEMBER, WITHOUT ME, THIS TEAM WOULDN'T EVEN EXIST.
I'VE MADE THE HARD DECISIONS FROM THE VERY BEGINNING-- INCLUDING FIRING KID FLASH.
YOU THINK YOU CAN LEAD THIS TEAM, STARFIRE?
LET'S SEE HOW THAT WORKS OUT FOR YOU.
IF YOU WANT KID FLASH BACK SO BADLY...

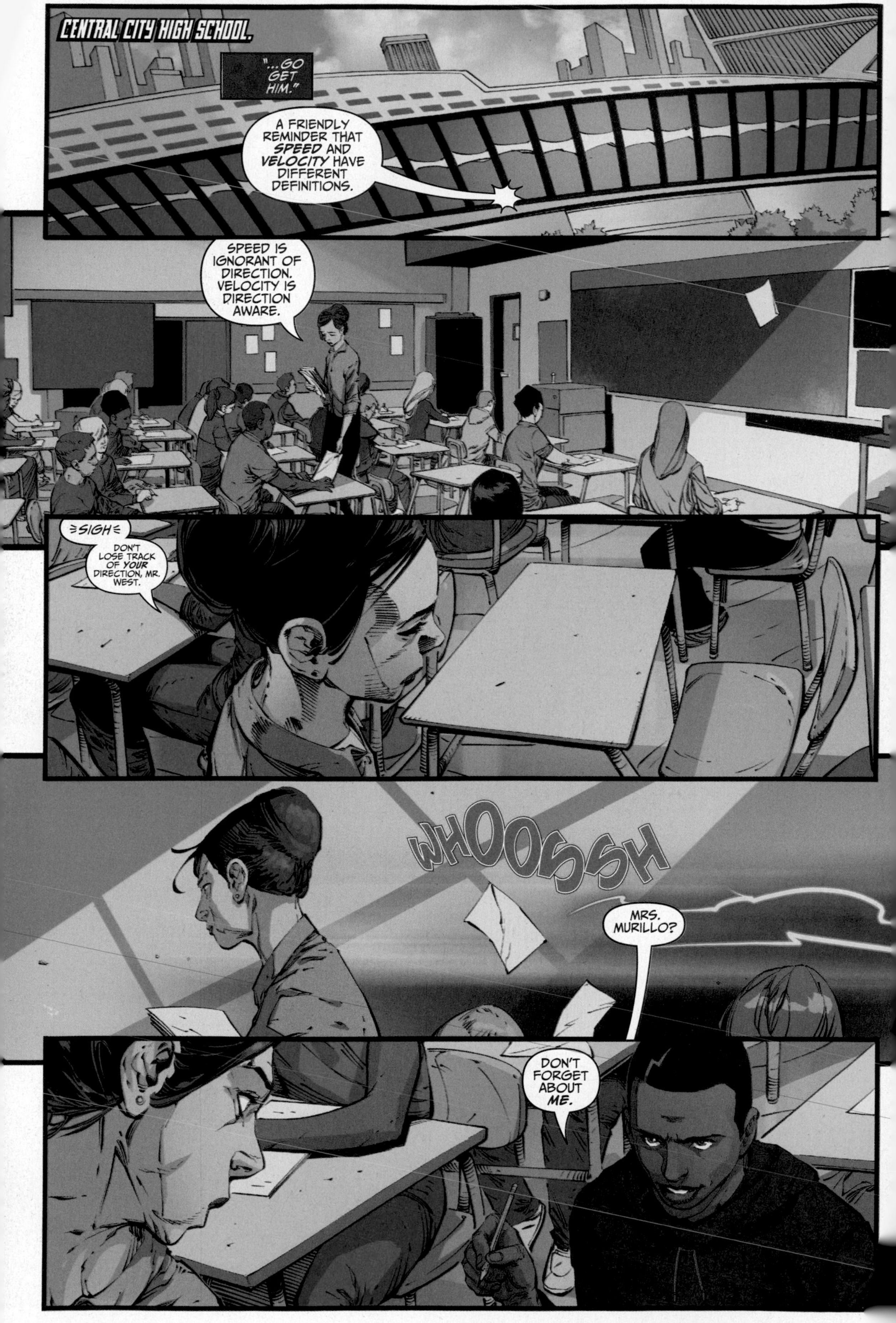
CENTRAL CITY HIGH SCHOOL.
"...GO GET HIM."
A FRIENDLY REMINDER THAT SPEED AND VELOCITY HAVE DIFFERENT DEFINITIONS.
SPEED IS IGNORANT OF DIRECTION. VELOCITY IS DIRECTION AWARE.
SIGH
DON'T LOSE TRACK OF YOUR DIRECTION, MR. WEST.
WHOOOSSH
MRS. MURILLO?
DON'T FORGET ABOUT ME.

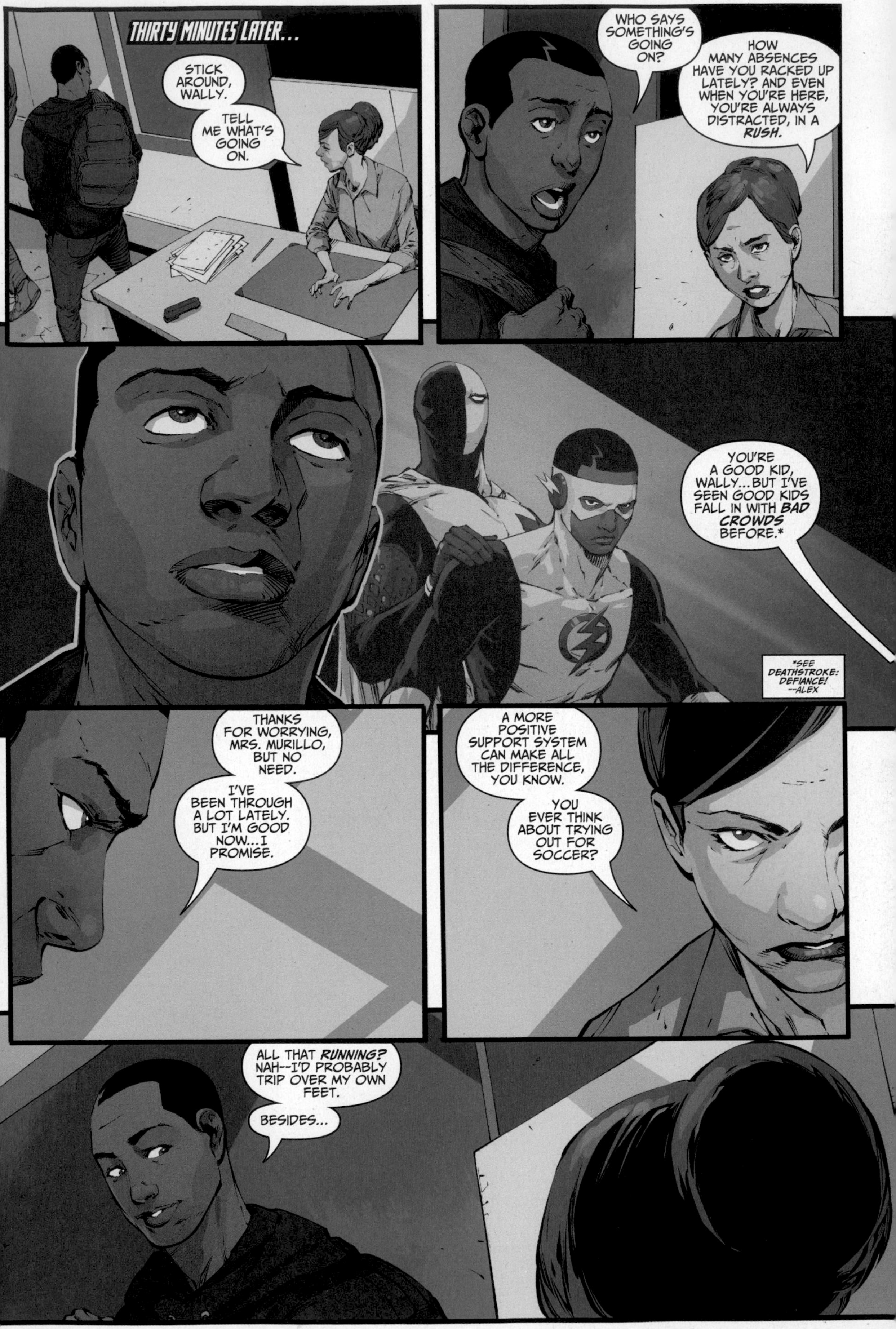
THIRTY MINUTES LATER...
STICK AROUND, WALLY.
TELL ME WHAT'S GOING ON.
WHO SAYS SOMETHING'S GOING ON?
HOW MANY ABSENCES HAVE YOU RACKED UP LATELY? AND EVEN WHEN YOU'RE HERE, YOU'RE ALWAYS DISTRACTED, IN A RUSH.
YOU'RE A GOOD KID, WALLY...BUT I'VE SEEN GOOD KIDS FALL IN WITH BAD CROWDS BEFORE.*
*SEE DEATHSTROKE: DEFIANCE! --ALEX
THANKS FOR WORRYING, MRS. MURILLO, BUT NO NEED.
I'VE BEEN THROUGH A LOT LATELY. BUT I'M GOOD NOW...I PROMISE.
A MORE POSITIVE SUPPORT SYSTEM CAN MAKE ALL THE DIFFERENCE, YOU KNOW.
YOU EVER THINK ABOUT TRYING OUT FOR SOCCER?
ALL THAT RUNNING? NAH--I'D PROBABLY TRIP OVER MY OWN FEET.
BESIDES...

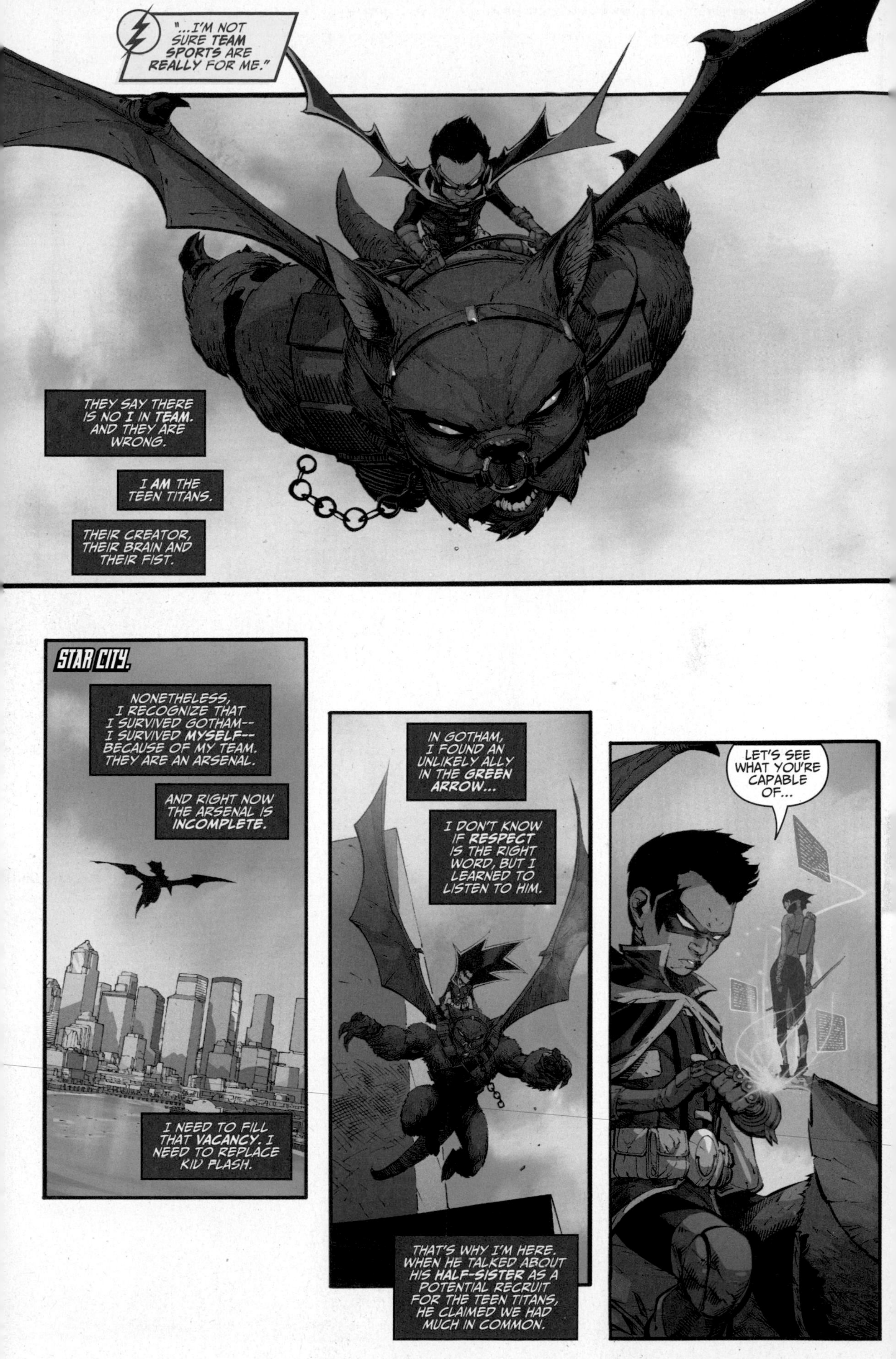

"...I'M NOT SURE TEAM SPORTS ARE REALLY FOR ME."
THEY SAY THERE IS NO I IN TEAM. AND THEY ARE WRONG.
I AM THE TEEN TITANS.
THEIR CREATOR, THEIR BRAIN AND THEIR FIST.
STAR CITY.
NONETHELESS, I RECOGNIZE THAT I SURVIVED GOTHAM-- I SURVIVED MYSELF-- BECAUSE OF MY TEAM. THEY ARE AN ARSENAL.
AND RIGHT NOW THE ARSENAL IS INCOMPLETE.
I NEED TO FILL THAT VACANCY. I NEED TO REPLACE KID FLASH.
IN GOTHAM, I FOUND AN UNLIKELY ALLY IN THE GREEN ARROW...
I DON'T KNOW IF RESPECT IS THE RIGHT WORD, BUT I LEARNED TO LISTEN TO HIM.
THAT'S WHY I'M HERE. WHEN HE TALKED ABOUT HIS HALF-SISTER AS A POTENTIAL RECRUIT FOR THE TEEN TITANS, HE CLAIMED WE HAD MUCH IN COMMON.
LET'S SEE WHAT YOU'RE CAPABLE OF...

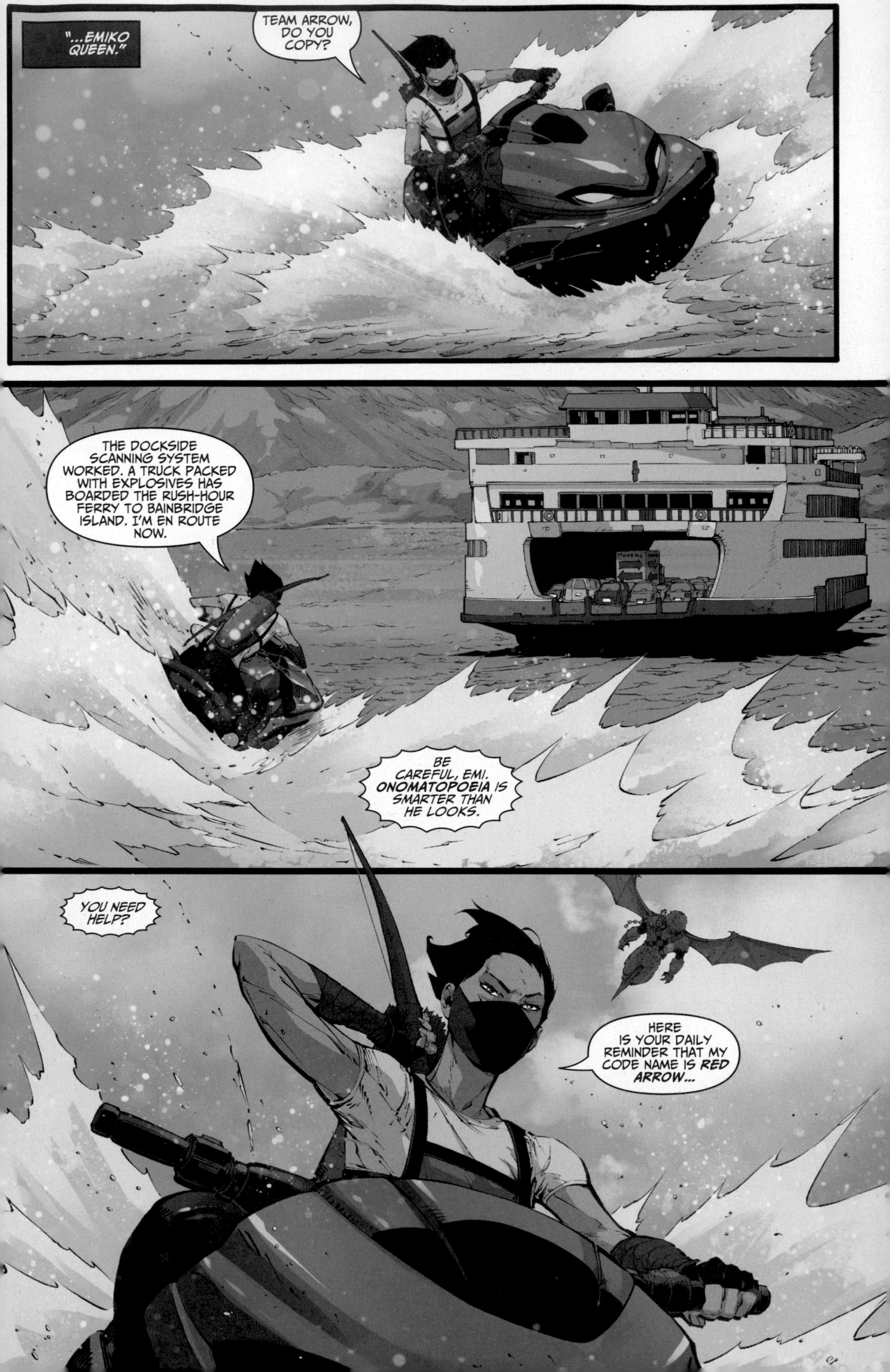
"...EMIKO QUEEN."
TEAM ARROW, DO YOU COPY?
THE DOCKSIDE SCANNING SYSTEM WORKED. A TRUCK PACKED WITH EXPLOSIVES HAS BOARDED THE RUSH-HOUR FERRY TO BAINBRIDGE ISLAND. I'M EN ROUTE NOW.
MOVERS
BE CAREFUL, EMI. ONOMATOPOEIA IS SMARTER THAN HE LOOKS.
YOU NEED HELP?
HERE IS YOUR DAILY REMINDER THAT MY CODE NAME IS RED ARROW...

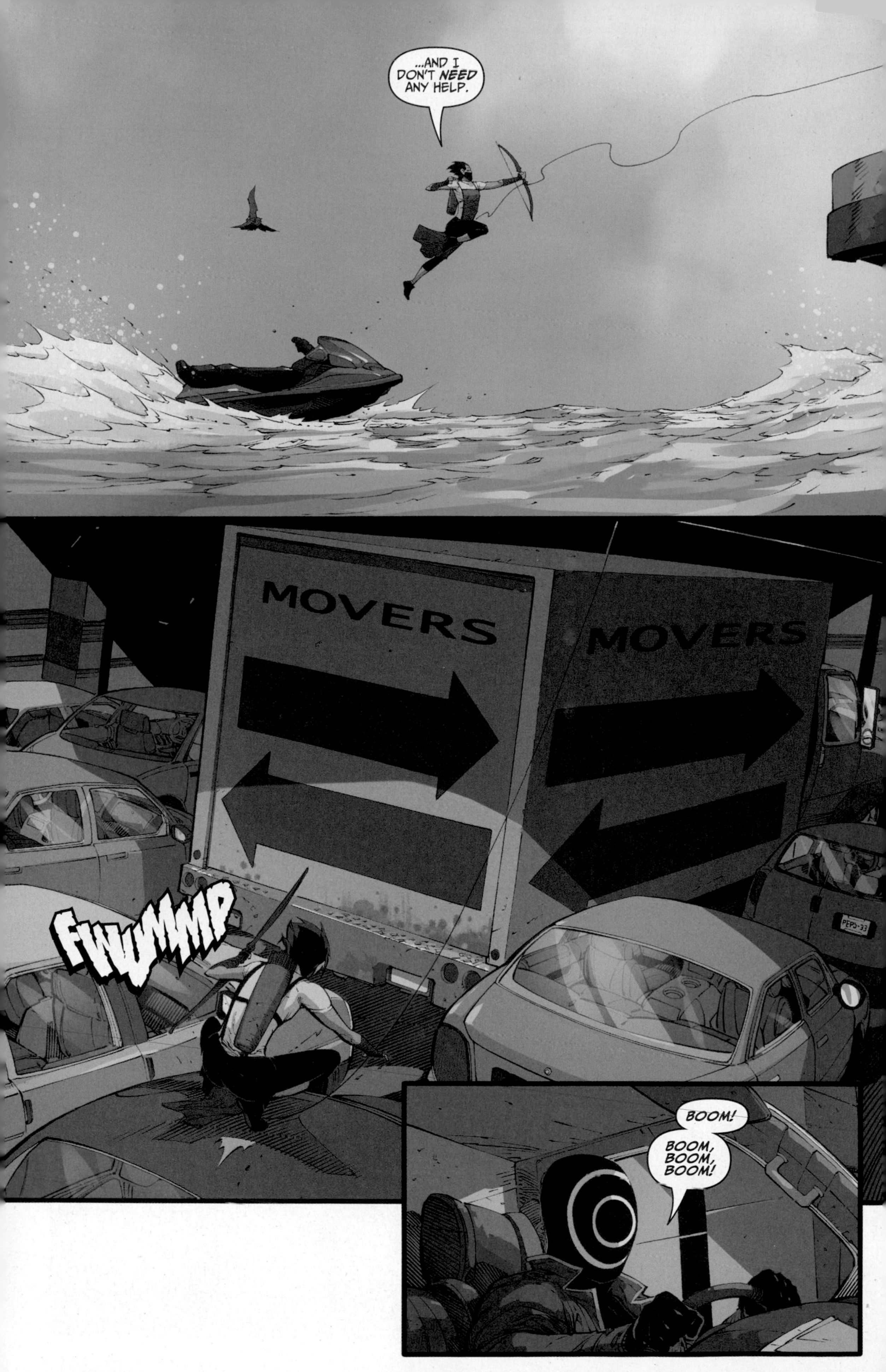
...AND I DON'T NEED ANY HELP.
MOVERS
MOVERS
FWUMMP
BOOM!
BOOM, BOOM, BOOM!

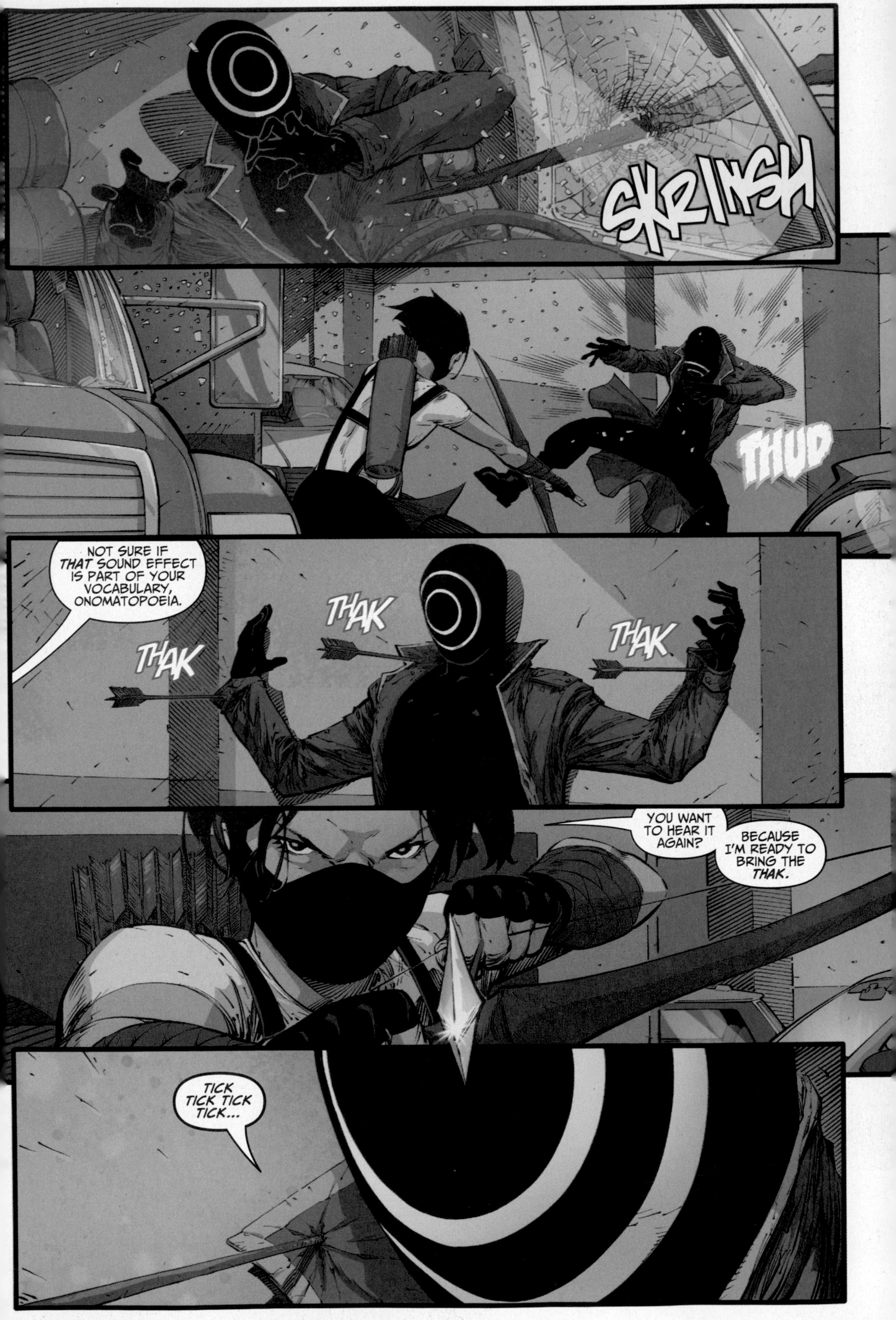
SKRISH
THUD
NOT SURE IF *THAT* SOUND EFFECT IS PART OF YOUR VOCABULARY, ONOMATOPOEIA.
THAK
THAK
THAK
YOU WANT TO HEAR IT AGAIN?
BECAUSE I'M READY TO BRING THE *THAK*.
TICK TICK TICK TICK...

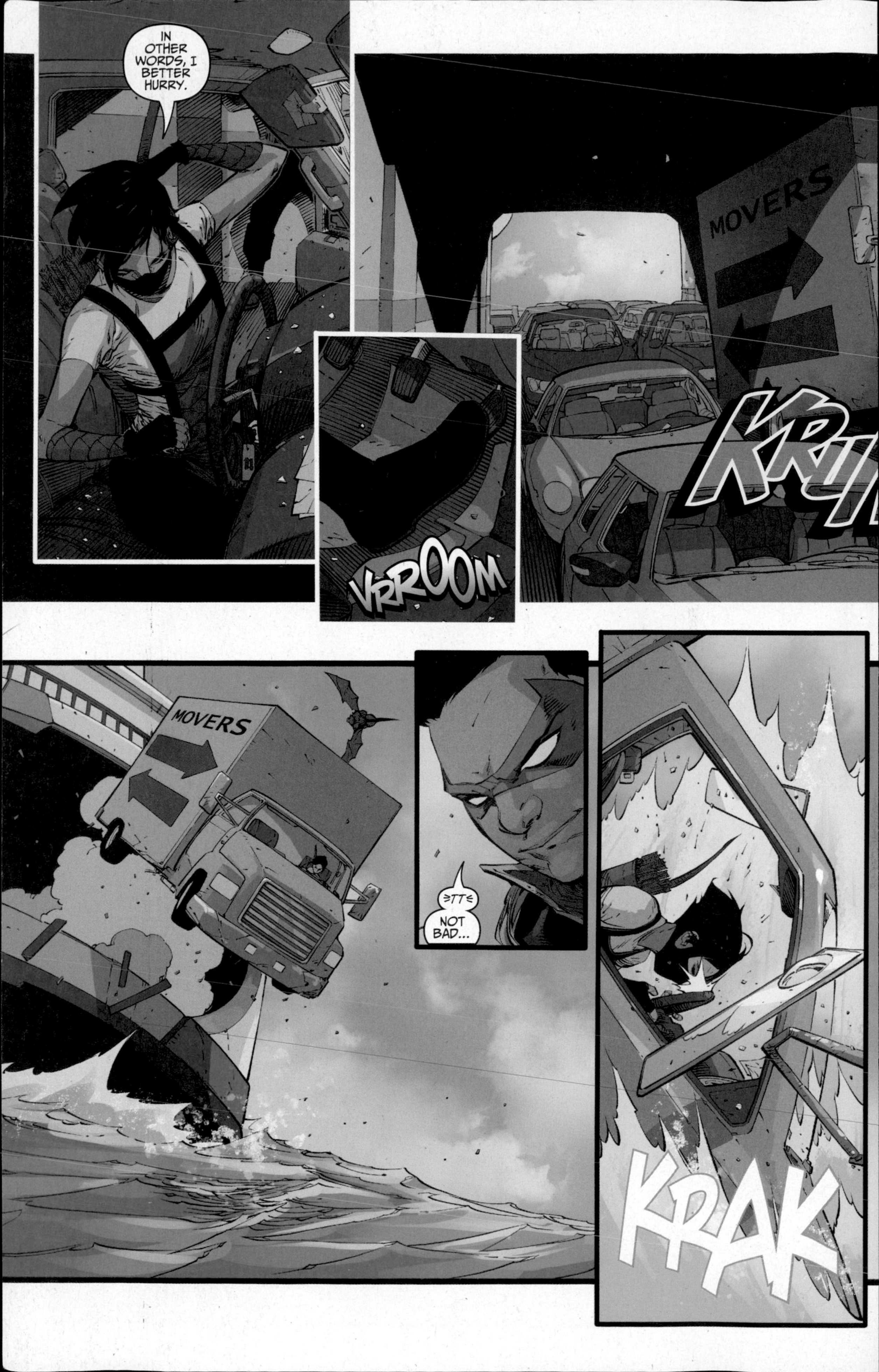

IN OTHER WORDS, I BETTER HURRY.
MOVERS
VRROOM
KRU
MOVERS
TT
NOT BAD...
KRAK

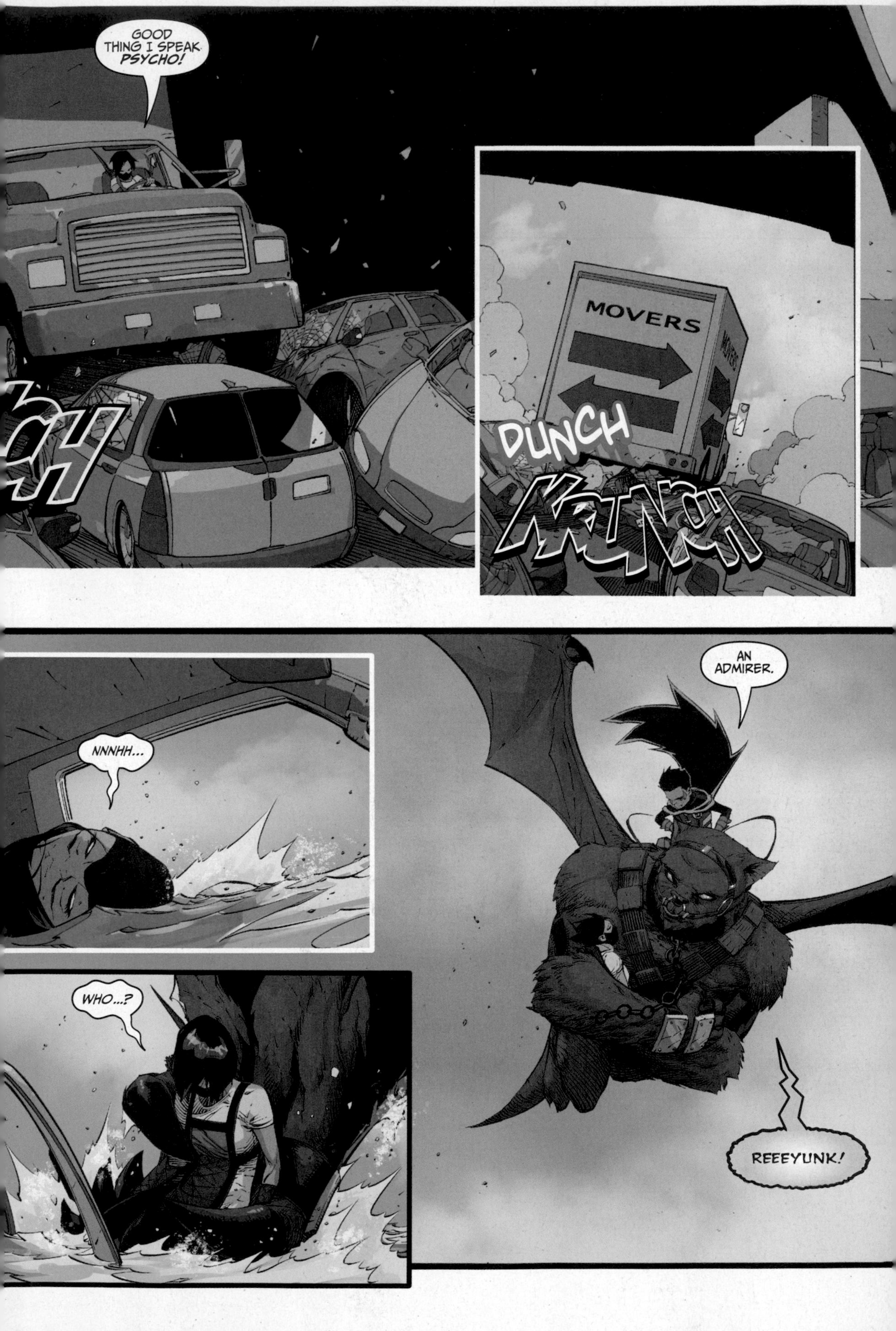
GOOD THING I SPEAK PSYCHO!
MOVERS
MOVERS
DUNCH
KRUNCH
NNNHH...
WHO...?
AN ADMIRER.
REEEYUNK!

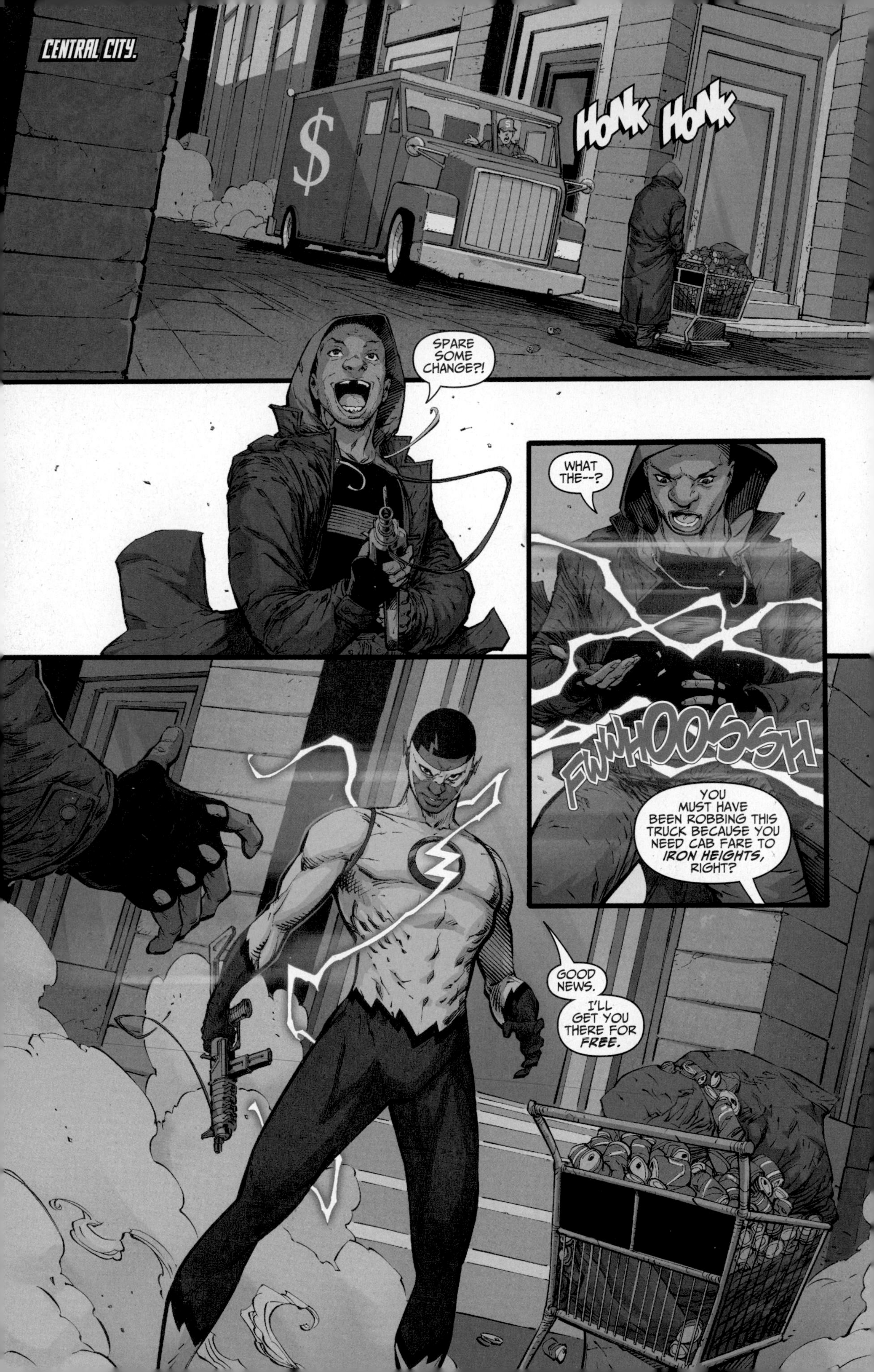
CENTRAL CITY.
HONK HONK
SPARE SOME CHANGE?!
WHAT THE--?
FWWHOOSSH
YOU MUST HAVE BEEN ROBBING THIS TRUCK BECAUSE YOU NEED CAB FARE TO IRON HEIGHTS, RIGHT?
GOOD NEWS.
I'LL GET YOU THERE FOR FREE.

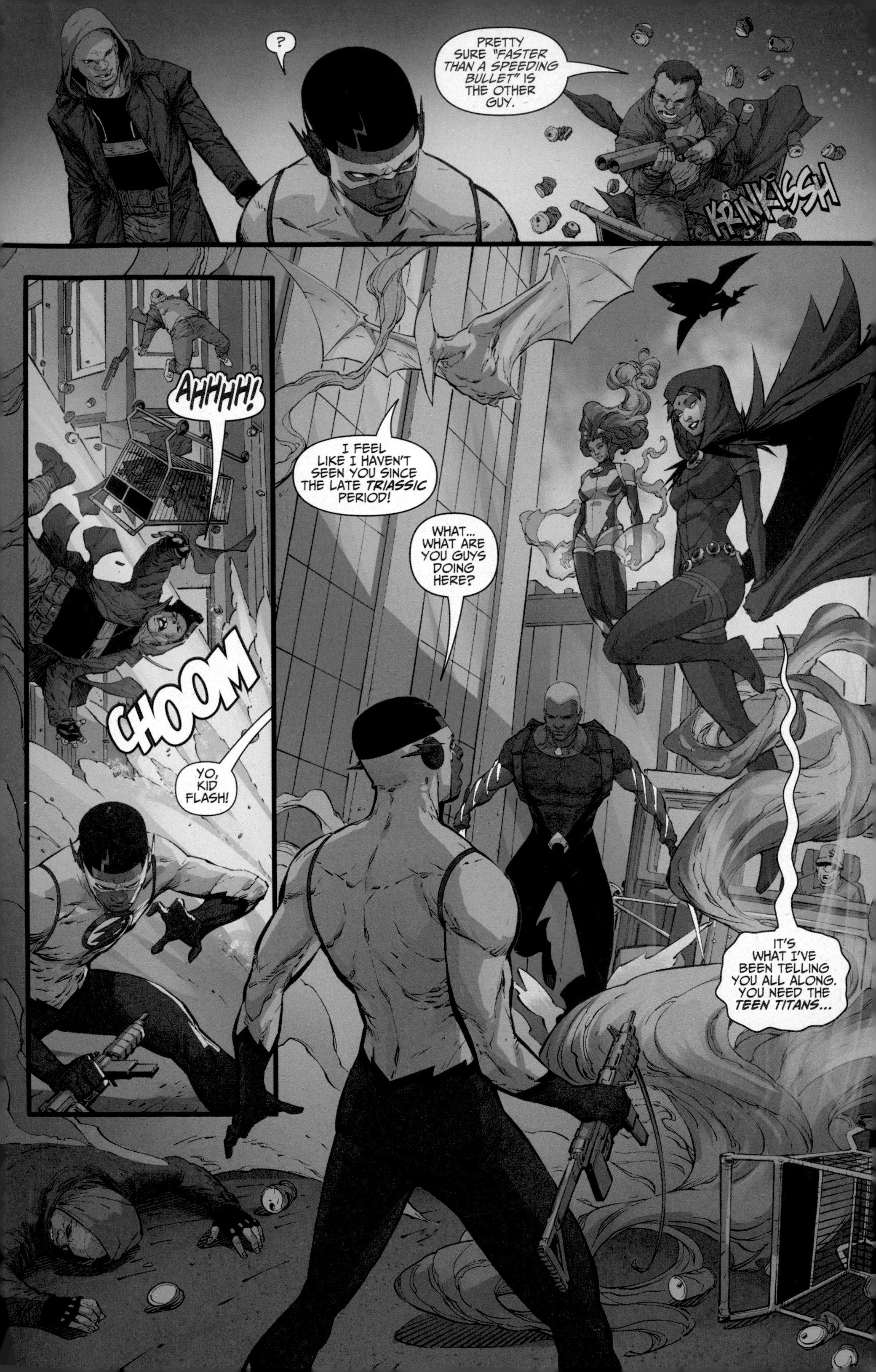
?
PRETTY SURE "FASTER THAN A SPEEDING BULLET" IS THE OTHER GUY.
KRINKSSH
AHHHH!
CHOOM
YO, KID FLASH!
I FEEL LIKE I HAVEN'T SEEN YOU SINCE THE LATE TRIASSIC PERIOD!
WHAT... WHAT ARE YOU GUYS DOING HERE?
IT'S WHAT I'VE BEEN TELLING YOU ALL ALONG. YOU NEED THE TEEN TITANS...

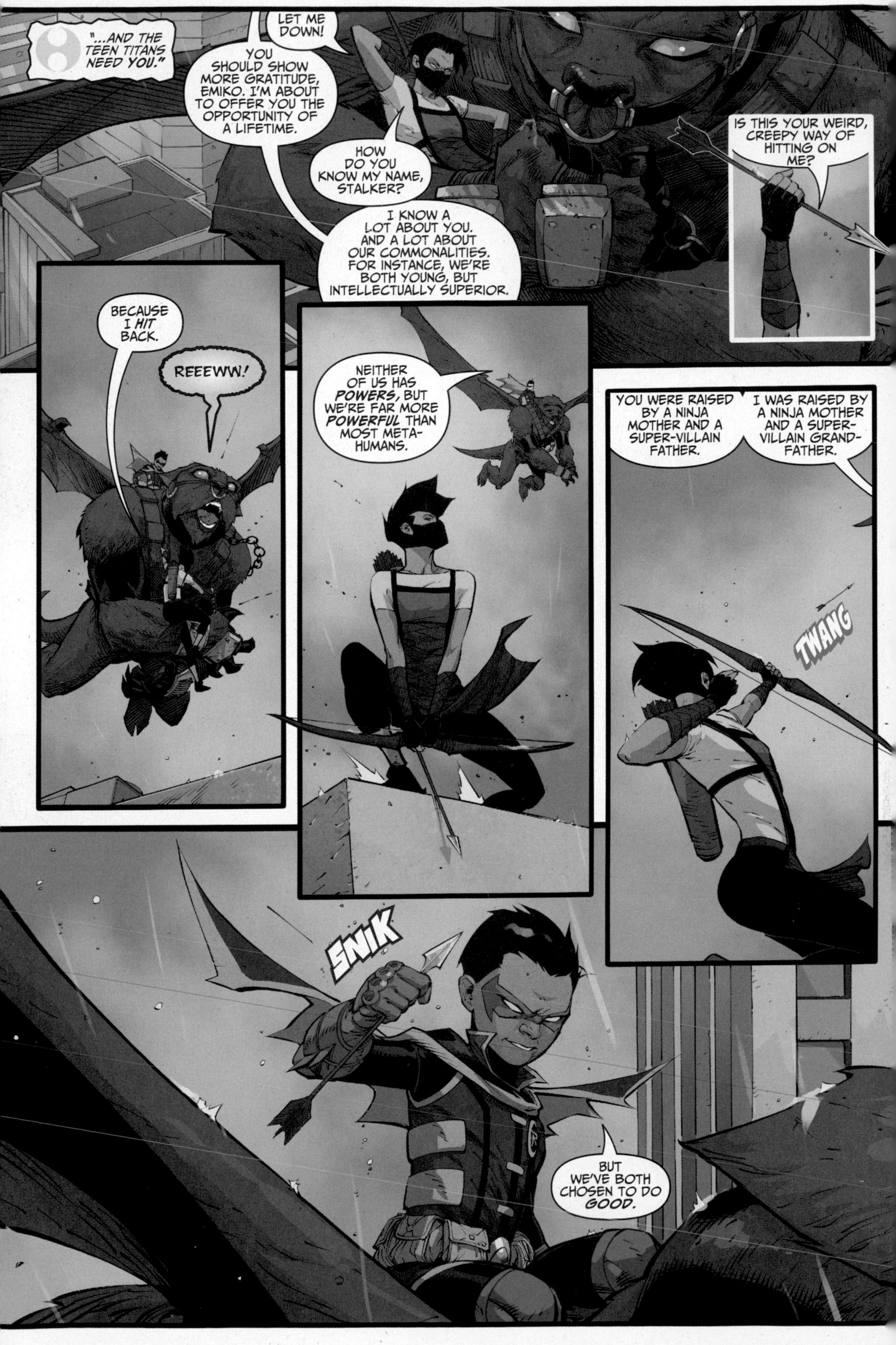
"...AND THE TEEN TITANS NEED YOU."
LET ME DOWN!
YOU SHOULD SHOW MORE GRATITUDE, EMIKO. I'M ABOUT TO OFFER YOU THE OPPORTUNITY OF A LIFETIME.
HOW DO YOU KNOW MY NAME, STALKER?
I KNOW A LOT ABOUT YOU. AND A LOT ABOUT OUR COMMONALITIES. FOR INSTANCE, WE'RE BOTH YOUNG, BUT INTELLECTUALLY SUPERIOR.
IS THIS YOUR WEIRD, CREEPY WAY OF HITTING ON ME?
BECAUSE I HIT BACK.
REEEWW!
NEITHER OF US HAS POWERS, BUT WE'RE FAR MORE POWERFUL THAN MOST META-HUMANS.
YOU WERE RAISED BY A NINJA MOTHER AND A SUPER-VILLAIN FATHER.
I WAS RAISED BY A NINJA MOTHER AND A SUPER-VILLAIN GRAND-FATHER.
TWANG
SNIK
BUT WE'VE BOTH CHOSEN TO DO GOOD.

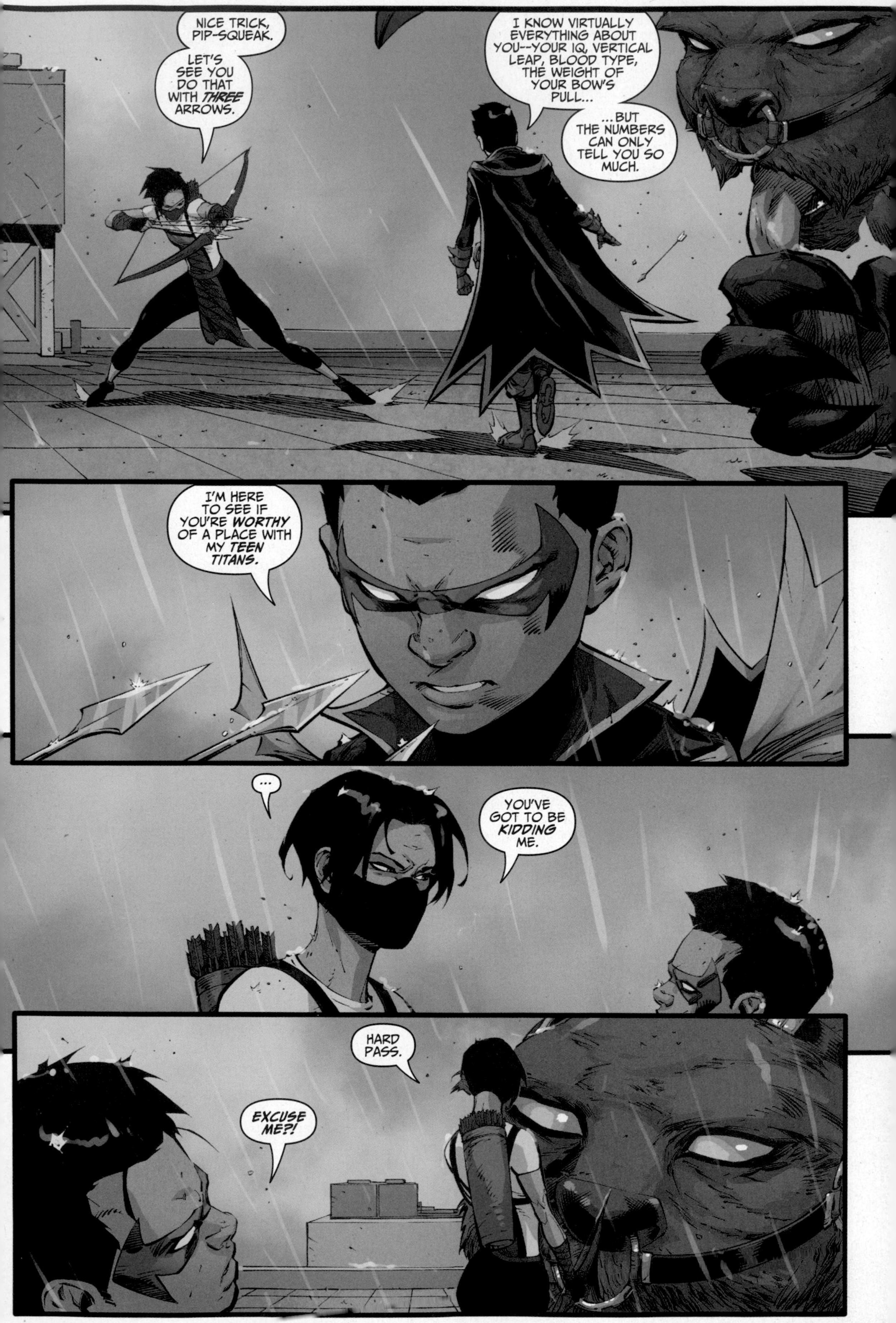
NICE TRICK, PIP-SQUEAK.
LET'S SEE YOU DO THAT WITH THREE ARROWS.
I KNOW VIRTUALLY EVERYTHING ABOUT YOU--YOUR IQ, VERTICAL LEAP, BLOOD TYPE, THE WEIGHT OF YOUR BOW'S PULL...
...BUT THE NUMBERS CAN ONLY TELL YOU SO MUCH.
I'M HERE TO SEE IF YOU'RE WORTHY OF A PLACE WITH MY TEEN TITANS.
...
YOU'VE GOT TO BE KIDDING ME.
HARD PASS.
EXCUSE ME?!

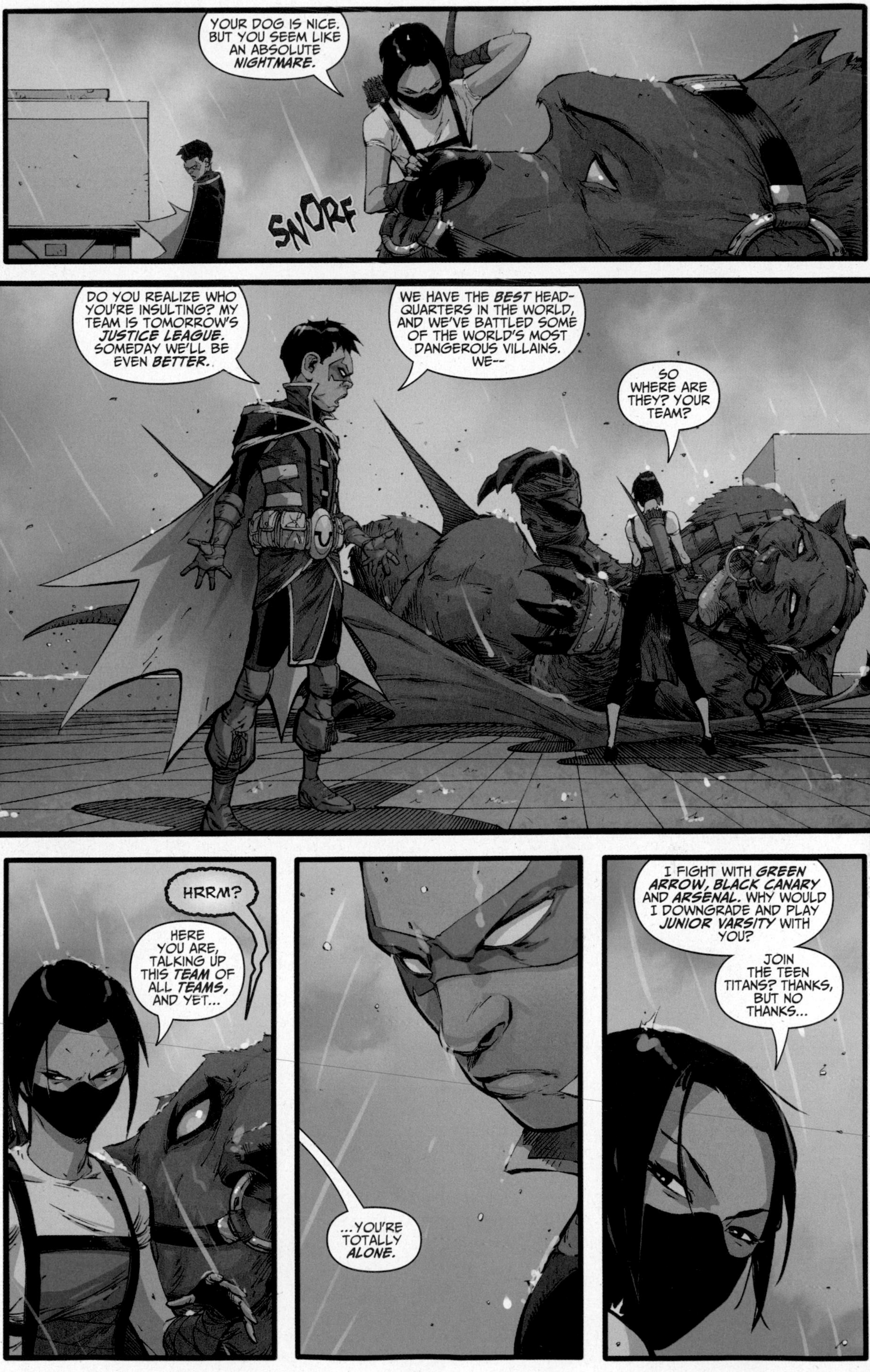
YOUR DOG IS NICE. BUT YOU SEEM LIKE AN ABSOLUTE NIGHTMARE.
SNORF
DO YOU REALIZE WHO YOU'RE INSULTING? MY TEAM IS TOMORROW'S JUSTICE LEAGUE. SOMEDAY WE'LL BE EVEN BETTER.
WE HAVE THE BEST HEAD-QUARTERS IN THE WORLD, AND WE'VE BATTLED SOME OF THE WORLD'S MOST DANGEROUS VILLAINS. WE--
SO WHERE ARE THEY? YOUR TEAM?
HRRM?
HERE YOU ARE, TALKING UP THIS TEAM OF ALL TEAMS, AND YET...
...YOU'RE TOTALLY ALONE.
I FIGHT WITH GREEN ARROW, BLACK CANARY AND ARSENAL. WHY WOULD I DOWNGRADE AND PLAY JUNIOR VARSITY WITH YOU?
JOIN THE TEEN TITANS? THANKS, BUT NO THANKS...

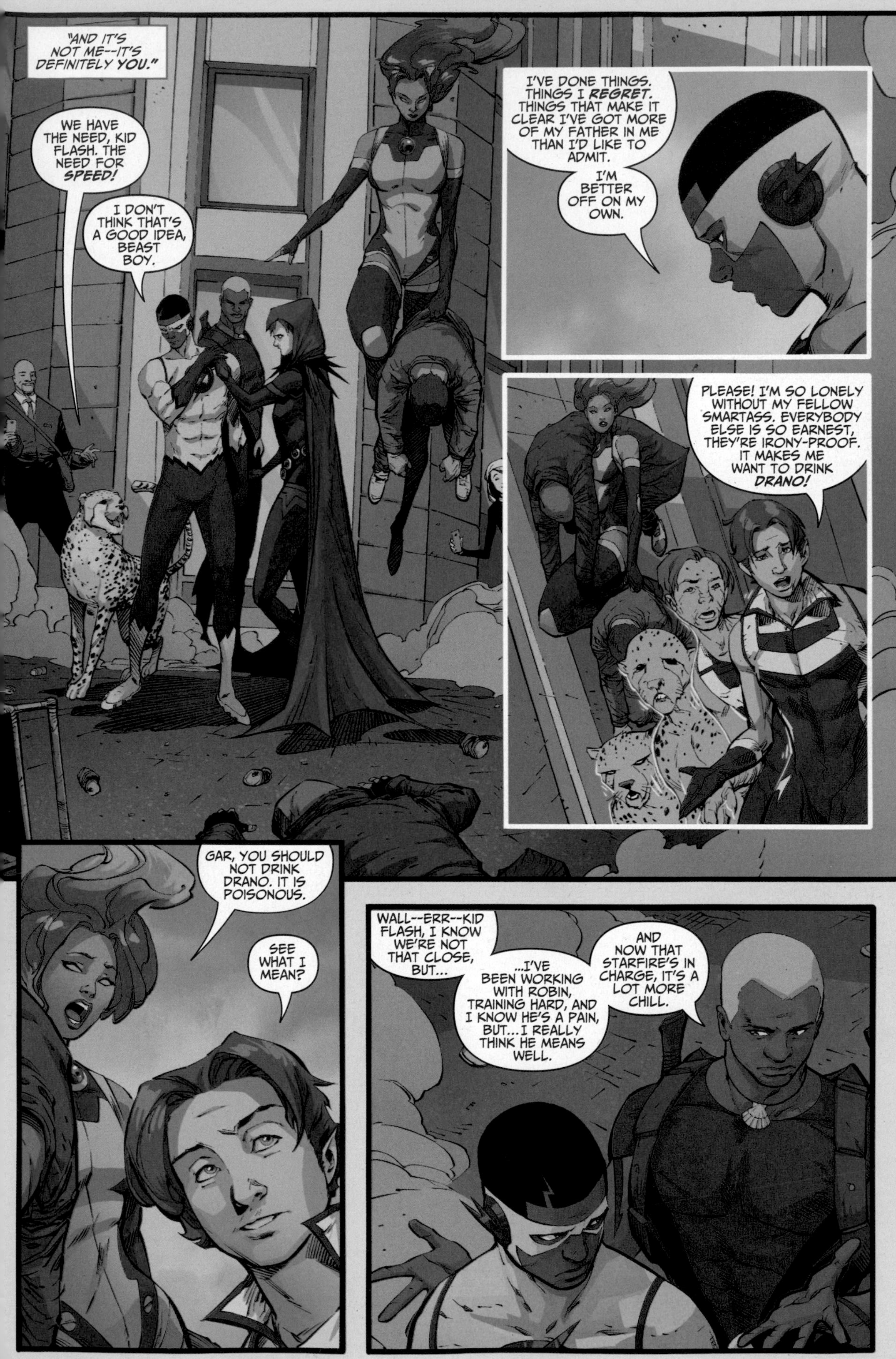
"AND IT'S NOT ME--IT'S DEFINITELY YOU."
WE HAVE THE NEED, KID FLASH. THE NEED FOR SPEED!
I DON'T THINK THAT'S A GOOD IDEA, BEAST BOY.
I'VE DONE THINGS. THINGS I REGRET. THINGS THAT MAKE IT CLEAR I'VE GOT MORE OF MY FATHER IN ME THAN I'D LIKE TO ADMIT.
I'M BETTER OFF ON MY OWN.
PLEASE! I'M SO LONELY WITHOUT MY FELLOW SMARTASS. EVERYBODY ELSE IS SO EARNEST, THEY'RE IRONY-PROOF. IT MAKES ME WANT TO DRINK DRANO!
GAR, YOU SHOULD NOT DRINK DRANO. IT IS POISONOUS.
SEE WHAT I MEAN?
WALL--ERR--KID FLASH, I KNOW WE'RE NOT THAT CLOSE, BUT...
...I'VE BEEN WORKING WITH ROBIN, TRAINING HARD, AND I KNOW HE'S A PAIN, BUT...I REALLY THINK HE MEANS WELL.
AND NOW THAT STARFIRE'S IN CHARGE, IT'S A LOT MORE CHILL.

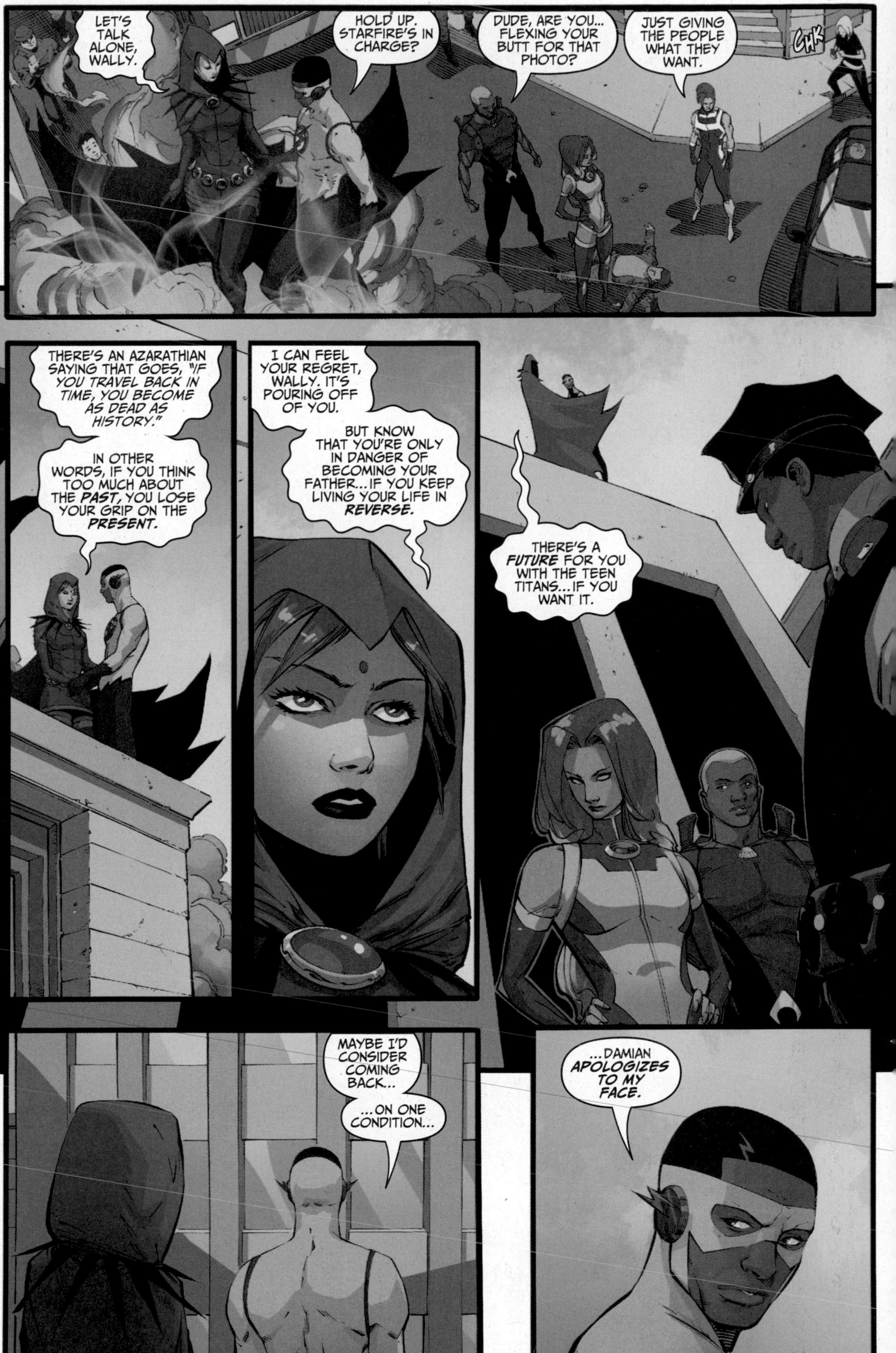
LET'S TALK ALONE, WALLY.
HOLD UP. STARFIRE'S IN CHARGE?
DUDE, ARE YOU... FLEXING YOUR BUTT FOR THAT PHOTO?
JUST GIVING THE PEOPLE WHAT THEY WANT.
CHK
THERE'S AN AZARATHIAN SAYING THAT GOES, "IF YOU TRAVEL BACK IN TIME, YOU BECOME AS DEAD AS HISTORY."
IN OTHER WORDS, IF YOU THINK TOO MUCH ABOUT THE PAST, YOU LOSE YOUR GRIP ON THE PRESENT.
I CAN FEEL YOUR REGRET, WALLY. IT'S POURING OFF OF YOU.
BUT KNOW THAT YOU'RE ONLY IN DANGER OF BECOMING YOUR FATHER...IF YOU KEEP LIVING YOUR LIFE IN REVERSE.
THERE'S A FUTURE FOR YOU WITH THE TEEN TITANS...IF YOU WANT IT.
MAYBE I'D CONSIDER COMING BACK...
...ON ONE CONDITION...
...DAMIAN APOLOGIZES TO MY FACE.

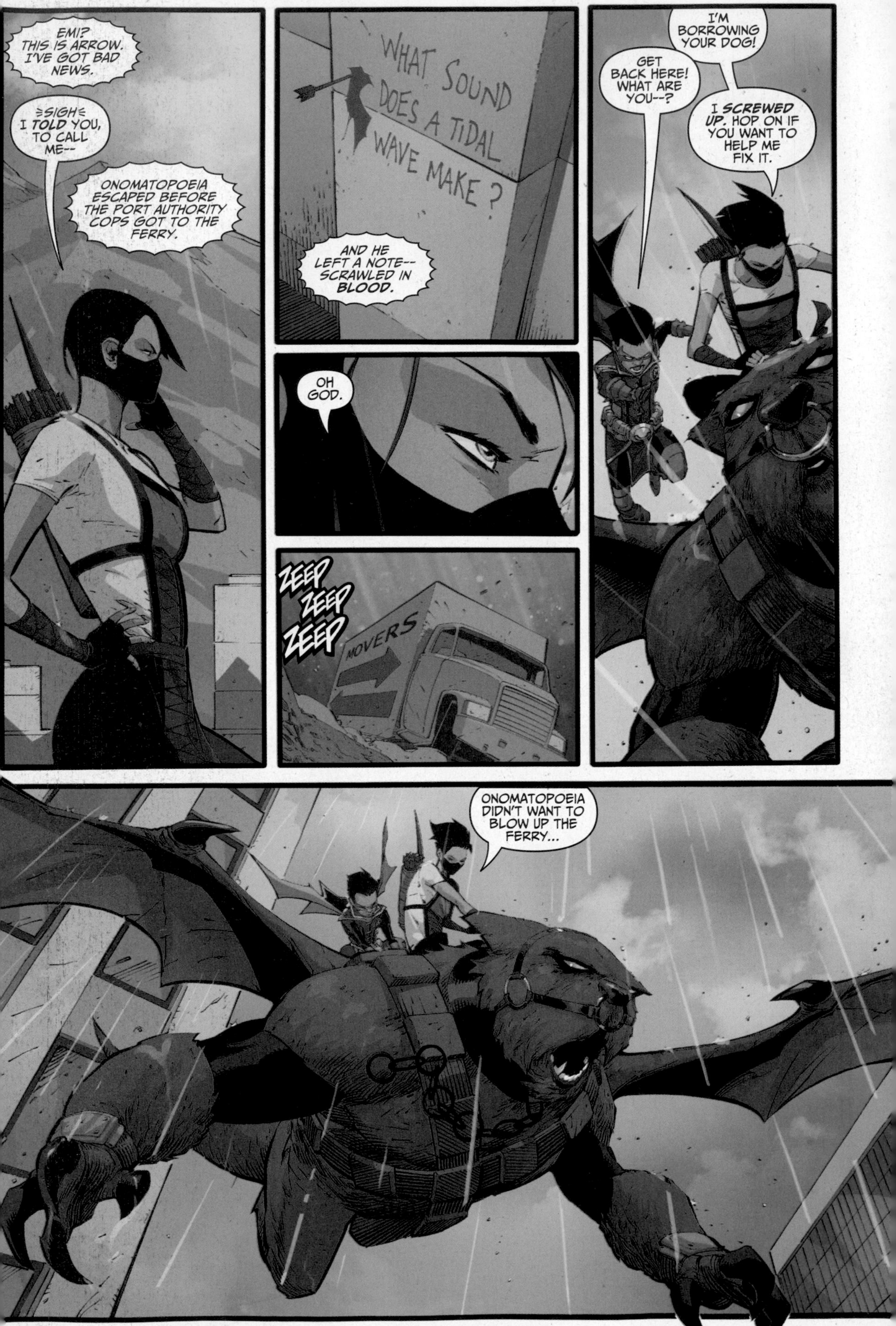

EMI? THIS IS ARROW. I'VE GOT BAD NEWS.
≈SIGH≈ I TOLD YOU, TO CALL ME--
ONOMATOPOEIA ESCAPED BEFORE THE PORT AUTHORITY COPS GOT TO THE FERRY.
WHAT SOUND DOES A TIDAL WAVE MAKE ?
AND HE LEFT A NOTE-- SCRAWLED IN BLOOD.
OH GOD.
ZEEP ZEEP ZEEP
MOVERS
I'M BORROWING YOUR DOG!
GET BACK HERE! WHAT ARE YOU--?
I SCREWED UP. HOP ON IF YOU WANT TO HELP ME FIX IT.
ONOMATOPOEIA DIDN'T WANT TO BLOW UP THE FERRY...

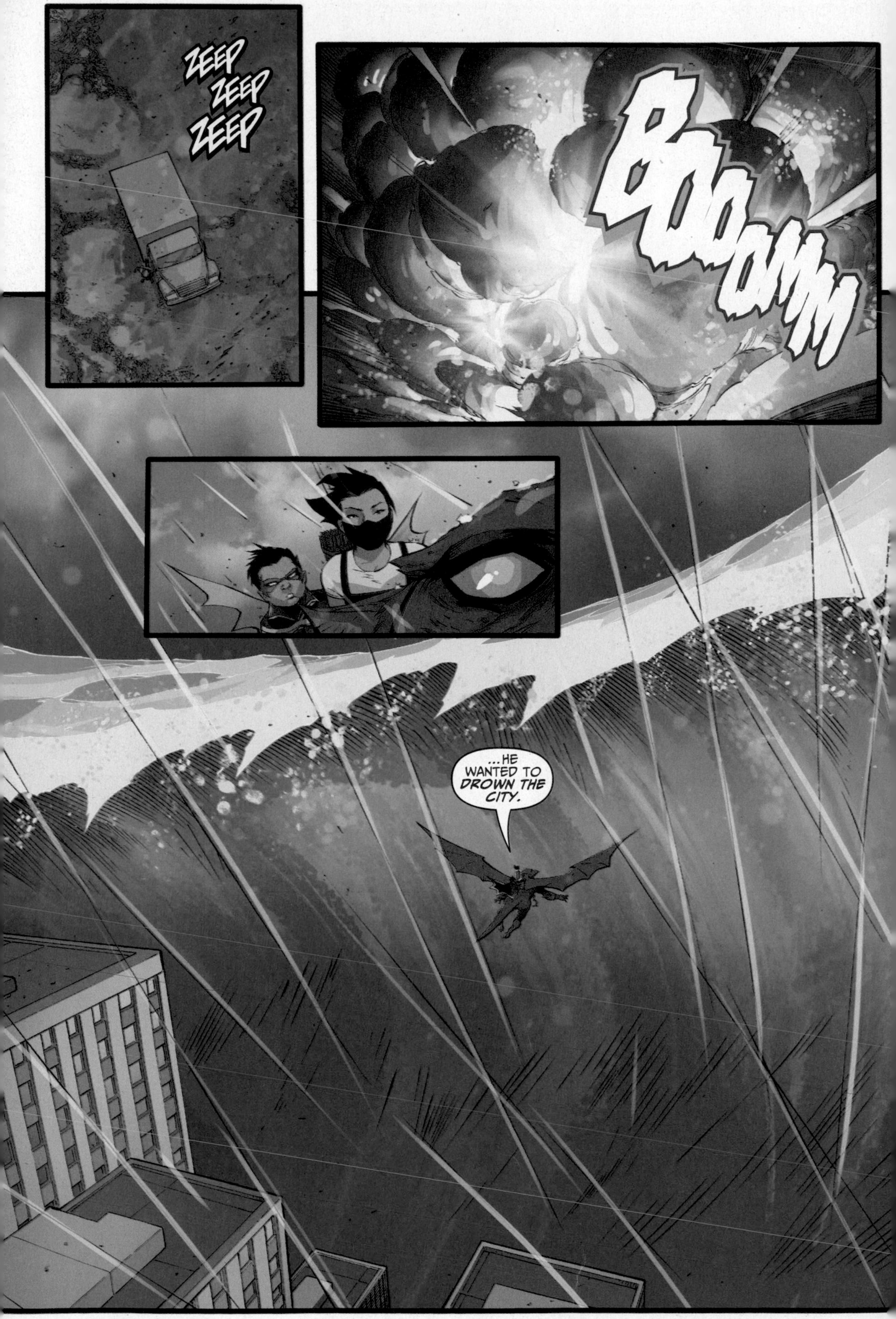
ZEEP ZEEP ZEEP
BOOOMMM
...HE WANTED TO DROWN THE CITY.

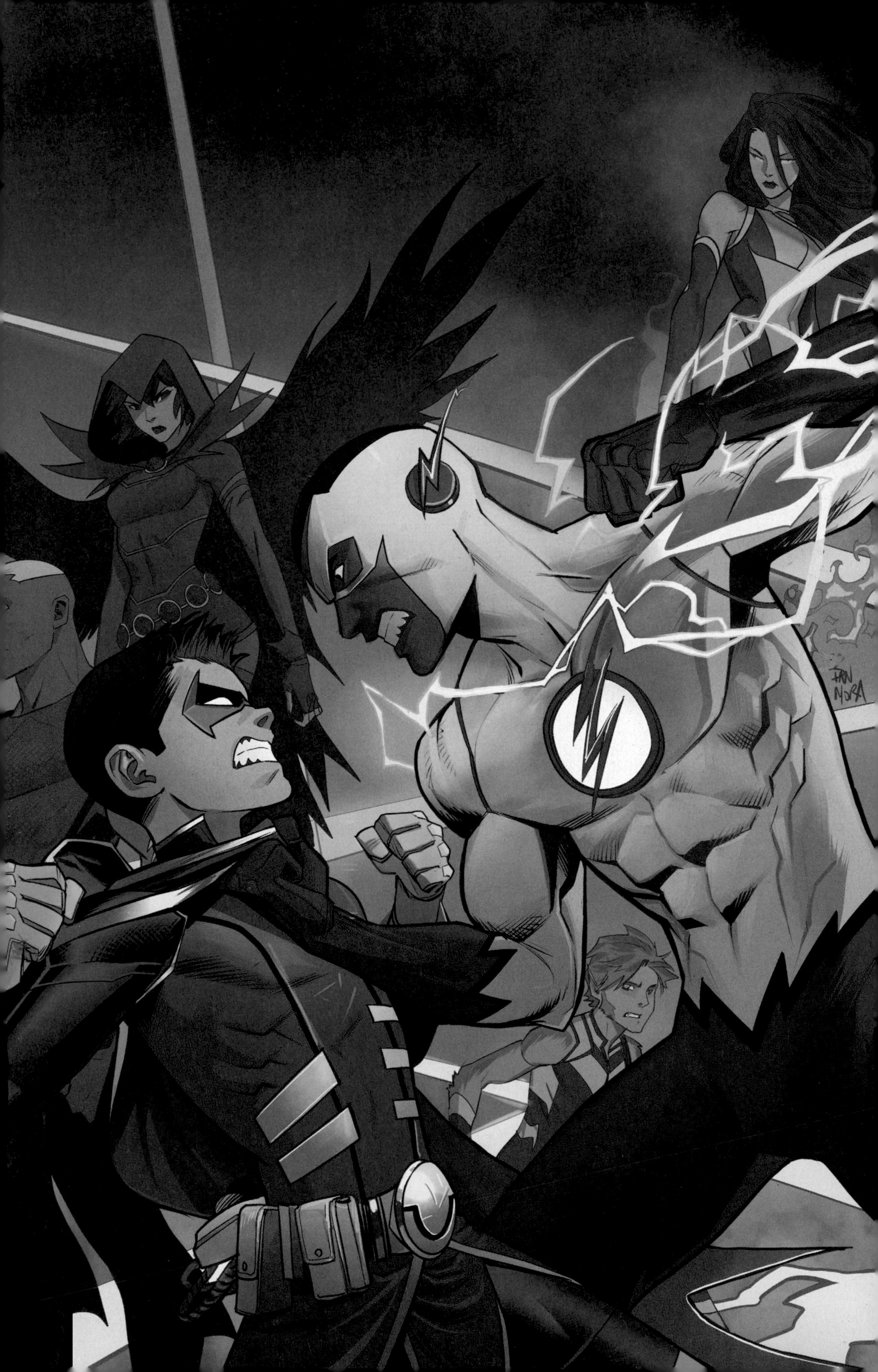

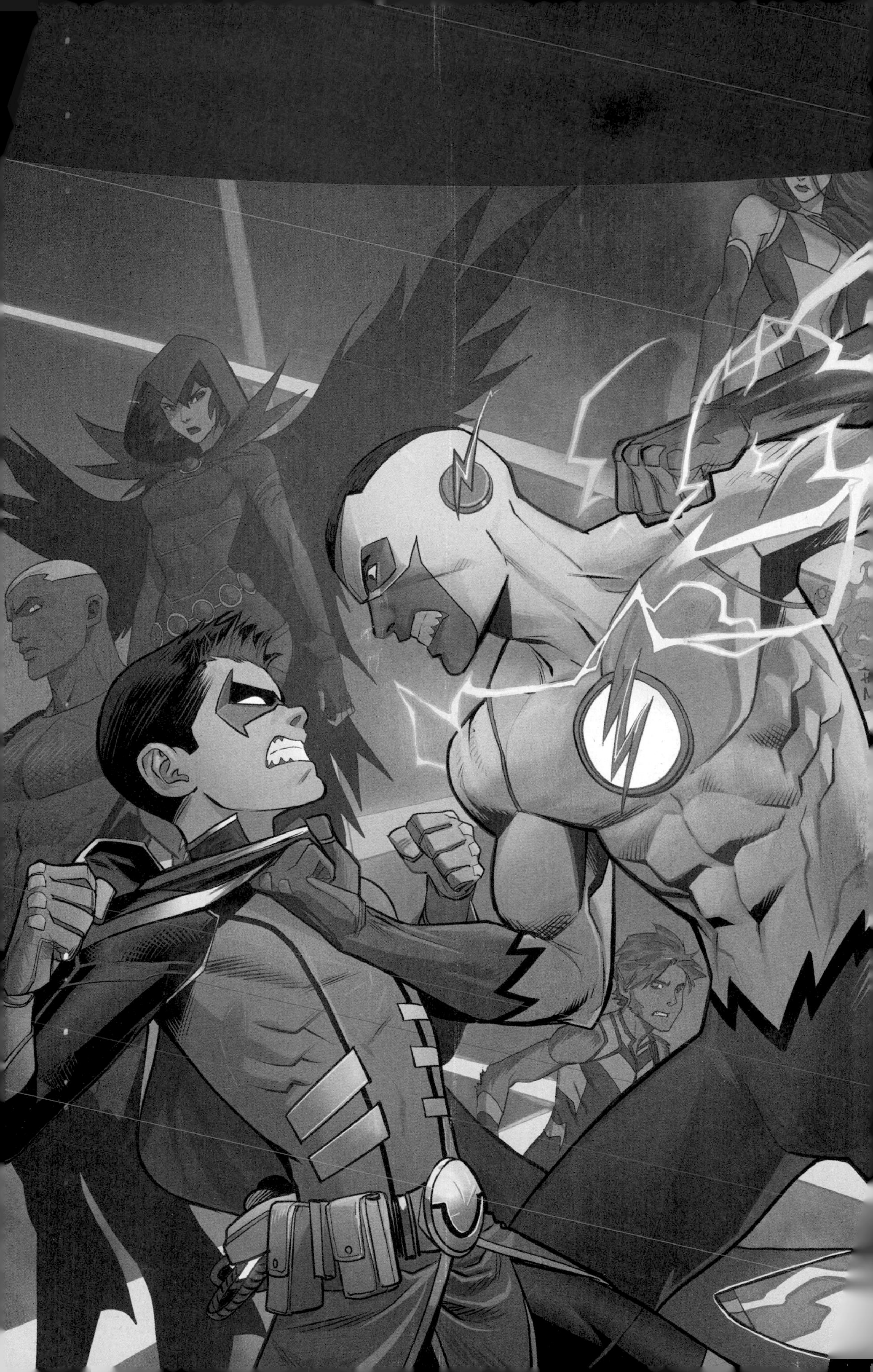

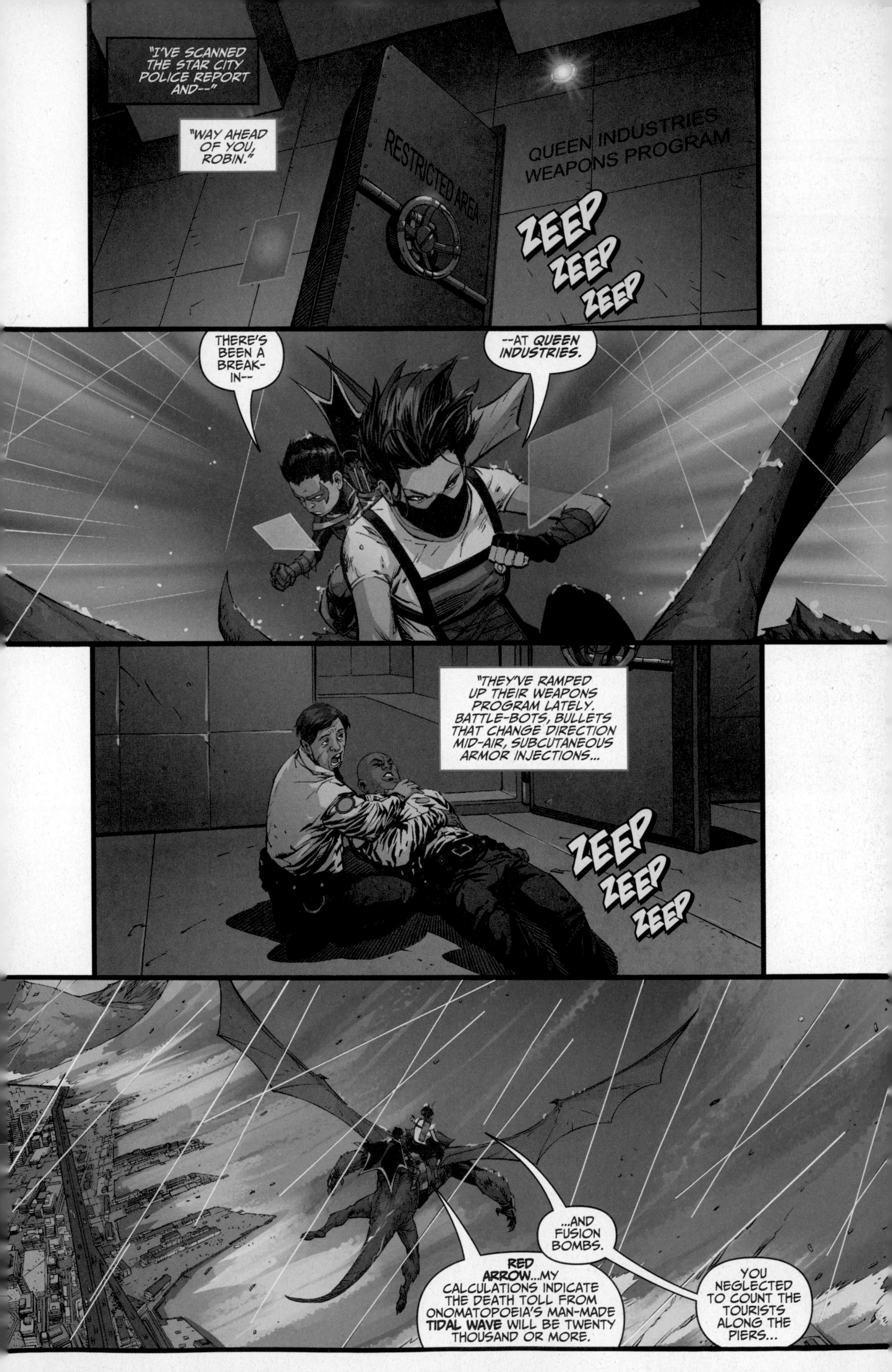
"I'VE SCANNED THE STAR CITY POLICE REPORT AND--"
"WAY AHEAD OF YOU, ROBIN."
RESTRICTED AREA
QUEEN INDUSTRIES WEAPONS PROGRAM
ZEEP ZEEP ZEEP
THERE'S BEEN A BREAK-IN--
--AT QUEEN INDUSTRIES.
"THEY'VE RAMPED UP THEIR WEAPONS PROGRAM LATELY. BATTLE-BOTS, BULLETS THAT CHANGE DIRECTION MID-AIR, SUBCUTANEOUS ARMOR INJECTIONS...
ZEEP ZEEP ZEEP
...AND FUSION BOMBS.
RED ARROW...MY CALCULATIONS INDICATE THE DEATH TOLL FROM ONOMATOPOEIA'S MAN-MADE TIDAL WAVE WILL BE TWENTY THOUSAND OR MORE.
YOU NEGLECTED TO COUNT THE TOURISTS ALONG THE PIERS...

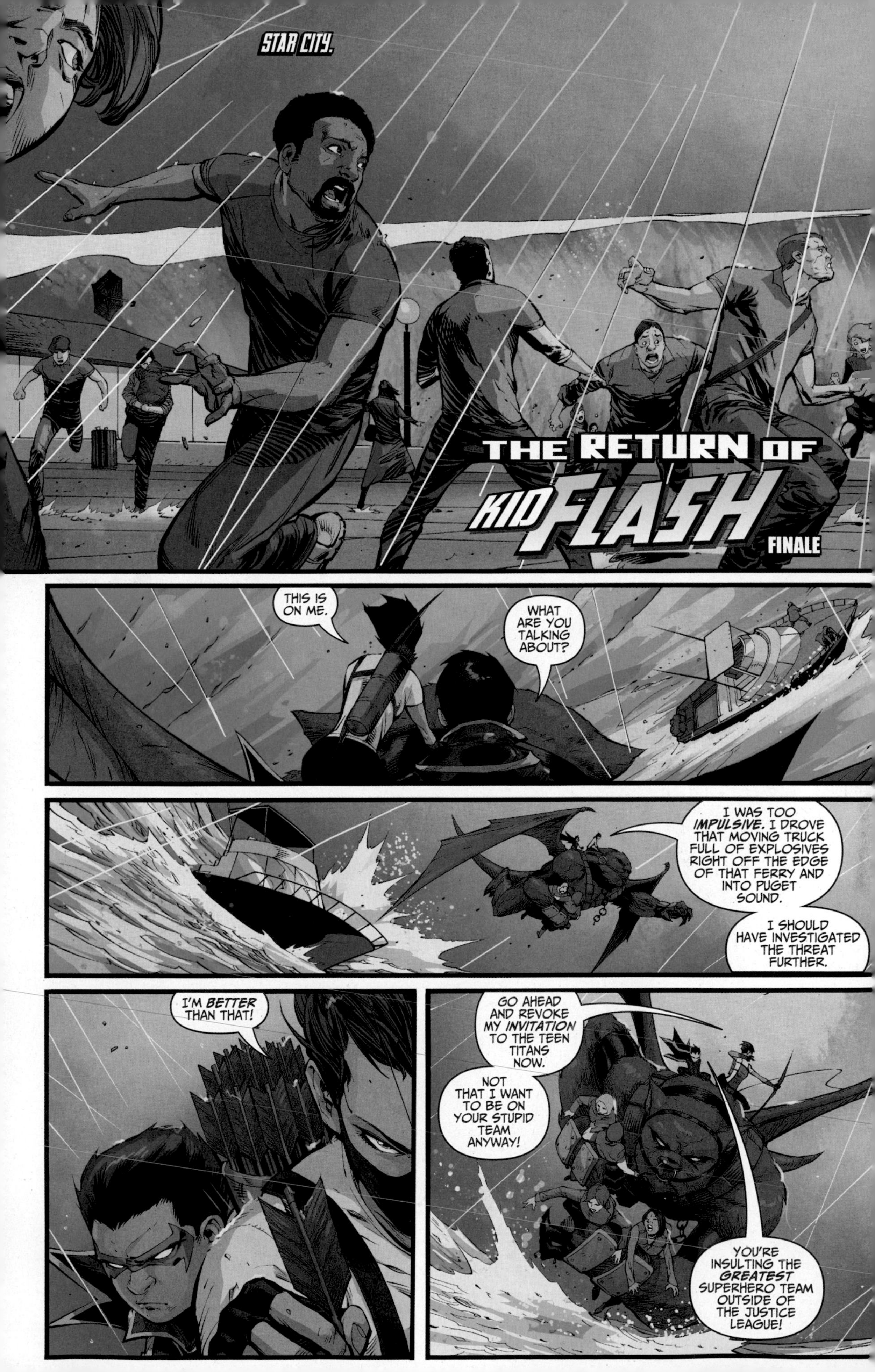
STAR CITY.
THE RETURN OF
KID FLASH
FINALE
THIS IS ON ME.
WHAT ARE YOU TALKING ABOUT?
I WAS TOO IMPULSIVE. I DROVE THAT MOVING TRUCK FULL OF EXPLOSIVES RIGHT OFF THE EDGE OF THAT FERRY AND INTO PUGET SOUND.
I SHOULD HAVE INVESTIGATED THE THREAT FURTHER.
I'M BETTER THAN THAT!
GO AHEAD AND REVOKE MY INVITATION TO THE TEEN TITANS NOW.
NOT THAT I WANT TO BE ON YOUR STUPID TEAM ANYWAY!
YOU'RE INSULTING THE GREATEST SUPERHERO TEAM OUTSIDE OF THE JUSTICE LEAGUE!

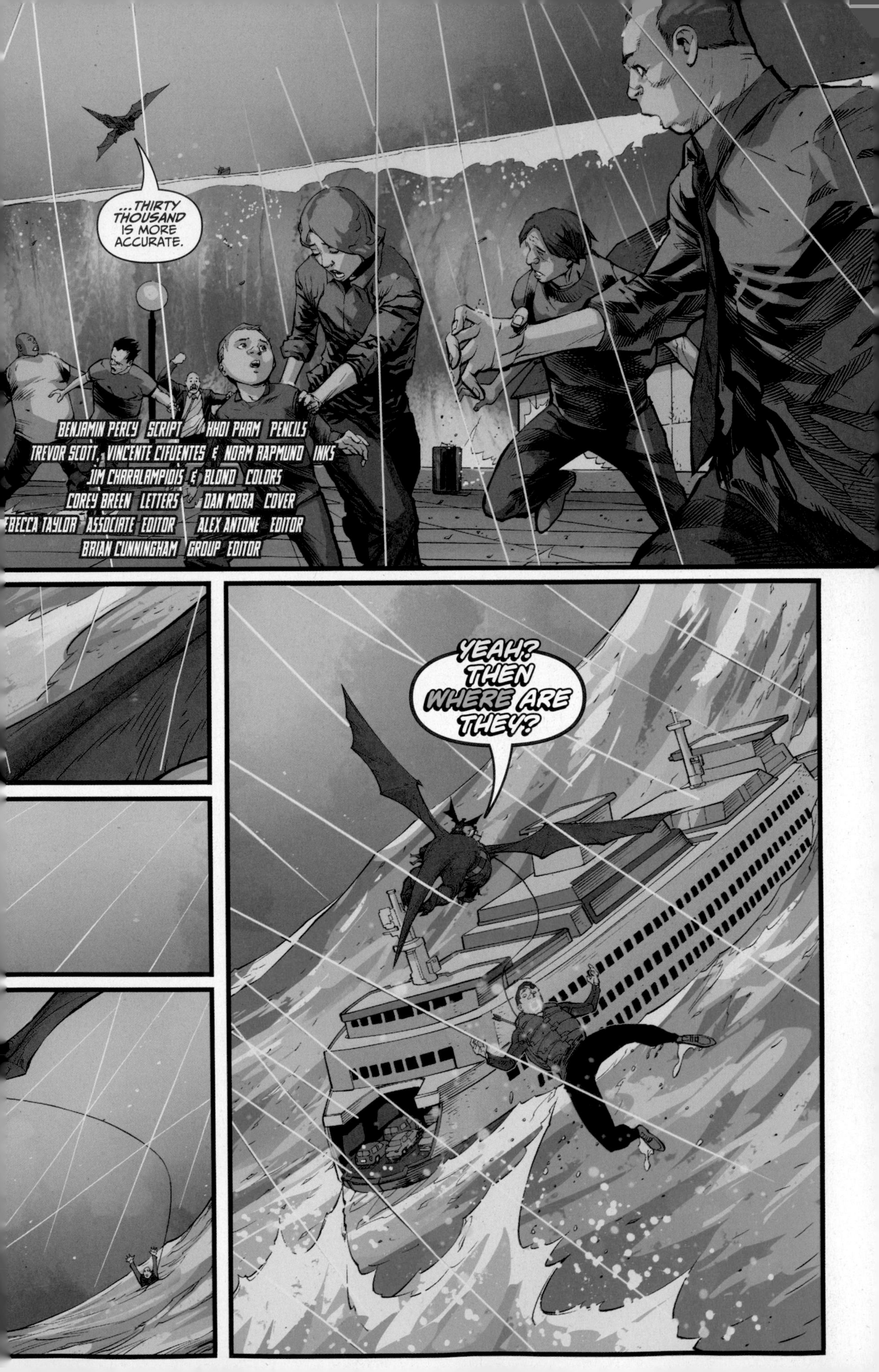
...THIRTY THOUSAND IS MORE ACCURATE.
BENJAMIN PERCY SCRIPT KHOI PHAM PENCILS
TREVOR SCOTT, VINCENTE CIFUENTES & NORM RAPMUND INKS
JIM CHARALAMPIDIS & BLOND COLORS
COREY BREEN LETTERS DAN MORA COVER
EBECCA TAYLOR ASSOCIATE EDITOR ALEX ANTONE EDITOR
BRIAN CUNNINGHAM GROUP EDITOR
YEAH? THEN WHERE ARE THEY?

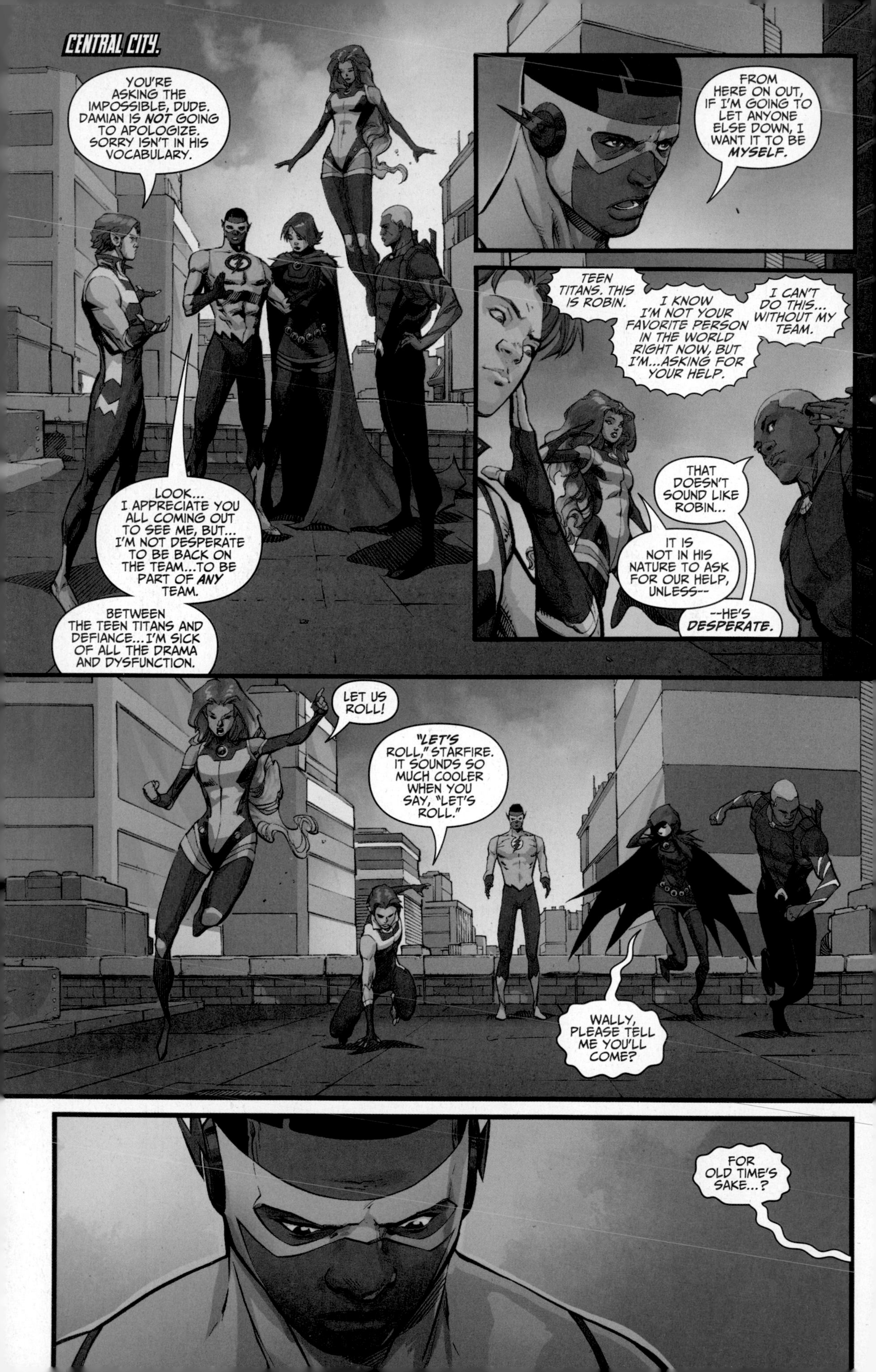
CENTRAL CITY.
YOU'RE ASKING THE IMPOSSIBLE, DUDE. DAMIAN IS NOT GOING TO APOLOGIZE. SORRY ISN'T IN HIS VOCABULARY.
LOOK... I APPRECIATE YOU ALL COMING OUT TO SEE ME, BUT... I'M NOT DESPERATE TO BE BACK ON THE TEAM...TO BE PART OF ANY TEAM.
BETWEEN THE TEEN TITANS AND DEFIANCE...I'M SICK OF ALL THE DRAMA AND DYSFUNCTION.
FROM HERE ON OUT, IF I'M GOING TO LET ANYONE ELSE DOWN, I WANT IT TO BE MYSELF.
TEEN TITANS. THIS IS ROBIN.
I KNOW I'M NOT YOUR FAVORITE PERSON IN THE WORLD RIGHT NOW, BUT I'M...ASKING FOR YOUR HELP.
I CAN'T DO THIS... WITHOUT MY TEAM.
THAT DOESN'T SOUND LIKE ROBIN...
IT IS NOT IN HIS NATURE TO ASK FOR OUR HELP, UNLESS--
--HE'S DESPERATE.
LET US ROLL!
"LET'S ROLL," STARFIRE. IT SOUNDS SO MUCH COOLER WHEN YOU SAY, "LET'S ROLL."
WALLY, PLEASE TELL ME YOU'LL COME?
FOR OLD TIME'S SAKE...?

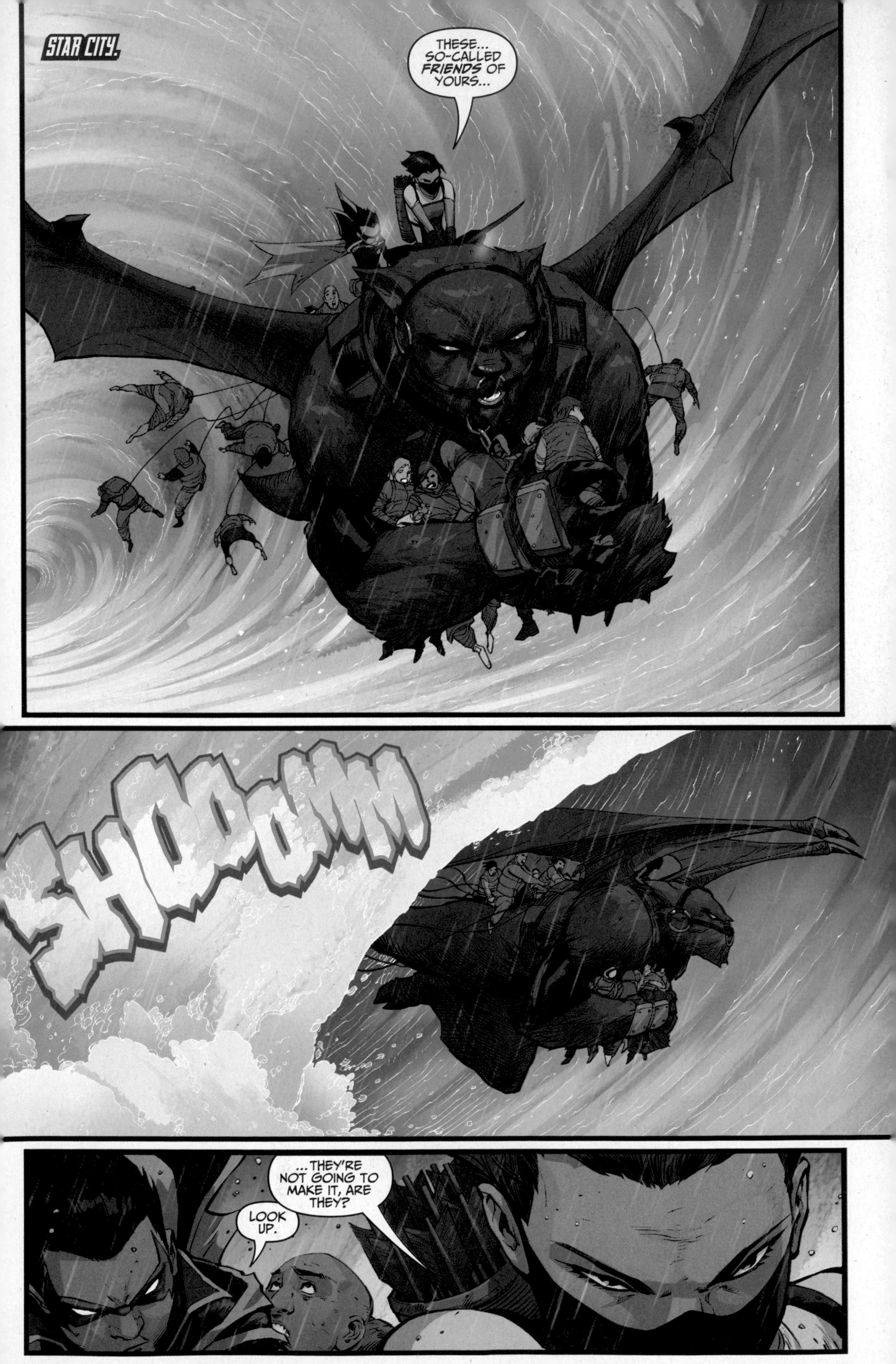
STAR CITY.
THESE... SO-CALLED FRIENDS OF YOURS...
SHOOOMM
...THEY'RE NOT GOING TO MAKE IT, ARE THEY?
LOOK UP.

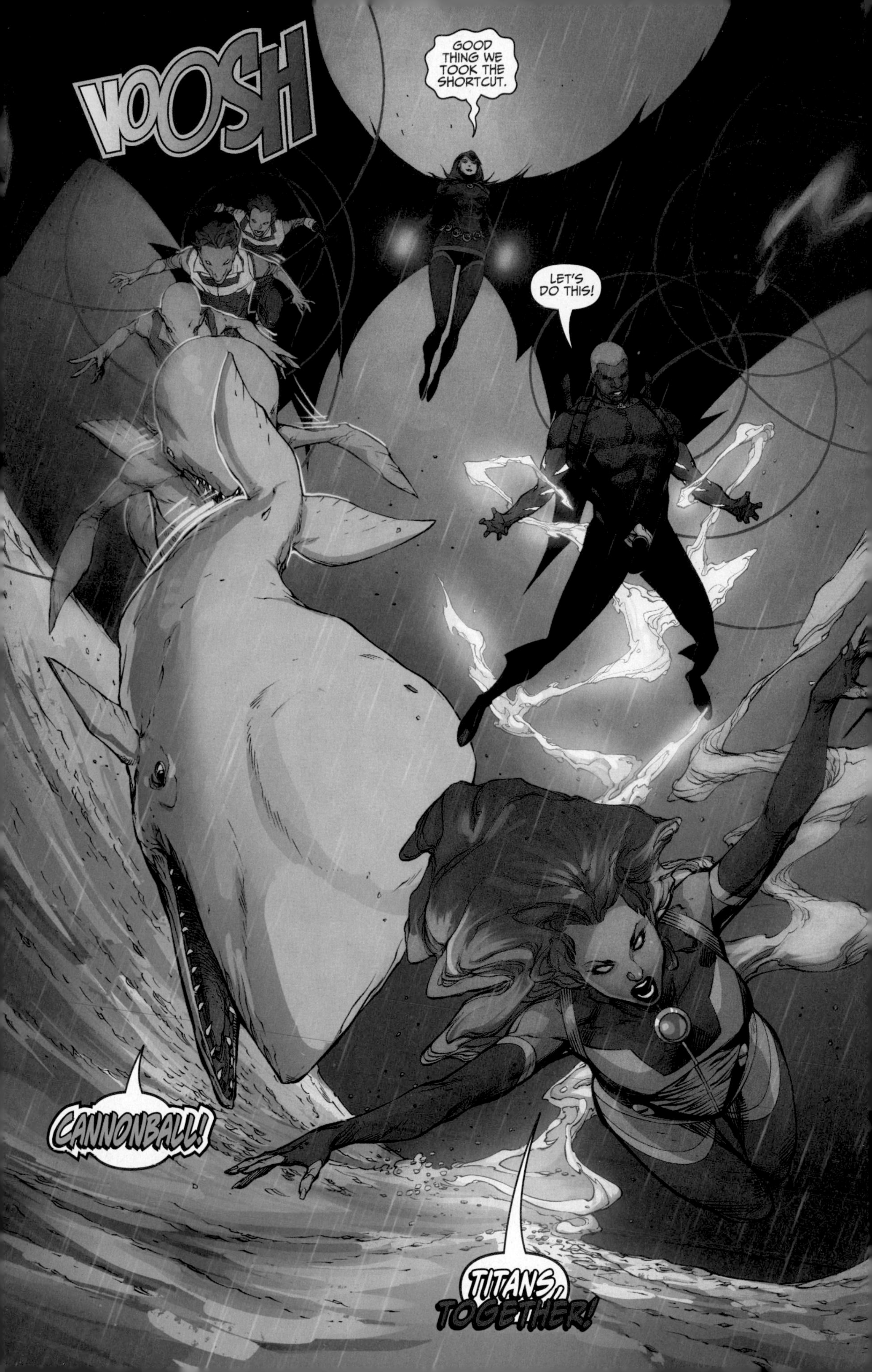
VOOSH
GOOD THING WE TOOK THE SHORTCUT.
LET'S DO THIS!
CANNONBALL!
TITANS, TOGETHER!

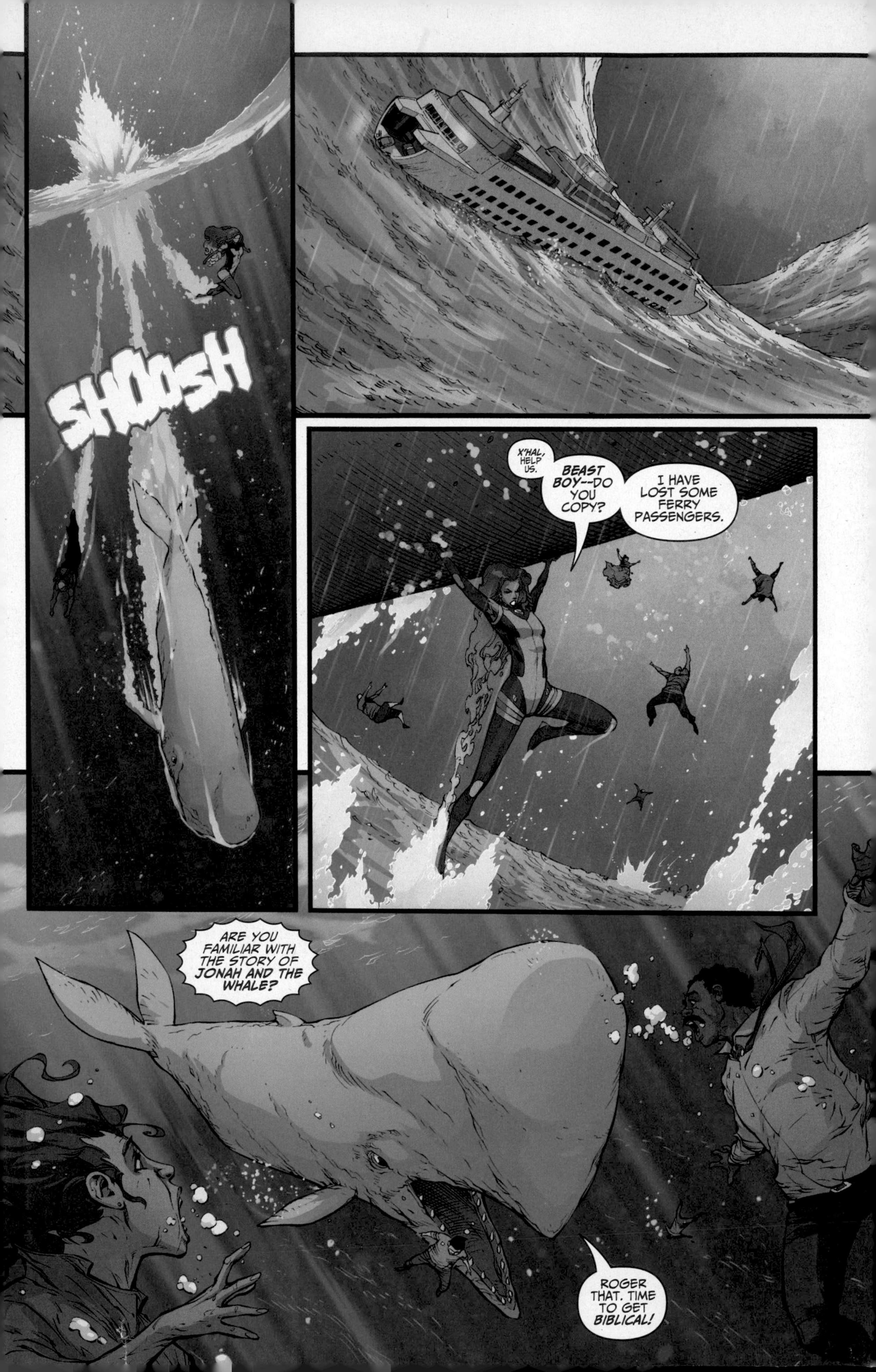
SHOOSH
X'HAL, HELP US.
BEAST BOY--DO YOU COPY?
I HAVE LOST SOME FERRY PASSENGERS.
ARE YOU FAMILIAR WITH THE STORY OF JONAH AND THE WHALE?
ROGER THAT. TIME TO GET BIBLICAL!

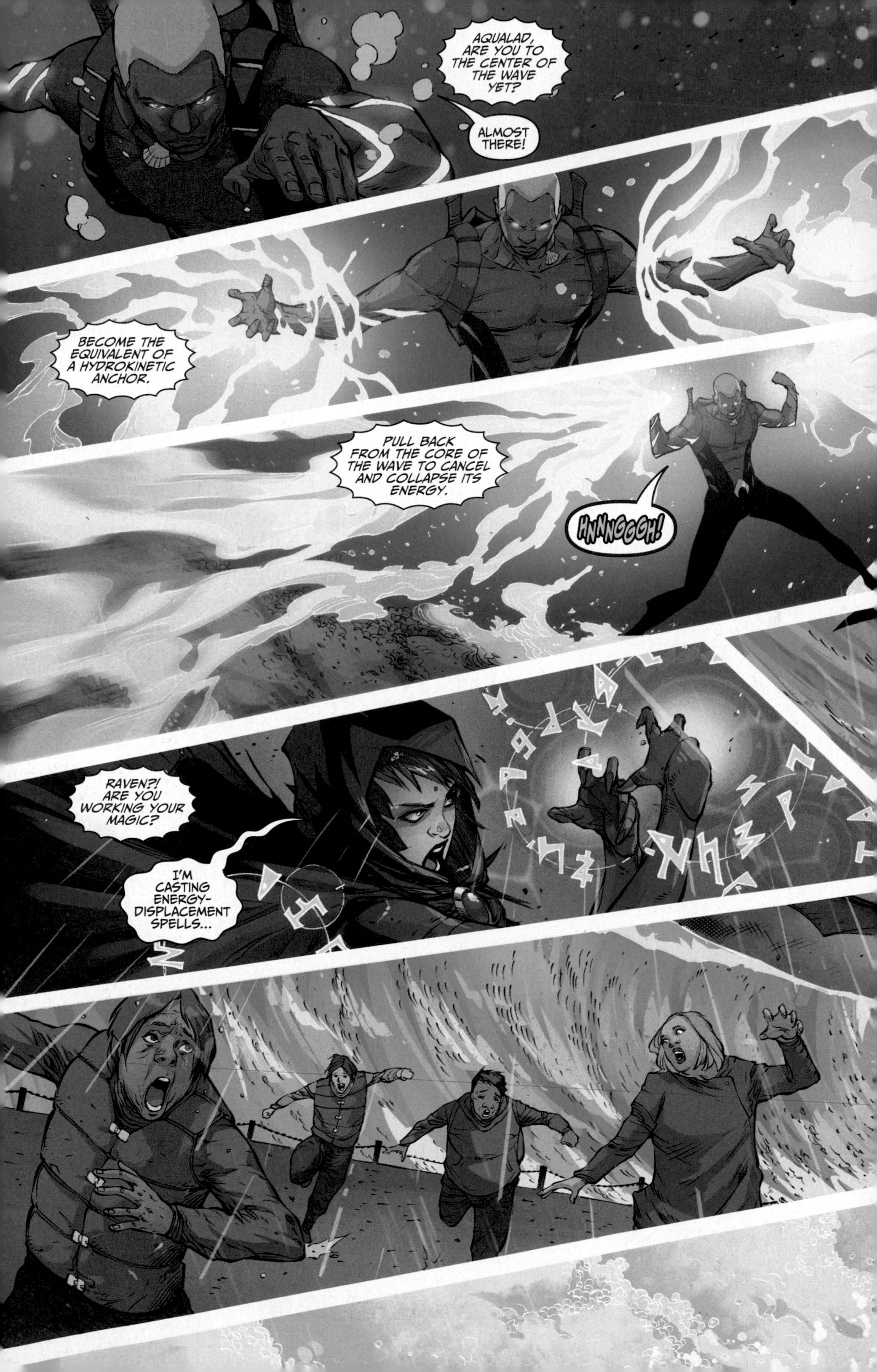
AQUALAD, ARE YOU TO THE CENTER OF THE WAVE YET?
ALMOST THERE!
BECOME THE EQUIVALENT OF A HYDROKINETIC ANCHOR.
PULL BACK FROM THE CORE OF THE WAVE TO CANCEL AND COLLAPSE ITS ENERGY.
HNNNGGGH!
RAVEN?! ARE YOU WORKING YOUR MAGIC?
I'M CASTING ENERGY-DISPLACEMENT SPELLS...

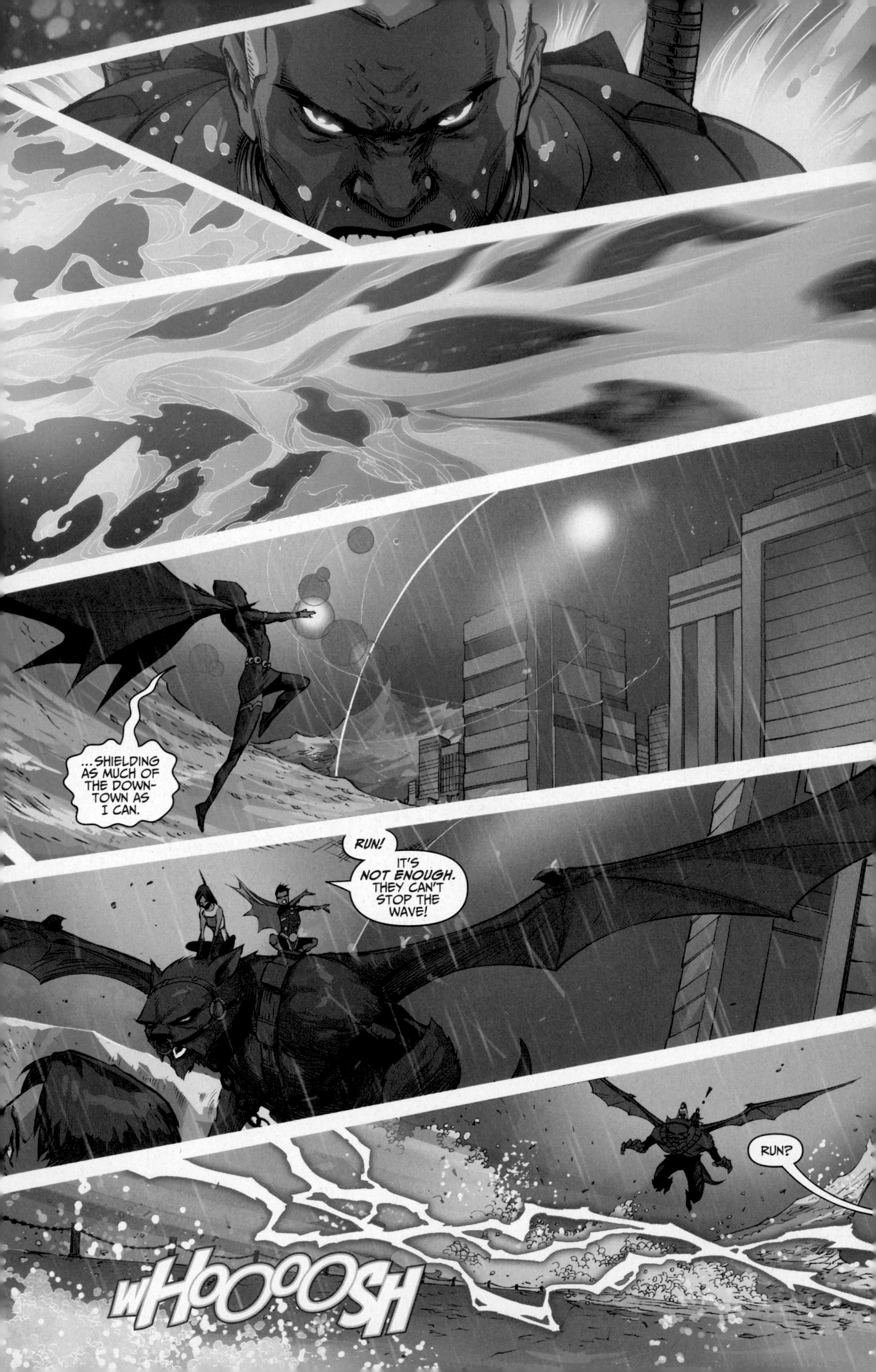
...SHIELDING AS MUCH OF THE DOWN-TOWN AS I CAN.
RUN!
IT'S NOT ENOUGH. THEY CAN'T STOP THE WAVE!
RUN?
WHOOOOSH

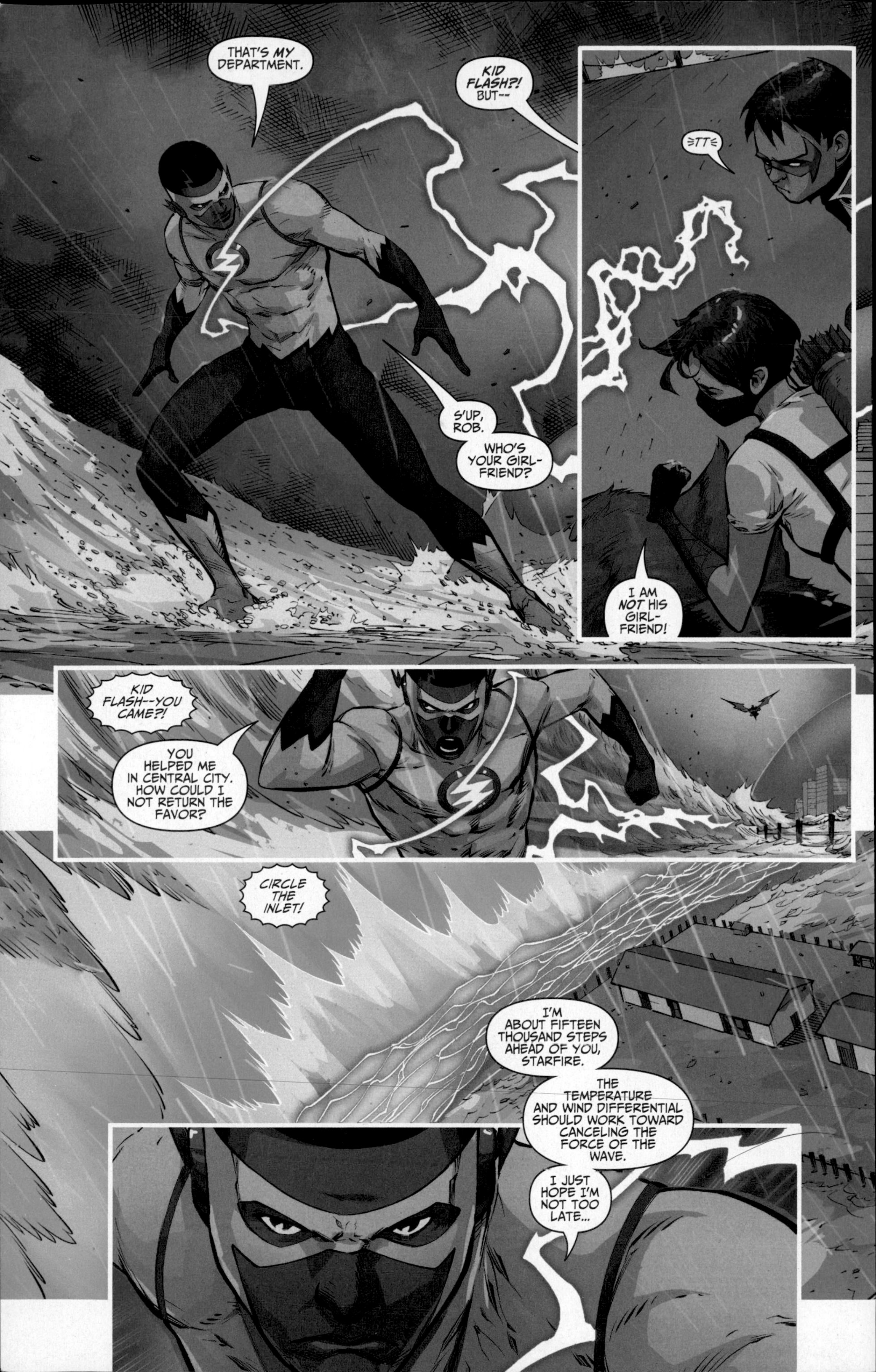
THAT'S MY DEPARTMENT.
KID FLASH?! BUT--
TT
S'UP, ROB.
WHO'S YOUR GIRL-FRIEND?
I AM NOT HIS GIRL-FRIEND!
KID FLASH--YOU CAME?!
YOU HELPED ME IN CENTRAL CITY. HOW COULD I NOT RETURN THE FAVOR?
CIRCLE THE INLET!
I'M ABOUT FIFTEEN THOUSAND STEPS AHEAD OF YOU, STARFIRE.
THE TEMPERATURE AND WIND DIFFERENTIAL SHOULD WORK TOWARD CANCELING THE FORCE OF THE WAVE.
I JUST HOPE I'M NOT TOO LATE...

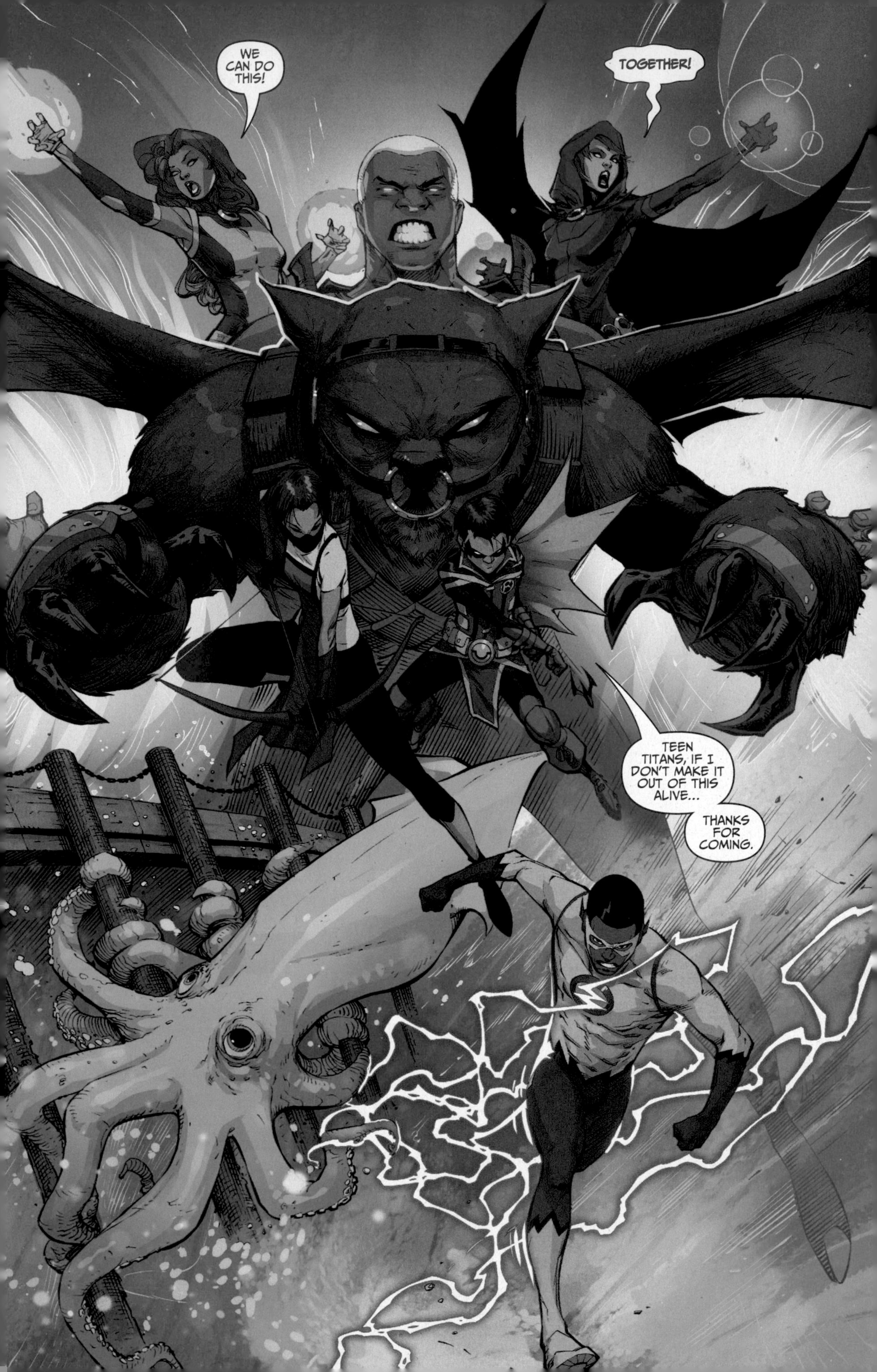
WE CAN DO THIS!
TOGETHER!
TEEN TITANS, IF I DON'T MAKE IT OUT OF THIS ALIVE...
THANKS FOR COMING.

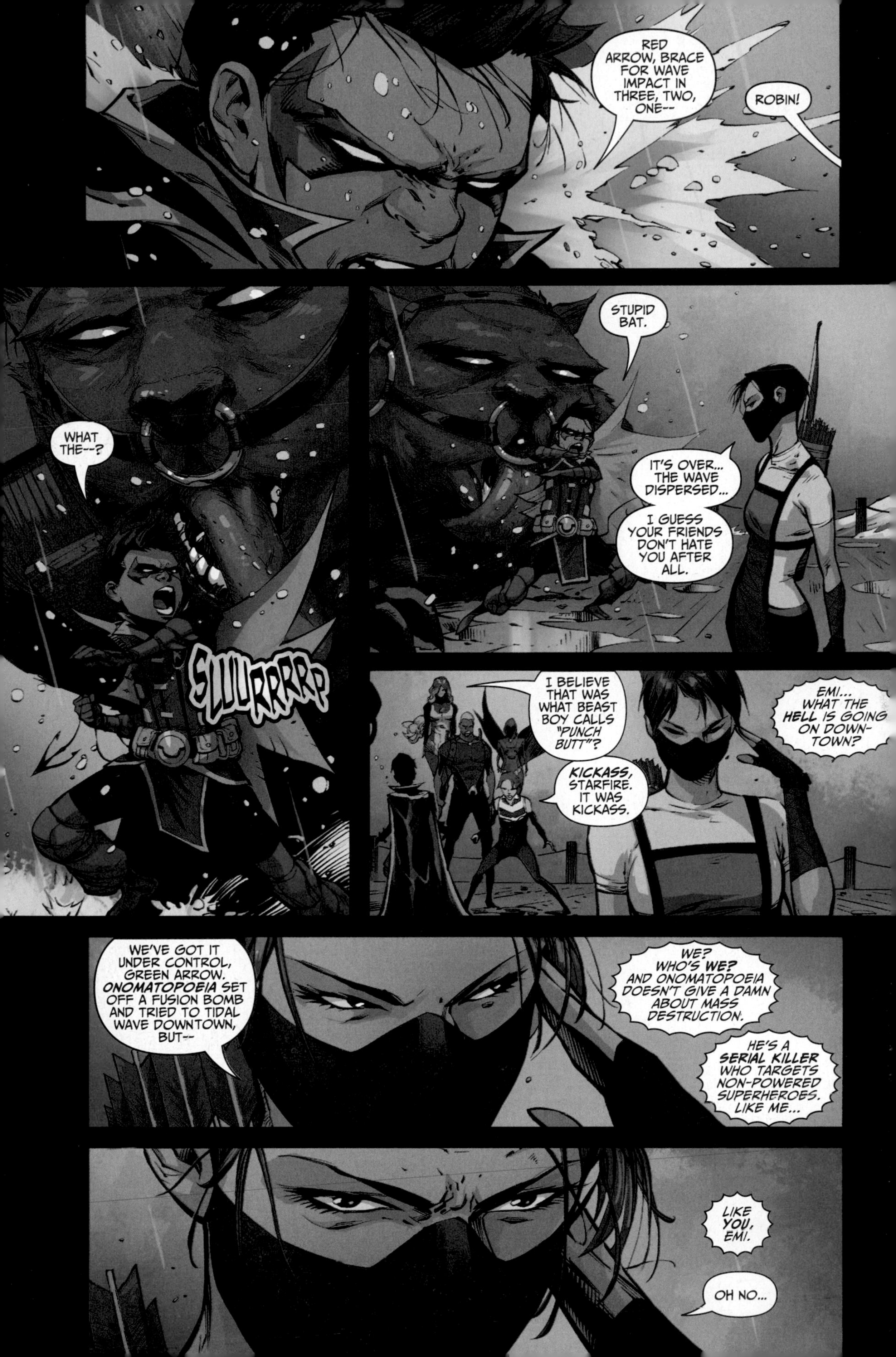
RED ARROW, BRACE FOR WAVE IMPACT IN THREE, TWO, ONE--
ROBIN!
WHAT THE--?
SLUURRRRP
STUPID BAT.
IT'S OVER... THE WAVE DISPERSED...
I GUESS YOUR FRIENDS DON'T HATE YOU AFTER ALL.
I BELIEVE THAT WAS WHAT BEAST BOY CALLS "PUNCH BUTT"?
KICKASS, STARFIRE. IT WAS KICKASS.
EMI... WHAT THE HELL IS GOING ON DOWN-TOWN?
WE'VE GOT IT UNDER CONTROL, GREEN ARROW. ONOMATOPOEIA SET OFF A FUSION BOMB AND TRIED TO TIDAL WAVE DOWNTOWN, BUT--
WE? WHO'S WE? AND ONOMATOPOEIA DOESN'T GIVE A DAMN ABOUT MASS DESTRUCTION.
HE'S A SERIAL KILLER WHO TARGETS NON-POWERED SUPERHEROES. LIKE ME...
LIKE YOU, EMI.
OH NO...

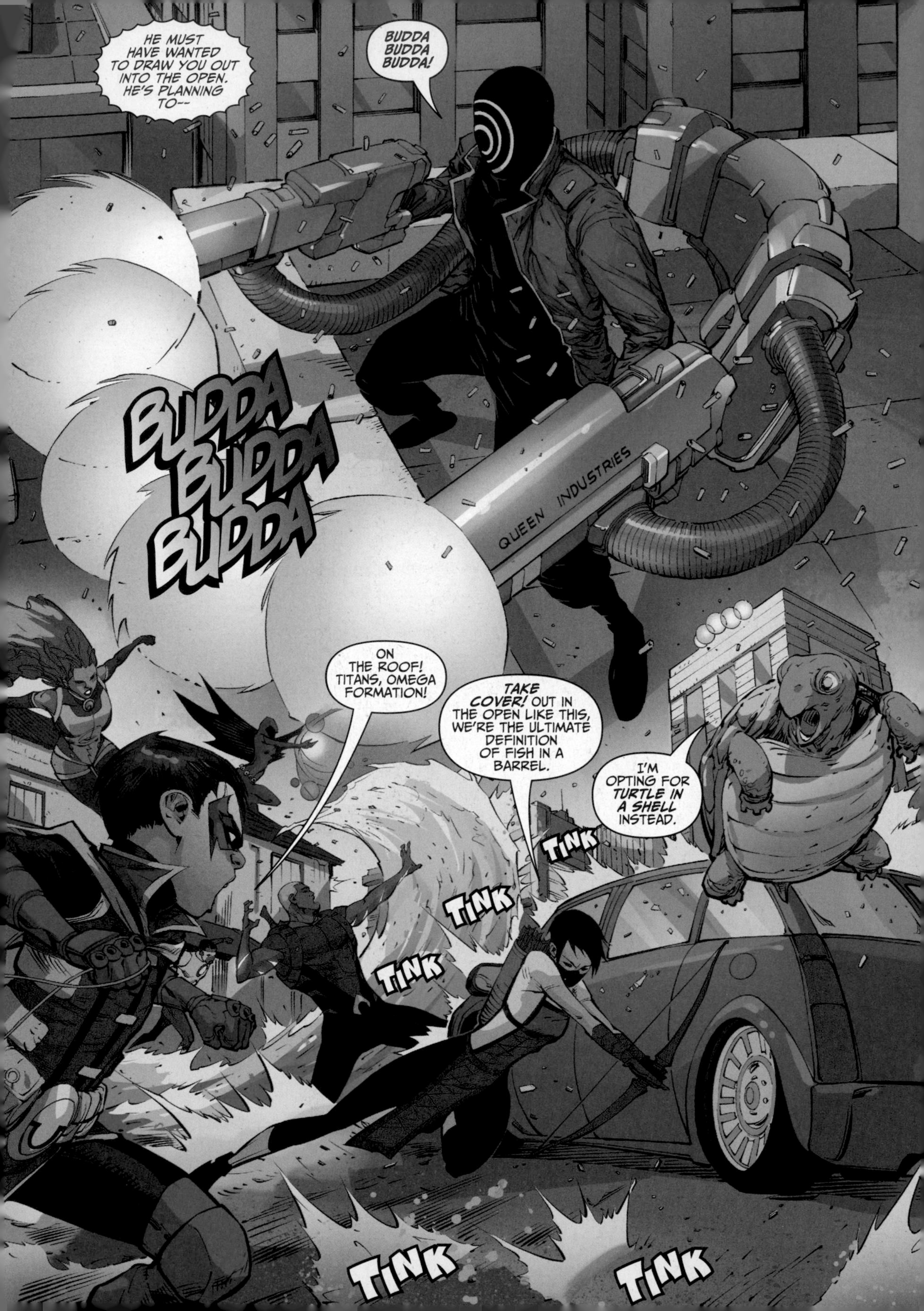
HE MUST HAVE WANTED TO DRAW YOU OUT INTO THE OPEN. HE'S PLANNING TO--
BUDDA BUDDA BUDDA!
BUDDA BUDDA BUDDA
QUEEN INDUSTRIES
ON THE ROOF! TITANS, OMEGA FORMATION!
TAKE COVER! OUT IN THE OPEN LIKE THIS, WE'RE THE ULTIMATE DEFINITION OF FISH IN A BARREL.
I'M OPTING FOR TURTLE IN A SHELL INSTEAD.
TINK
TINK
TINK
TINK
TINK

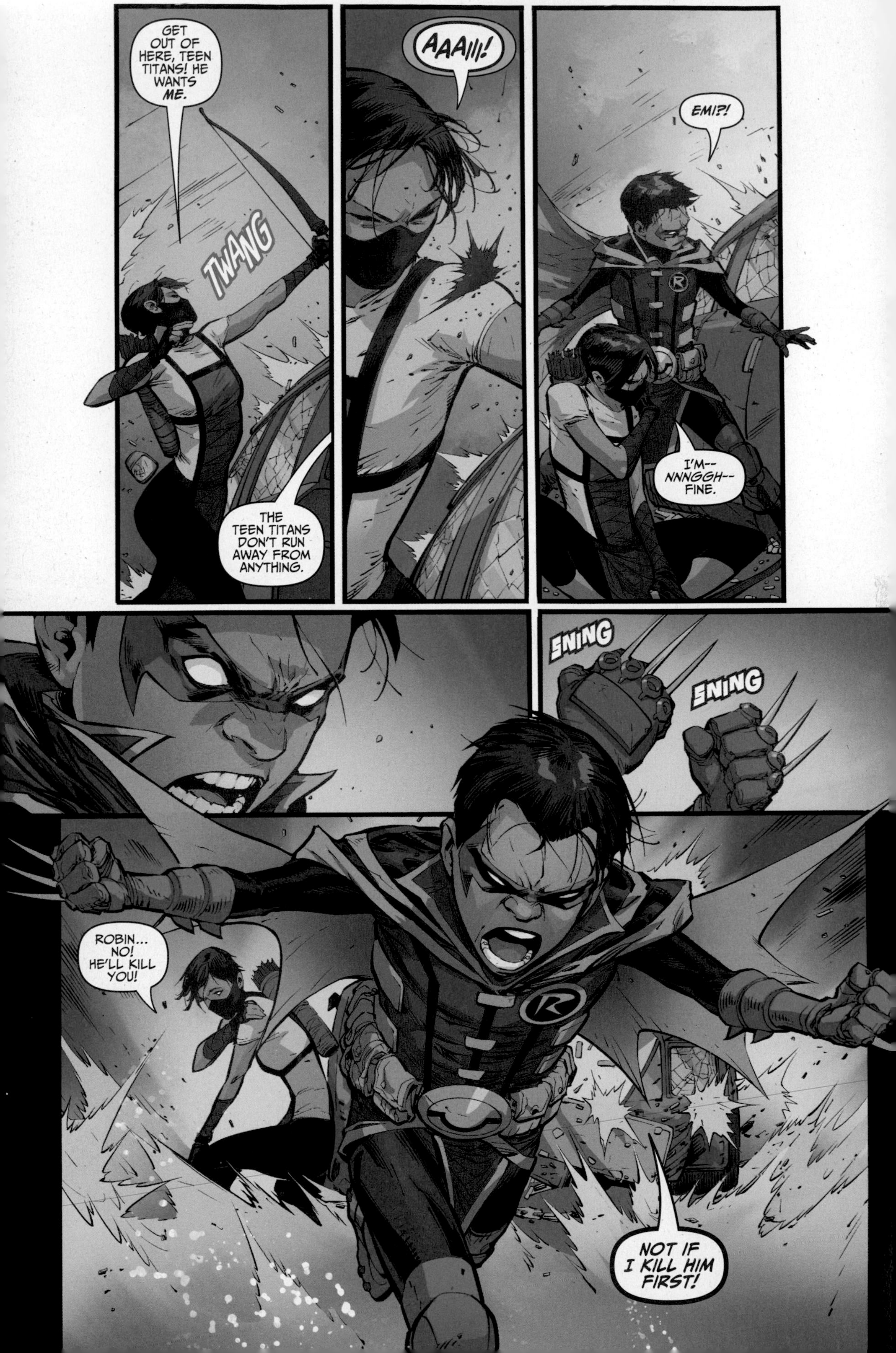

GET OUT OF HERE, TEEN TITANS! HE WANTS ME.
TWANG
THE TEEN TITANS DON'T RUN AWAY FROM ANYTHING.
AAAIII!
EMI?!
I'M-- NNNGGH-- FINE.
SNING
SNING
ROBIN... NO! HE'LL KILL YOU!
NOT IF I KILL HIM FIRST!

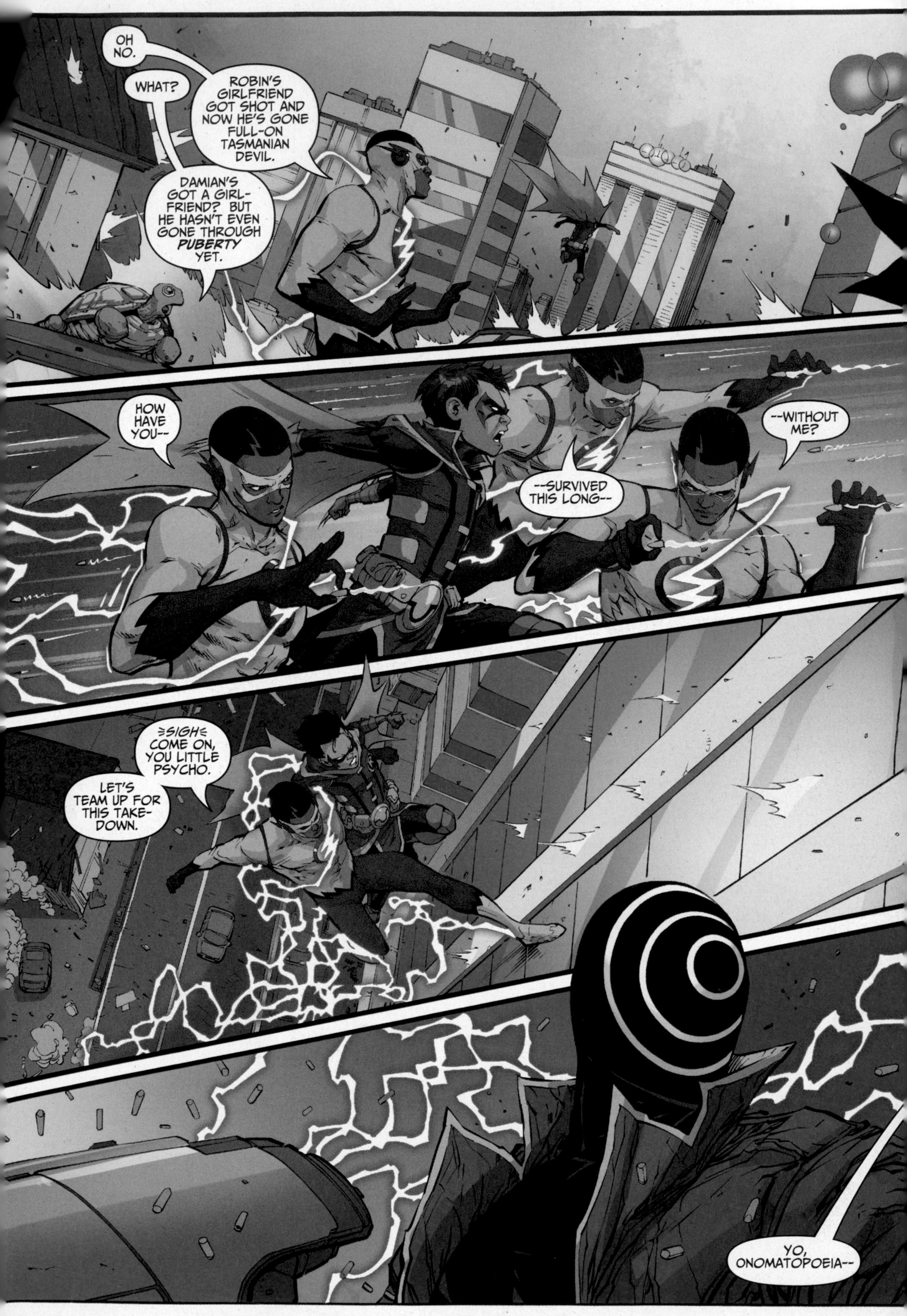
OH NO.
WHAT?
ROBIN'S GIRLFRIEND GOT SHOT AND NOW HE'S GONE FULL-ON TASMANIAN DEVIL.
DAMIAN'S GOT A GIRL-FRIEND? BUT HE HASN'T EVEN GONE THROUGH PUBERTY YET.
HOW HAVE YOU--
--SURVIVED THIS LONG--
--WITHOUT ME?
SIGH COME ON, YOU LITTLE PSYCHO.
LET'S TEAM UP FOR THIS TAKE-DOWN.
YO, ONOMATOPOEIA--

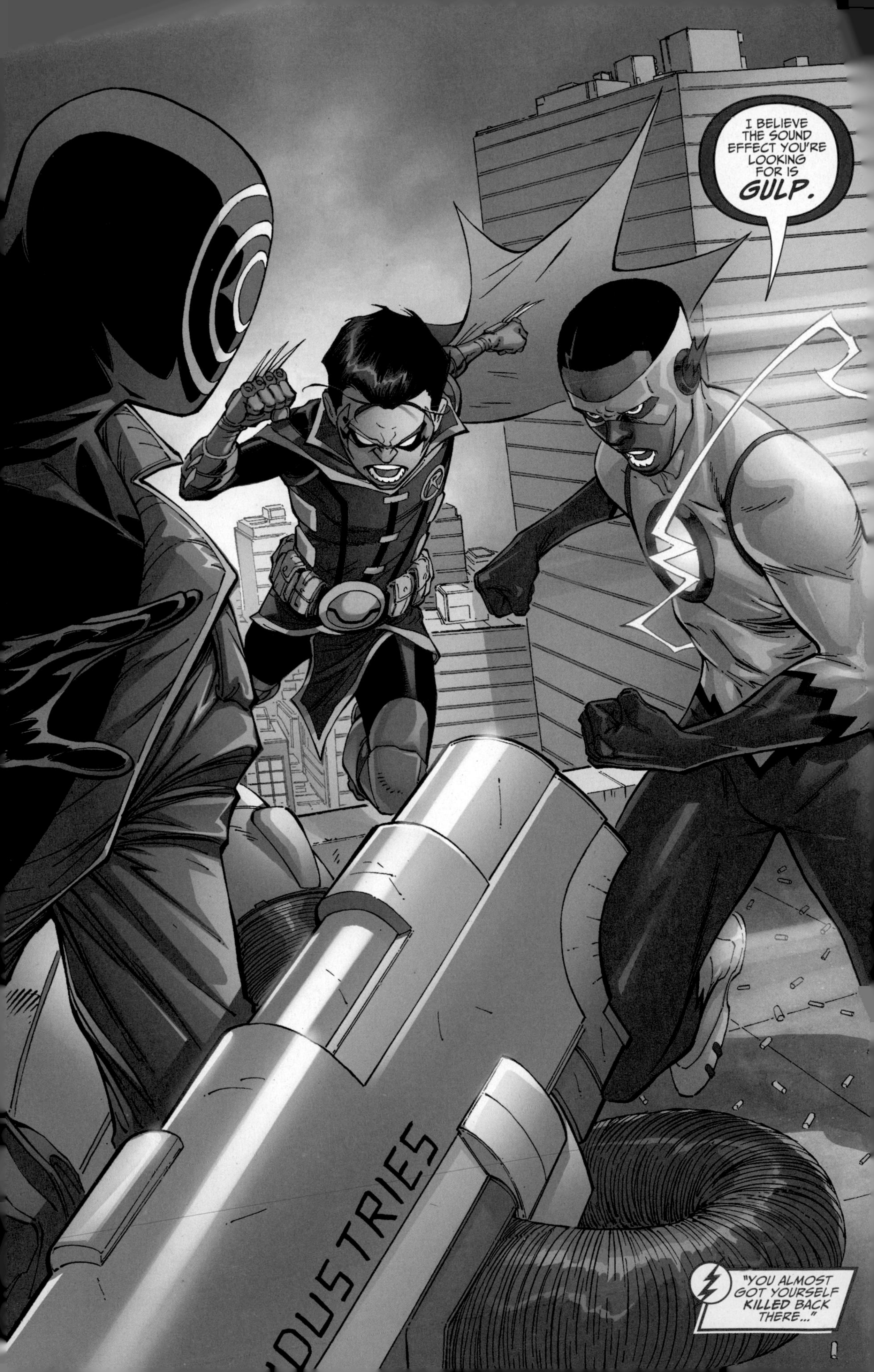
I BELIEVE THE SOUND EFFECT YOU'RE LOOKING FOR IS GULP.
"YOU ALMOST GOT YOURSELF KILLED BACK THERE..."

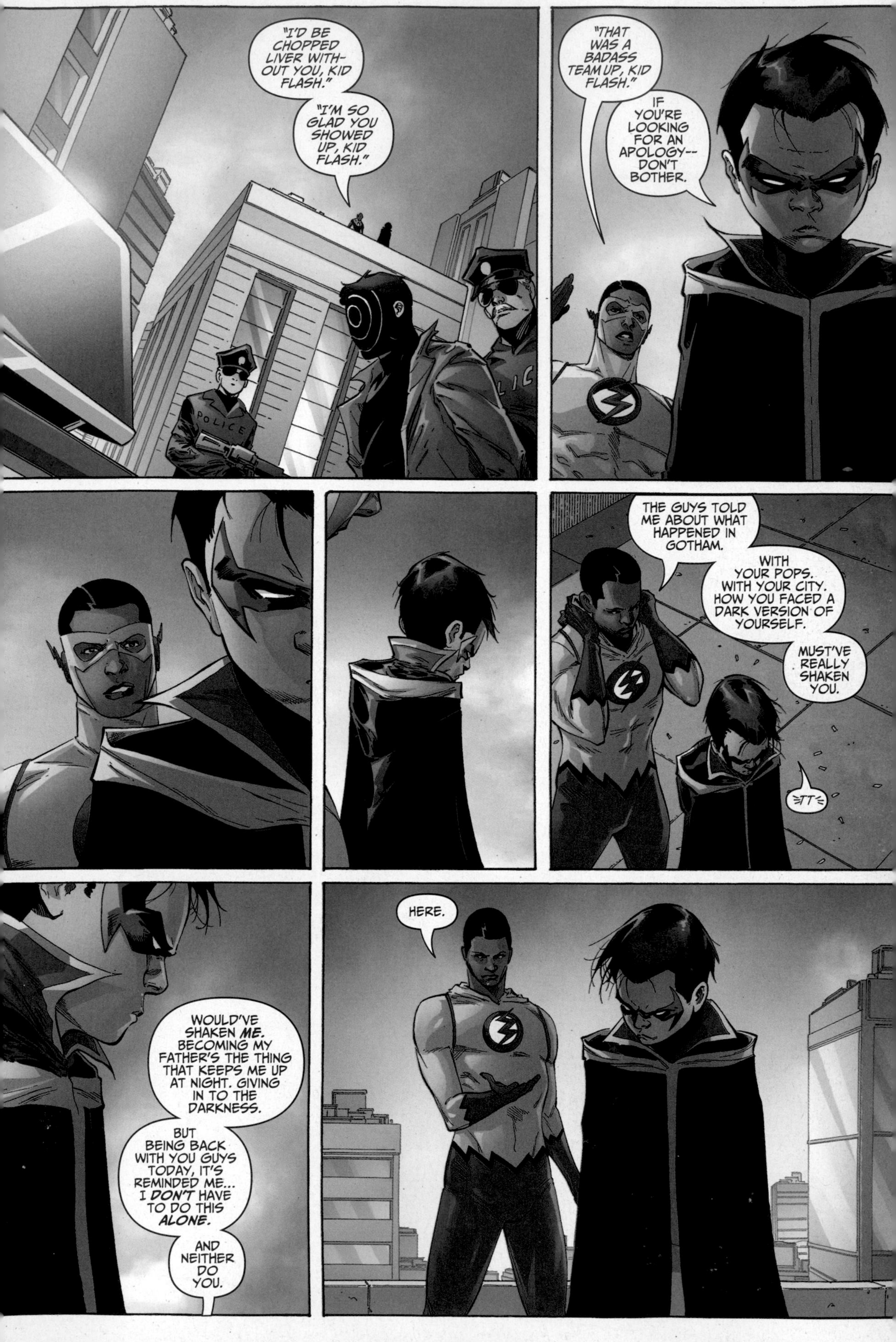
"I'D BE CHOPPED LIVER WITH-OUT YOU, KID FLASH."
"I'M SO GLAD YOU SHOWED UP, KID FLASH."
POLICE
"THAT WAS A BADASS TEAM UP, KID FLASH."
IF YOU'RE LOOKING FOR AN APOLOGY-- DON'T BOTHER.
THE GUYS TOLD ME ABOUT WHAT HAPPENED IN GOTHAM.
WITH YOUR POPS. WITH YOUR CITY. HOW YOU FACED A DARK VERSION OF YOURSELF.
MUST'VE REALLY SHAKEN YOU.
TT
WOULD'VE SHAKEN ME. BECOMING MY FATHER'S THE THING THAT KEEPS ME UP AT NIGHT. GIVING IN TO THE DARKNESS.
BUT BEING BACK WITH YOU GUYS TODAY, IT'S REMINDED ME... I DON'T HAVE TO DO THIS ALONE.
AND NEITHER DO YOU.
HERE.

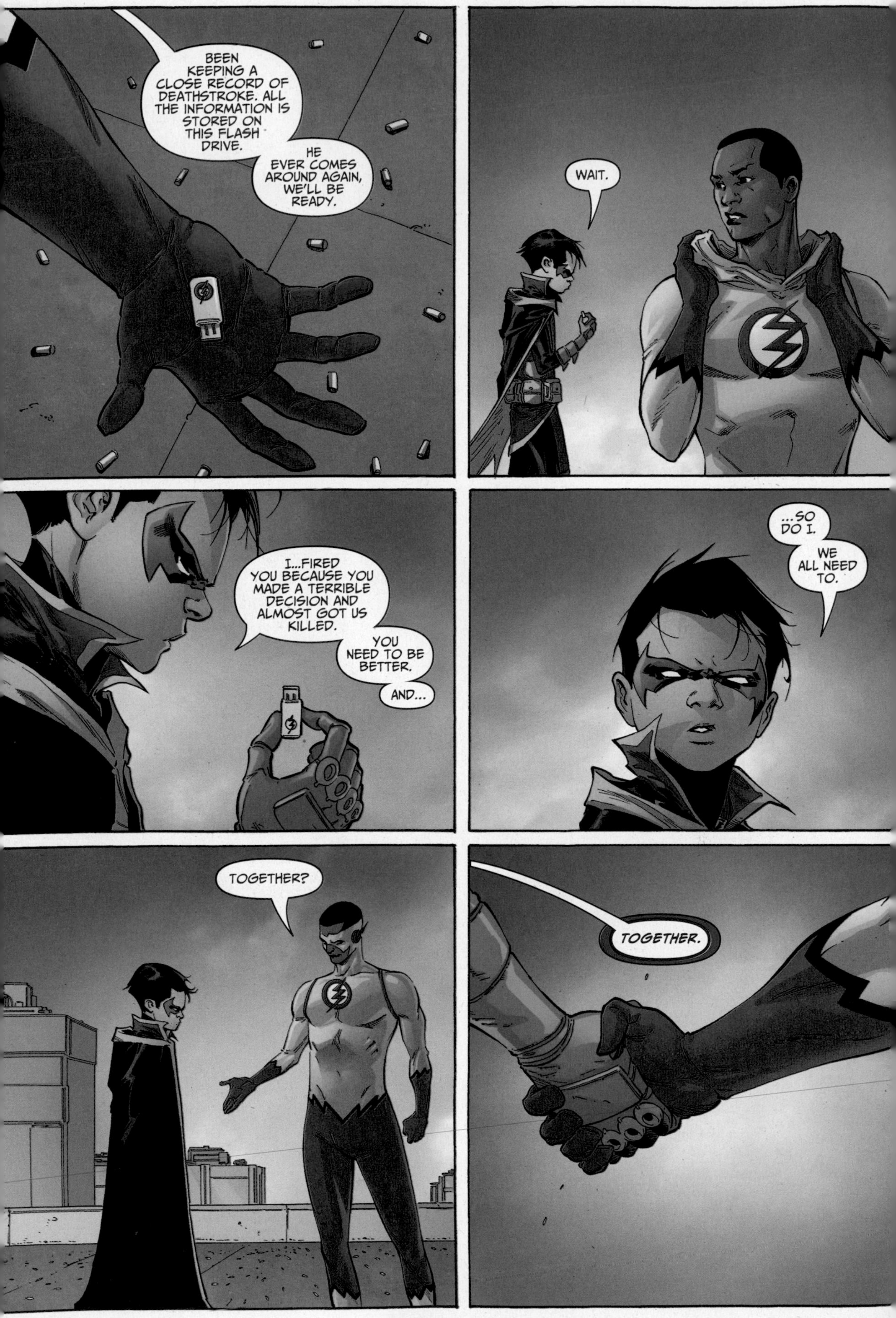
BEEN KEEPING A CLOSE RECORD OF DEATHSTROKE. ALL THE INFORMATION IS STORED ON THIS FLASH DRIVE.
HE EVER COMES AROUND AGAIN, WE'LL BE READY.
WAIT.
I...FIRED YOU BECAUSE YOU MADE A TERRIBLE DECISION AND ALMOST GOT US KILLED.
YOU NEED TO BE BETTER.
AND...
...SO DO I.
WE ALL NEED TO.
TOGETHER?
TOGETHER.

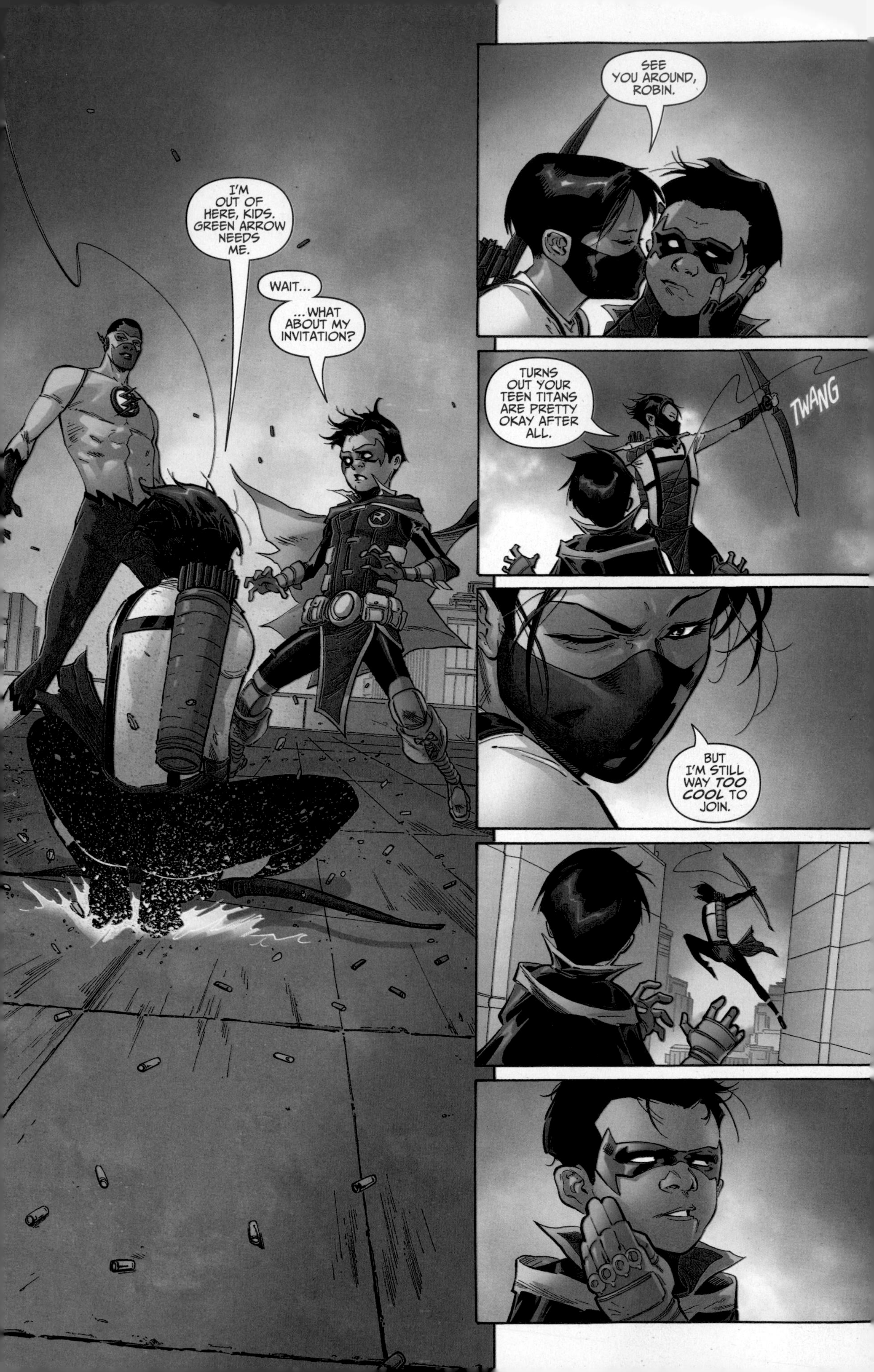
I'M OUT OF HERE, KIDS. GREEN ARROW NEEDS ME.
WAIT...
...WHAT ABOUT MY INVITATION?
SEE YOU AROUND, ROBIN.
TURNS OUT YOUR TEEN TITANS ARE PRETTY OKAY AFTER ALL.
TWANG
BUT I'M STILL WAY *TOO COOL* TO JOIN.

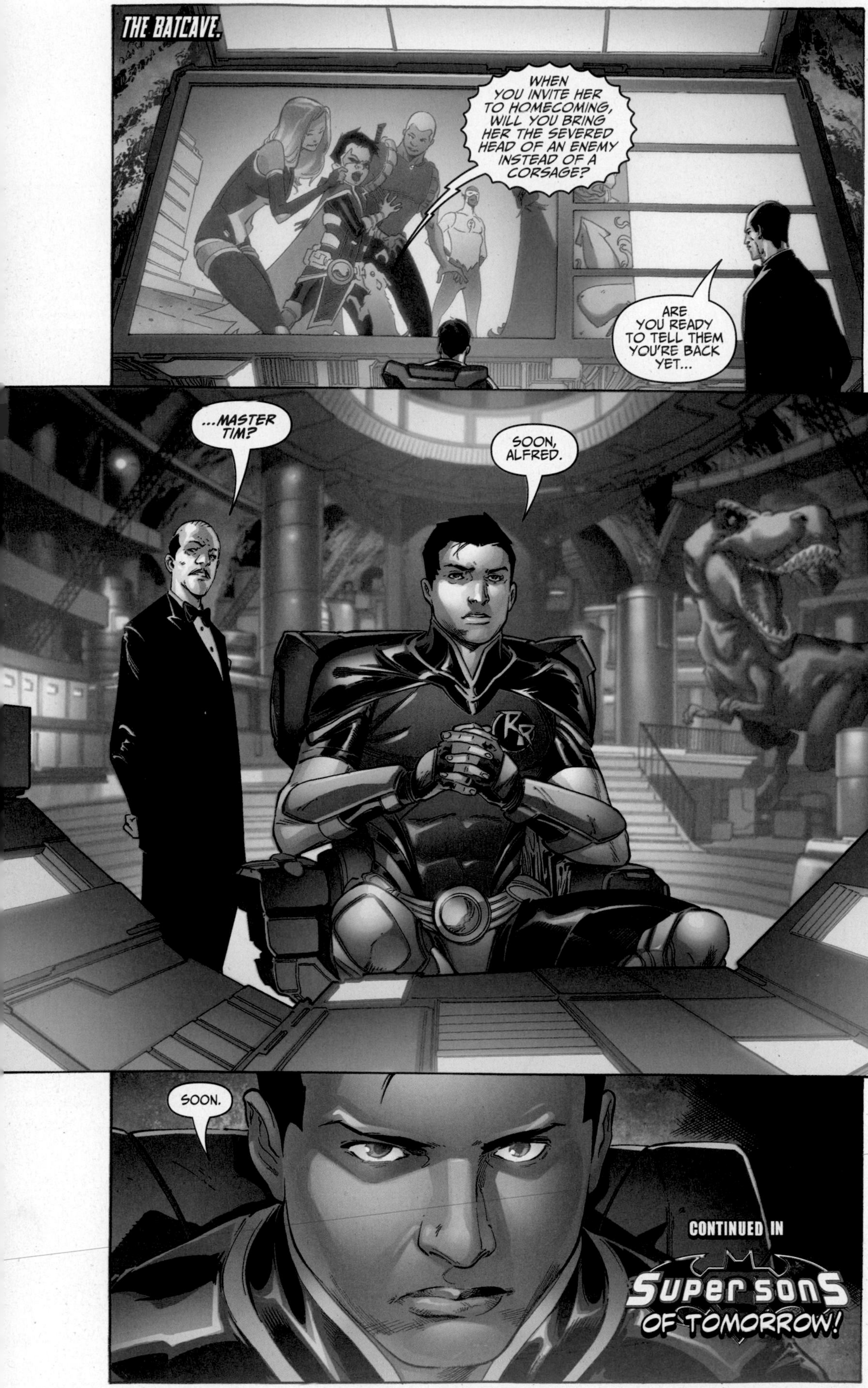
THE BATCAVE.
WHEN YOU INVITE HER TO HOMECOMING, WILL YOU BRING HER THE SEVERED HEAD OF AN ENEMY INSTEAD OF A CORSAGE?
ARE YOU READY TO TELL THEM YOU'RE BACK YET...
...MASTER TIM?
SOON, ALFRED.
SOON.
CONTINUED IN
SUPER SONS OF TOMORROW!

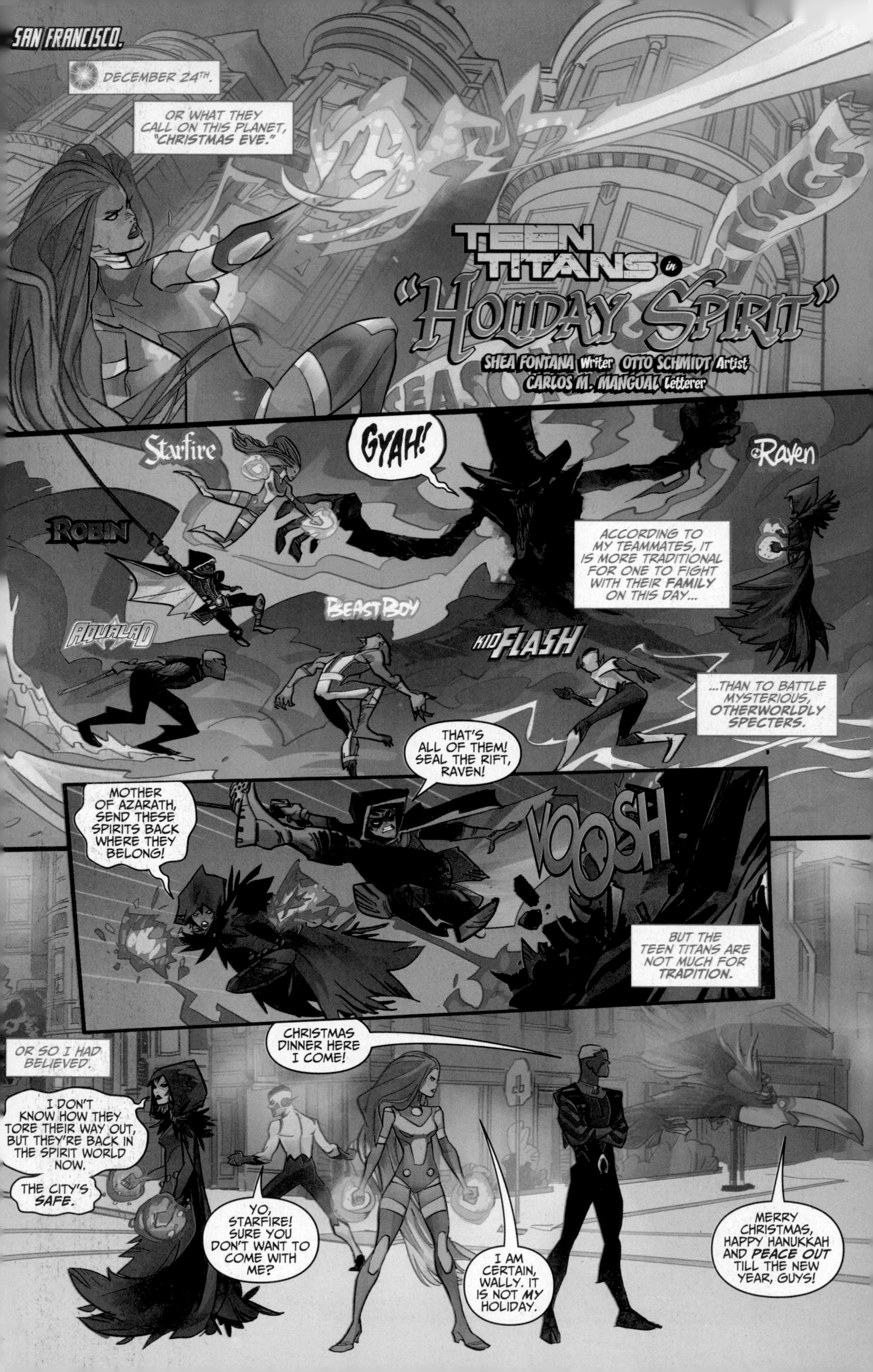

SAN FRANCISCO.
DECEMBER 24TH.
OR WHAT THEY CALL ON THIS PLANET, "CHRISTMAS EVE."
TEEN TITANS in "HOLIDAY SPIRIT"
SHEA FONTANA Writer OTTO SCHMIDT Artist
CARLOS M. MANGUAL Letterer
Starfire
GYAH!
Raven
ROBIN
ACCORDING TO MY TEAMMATES, IT IS MORE TRADITIONAL FOR ONE TO FIGHT WITH THEIR FAMILY ON THIS DAY...
BEAST BOY
AQUALAD
KID FLASH
...THAN TO BATTLE MYSTERIOUS, OTHERWORLDLY SPECTERS.
THAT'S ALL OF THEM! SEAL THE RIFT, RAVEN!
MOTHER OF AZARATH, SEND THESE SPIRITS BACK WHERE THEY BELONG!
VOOSH
BUT THE TEEN TITANS ARE NOT MUCH FOR TRADITION.
OR SO I HAD BELIEVED.
CHRISTMAS DINNER HERE I COME!
I DON'T KNOW HOW THEY TORE THEIR WAY OUT, BUT THEY'RE BACK IN THE SPIRIT WORLD NOW.
THE CITY'S SAFE.
YO, STARFIRE! SURE YOU DON'T WANT TO COME WITH ME?
I AM CERTAIN, WALLY. IT IS NOT MY HOLIDAY.
MERRY CHRISTMAS, HAPPY HANUKKAH AND PEACE OUT TILL THE NEW YEAR, GUYS!

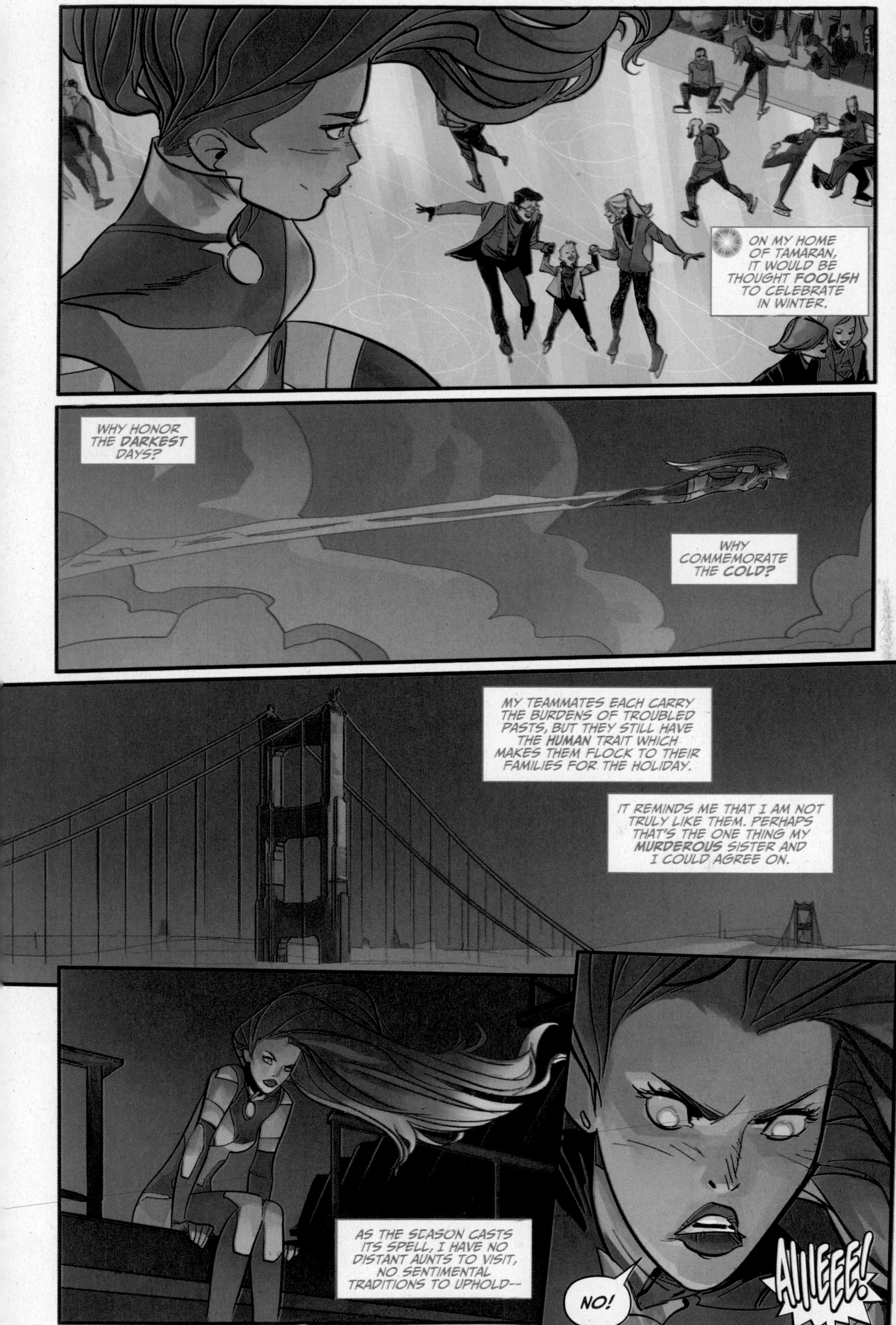
ON MY HOME OF TAMARAN, IT WOULD BE THOUGHT FOOLISH TO CELEBRATE IN WINTER.
WHY HONOR THE DARKEST DAYS?
WHY COMMEMORATE THE COLD?
MY TEAMMATES EACH CARRY THE BURDENS OF TROUBLED PASTS, BUT THEY STILL HAVE THE HUMAN TRAIT WHICH MAKES THEM FLOCK TO THEIR FAMILIES FOR THE HOLIDAY.
IT REMINDS ME THAT I AM NOT TRULY LIKE THEM. PERHAPS THAT'S THE ONE THING MY MURDEROUS SISTER AND I COULD AGREE ON.
AS THE SEASON CASTS ITS SPELL, I HAVE NO DISTANT AUNTS TO VISIT, NO SENTIMENTAL TRADITIONS TO UPHOLD--
NO!
AIIIEEE!

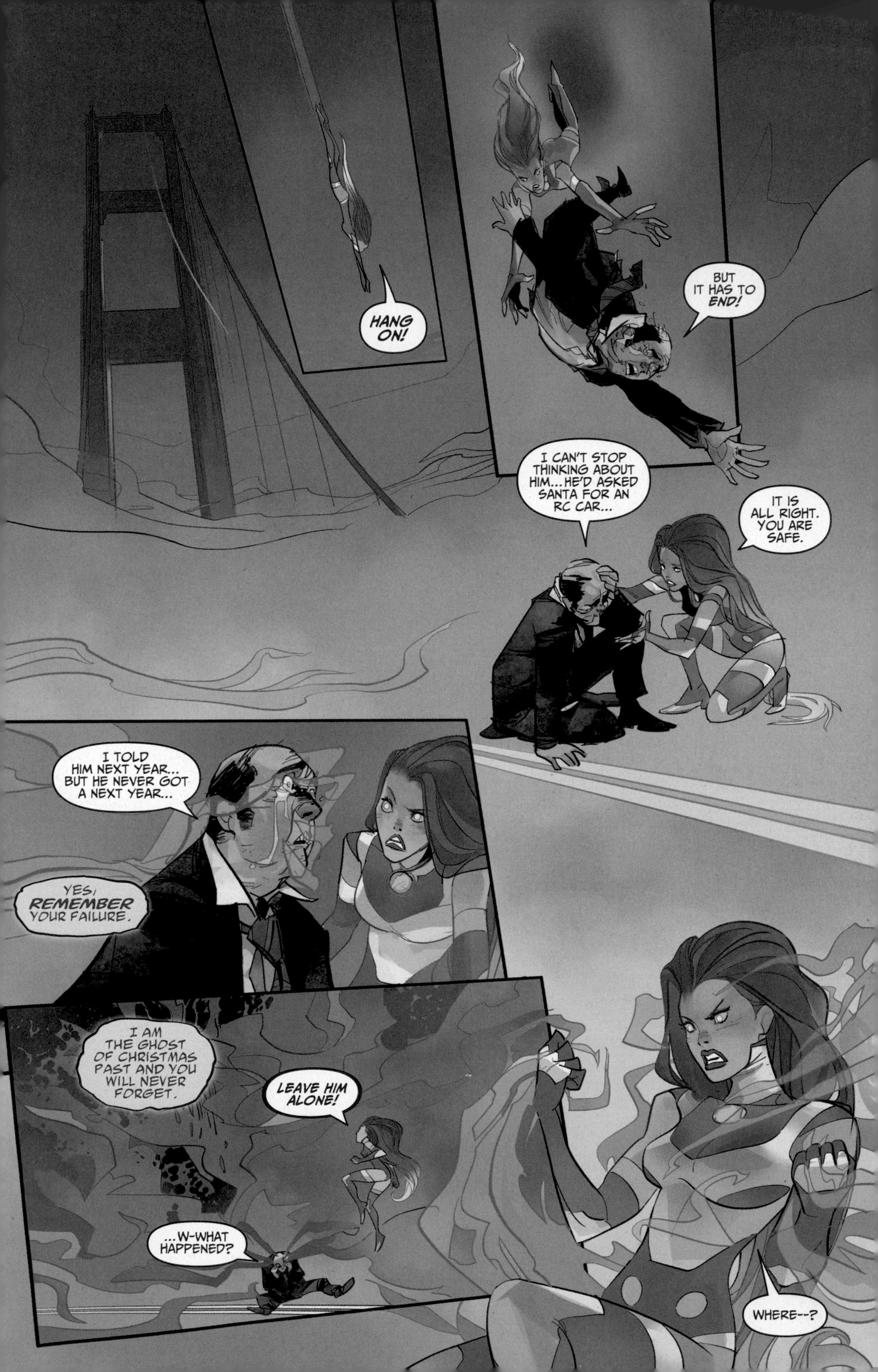

HANG ON!
BUT IT HAS TO END!
I CAN'T STOP THINKING ABOUT HIM...HE'D ASKED SANTA FOR AN RC CAR...
IT IS ALL RIGHT. YOU ARE SAFE.
I TOLD HIM NEXT YEAR... BUT HE NEVER GOT A NEXT YEAR...
YES, REMEMBER YOUR FAILURE.
I AM THE GHOST OF CHRISTMAS PAST AND YOU WILL NEVER FORGET.
LEAVE HIM ALONE!
...W-WHAT HAPPENED?
WHERE--?

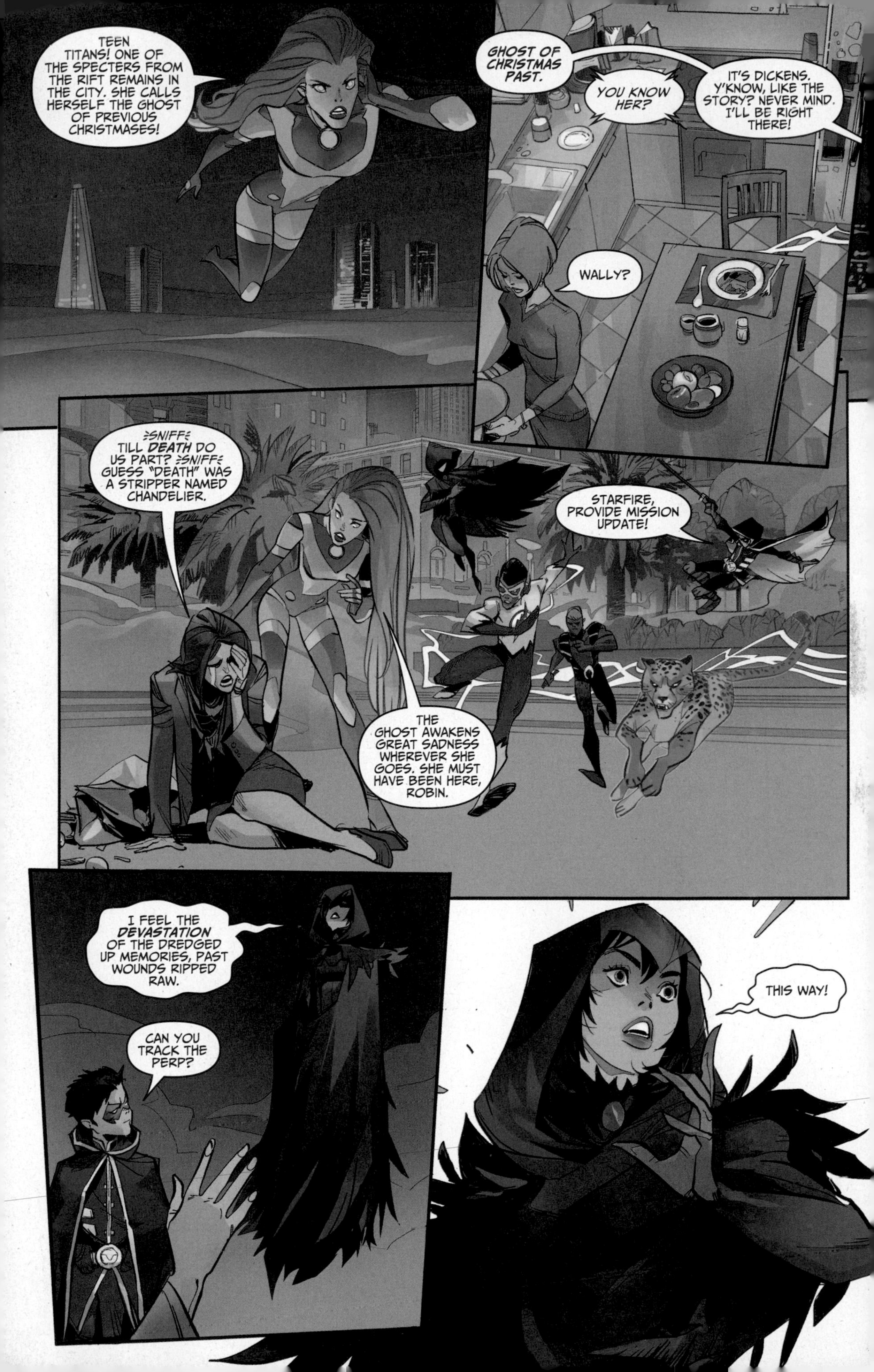
TEEN TITANS! ONE OF THE SPECTERS FROM THE RIFT REMAINS IN THE CITY. SHE CALLS HERSELF THE GHOST OF PREVIOUS CHRISTMASES!
GHOST OF CHRISTMAS PAST.
YOU KNOW HER?
IT'S DICKENS. Y'KNOW, LIKE THE STORY? NEVER MIND. I'LL BE RIGHT THERE!
WALLY?
SNIFF TILL DEATH DO US PART? SNIFF GUESS "DEATH" WAS A STRIPPER NAMED CHANDELIER.
STARFIRE, PROVIDE MISSION UPDATE!
THE GHOST AWAKENS GREAT SADNESS WHEREVER SHE GOES. SHE MUST HAVE BEEN HERE, ROBIN.
I FEEL THE DEVASTATION OF THE DREDGED UP MEMORIES, PAST WOUNDS RIPPED RAW.
CAN YOU TRACK THE PERP?
THIS WAY!

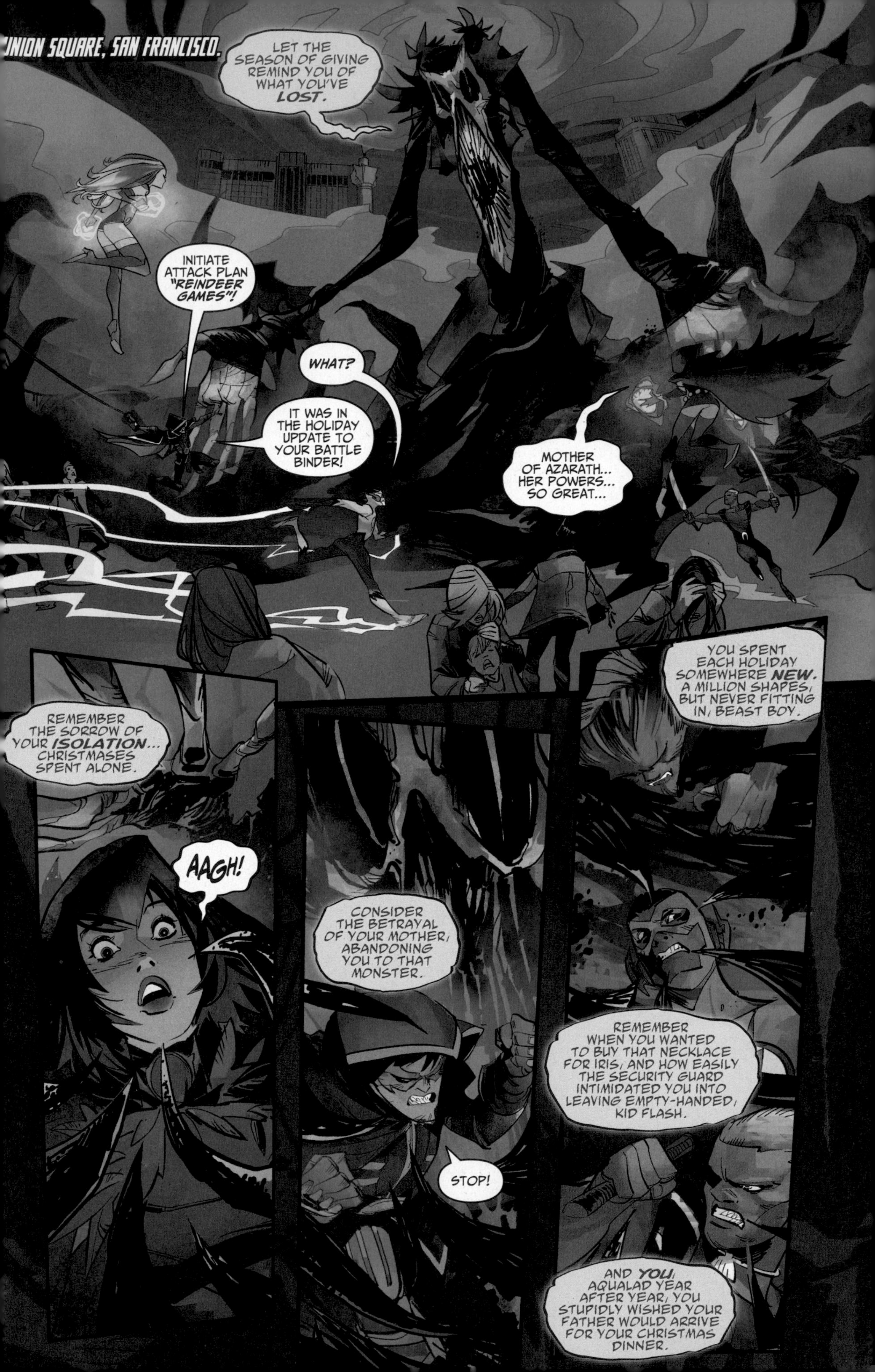
UNION SQUARE, SAN FRANCISCO.
LET THE SEASON OF GIVING REMIND YOU OF WHAT YOU'VE LOST.
INITIATE ATTACK PLAN "REINDEER GAMES"!
WHAT?
IT WAS IN THE HOLIDAY UPDATE TO YOUR BATTLE BINDER!
MOTHER OF AZARATH... HER POWERS... SO GREAT...
REMEMBER THE SORROW OF YOUR ISOLATION... CHRISTMASES SPENT ALONE.
AAGH!
CONSIDER THE BETRAYAL OF YOUR MOTHER, ABANDONING YOU TO THAT MONSTER.
STOP!
YOU SPENT EACH HOLIDAY SOMEWHERE NEW. A MILLION SHAPES, BUT NEVER FITTING IN, BEAST BOY.
REMEMBER WHEN YOU WANTED TO BUY THAT NECKLACE FOR IRIS, AND HOW EASILY THE SECURITY GUARD INTIMIDATED YOU INTO LEAVING EMPTY-HANDED, KID FLASH.
AND YOU, AQUALAD YEAR AFTER YEAR, YOU STUPIDLY WISHED YOUR FATHER WOULD ARRIVE FOR YOUR CHRISTMAS DINNER.

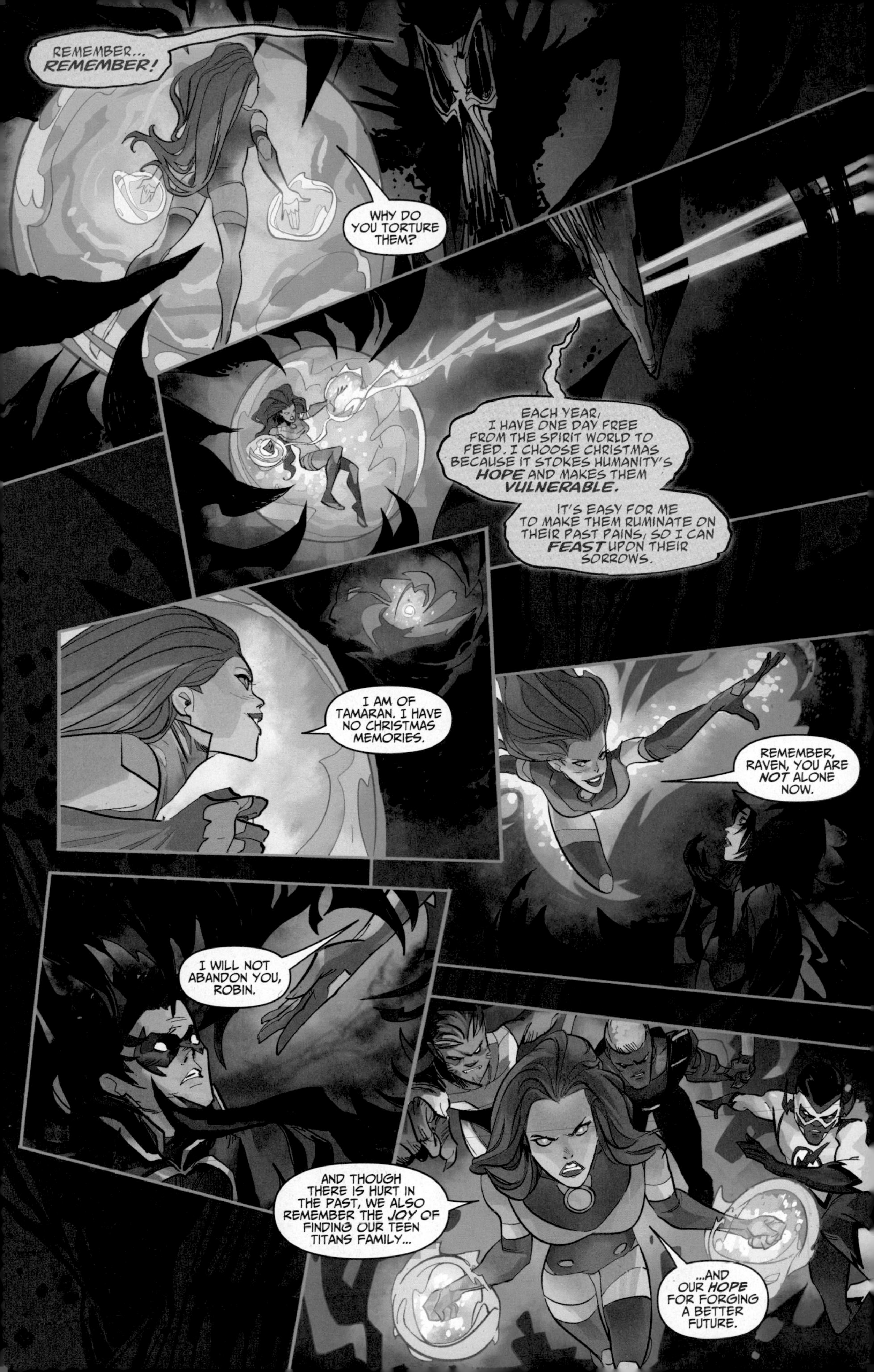
REMEMBER... REMEMBER!
WHY DO YOU TORTURE THEM?
EACH YEAR, I HAVE ONE DAY FREE FROM THE SPIRIT WORLD TO FEED. I CHOOSE CHRISTMAS BECAUSE IT STOKES HUMANITY'S HOPE AND MAKES THEM VULNERABLE.
IT'S EASY FOR ME TO MAKE THEM RUMINATE ON THEIR PAST PAINS, SO I CAN FEAST UPON THEIR SORROWS.
I AM OF TAMARAN. I HAVE NO CHRISTMAS MEMORIES.
REMEMBER, RAVEN, YOU ARE NOT ALONE NOW.
I WILL NOT ABANDON YOU, ROBIN.
AND THOUGH THERE IS HURT IN THE PAST, WE ALSO REMEMBER THE JOY OF FINDING OUR TEEN TITANS FAMILY...
...AND OUR HOPE FOR FORGING A BETTER FUTURE.

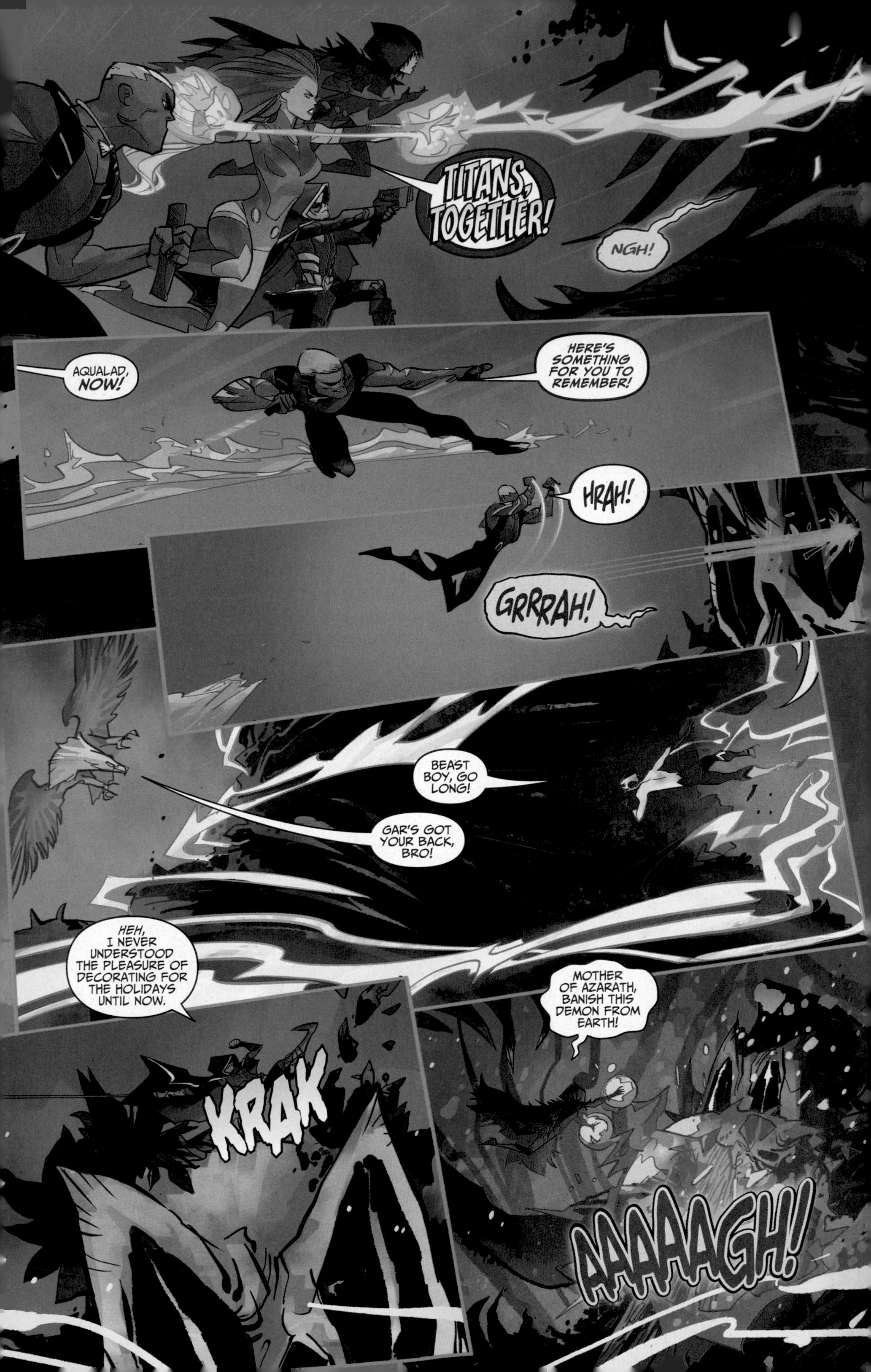
TITANS, TOGETHER!
NGH!
AQUALAD, NOW!
HERE'S SOMETHING FOR YOU TO REMEMBER!
HRAH!
GRRRAH!
BEAST BOY, GO LONG!
GAR'S GOT YOUR BACK, BRO!
HEH, I NEVER UNDERSTOOD THE PLEASURE OF DECORATING FOR THE HOLIDAYS UNTIL NOW.
MOTHER OF AZARATH, BANISH THIS DEMON FROM EARTH!
KRAK
AAAAAGH!

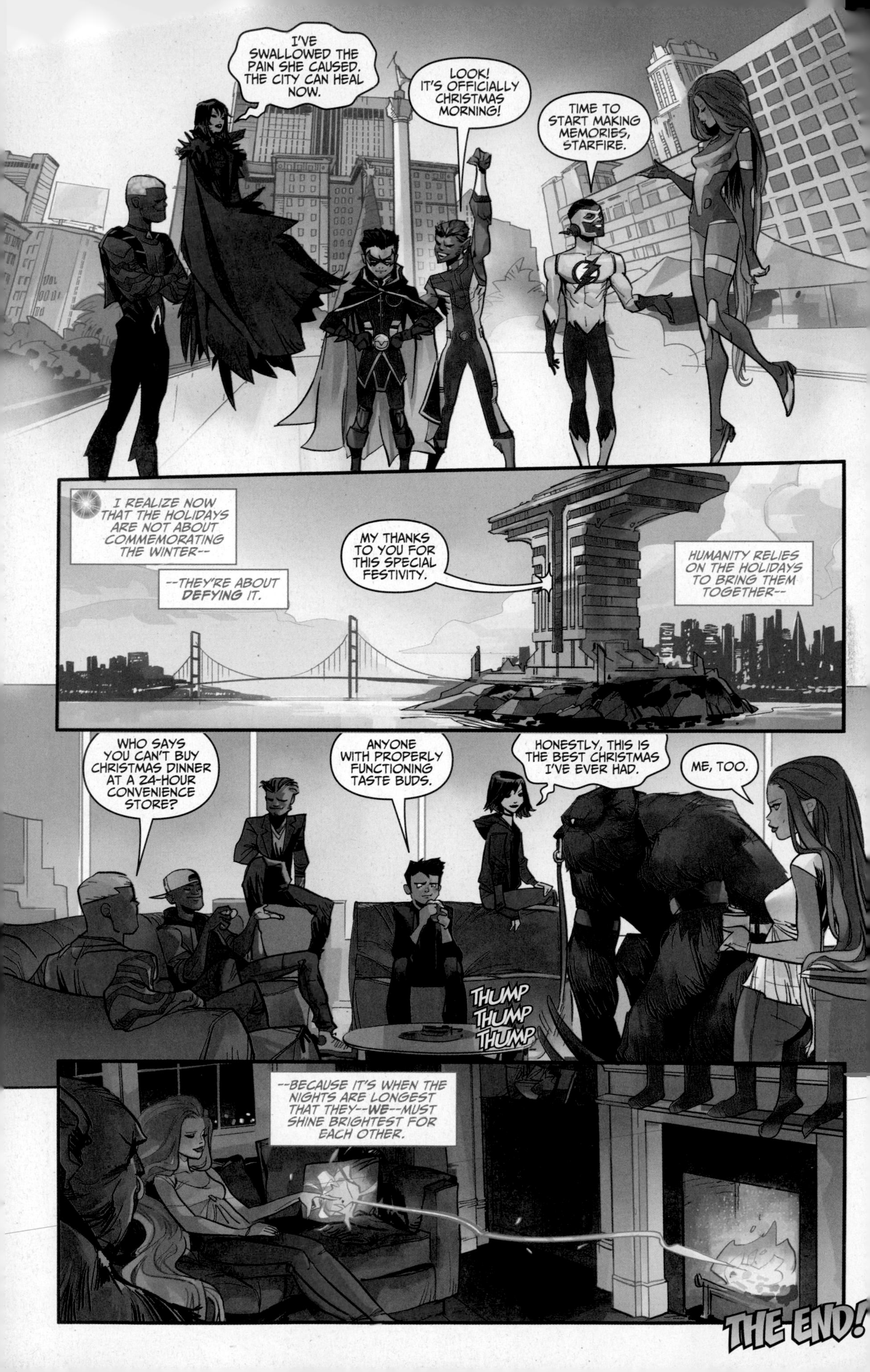
I'VE SWALLOWED THE PAIN SHE CAUSED. THE CITY CAN HEAL NOW.
LOOK! IT'S OFFICIALLY CHRISTMAS MORNING!
TIME TO START MAKING MEMORIES, STARFIRE.
I REALIZE NOW THAT THE HOLIDAYS ARE NOT ABOUT COMMEMORATING THE WINTER--
--THEY'RE ABOUT DEFYING IT.
MY THANKS TO YOU FOR THIS SPECIAL FESTIVITY.
HUMANITY RELIES ON THE HOLIDAYS TO BRING THEM TOGETHER--
WHO SAYS YOU CAN'T BUY CHRISTMAS DINNER AT A 24-HOUR CONVENIENCE STORE?
ANYONE WITH PROPERLY FUNCTIONING TASTE BUDS.
HONESTLY, THIS IS THE BEST CHRISTMAS I'VE EVER HAD.
ME, TOO.
THUMP THUMP THUMP
--BECAUSE IT'S WHEN THE NIGHTS ARE LONGEST THAT THEY--WE--MUST SHINE BRIGHTEST FOR EACH OTHER.
THE END!

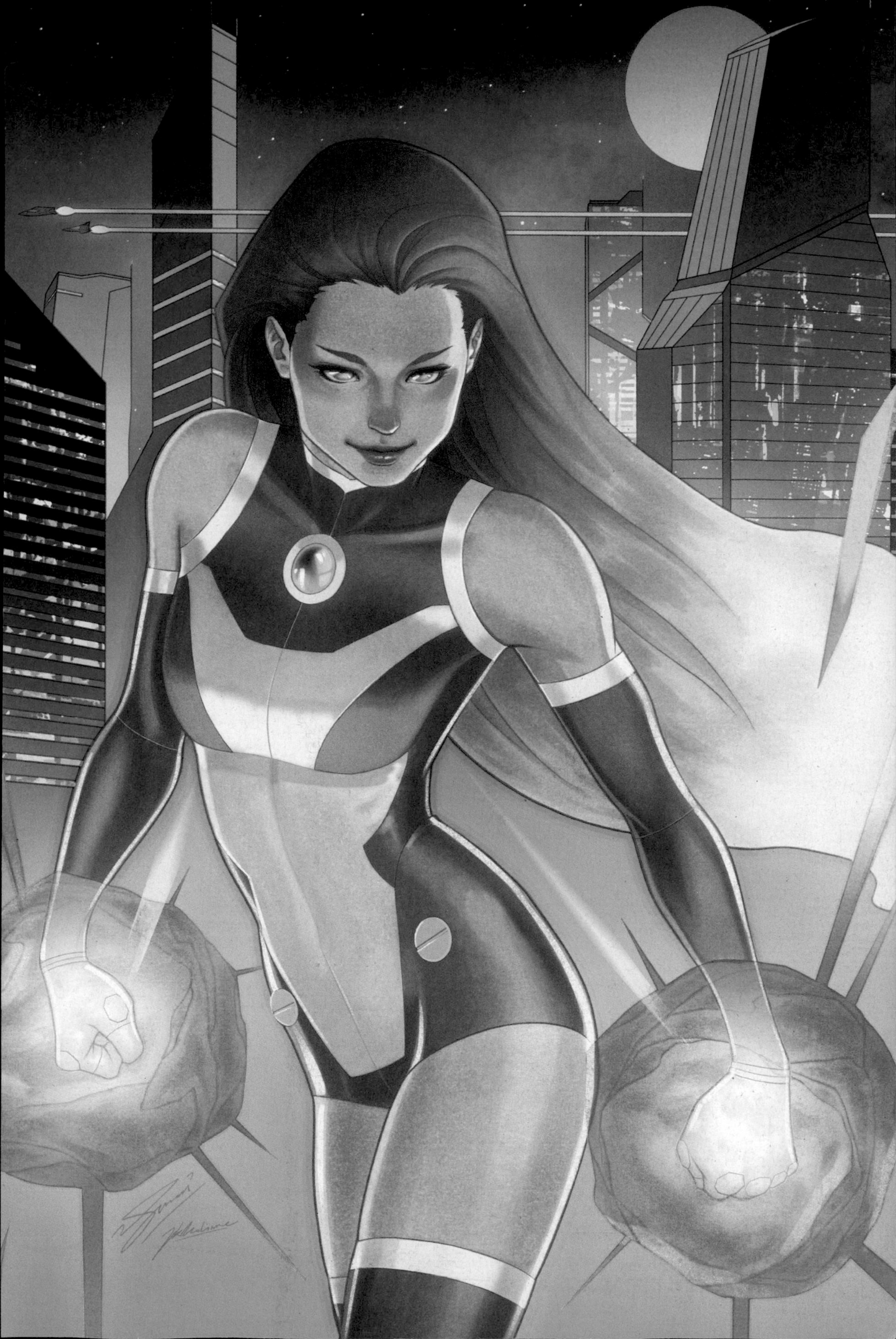

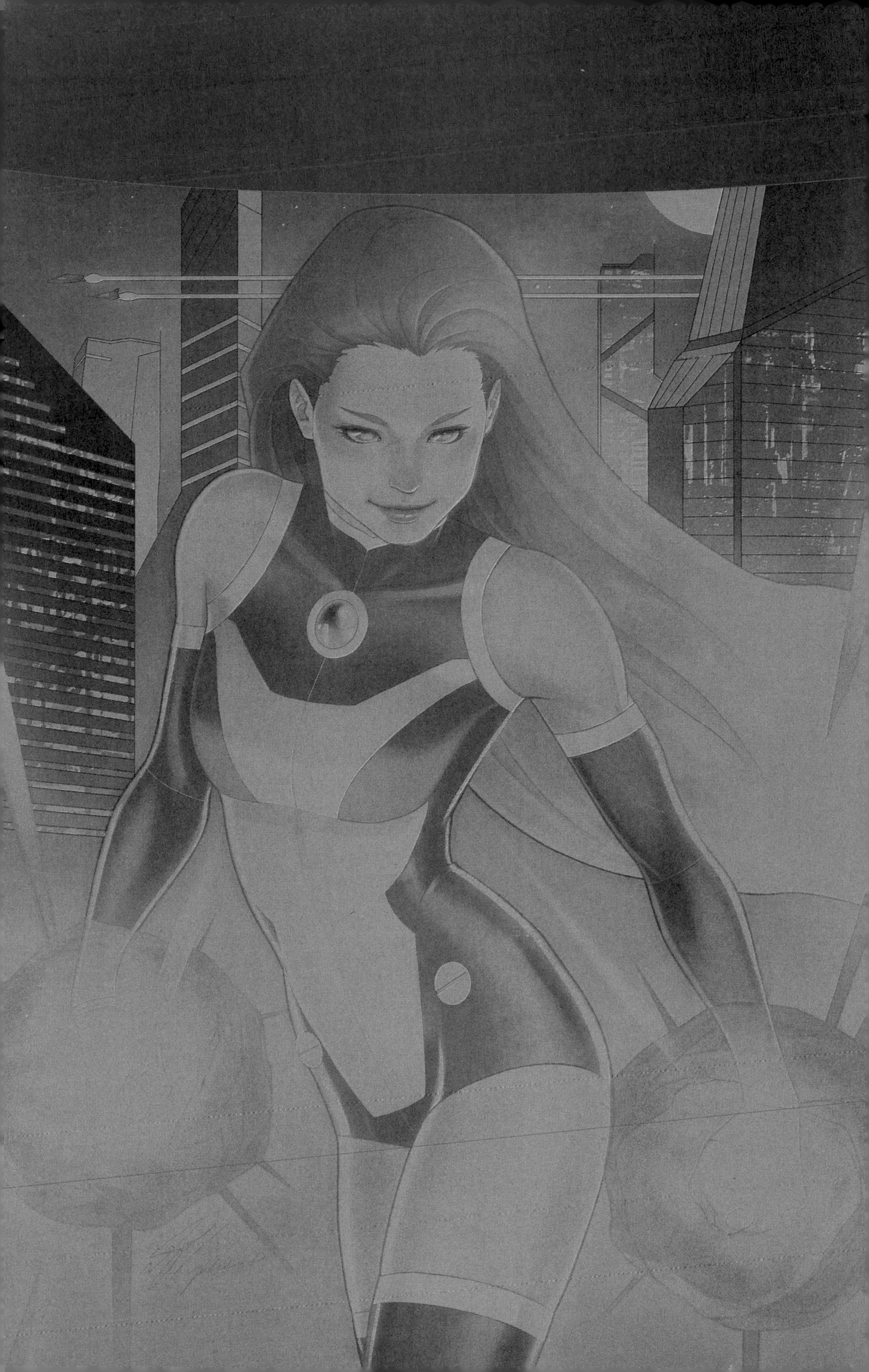

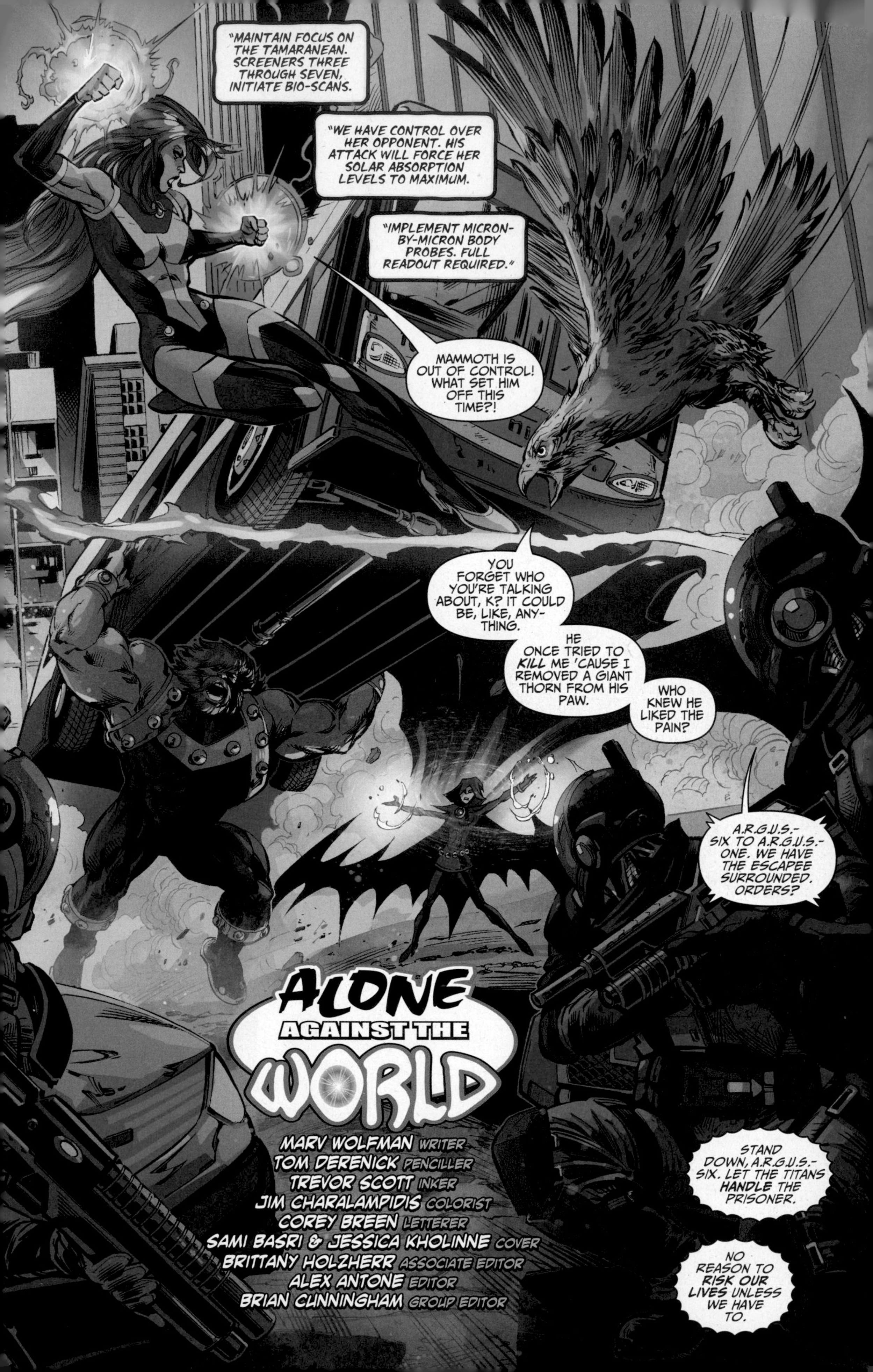
"MAINTAIN FOCUS ON THE TAMARANEAN. SCREENERS THREE THROUGH SEVEN, INITIATE BIO-SCANS.
"WE HAVE CONTROL OVER HER OPPONENT. HIS ATTACK WILL FORCE HER SOLAR ABSORPTION LEVELS TO MAXIMUM.
"IMPLEMENT MICRON-BY-MICRON BODY PROBES. FULL READOUT REQUIRED."
MAMMOTH IS OUT OF CONTROL! WHAT SET HIM OFF THIS TIME?!
YOU FORGET WHO YOU'RE TALKING ABOUT, K? IT COULD BE, LIKE, ANY-THING.
HE ONCE TRIED TO KILL ME 'CAUSE I REMOVED A GIANT THORN FROM HIS PAW.
WHO KNEW HE LIKED THE PAIN?
A.R.G.U.S.-SIX TO A.R.G.U.S.-ONE. WE HAVE THE ESCAPEE SURROUNDED. ORDERS?
ALONE AGAINST THE WORLD
MARV WOLFMAN WRITER
TOM DERENICK PENCILLER
TREVOR SCOTT INKER
JIM CHARALAMPIDIS COLORIST
COREY BREEN LETTERER
SAMI BASRI & JESSICA KHOLINNE COVER
BRITTANY HOLZHERR ASSOCIATE EDITOR
ALEX ANTONE EDITOR
BRIAN CUNNINGHAM GROUP EDITOR
STAND DOWN, A.R.G.U.S.-SIX. LET THE TITANS HANDLE THE PRISONER.
NO REASON TO RISK OUR LIVES UNLESS WE HAVE TO.

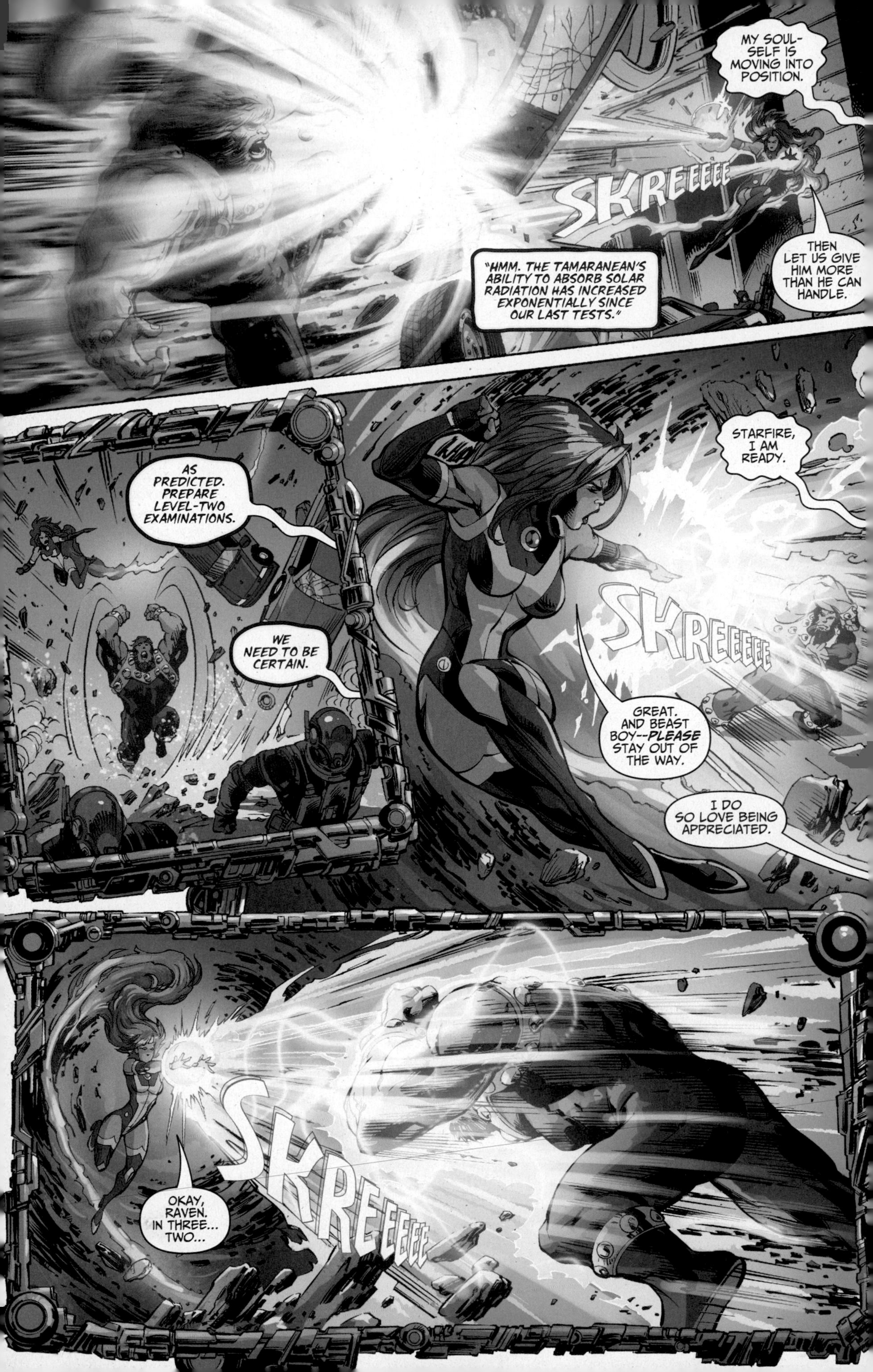

MY SOUL-SELF IS MOVING INTO POSITION.
SKREEEEE
"HMM. THE TAMARANEAN'S ABILITY TO ABSORB SOLAR RADIATION HAS INCREASED EXPONENTIALLY SINCE OUR LAST TESTS."
THEN LET US GIVE HIM MORE THAN HE CAN HANDLE.
AS PREDICTED. PREPARE LEVEL-TWO EXAMINATIONS.
STARFIRE, I AM READY.
WE NEED TO BE CERTAIN.
SKREEEEEE
GREAT. AND BEAST BOY--*PLEASE* STAY OUT OF THE WAY.
I DO SO LOVE BEING APPRECIATED.
SKREEEEEE
OKAY, RAVEN. IN THREE... TWO...

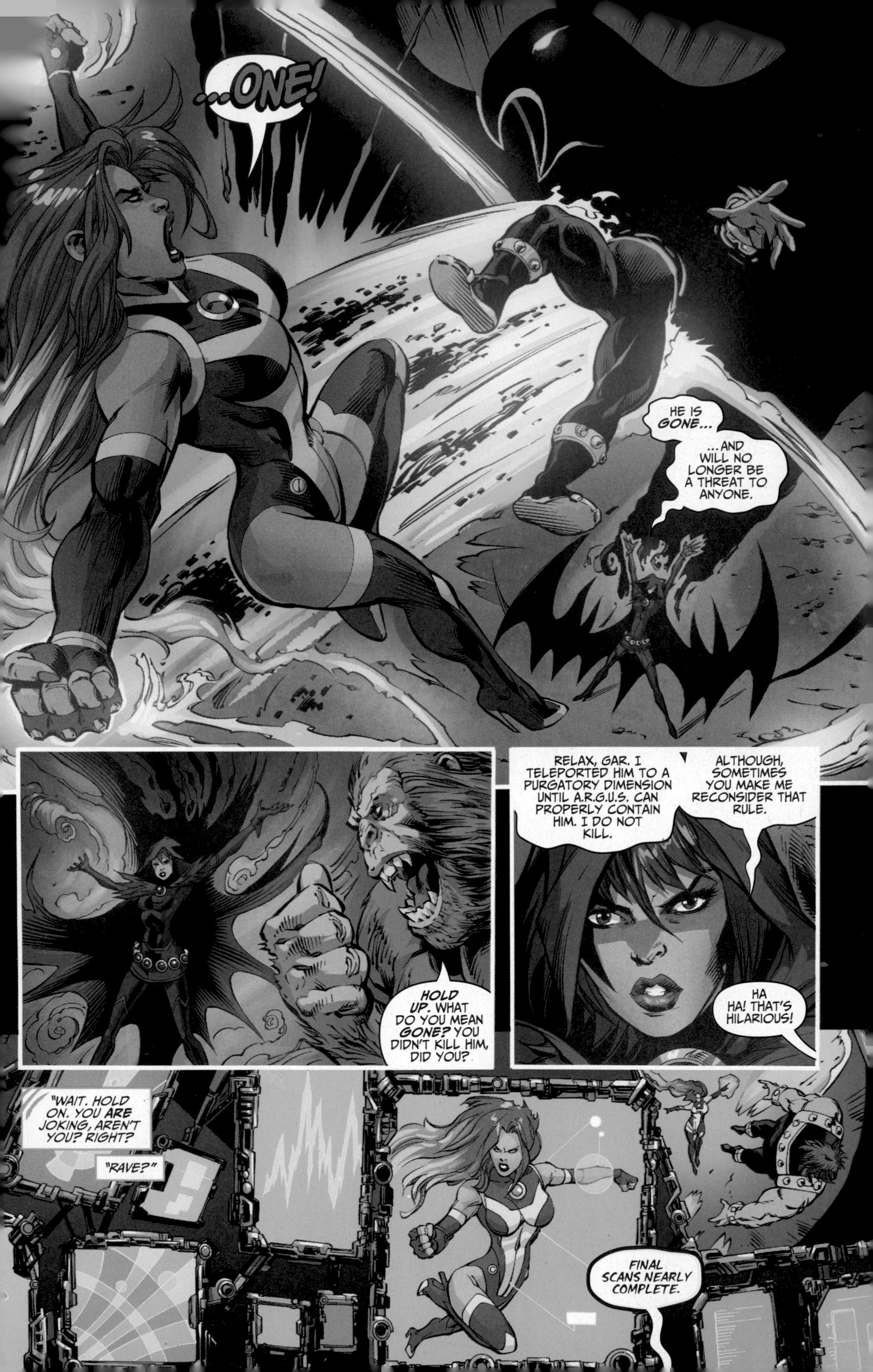
...ONE!
HE IS GONE...
...AND WILL NO LONGER BE A THREAT TO ANYONE.
HOLD UP. WHAT DO YOU MEAN GONE? YOU DIDN'T KILL HIM, DID YOU?
RELAX, GAR. I TELEPORTED HIM TO A PURGATORY DIMENSION UNTIL A.R.G.U.S. CAN PROPERLY CONTAIN HIM. I DO NOT KILL.
ALTHOUGH, SOMETIMES YOU MAKE ME RECONSIDER THAT RULE.
HA HA! THAT'S HILARIOUS!
"WAIT. HOLD ON. YOU ARE JOKING, AREN'T YOU? RIGHT?
"RAVE?"
FINAL SCANS NEARLY COMPLETE.

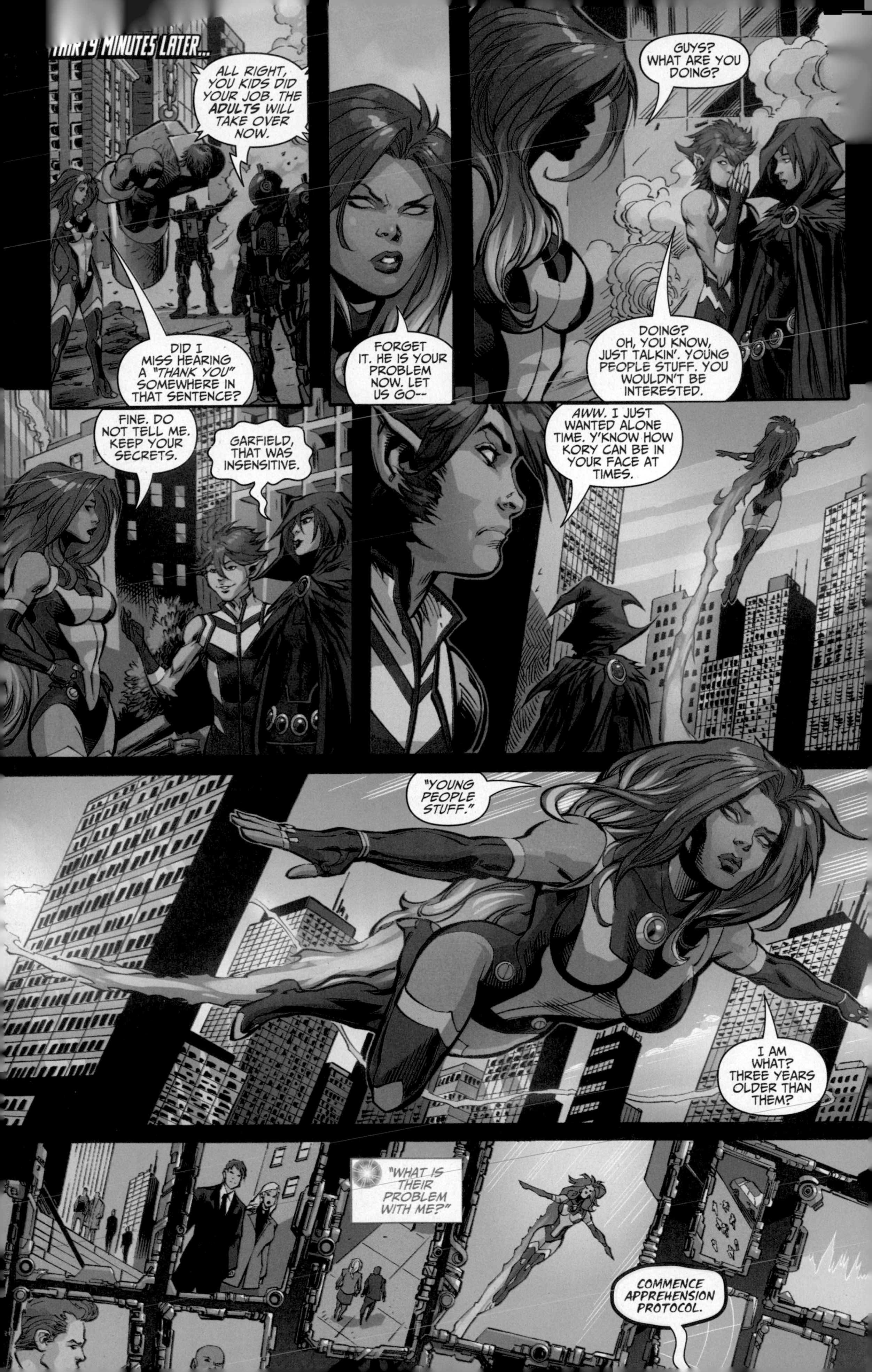
THIRTY MINUTES LATER...
ALL RIGHT, YOU KIDS DID YOUR JOB. THE ADULTS WILL TAKE OVER NOW.
DID I MISS HEARING A "THANK YOU" SOMEWHERE IN THAT SENTENCE?
FORGET IT. HE IS YOUR PROBLEM NOW. LET US GO--
GUYS? WHAT ARE YOU DOING?
DOING? OH, YOU KNOW, JUST TALKIN'. YOUNG PEOPLE STUFF. YOU WOULDN'T BE INTERESTED.
FINE. DO NOT TELL ME. KEEP YOUR SECRETS.
GARFIELD, THAT WAS INSENSITIVE.
AWW. I JUST WANTED ALONE TIME. Y'KNOW HOW KORY CAN BE IN YOUR FACE AT TIMES.
"YOUNG PEOPLE STUFF."
I AM WHAT? THREE YEARS OLDER THAN THEM?
"WHAT IS THEIR PROBLEM WITH ME?"
COMMENCE APPREHENSION PROTOCOL.

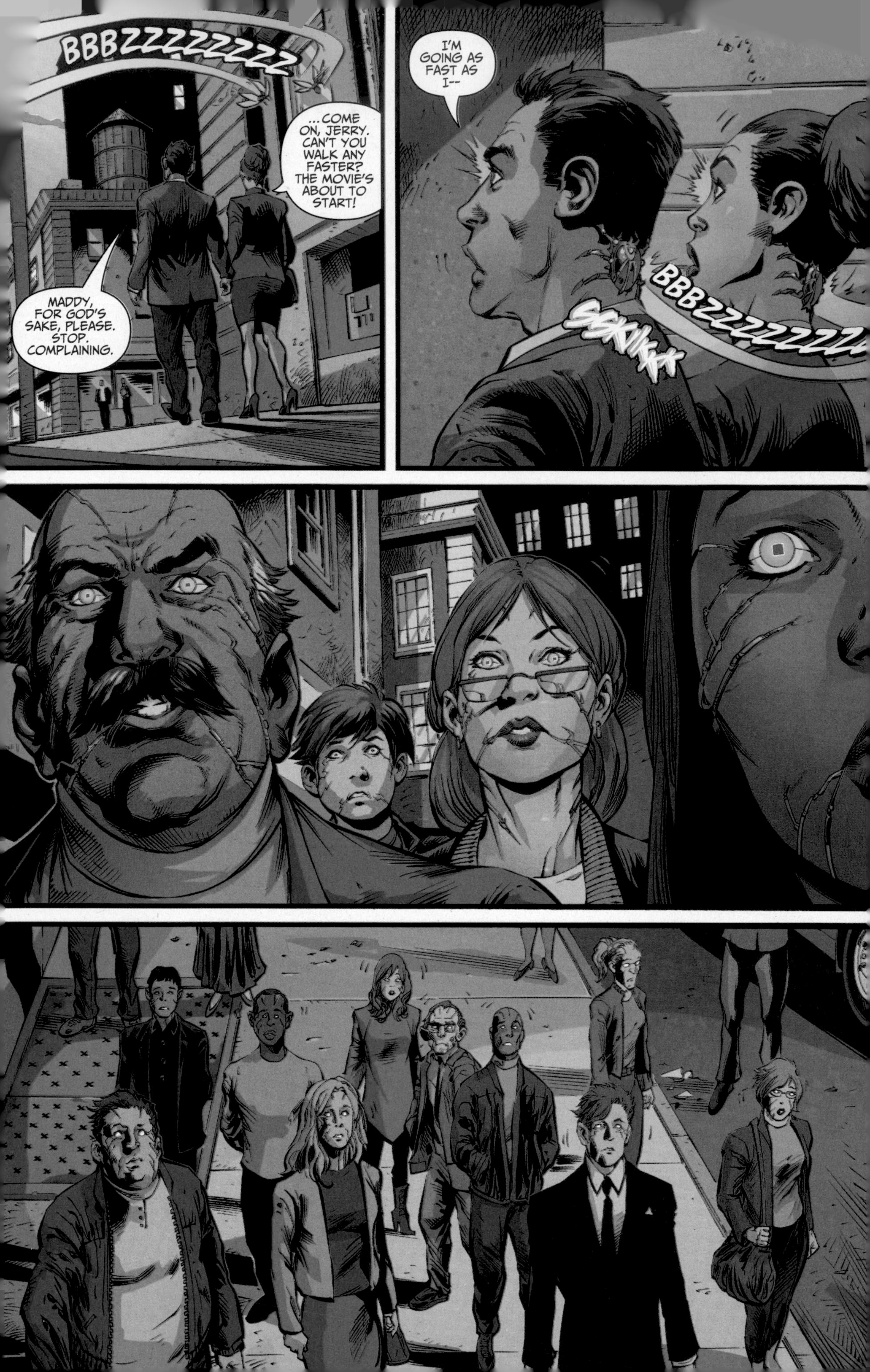
BBBZZZZZZZZZ
...COME ON, JERRY. CAN'T YOU WALK ANY FASTER? THE MOVIE'S ABOUT TO START!
MADDY, FOR GOD'S SAKE, PLEASE. STOP. COMPLAINING.
I'M GOING AS FAST AS I--
SSSKKKK
BBBZZZZZZZZZ

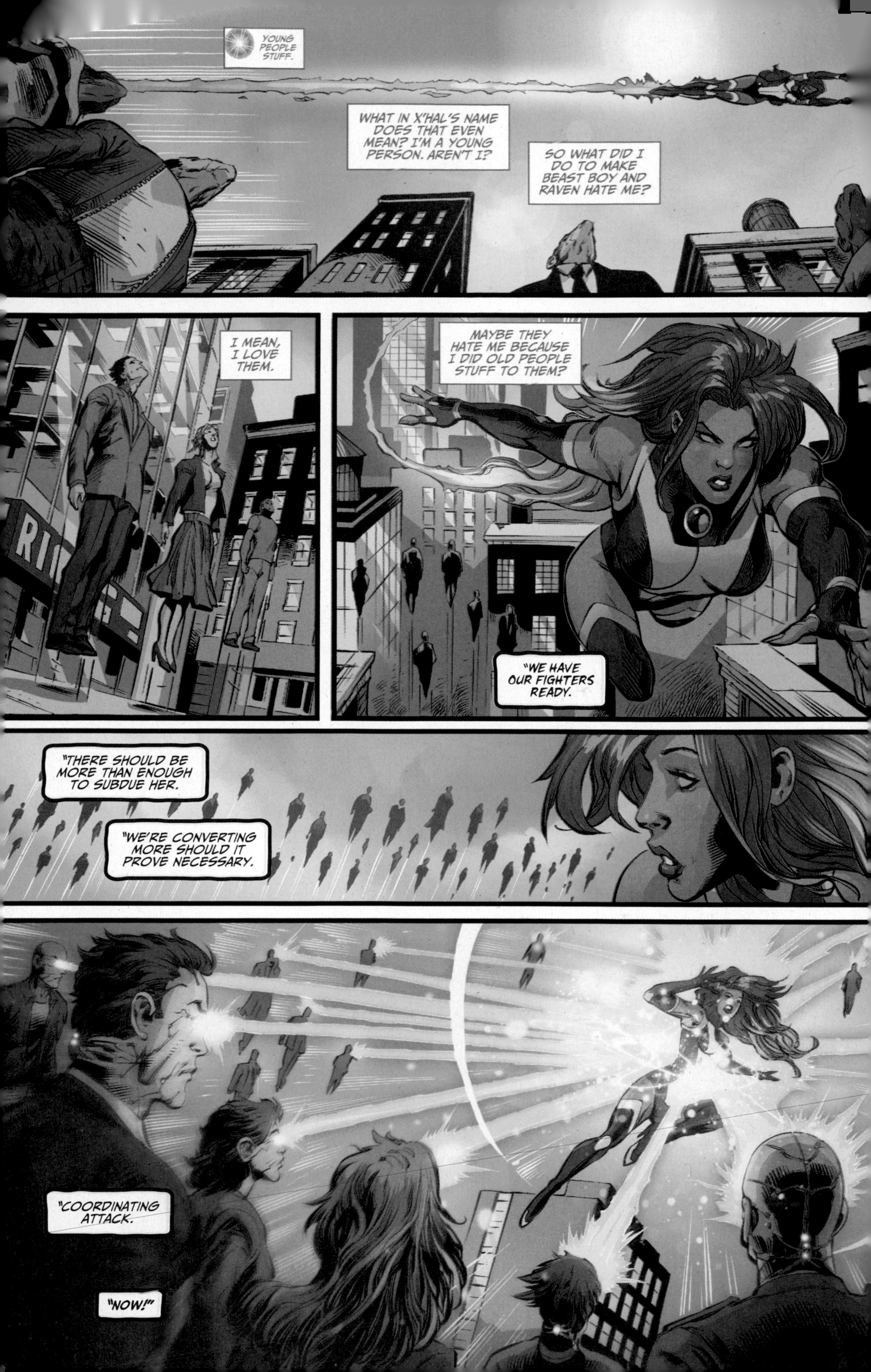
YOUNG PEOPLE STUFF.
WHAT IN X'HAL'S NAME DOES THAT EVEN MEAN? I'M A YOUNG PERSON. AREN'T I?
SO WHAT DID I DO TO MAKE BEAST BOY AND RAVEN HATE ME?
I MEAN, I LOVE THEM.
MAYBE THEY HATE ME BECAUSE I DID OLD PEOPLE STUFF TO THEM?
"WE HAVE OUR FIGHTERS READY.
"THERE SHOULD BE MORE THAN ENOUGH TO SUBDUE HER.
"WE'RE CONVERTING MORE SHOULD IT PROVE NECESSARY.
"COORDINATING ATTACK.
"NOW!"

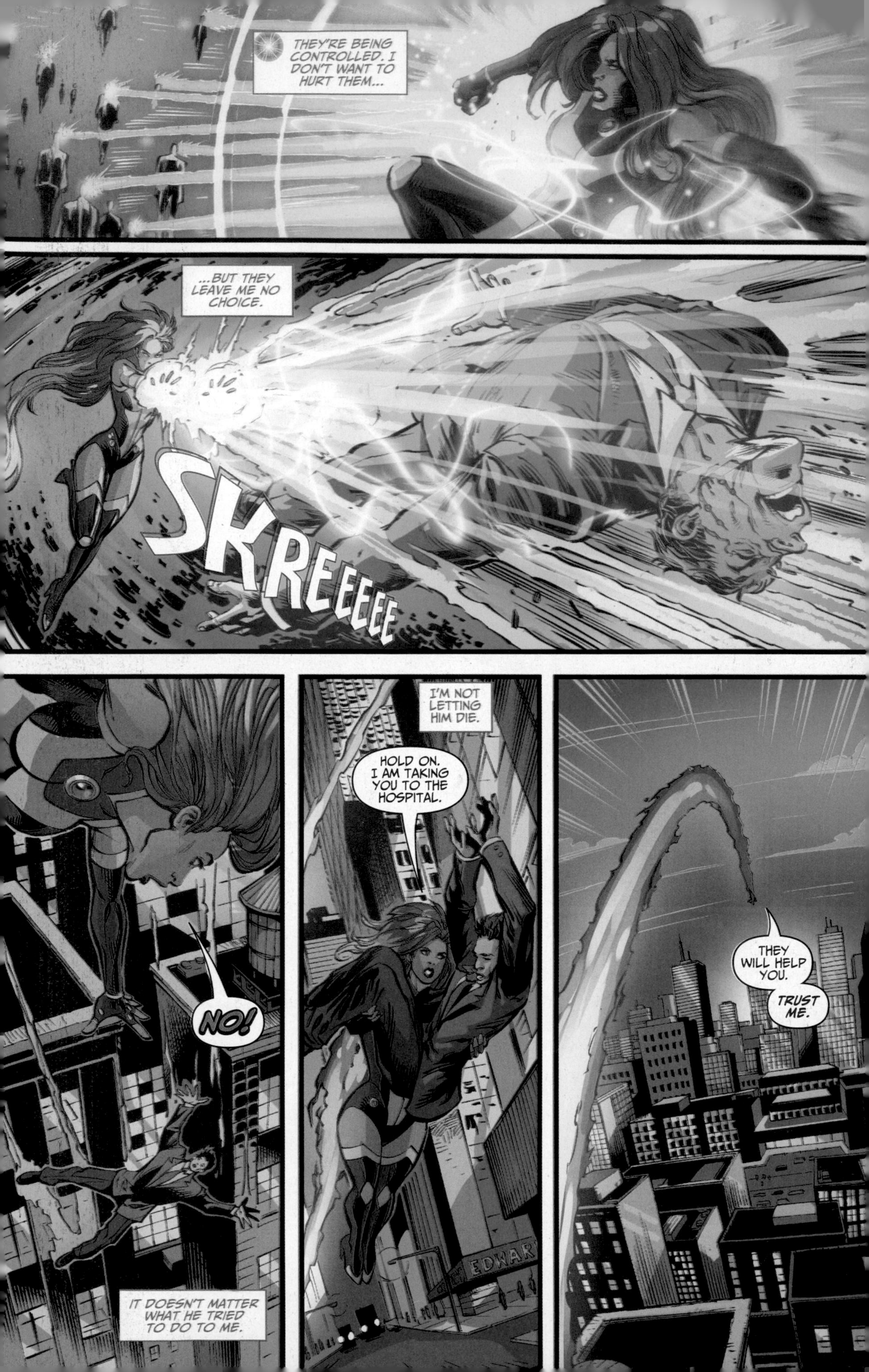
THEY'RE BEING CONTROLLED. I DON'T WANT TO HURT THEM...
...BUT THEY LEAVE ME NO CHOICE.
SKREEEEEE
NO!
IT DOESN'T MATTER WHAT HE TRIED TO DO TO ME.
I'M NOT LETTING HIM DIE.
HOLD ON. I AM TAKING YOU TO THE HOSPITAL.
EDWAR
THEY WILL HELP YOU.
TRUST ME.

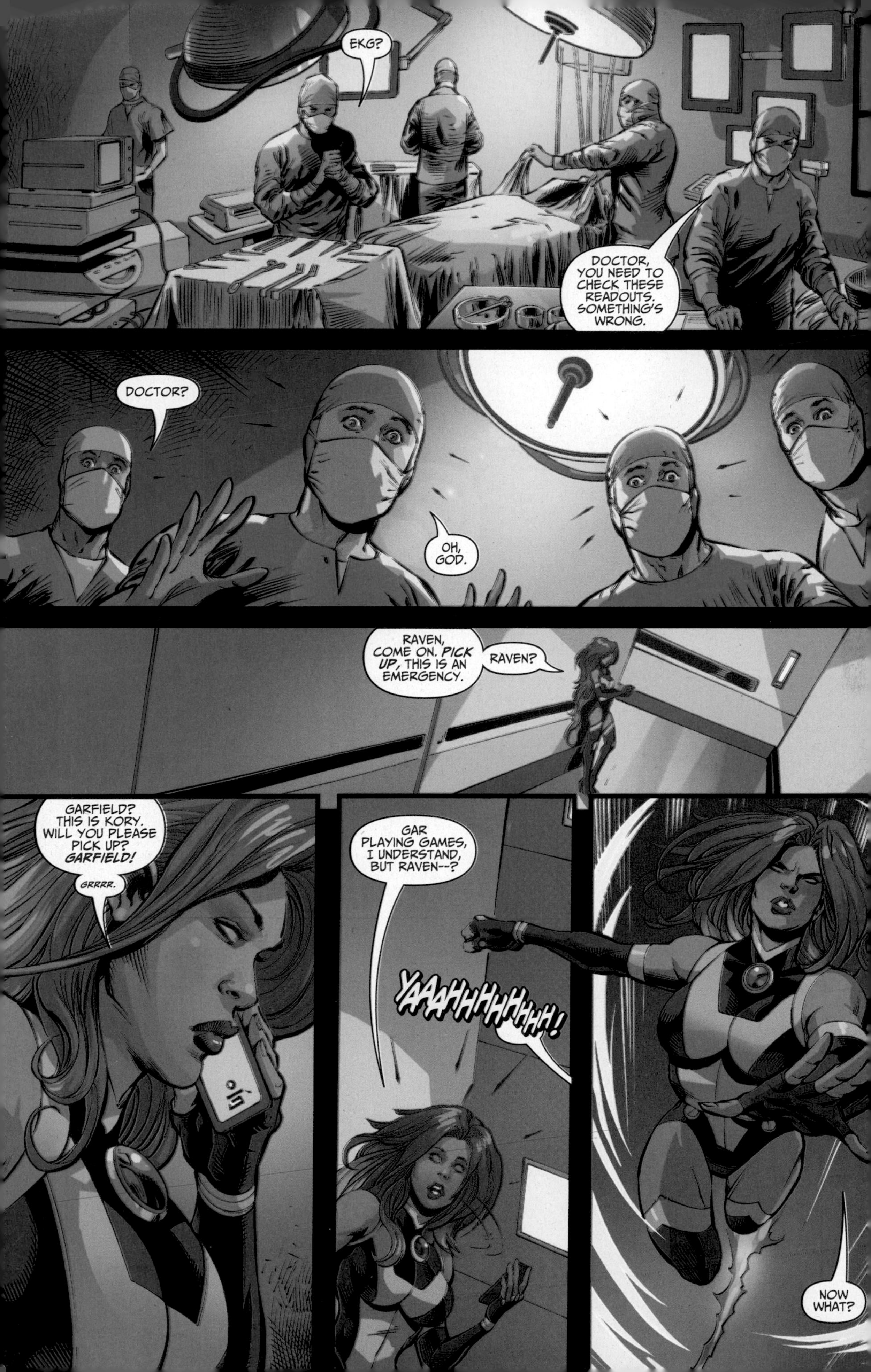
EKG?
DOCTOR, YOU NEED TO CHECK THESE READOUTS. SOMETHING'S WRONG.
DOCTOR?
OH, GOD.
RAVEN, COME ON. PICK UP, THIS IS AN EMERGENCY.
RAVEN?
GARFIELD? THIS IS KORY. WILL YOU PLEASE PICK UP? GARFIELD!
GRRRR.
GAR PLAYING GAMES, I UNDERSTAND, BUT RAVEN--?
YAAAHHHHHHHH!
NOW WHAT?

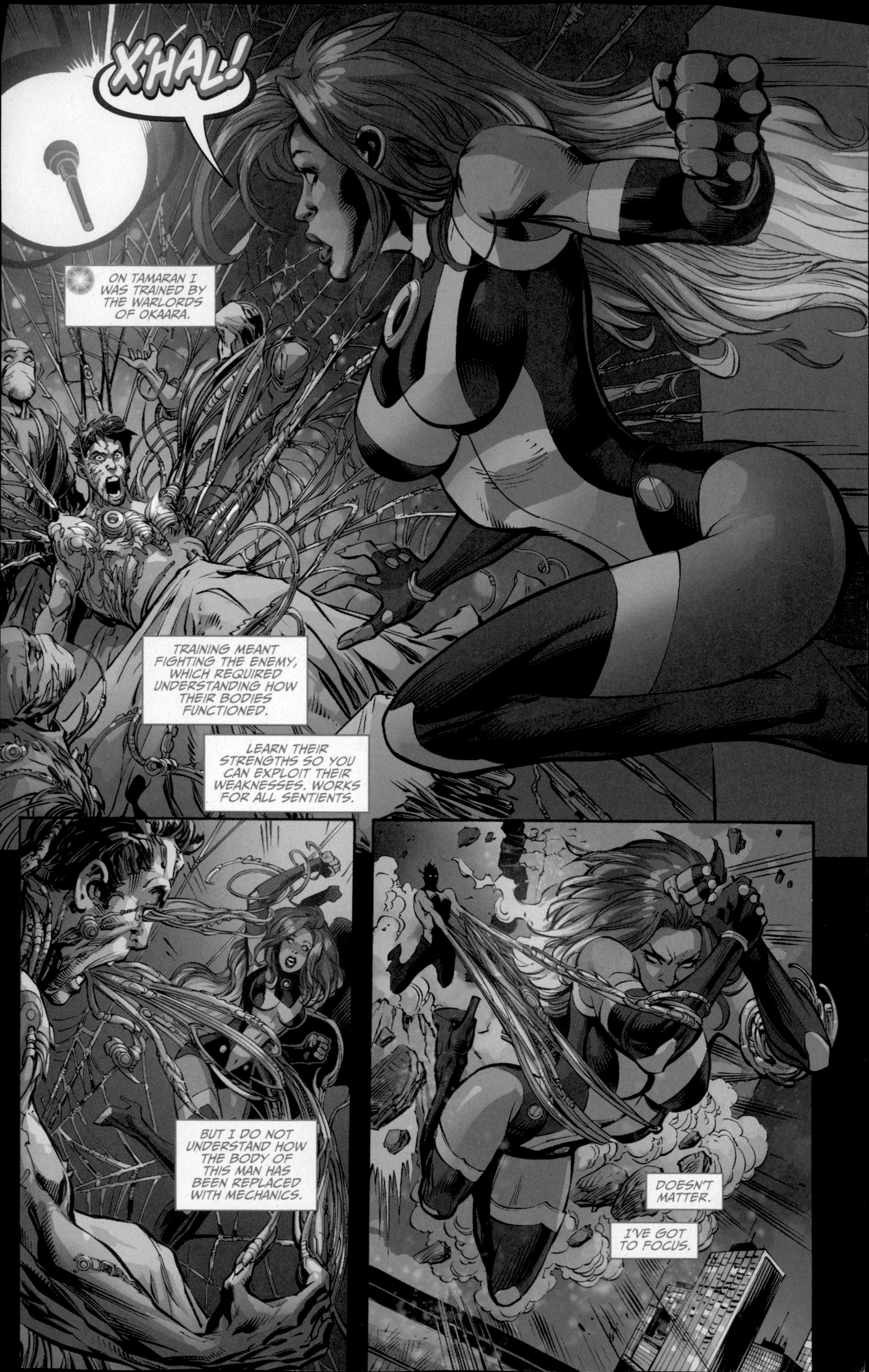
X'HAL!
ON TAMARAN I WAS TRAINED BY THE WARLORDS OF OKAARA.
TRAINING MEANT FIGHTING THE ENEMY, WHICH REQUIRED UNDERSTANDING HOW THEIR BODIES FUNCTIONED.
LEARN THEIR STRENGTHS SO YOU CAN EXPLOIT THEIR WEAKNESSES. WORKS FOR ALL SENTIENTS.
BUT I DO NOT UNDERSTAND HOW THE BODY OF THIS MAN HAS BEEN REPLACED WITH MECHANICS.
DOESN'T MATTER.
I'VE GOT TO FOCUS.

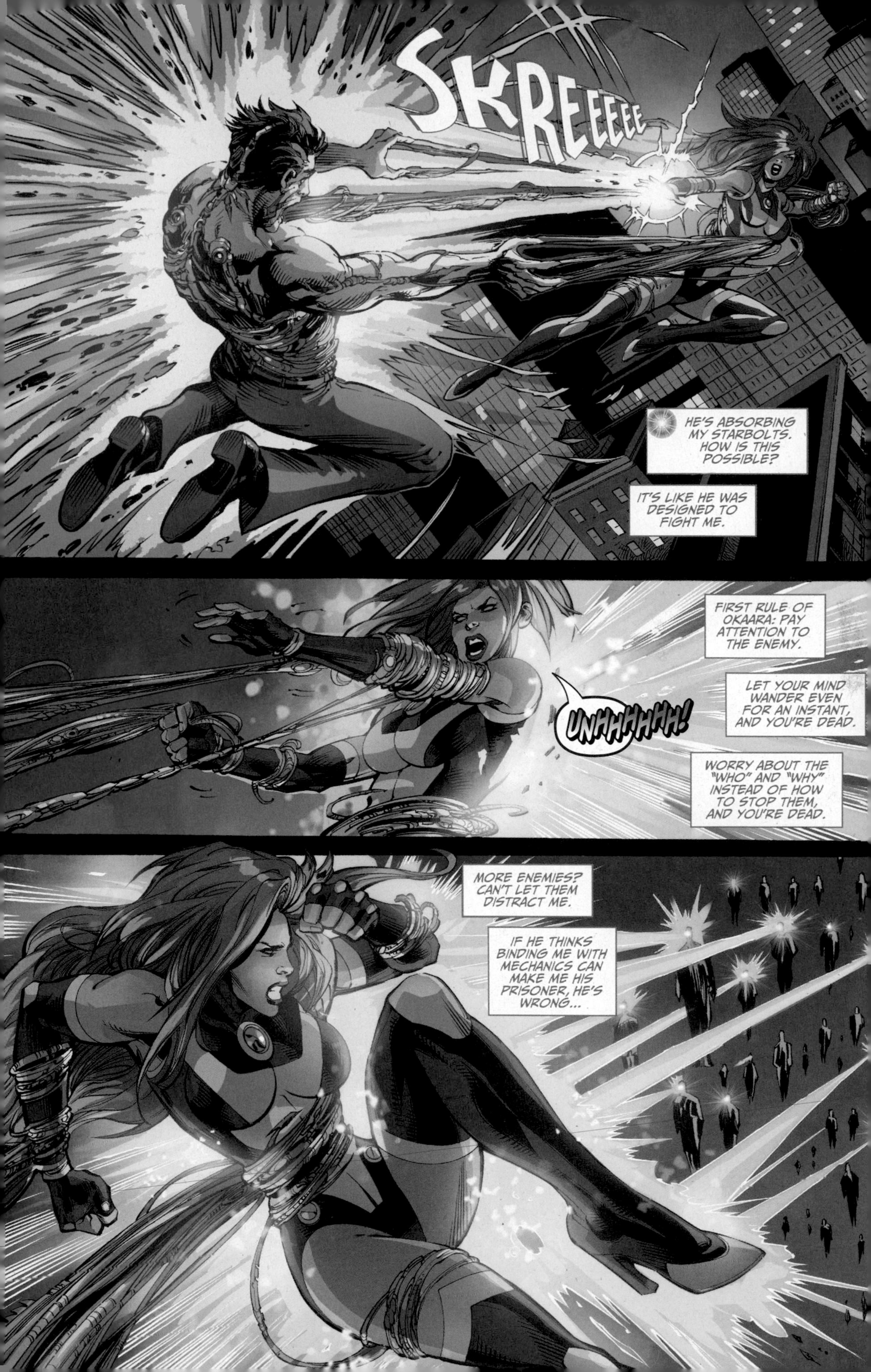
SKREEEEE
HE'S ABSORBING MY STARBOLTS. HOW IS THIS POSSIBLE?
IT'S LIKE HE WAS DESIGNED TO FIGHT ME.
FIRST RULE OF OKAARA: PAY ATTENTION TO THE ENEMY.
UNHHHHHH!
LET YOUR MIND WANDER EVEN FOR AN INSTANT, AND YOU'RE DEAD.
WORRY ABOUT THE "WHO" AND "WHY" INSTEAD OF HOW TO STOP THEM, AND YOU'RE DEAD.
MORE ENEMIES? CAN'T LET THEM DISTRACT ME.
IF HE THINKS BINDING ME WITH MECHANICS CAN MAKE ME HIS PRISONER, HE'S WRONG...

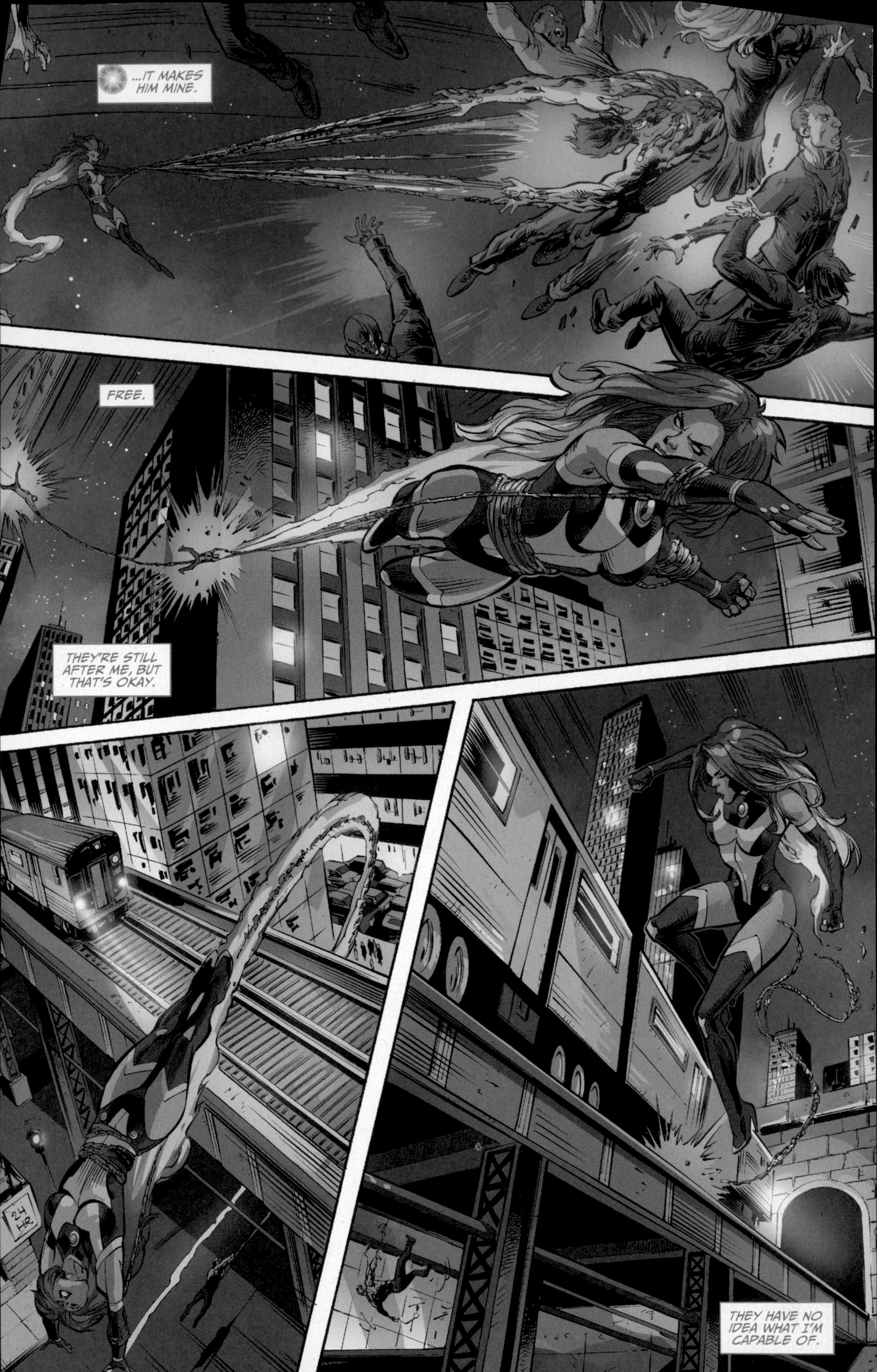
...IT MAKES HIM MINE.
FREE.
THEY'RE STILL AFTER ME, BUT THAT'S OKAY.
24 HR.
THEY HAVE NO IDEA WHAT I'M CAPABLE OF.

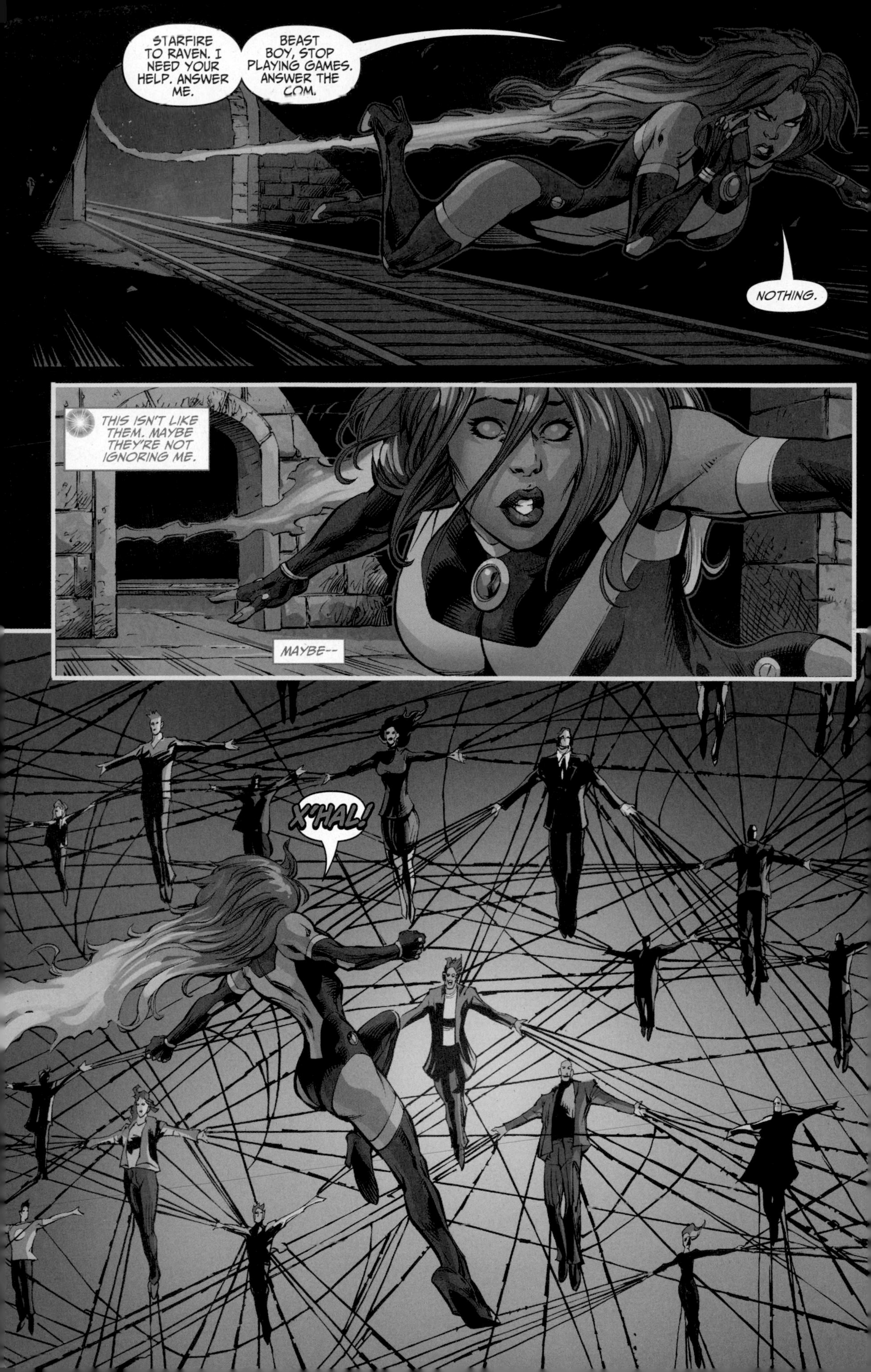
STARFIRE TO RAVEN. I NEED YOUR HELP. ANSWER ME.
BEAST BOY, STOP PLAYING GAMES. ANSWER THE COM.
NOTHING.
THIS ISN'T LIKE THEM. MAYBE THEY'RE NOT IGNORING ME.
MAYBE--
X'HAL!

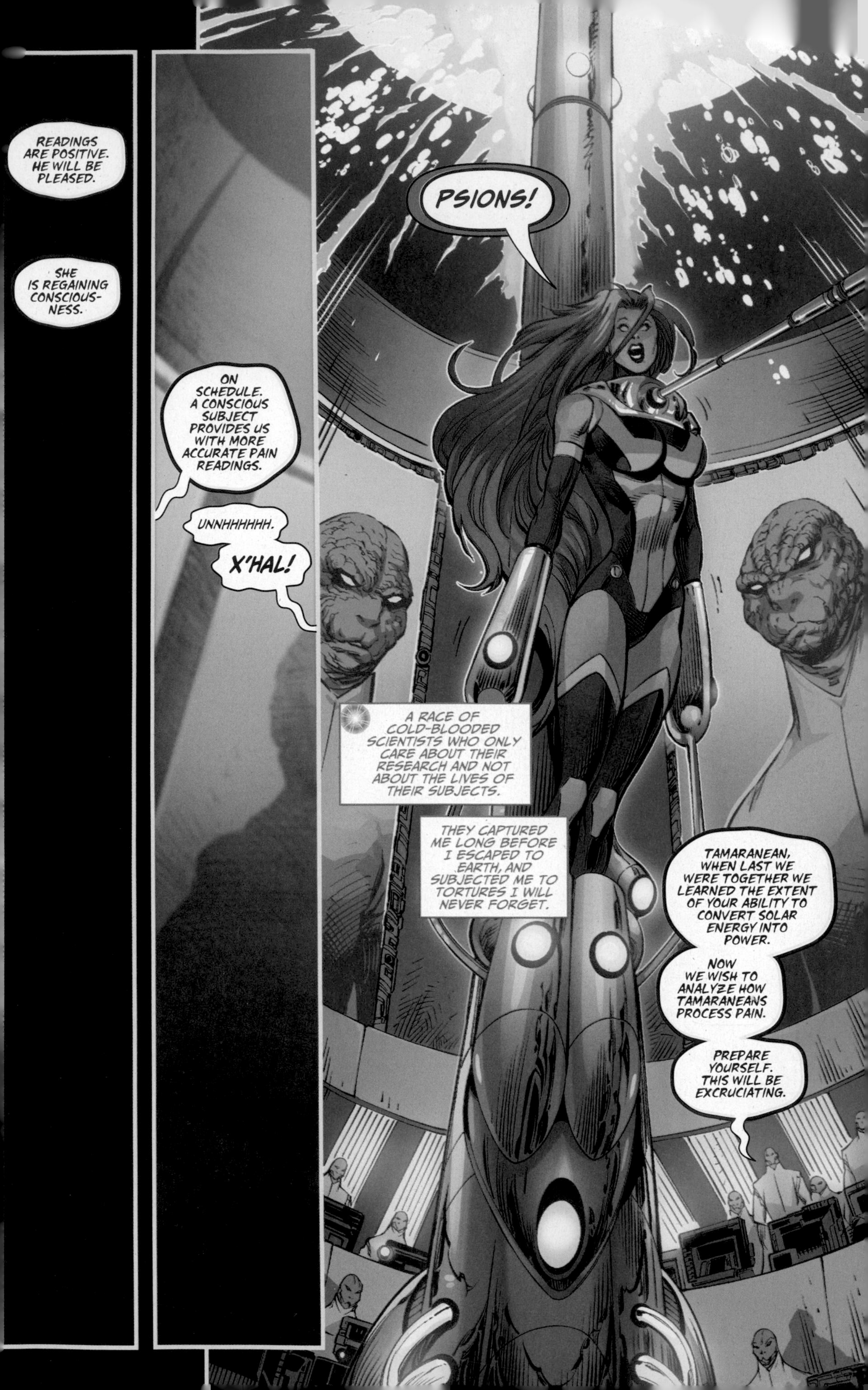
READINGS ARE POSITIVE. HE WILL BE PLEASED.
SHE IS REGAINING CONSCIOUS-NESS.
ON SCHEDULE. A CONSCIOUS SUBJECT PROVIDES US WITH MORE ACCURATE PAIN READINGS.
UNNHHHHHH.
X'HAL!
PSIONS!
A RACE OF COLD-BLOODED SCIENTISTS WHO ONLY CARE ABOUT THEIR RESEARCH AND NOT ABOUT THE LIVES OF THEIR SUBJECTS.
THEY CAPTURED ME LONG BEFORE I ESCAPED TO EARTH, AND SUBJECTED ME TO TORTURES I WILL NEVER FORGET.
TAMARANEAN, WHEN LAST WE WERE TOGETHER WE LEARNED THE EXTENT OF YOUR ABILITY TO CONVERT SOLAR ENERGY INTO POWER.
NOW WE WISH TO ANALYZE HOW TAMARANEANS PROCESS PAIN.
PREPARE YOURSELF. THIS WILL BE EXCRUCIATING.

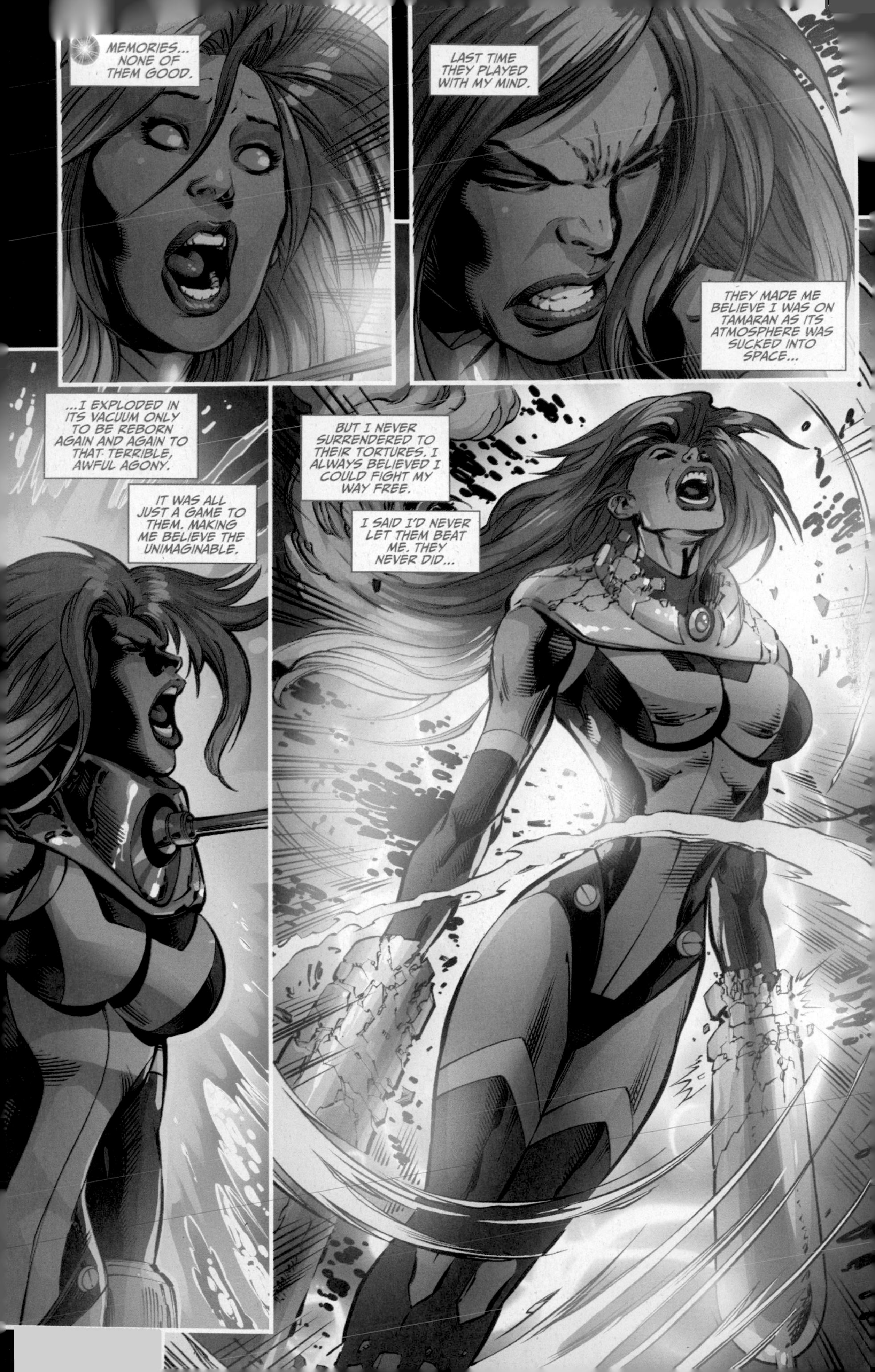
MEMORIES... NONE OF THEM GOOD.
LAST TIME THEY PLAYED WITH MY MIND.
THEY MADE ME BELIEVE I WAS ON TAMARAN AS ITS ATMOSPHERE WAS SUCKED INTO SPACE...
...I EXPLODED IN ITS VACUUM ONLY TO BE REBORN AGAIN AND AGAIN TO THAT TERRIBLE, AWFUL AGONY.
IT WAS ALL JUST A GAME TO THEM. MAKING ME BELIEVE THE UNIMAGINABLE.
BUT I NEVER SURRENDERED TO THEIR TORTURES. I ALWAYS BELIEVED I COULD FIGHT MY WAY FREE.
I SAID I'D NEVER LET THEM BEAT ME. THEY NEVER DID...

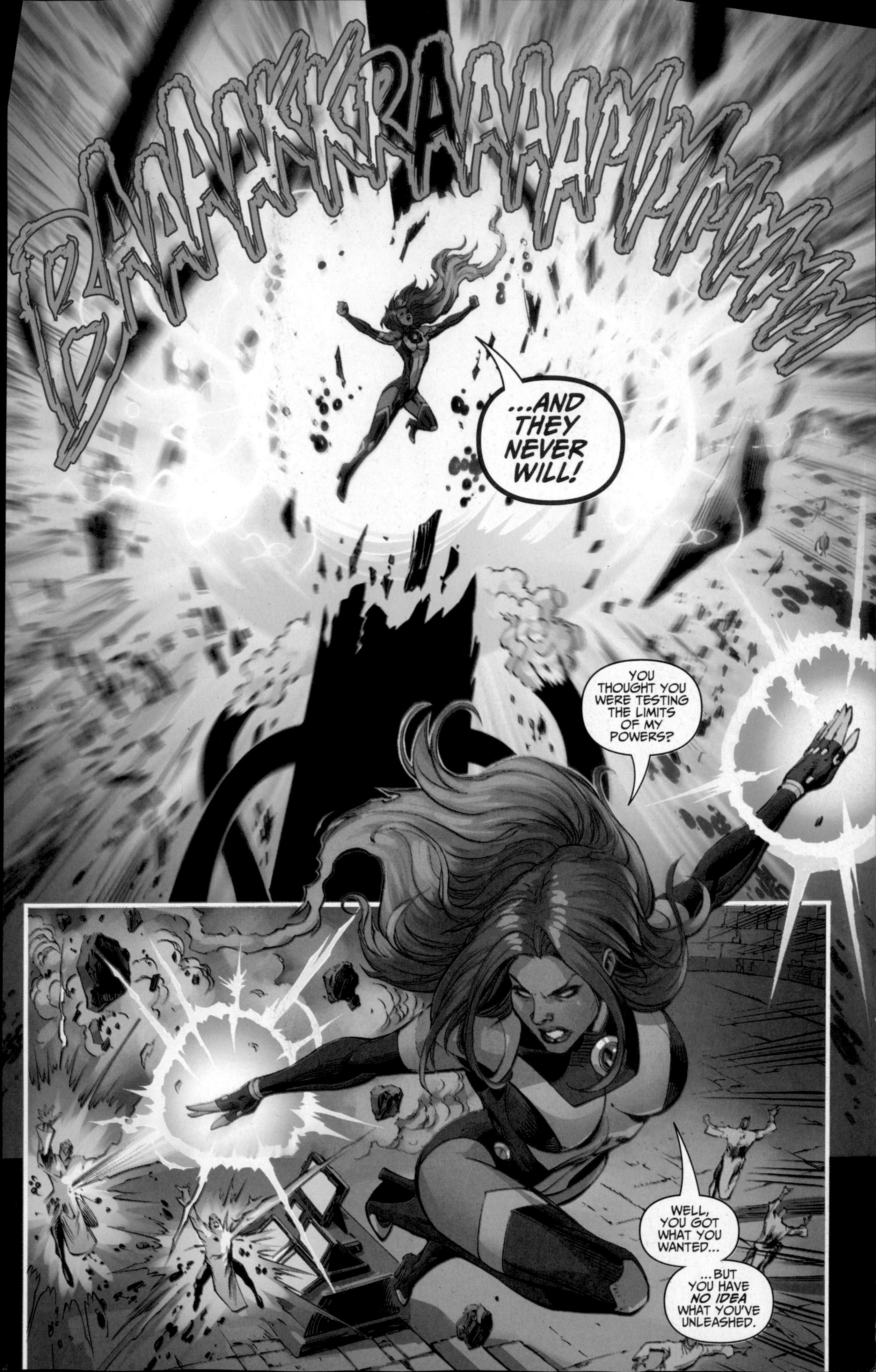
...AND THEY NEVER WILL!
YOU THOUGHT YOU WERE TESTING THE LIMITS OF MY POWERS?
WELL, YOU GOT WHAT YOU WANTED...
...BUT YOU HAVE *NO IDEA* WHAT YOU'VE UNLEASHED.

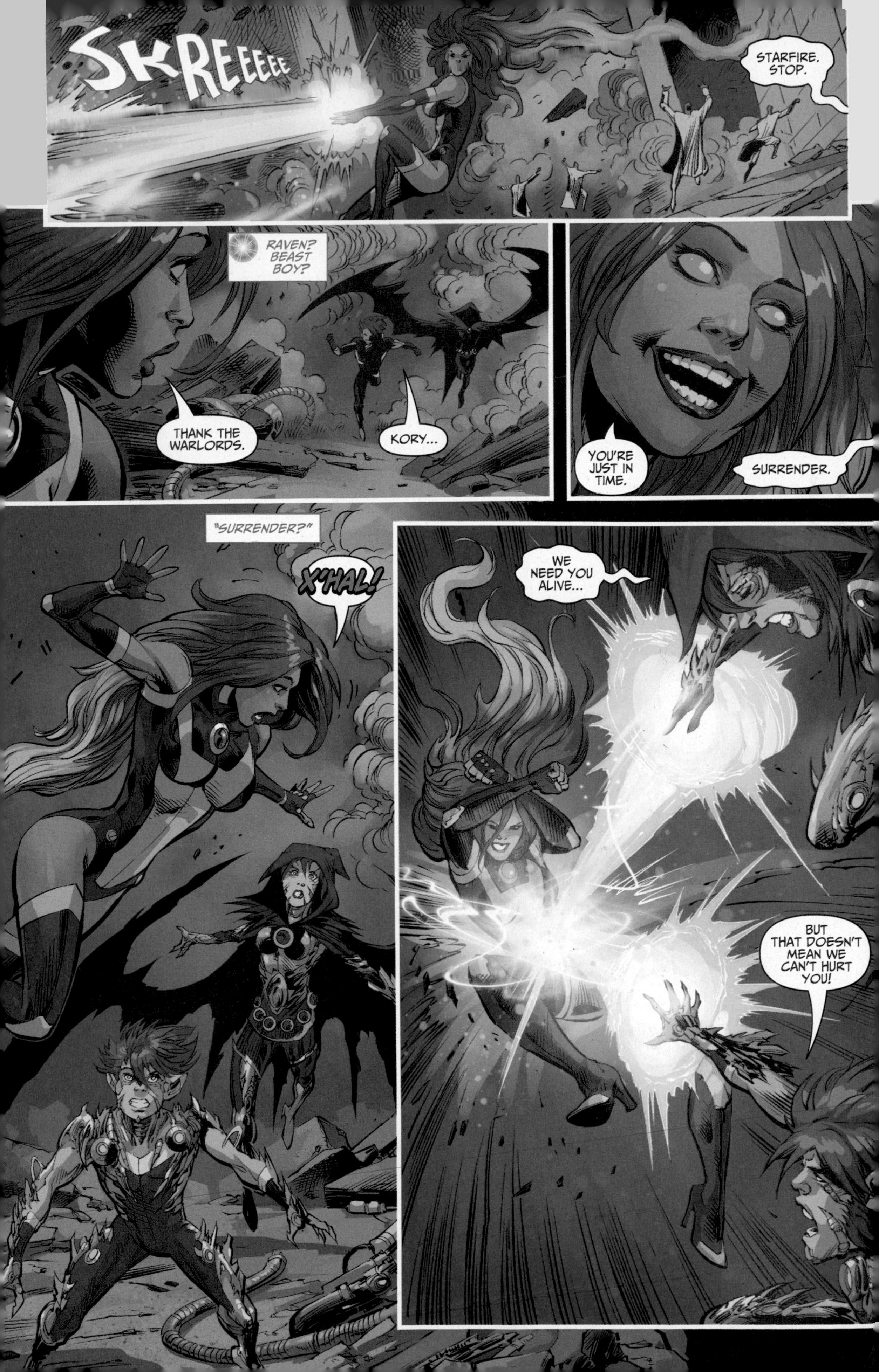
SKREEEEEE
STARFIRE. STOP.
RAVEN? BEAST BOY?
THANK THE WARLORDS.
KORY...
YOU'RE JUST IN TIME.
SURRENDER.
"SURRENDER?"
X'HAL!
WE NEED YOU ALIVE...
BUT THAT DOESN'T MEAN WE CAN'T HURT YOU!

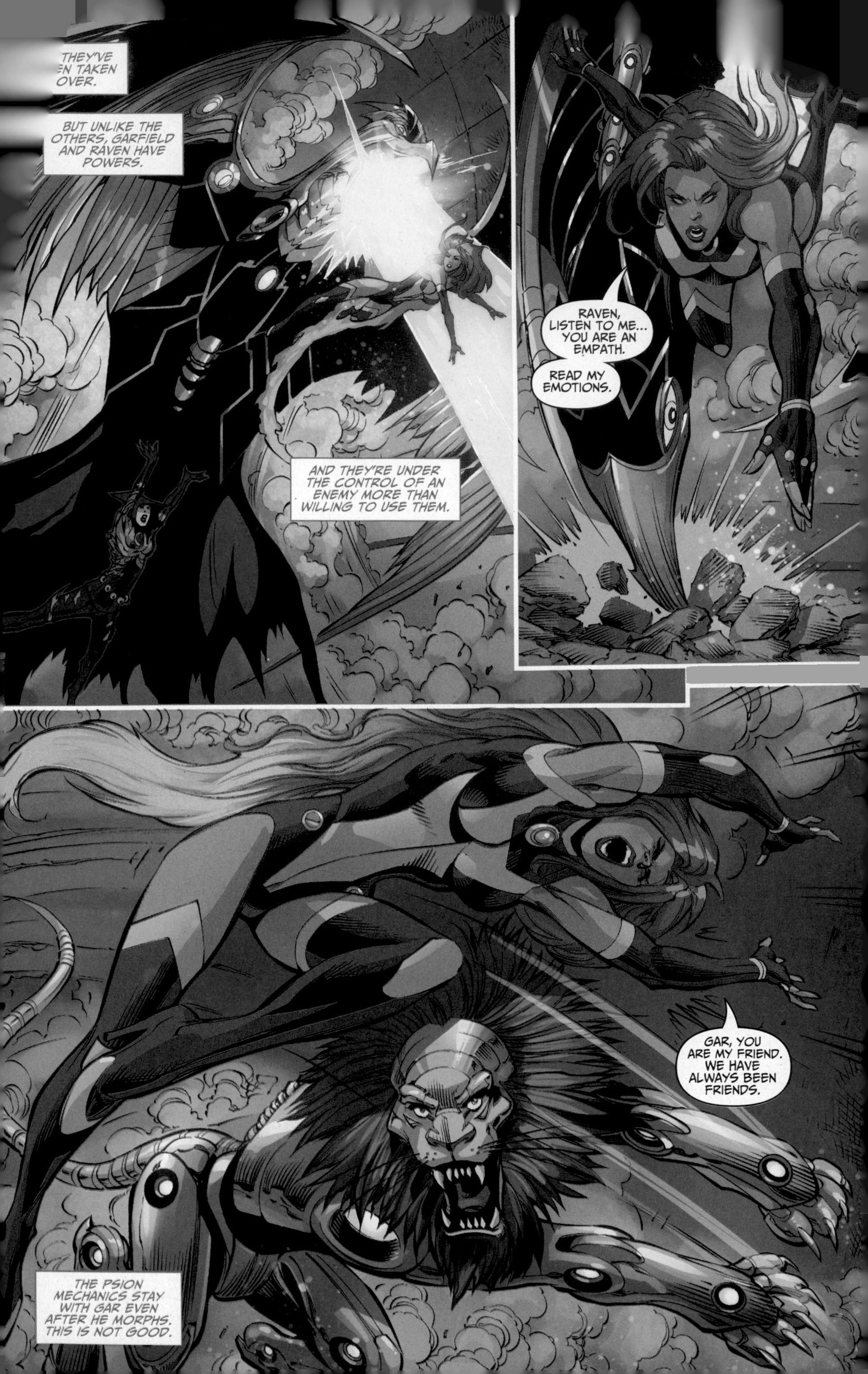
THEY'VE
EN TAKEN
OVER.
BUT UNLIKE THE OTHERS, GARFIELD AND RAVEN HAVE POWERS.
AND THEY'RE UNDER THE CONTROL OF AN ENEMY MORE THAN WILLING TO USE THEM.
RAVEN, LISTEN TO ME... YOU ARE AN EMPATH.
READ MY EMOTIONS.
GAR, YOU ARE MY FRIEND. WE HAVE ALWAYS BEEN FRIENDS.
THE PSION MECHANICS STAY WITH GAR EVEN AFTER HE MORPHS. THIS IS NOT GOOD.

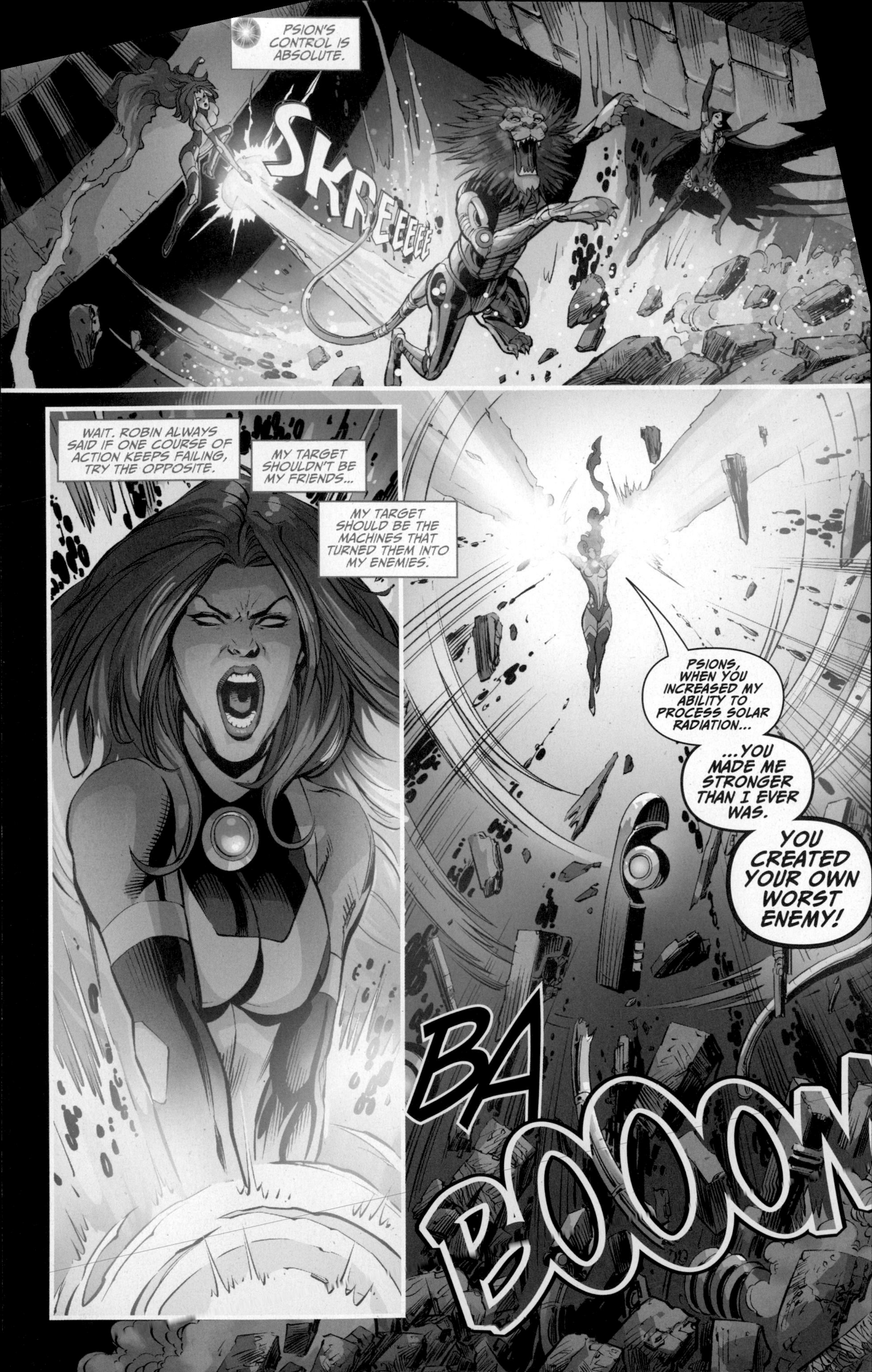
PSION'S CONTROL IS ABSOLUTE.
SKREEEEEE
WAIT. ROBIN ALWAYS SAID IF ONE COURSE OF ACTION KEEPS FAILING, TRY THE OPPOSITE.
MY TARGET SHOULDN'T BE MY FRIENDS...
MY TARGET SHOULD BE THE MACHINES THAT TURNED THEM INTO MY ENEMIES.
PSIONS, WHEN YOU INCREASED MY ABILITY TO PROCESS SOLAR RADIATION...
...YOU MADE ME STRONGER THAN I EVER WAS.
YOU CREATED YOUR OWN WORST ENEMY!
BA BOOOOM

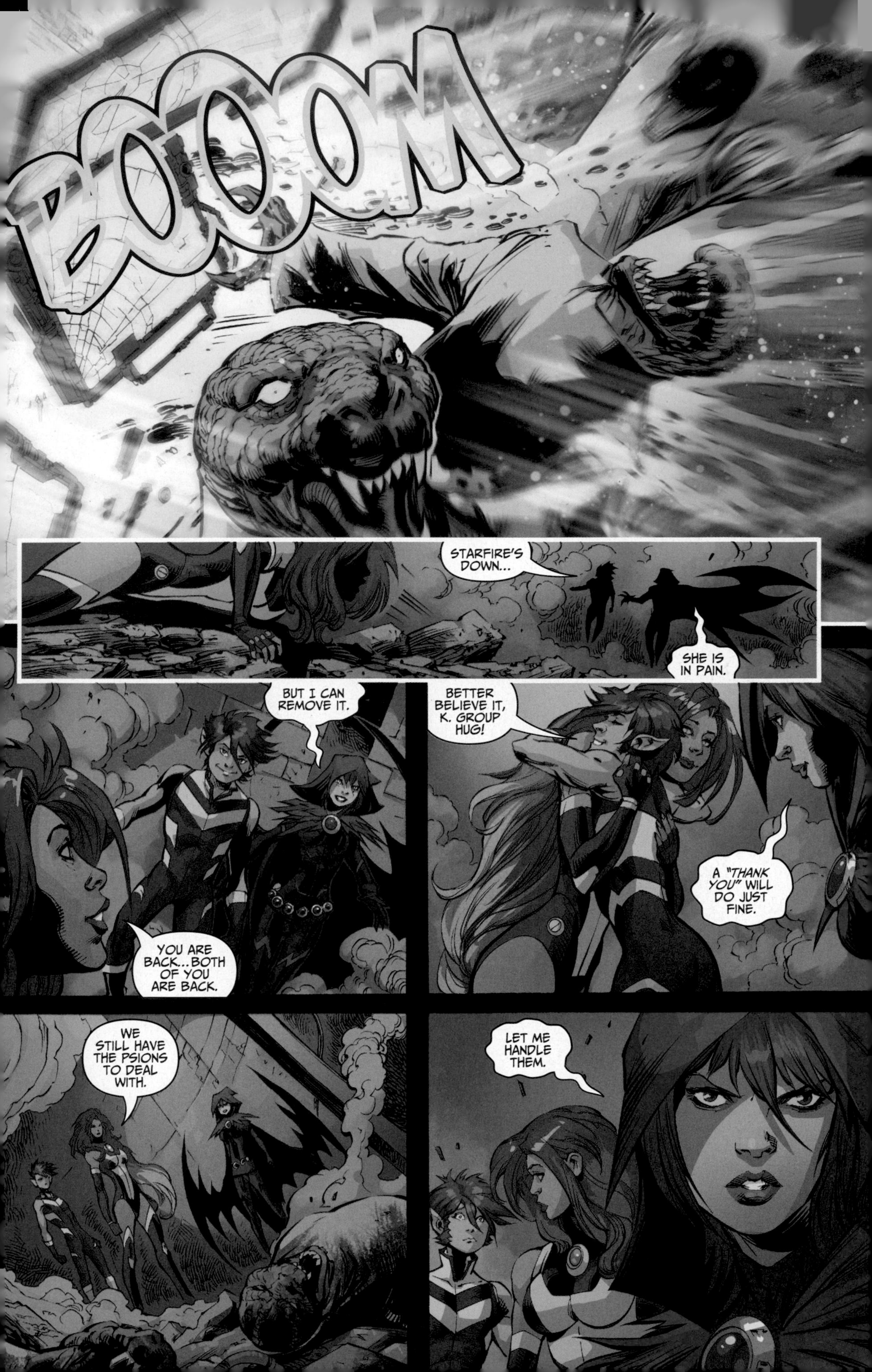
BOOOM
STARFIRE'S DOWN...
SHE IS IN PAIN.
BUT I CAN REMOVE IT.
YOU ARE BACK...BOTH OF YOU ARE BACK.
BETTER BELIEVE IT, K. GROUP HUG!
A "THANK YOU" WILL DO JUST FINE.
WE STILL HAVE THE PSIONS TO DEAL WITH.
LET ME HANDLE THEM.

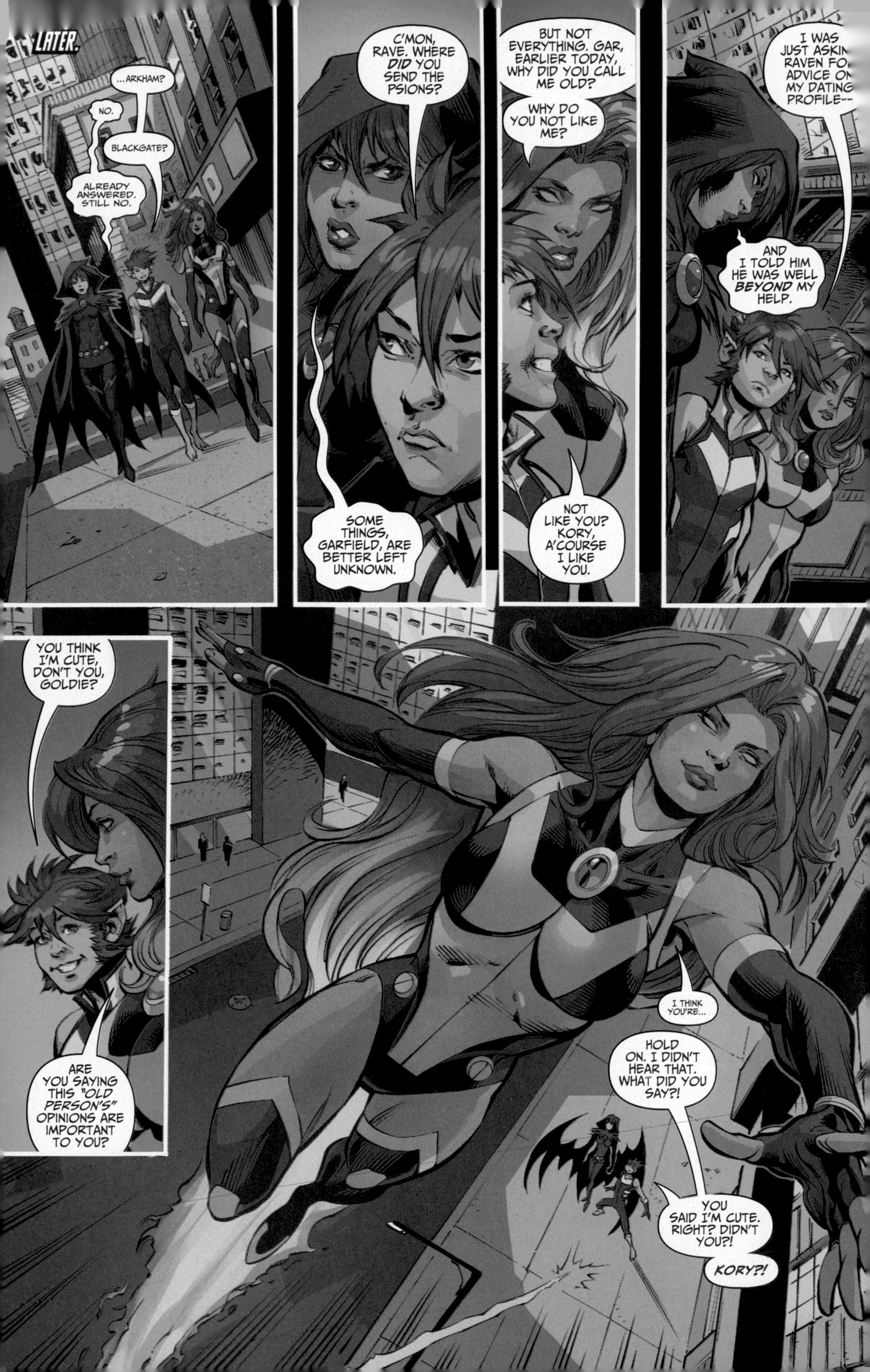
LATER.
...ARKHAM?
NO.
BLACKGATE?
ALREADY ANSWERED. STILL NO.
C'MON, RAVE. WHERE *DID* YOU SEND THE PSIONS?
SOME THINGS, GARFIELD, ARE BETTER LEFT UNKNOWN.
BUT NOT EVERYTHING. GAR, EARLIER TODAY, WHY DID YOU CALL ME OLD?
WHY DO YOU NOT LIKE ME?
NOT LIKE YOU? KORY, A'COURSE I LIKE YOU.
I WAS JUST ASKIN RAVEN FO ADVICE ON MY DATING PROFILE--
AND I TOLD HIM HE WAS WELL *BEYOND* MY HELP.
YOU THINK I'M CUTE, DON'T YOU, GOLDIE?
ARE YOU SAYING THIS "OLD PERSON'S" OPINIONS ARE IMPORTANT TO YOU?
I THINK YOU'RE...
HOLD ON. I DIDN'T HEAR THAT. WHAT DID YOU SAY?!
YOU SAID I'M CUTE. RIGHT? DIDN'T YOU?!
KORY?!

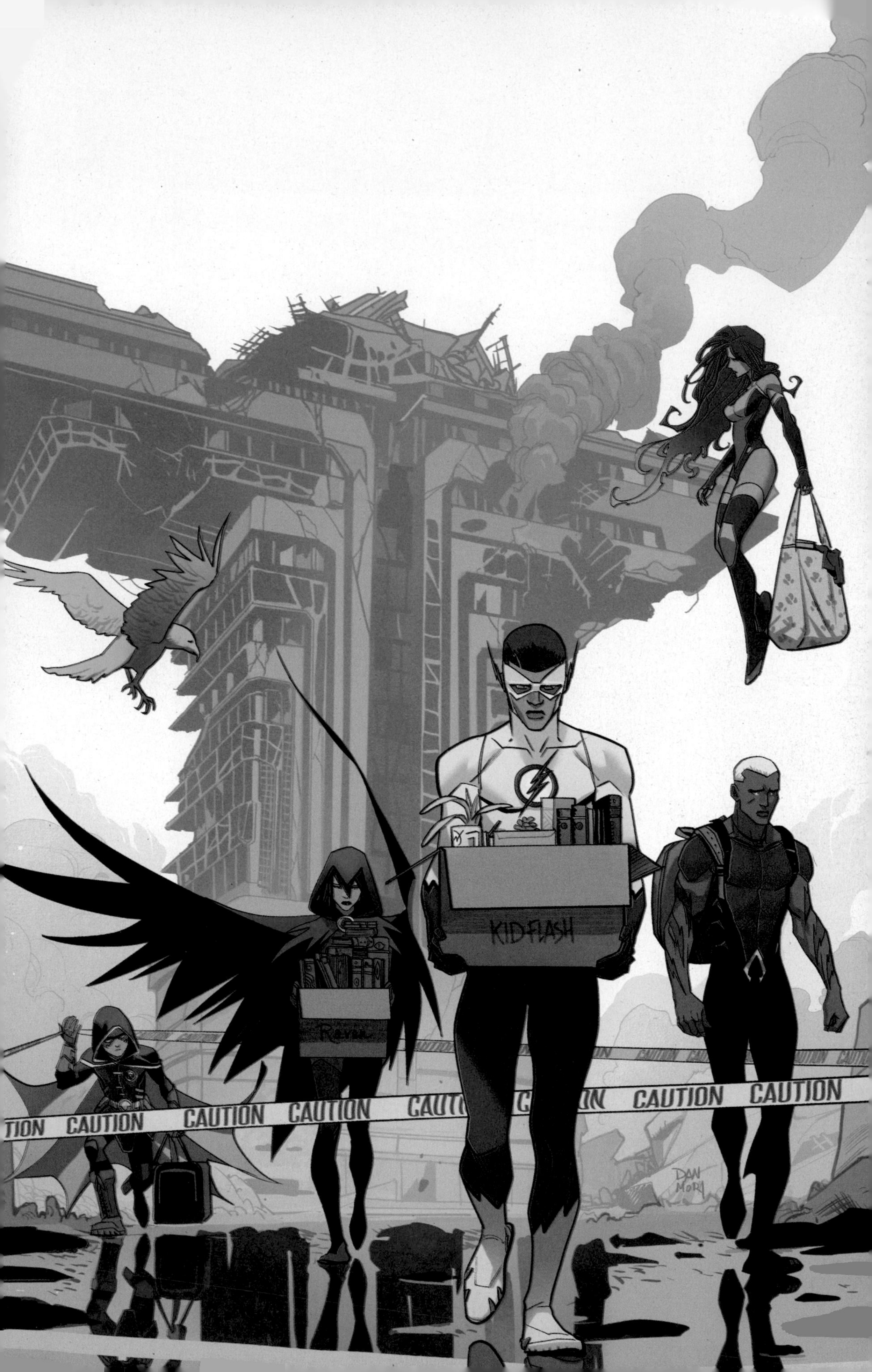
KID FLASH
CAUTION
CAUTION
CAUTION
CAUTION
CAUTION

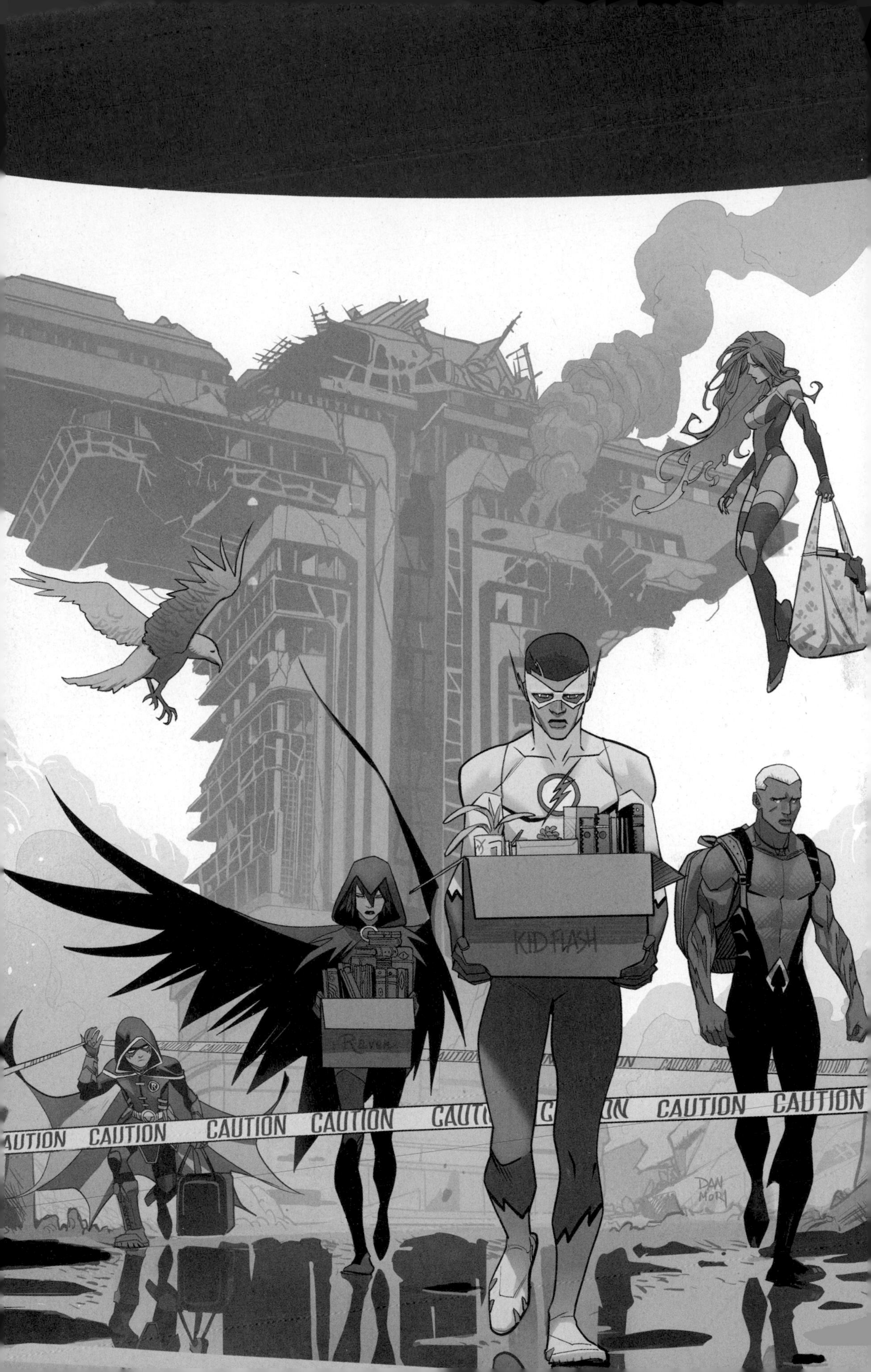
KID FLASH
Raven
CAUTION
DAN MORA

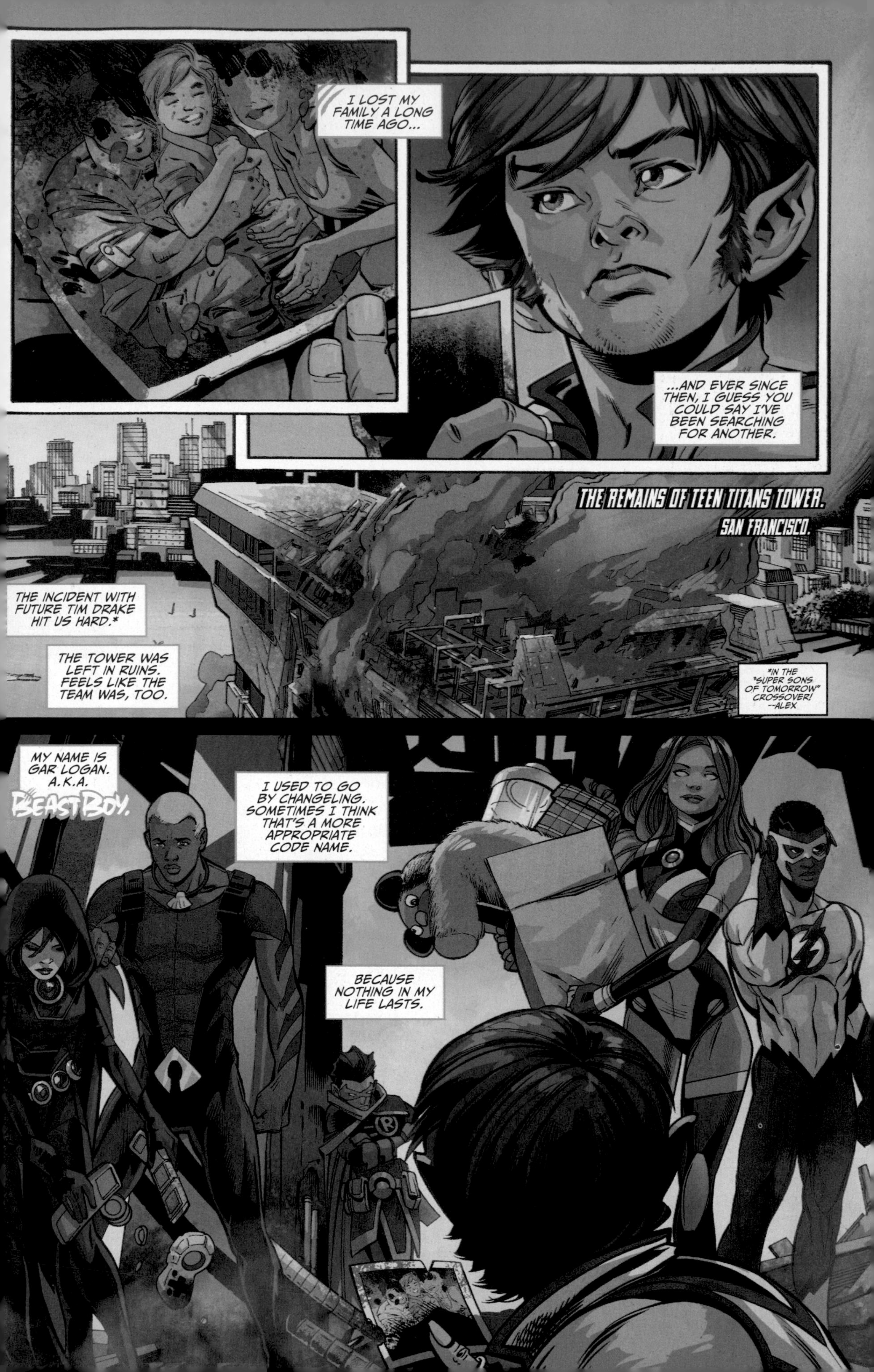
I LOST MY FAMILY A LONG TIME AGO...
...AND EVER SINCE THEN, I GUESS YOU COULD SAY I'VE BEEN SEARCHING FOR ANOTHER.
THE REMAINS OF TEEN TITANS TOWER.
SAN FRANCISCO.
THE INCIDENT WITH FUTURE TIM DRAKE HIT US HARD.*
THE TOWER WAS LEFT IN RUINS. FEELS LIKE THE TEAM WAS, TOO.
*IN THE "SUPER SONS OF TOMORROW" CROSSOVER! --ALEX
MY NAME IS GAR LOGAN. A.K.A.
BEAST BOY.
I USED TO GO BY CHANGELING. SOMETIMES I THINK THAT'S A MORE APPROPRIATE CODE NAME.
BECAUSE NOTHING IN MY LIFE LASTS.

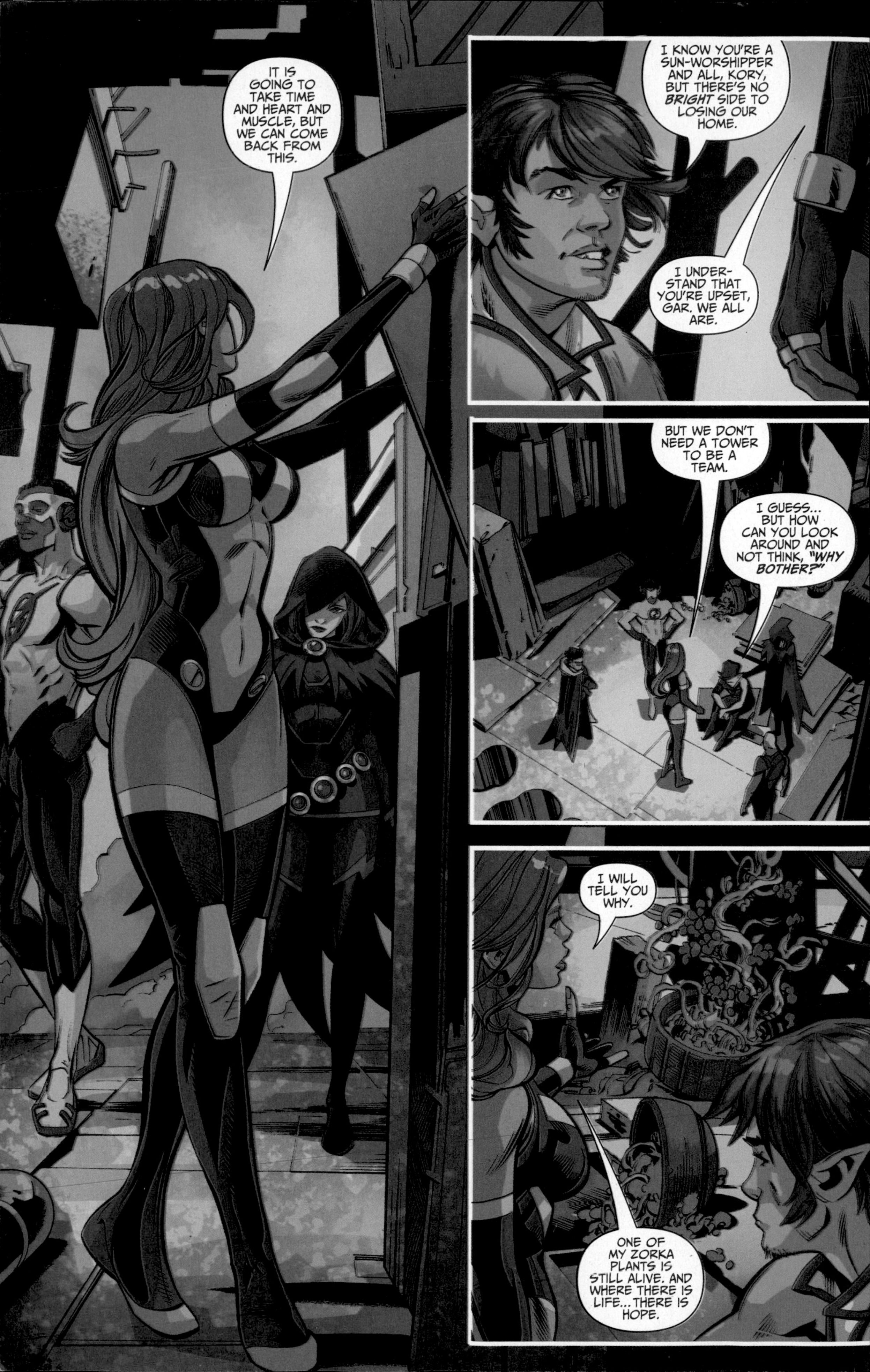
IT IS GOING TO TAKE TIME AND HEART AND MUSCLE, BUT WE CAN COME BACK FROM THIS.
I KNOW YOU'RE A SUN-WORSHIPPER AND ALL, KORY, BUT THERE'S NO BRIGHT SIDE TO LOSING OUR HOME.
I UNDER-STAND THAT YOU'RE UPSET, GAR. WE ALL ARE.
BUT WE DON'T NEED A TOWER TO BE A TEAM.
I GUESS... BUT HOW CAN YOU LOOK AROUND AND NOT THINK, "WHY BOTHER?"
I WILL TELL YOU WHY.
ONE OF MY ZORKA PLANTS IS STILL ALIVE. AND WHERE THERE IS LIFE... THERE IS HOPE.

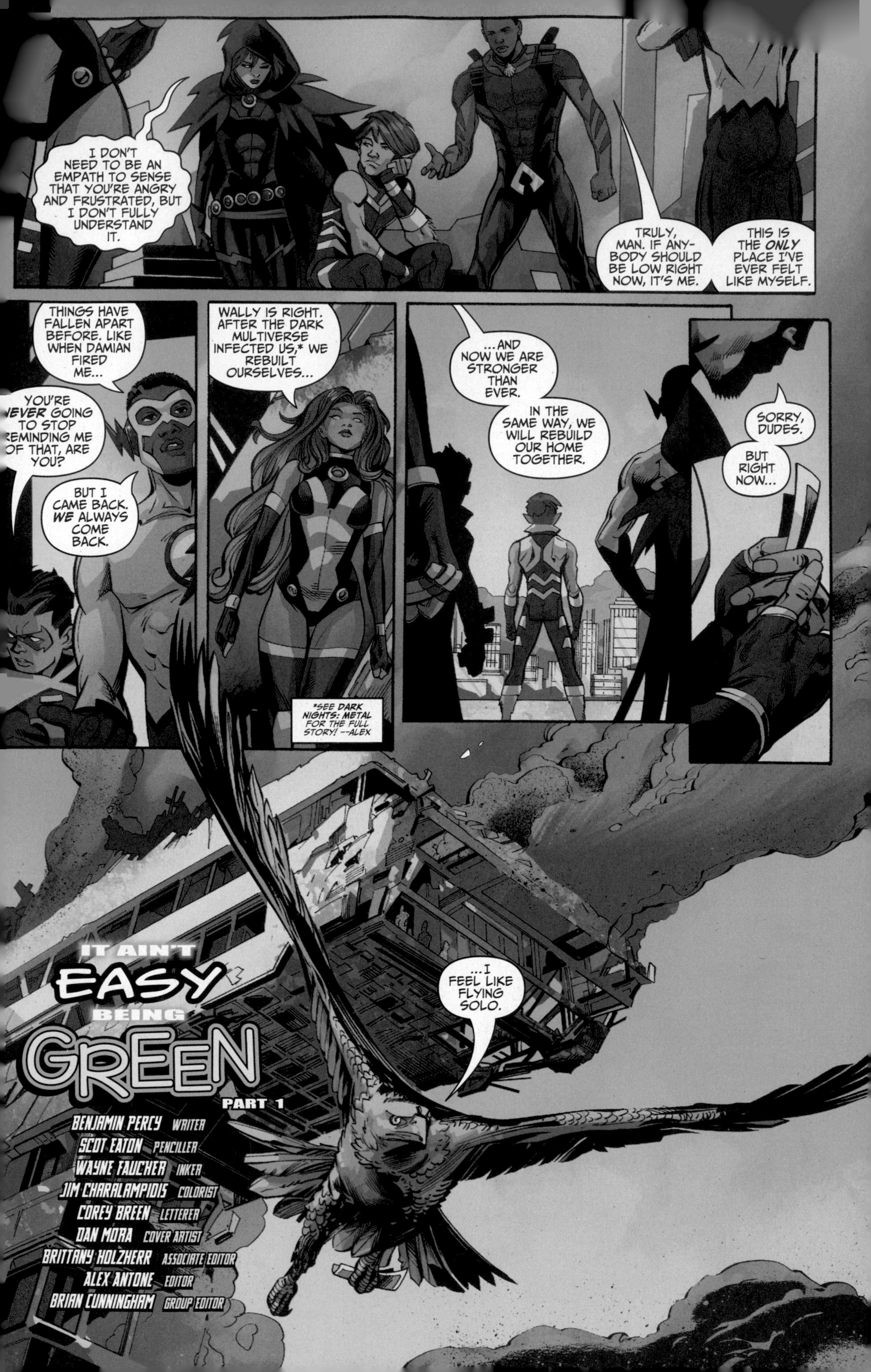

I DON'T NEED TO BE AN EMPATH TO SENSE THAT YOU'RE ANGRY AND FRUSTRATED, BUT I DON'T FULLY UNDERSTAND IT.
TRULY, MAN. IF ANY-BODY SHOULD BE LOW RIGHT NOW, IT'S ME.
THIS IS THE ONLY PLACE I'VE EVER FELT LIKE MYSELF.
THINGS HAVE FALLEN APART BEFORE. LIKE WHEN DAMIAN FIRED ME...
YOU'RE NEVER GOING TO STOP REMINDING ME OF THAT, ARE YOU?
BUT I CAME BACK. WE ALWAYS COME BACK.
WALLY IS RIGHT. AFTER THE DARK MULTIVERSE INFECTED US,* WE REBUILT OURSELVES...
*SEE DARK NIGHTS: METAL FOR THE FULL STORY! --ALEX
...AND NOW WE ARE STRONGER THAN EVER.
IN THE SAME WAY, WE WILL REBUILD OUR HOME TOGETHER.
SORRY, DUDES.
BUT RIGHT NOW...
...I FEEL LIKE FLYING SOLO.
IT AIN'T EASY BEING GREEN
PART 1
BENJAMIN PERCY WRITER
SCOT EATON PENCILLER
WAYNE FAUCHER INKER
JIM CHARALAMPIDIS COLORIST
COREY BREEN LETTERER
DAN MORA COVER ARTIST
BRITTANY HOLZHERR ASSOCIATE EDITOR
ALEX ANTONE EDITOR
BRIAN CUNNINGHAM GROUP EDITOR

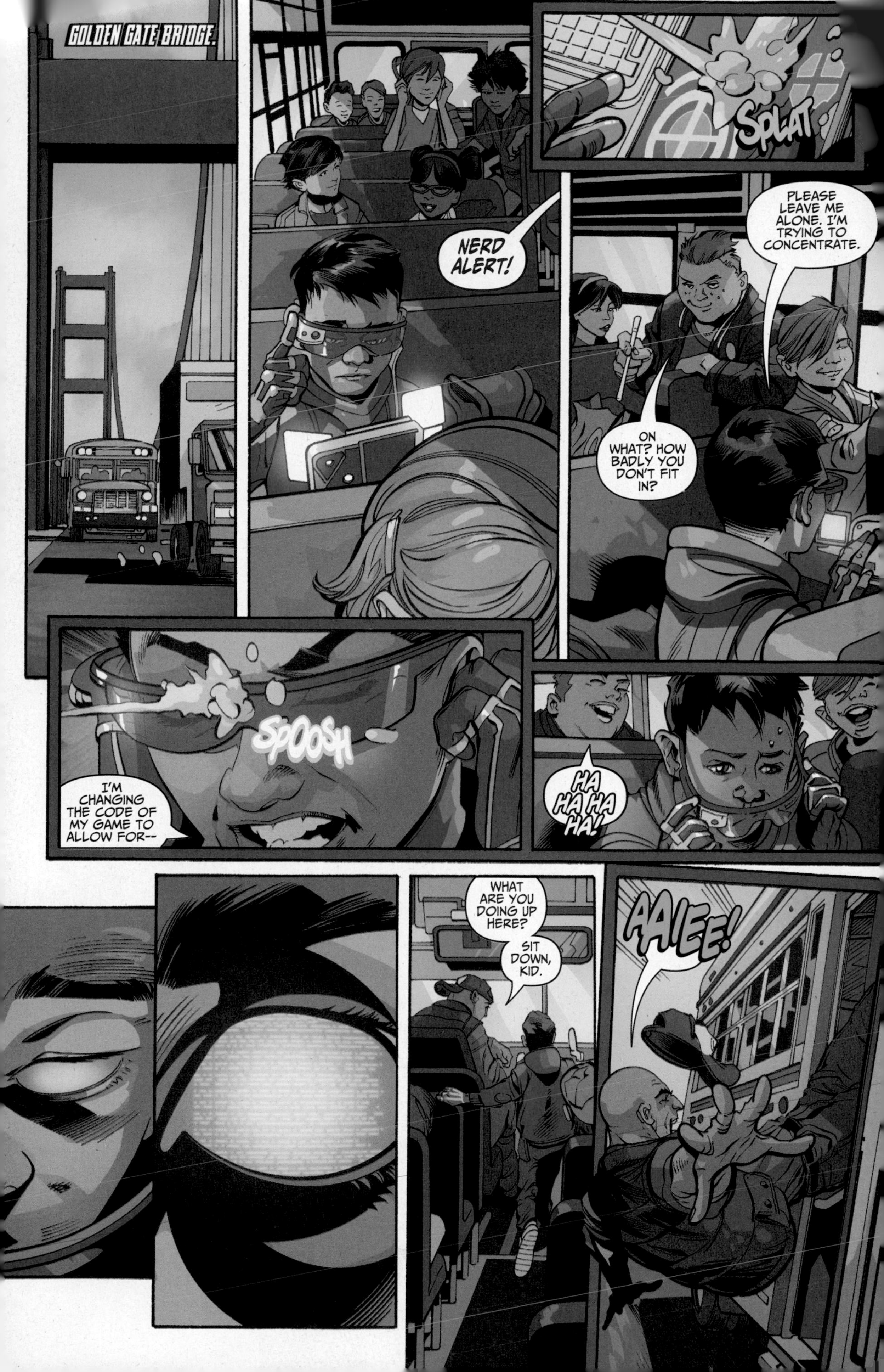
GOLDEN GATE BRIDGE.
SPLAT
NERD ALERT!
PLEASE LEAVE ME ALONE. I'M TRYING TO CONCENTRATE.
ON WHAT? HOW BADLY YOU DON'T FIT IN?
SPOOSH
I'M CHANGING THE CODE OF MY GAME TO ALLOW FOR--
HA HA HA HA HA!
WHAT ARE YOU DOING UP HERE?
SIT DOWN, KID.
AAIEE!

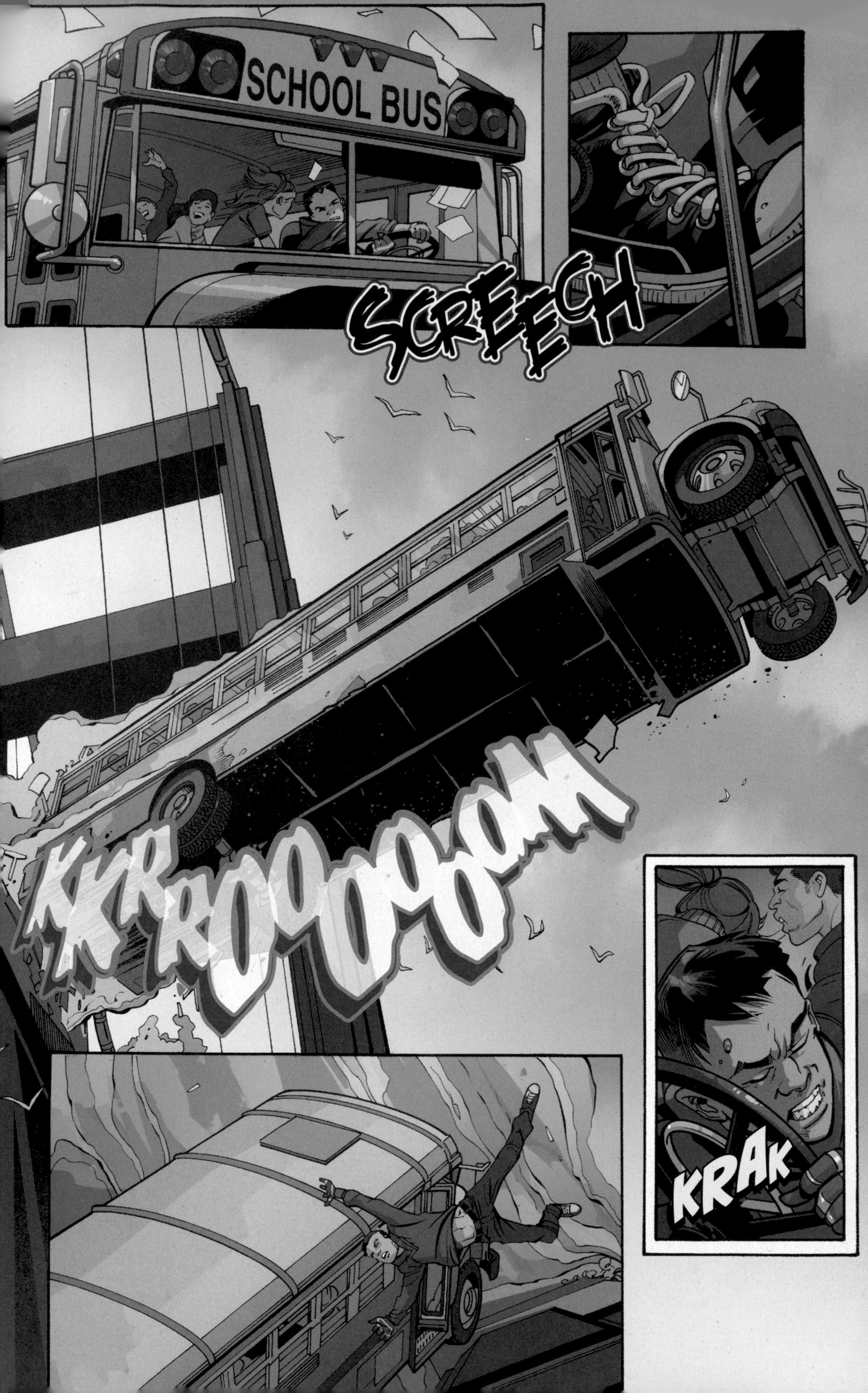
SCHOOL BUS
SCREECH
KKROOOOOOM
KRAK

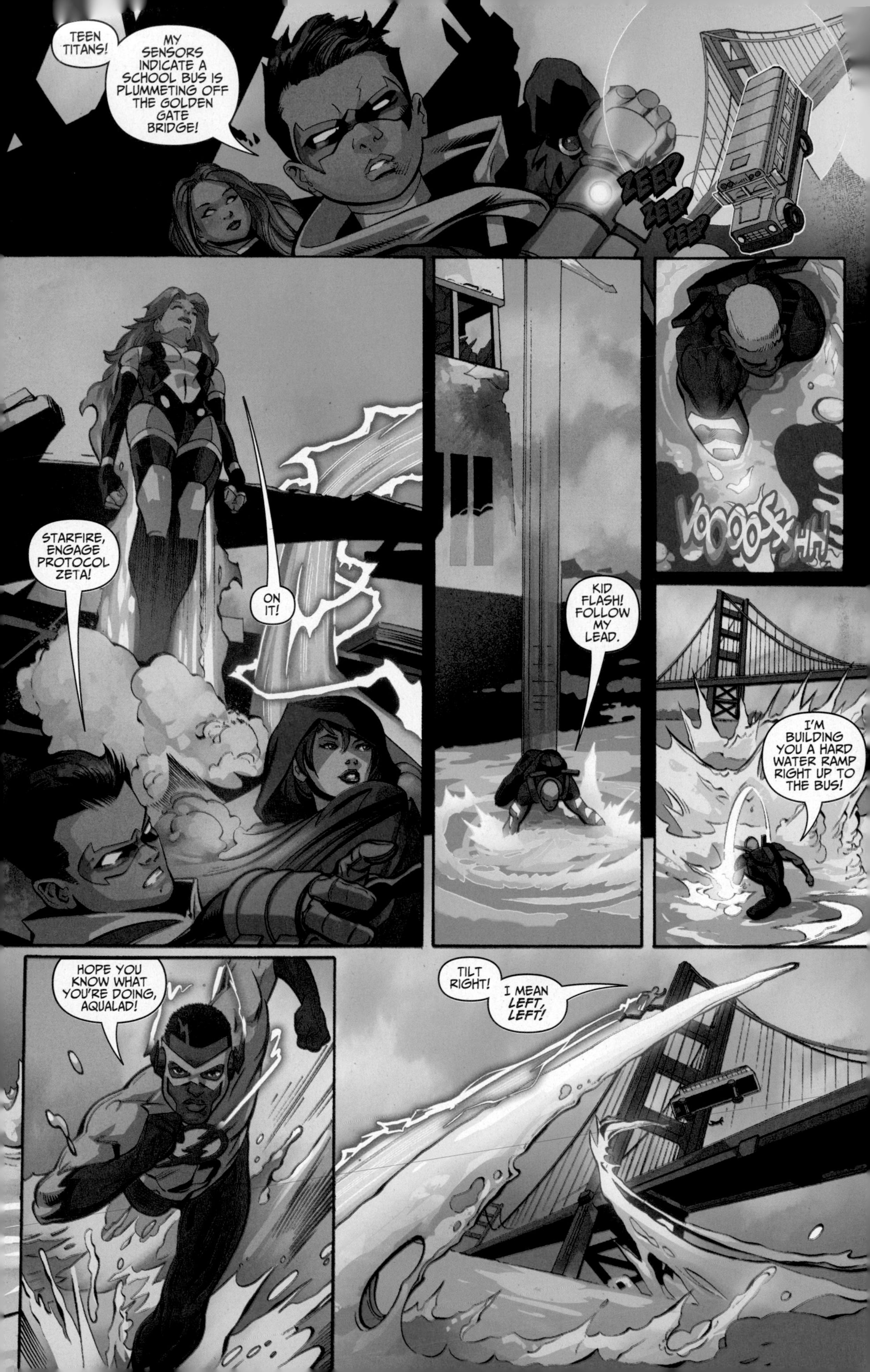
TEEN TITANS!
MY SENSORS INDICATE A SCHOOL BUS IS PLUMMETING OFF THE GOLDEN GATE BRIDGE!
ZEEP ZEEP ZEEP
STARFIRE, ENGAGE PROTOCOL ZETA!
ON IT!
KID FLASH! FOLLOW MY LEAD.
VOOOOSHH
I'M BUILDING YOU A HARD WATER RAMP RIGHT UP TO THE BUS!
HOPE YOU KNOW WHAT YOU'RE DOING, AQUALAD!
TILT RIGHT!
I MEAN *LEFT, LEFT!*

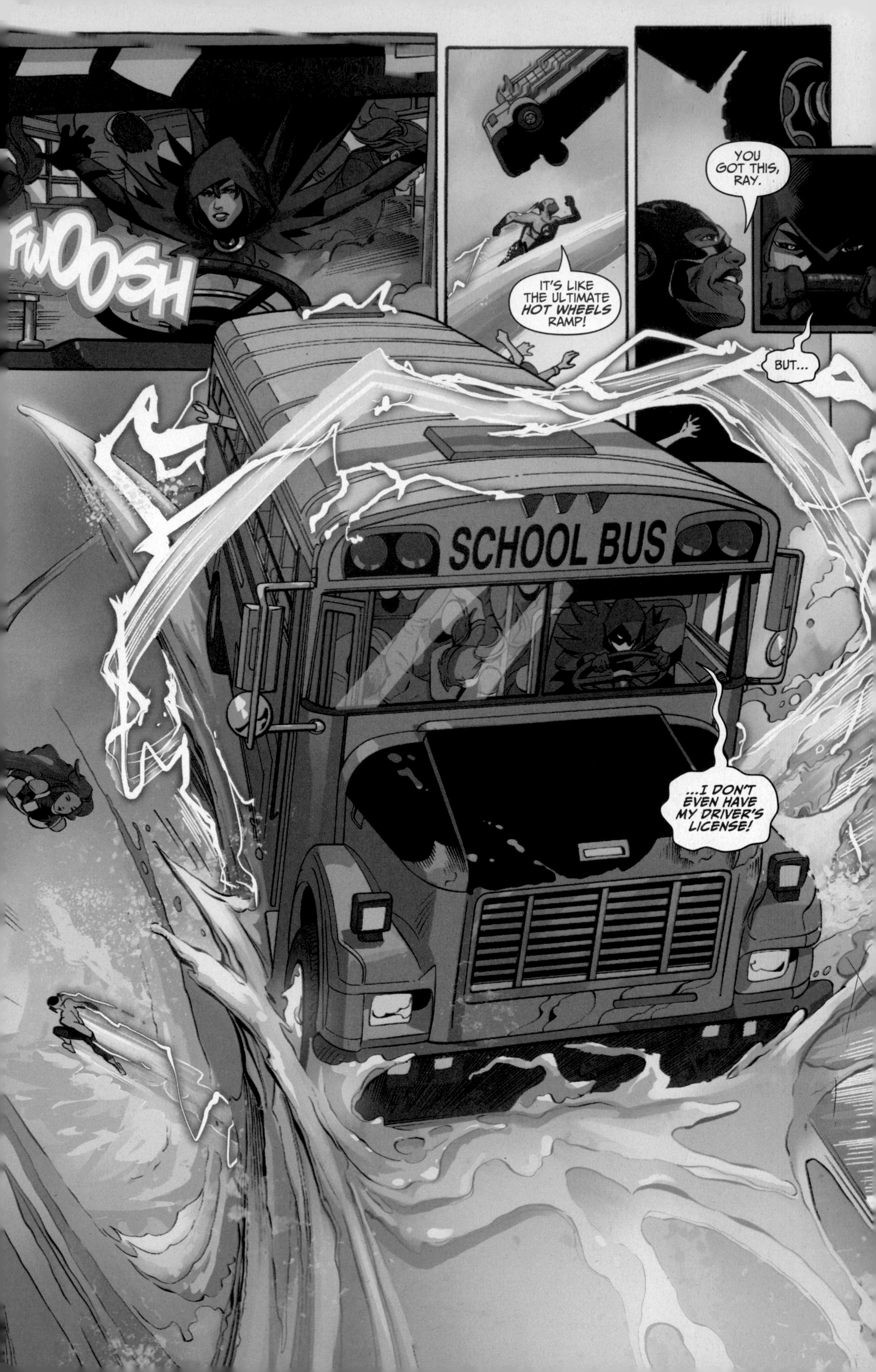
FWOOSH
IT'S LIKE THE ULTIMATE HOT WHEELS RAMP!
YOU GOT THIS, RAY.
BUT...
SCHOOL BUS
...I DON'T EVEN HAVE MY DRIVER'S LICENSE!

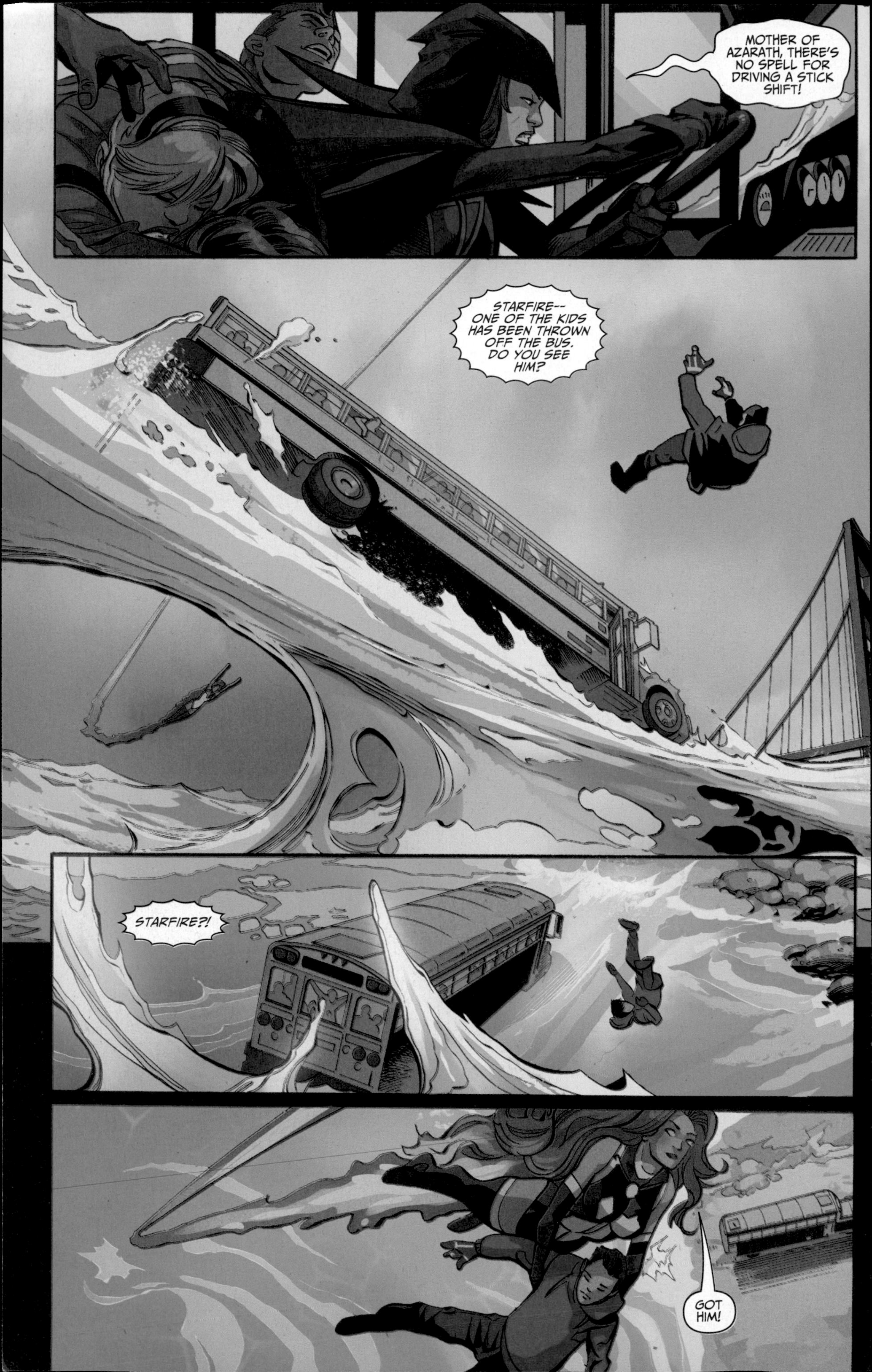
MOTHER OF AZARATH, THERE'S NO SPELL FOR DRIVING A STICK SHIFT!
STARFIRE-- ONE OF THE KIDS HAS BEEN THROWN OFF THE BUS. DO YOU SEE HIM?
STARFIRE?!
GOT HIM!

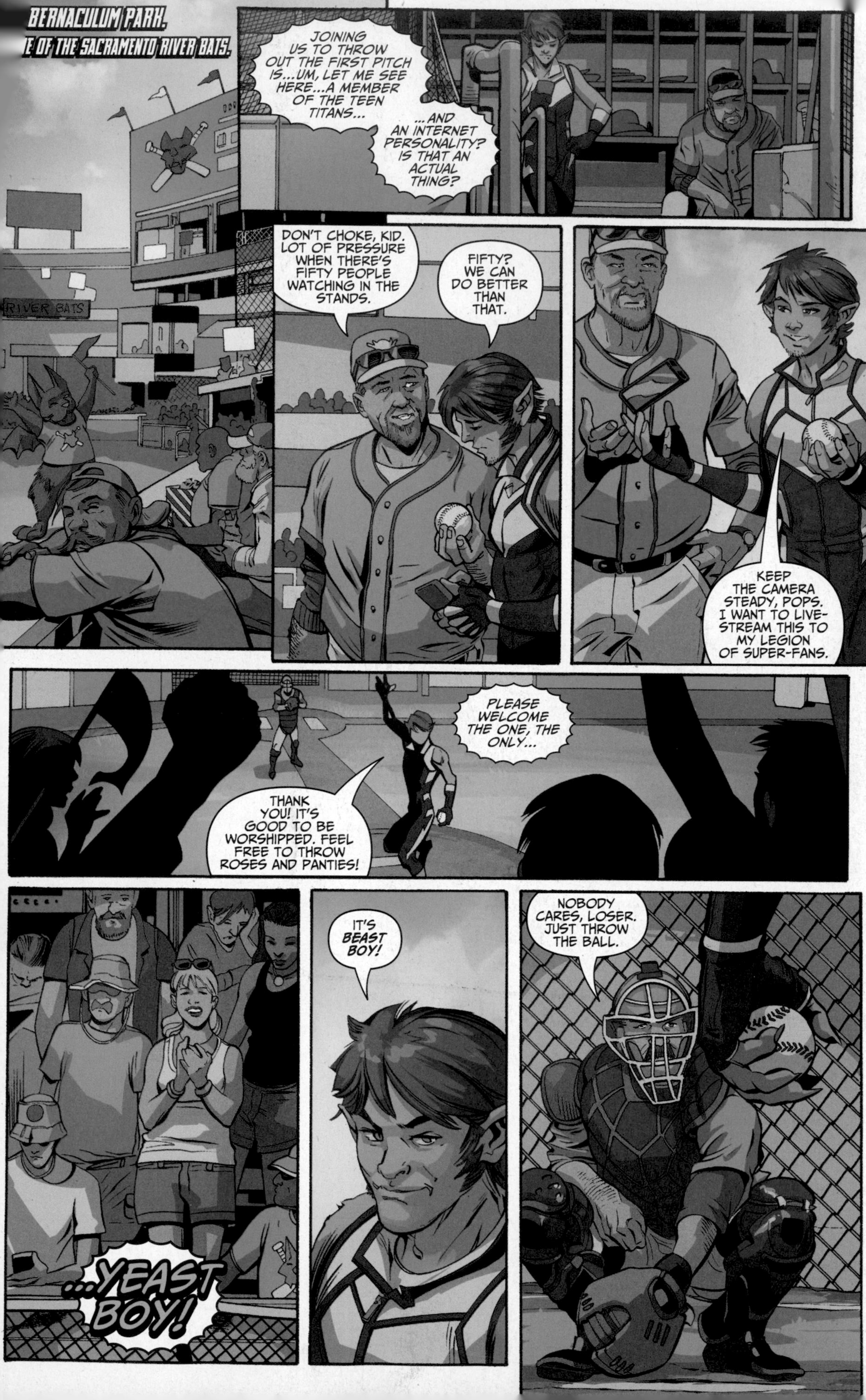
BERNACULUM PARK.
E OF THE SACRAMENTO RIVER BATS.
JOINING US TO THROW OUT THE FIRST PITCH IS...UM, LET ME SEE HERE...A MEMBER OF THE TEEN TITANS...
...AND AN INTERNET PERSONALITY? IS THAT AN ACTUAL THING?
RIVER BATS
DON'T CHOKE, KID. LOT OF PRESSURE WHEN THERE'S FIFTY PEOPLE WATCHING IN THE STANDS.
FIFTY? WE CAN DO BETTER THAN THAT.
KEEP THE CAMERA STEADY, POPS. I WANT TO LIVE-STREAM THIS TO MY LEGION OF SUPER-FANS.
PLEASE WELCOME THE ONE, THE ONLY...
THANK YOU! IT'S GOOD TO BE WORSHIPPED. FEEL FREE TO THROW ROSES AND PANTIES!
...YEAST BOY!
IT'S BEAST BOY!
NOBODY CARES, LOSER. JUST THROW THE BALL.

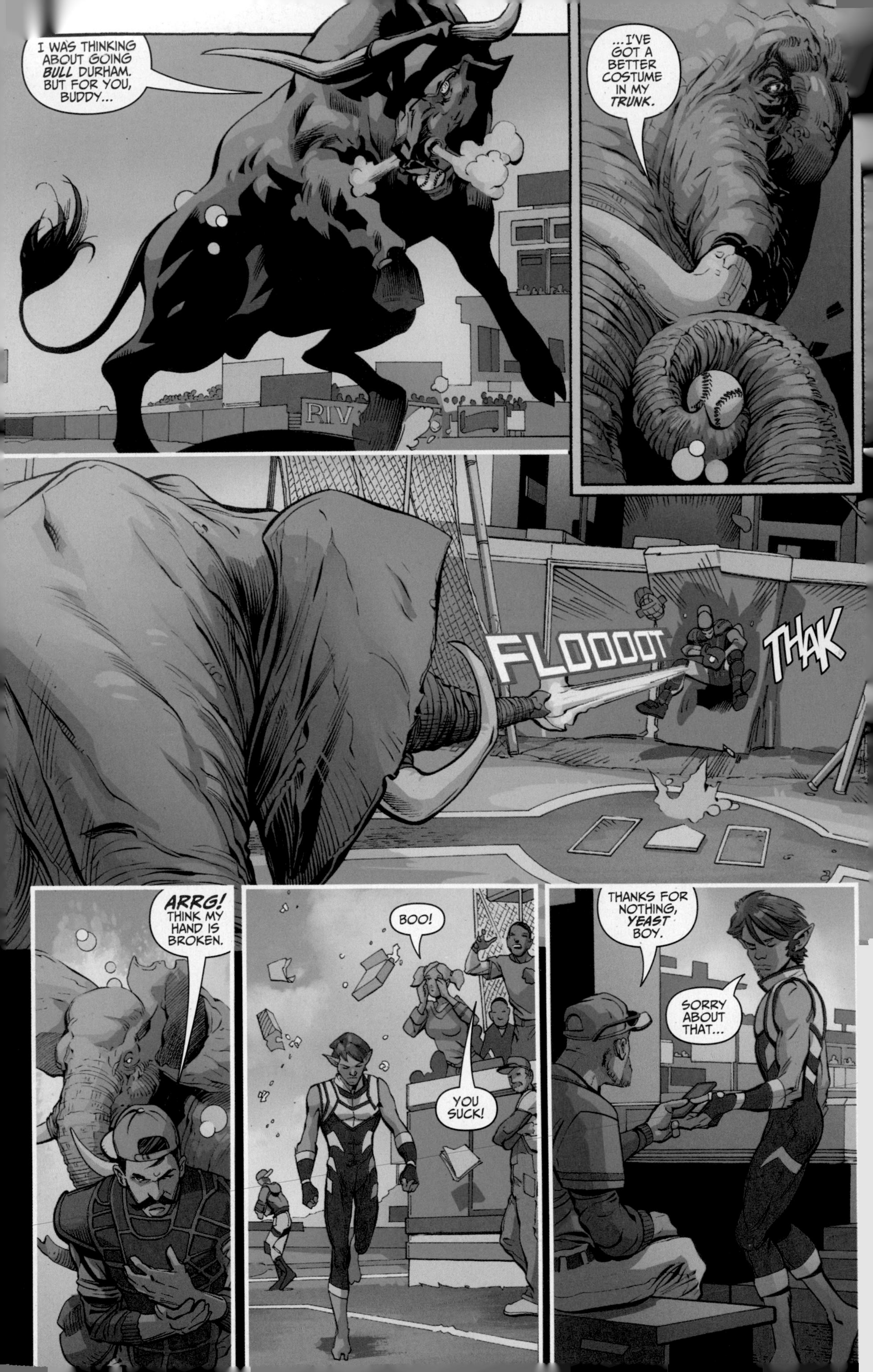
I WAS THINKING ABOUT GOING BULL DURHAM. BUT FOR YOU, BUDDY...
...I'VE GOT A BETTER COSTUME IN MY TRUNK.
FLOOOOT
THAK
ARRG! THINK MY HAND IS BROKEN.
BOO!
YOU SUCK!
THANKS FOR NOTHING, YEAST BOY.
SORRY ABOUT THAT...

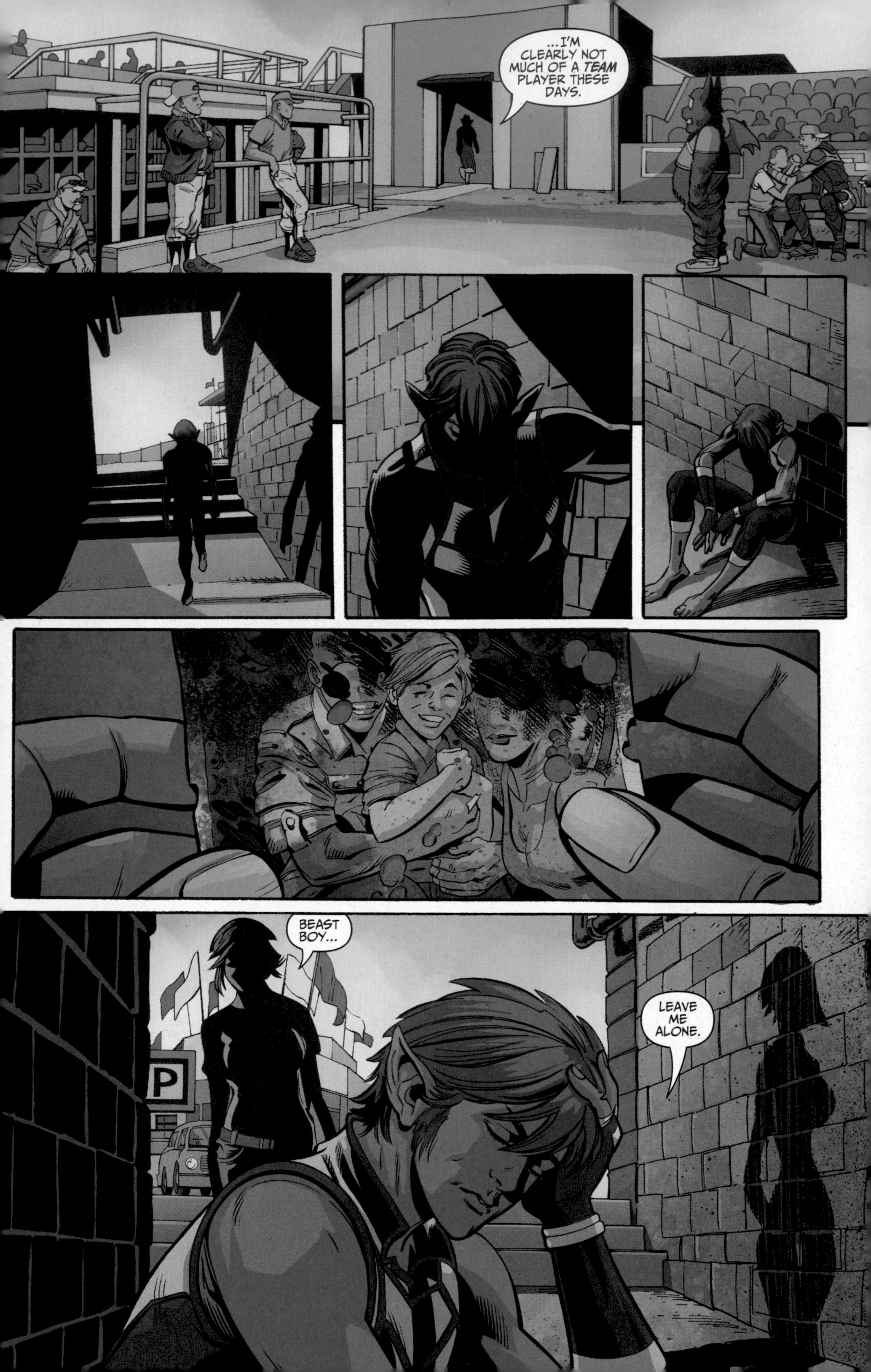
...I'M CLEARLY NOT MUCH OF A *TEAM* PLAYER THESE DAYS.
BEAST BOY...
LEAVE ME ALONE.

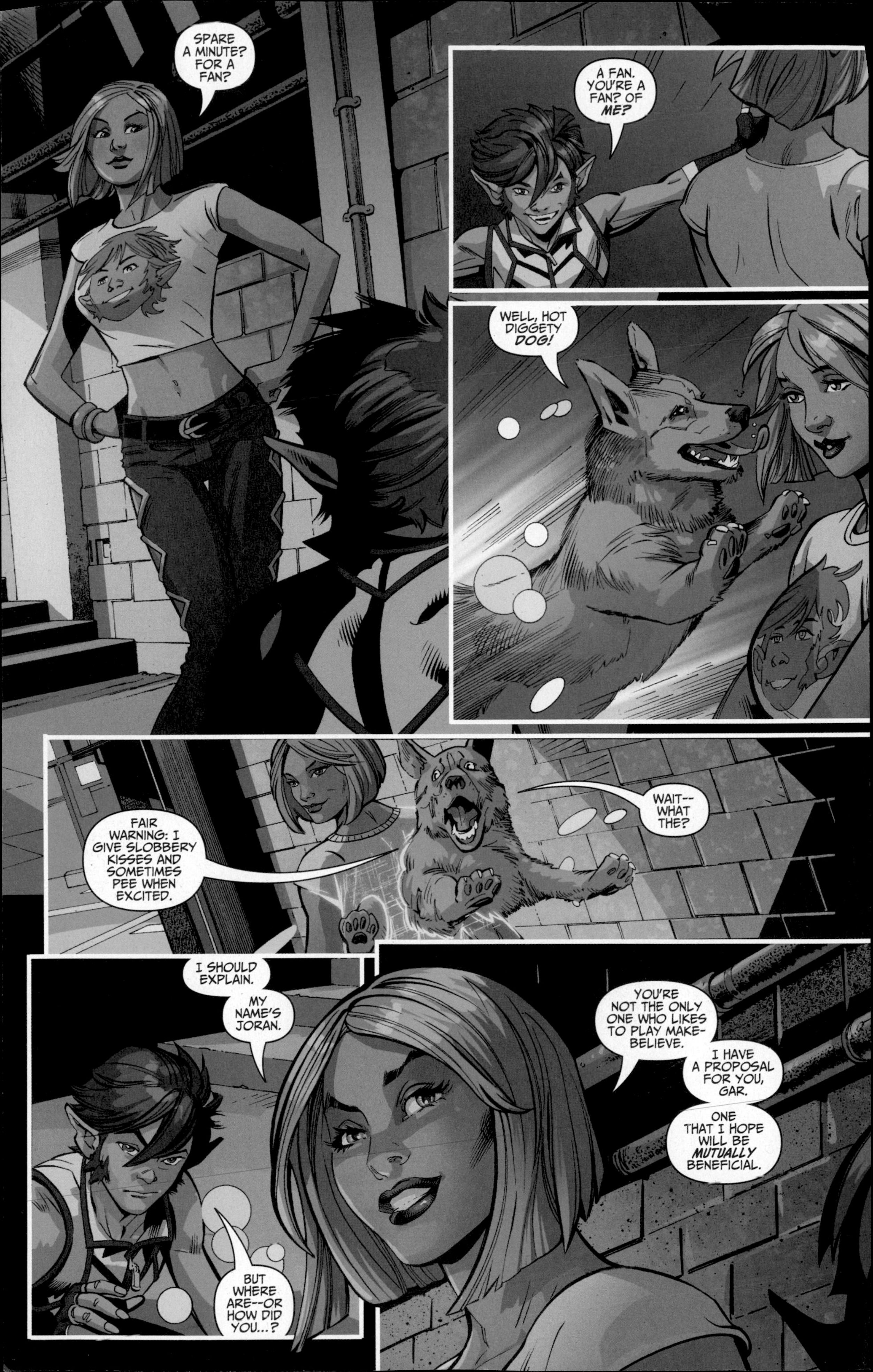
SPARE A MINUTE? FOR A FAN?
A FAN. YOU'RE A FAN? OF *ME?*
WELL, HOT DIGGETY *DOG!*
FAIR WARNING: I GIVE SLOBBERY KISSES AND SOMETIMES PEE WHEN EXCITED.
WAIT-- WHAT THE?
I SHOULD EXPLAIN.
MY NAME'S JORAN.
BUT WHERE ARE--OR HOW DID YOU...?
YOU'RE NOT THE ONLY ONE WHO LIKES TO PLAY MAKE-BELIEVE.
I HAVE A PROPOSAL FOR YOU, GAR.
ONE THAT I HOPE WILL BE *MUTUALLY* BENEFICIAL.

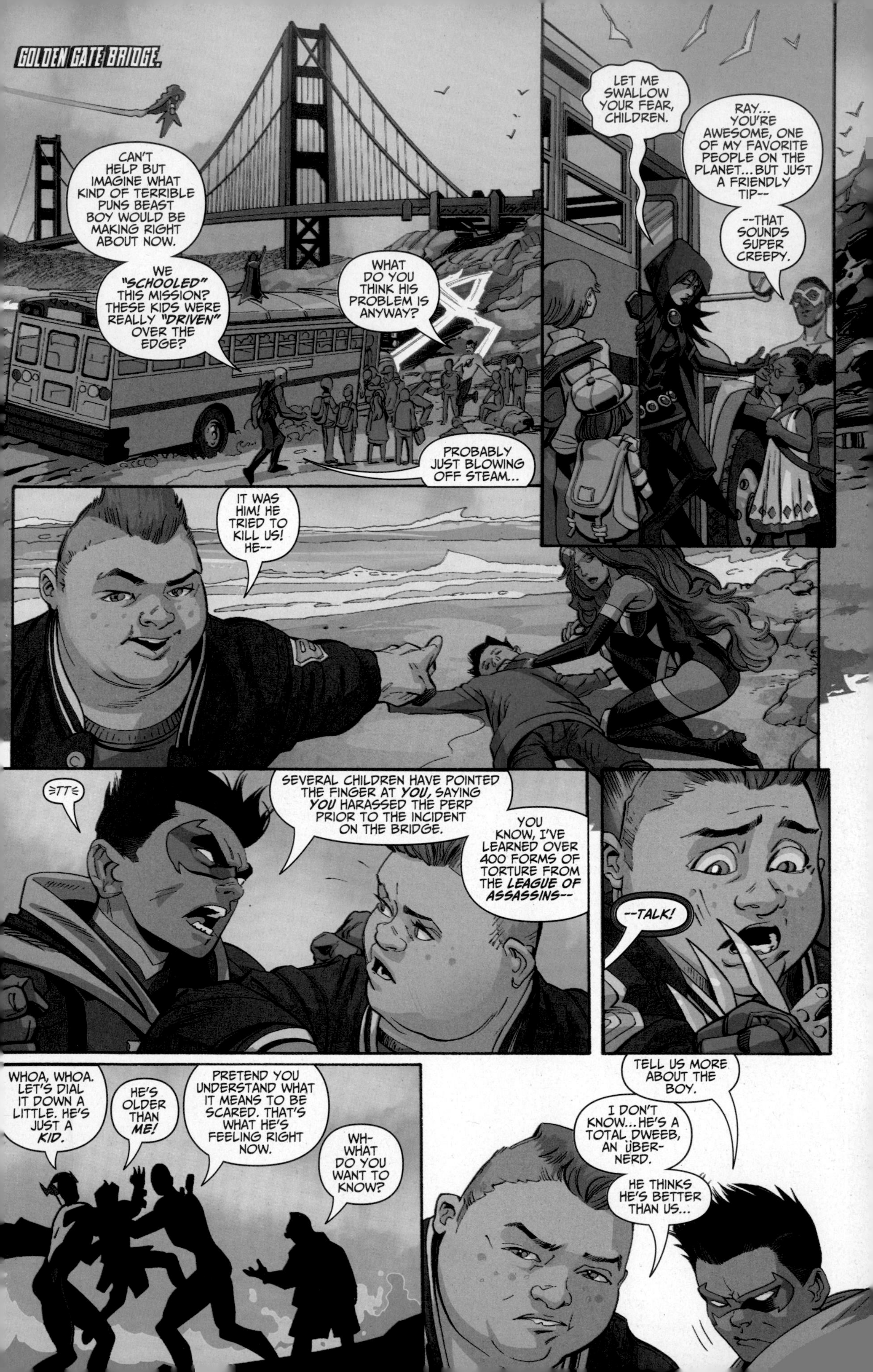
GOLDEN GATE BRIDGE.
CAN'T HELP BUT IMAGINE WHAT KIND OF TERRIBLE PUNS BEAST BOY WOULD BE MAKING RIGHT ABOUT NOW.
WE "SCHOOLED" THIS MISSION? THESE KIDS WERE REALLY "DRIVEN" OVER THE EDGE?
WHAT DO YOU THINK HIS PROBLEM IS ANYWAY?
PROBABLY JUST BLOWING OFF STEAM...
LET ME SWALLOW YOUR FEAR, CHILDREN.
RAY... YOU'RE AWESOME, ONE OF MY FAVORITE PEOPLE ON THE PLANET... BUT JUST A FRIENDLY TIP--
--THAT SOUNDS SUPER CREEPY.
IT WAS HIM! HE TRIED TO KILL US! HE--
TT
SEVERAL CHILDREN HAVE POINTED THE FINGER AT YOU, SAYING YOU HARASSED THE PERP PRIOR TO THE INCIDENT ON THE BRIDGE.
YOU KNOW, I'VE LEARNED OVER 400 FORMS OF TORTURE FROM THE LEAGUE OF ASSASSINS--
--TALK!
WHOA, WHOA. LET'S DIAL IT DOWN A LITTLE. HE'S JUST A KID.
HE'S OLDER THAN ME!
PRETEND YOU UNDERSTAND WHAT IT MEANS TO BE SCARED. THAT'S WHAT HE'S FEELING RIGHT NOW.
WH-WHAT DO YOU WANT TO KNOW?
TELL US MORE ABOUT THE BOY.
I DON'T KNOW... HE'S A TOTAL DWEEB, AN ÜBER-NERD.
HE THINKS HE'S BETTER THAN US...

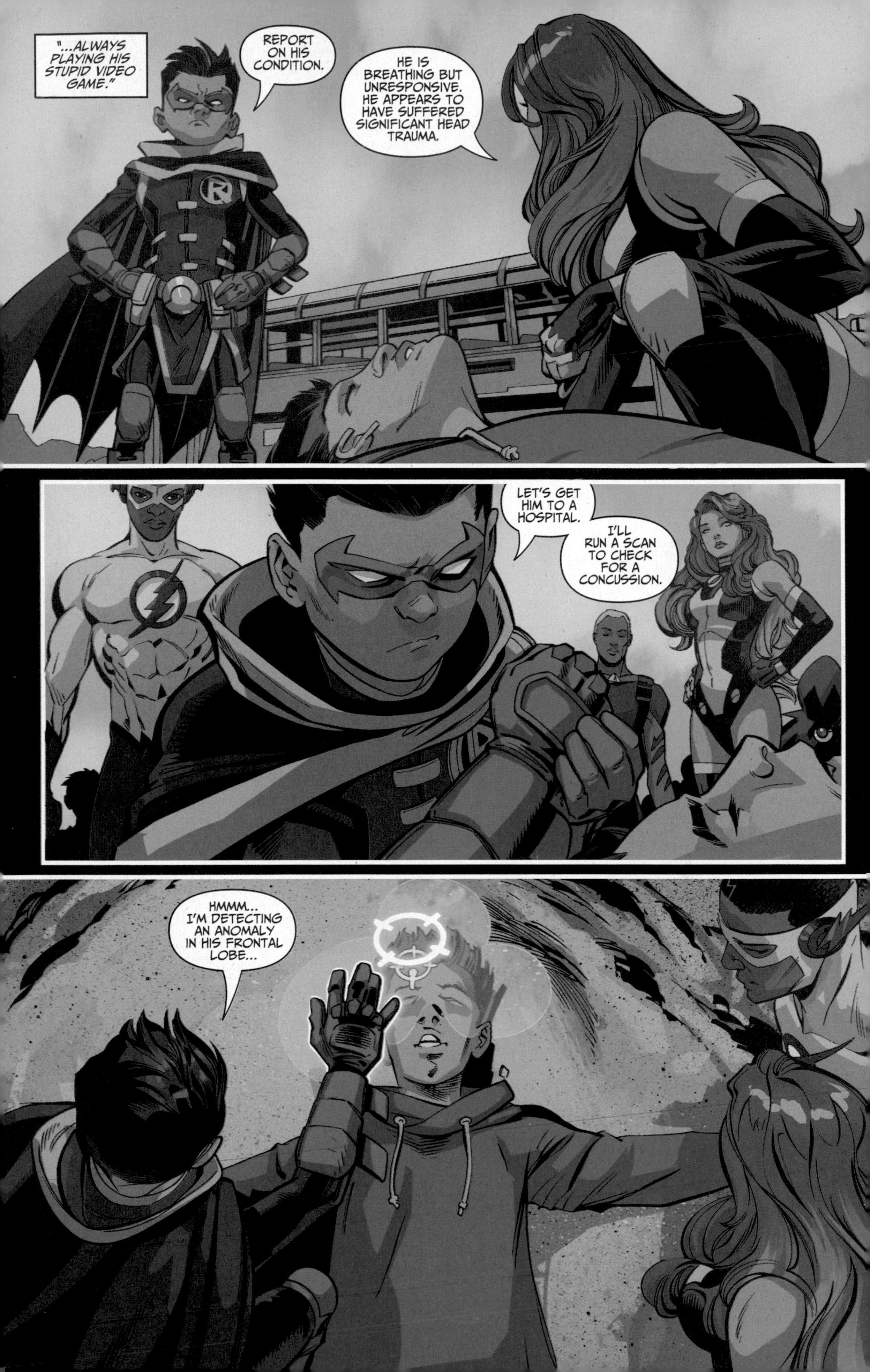
"...ALWAYS PLAYING HIS STUPID VIDEO GAME."
REPORT ON HIS CONDITION.
HE IS BREATHING BUT UNRESPONSIVE. HE APPEARS TO HAVE SUFFERED SIGNIFICANT HEAD TRAUMA.
LET'S GET HIM TO A HOSPITAL.
I'LL RUN A SCAN TO CHECK FOR A CONCUSSION.
HMMM... I'M DETECTING AN ANOMALY IN HIS FRONTAL LOBE...

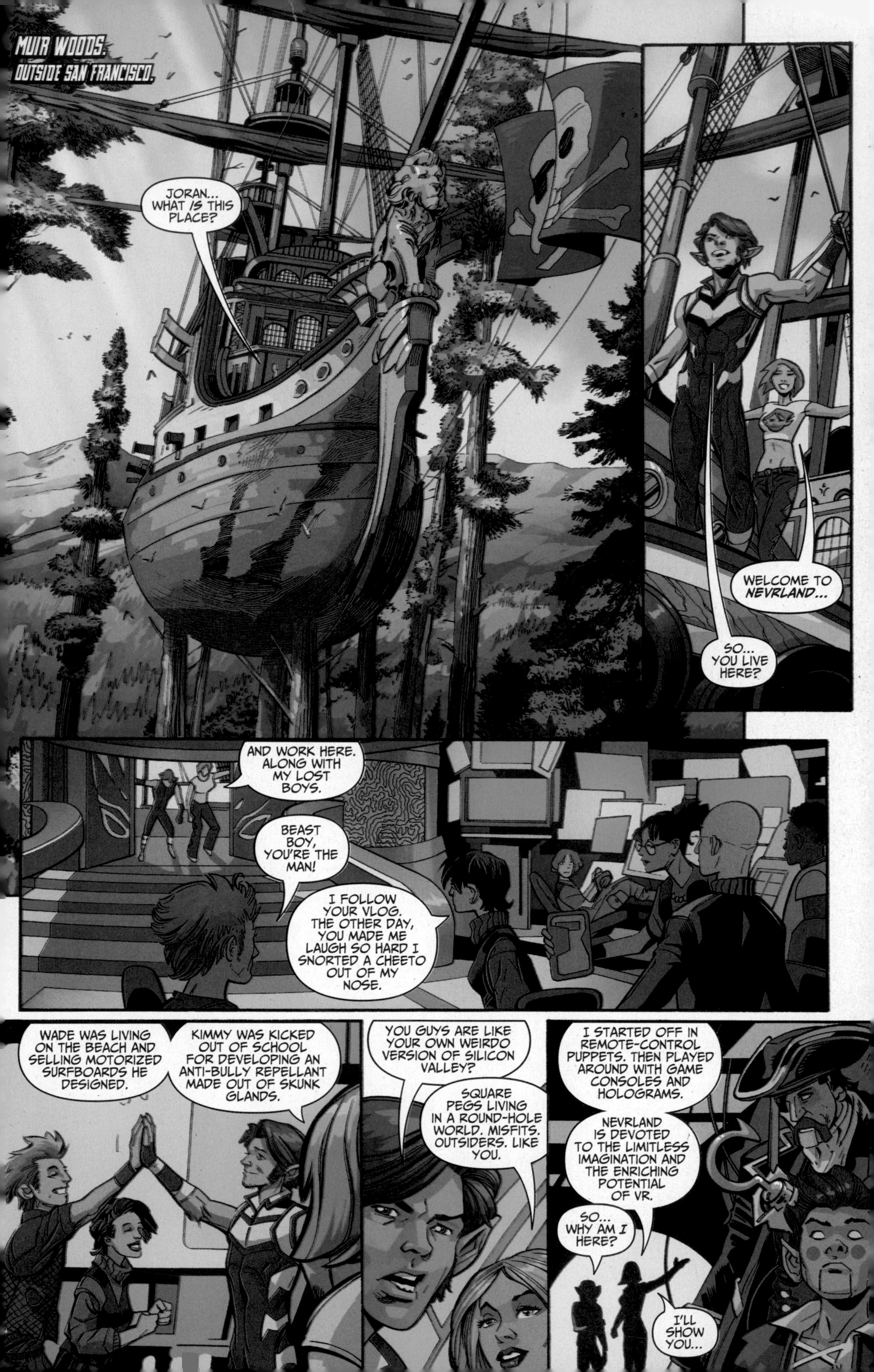

MUIR WOODS.
OUTSIDE SAN FRANCISCO.
JORAN... WHAT IS THIS PLACE?
WELCOME TO NEVRLAND...
SO... YOU LIVE HERE?
AND WORK HERE. ALONG WITH MY LOST BOYS.
BEAST BOY, YOU'RE THE MAN!
I FOLLOW YOUR VLOG. THE OTHER DAY, YOU MADE ME LAUGH SO HARD I SNORTED A CHEETO OUT OF MY NOSE.
WADE WAS LIVING ON THE BEACH AND SELLING MOTORIZED SURFBOARDS HE DESIGNED.
KIMMY WAS KICKED OUT OF SCHOOL FOR DEVELOPING AN ANTI-BULLY REPELLANT MADE OUT OF SKUNK GLANDS.
YOU GUYS ARE LIKE YOUR OWN WEIRDO VERSION OF SILICON VALLEY?
SQUARE PEGS LIVING IN A ROUND-HOLE WORLD. MISFITS. OUTSIDERS. LIKE YOU.
I STARTED OFF IN REMOTE-CONTROL PUPPETS. THEN PLAYED AROUND WITH GAME CONSOLES AND HOLOGRAMS.
NEVRLAND IS DEVOTED TO THE LIMITLESS IMAGINATION AND THE ENRICHING POTENTIAL OF VR.
SO... WHY AM I HERE?
I'LL SHOW YOU...

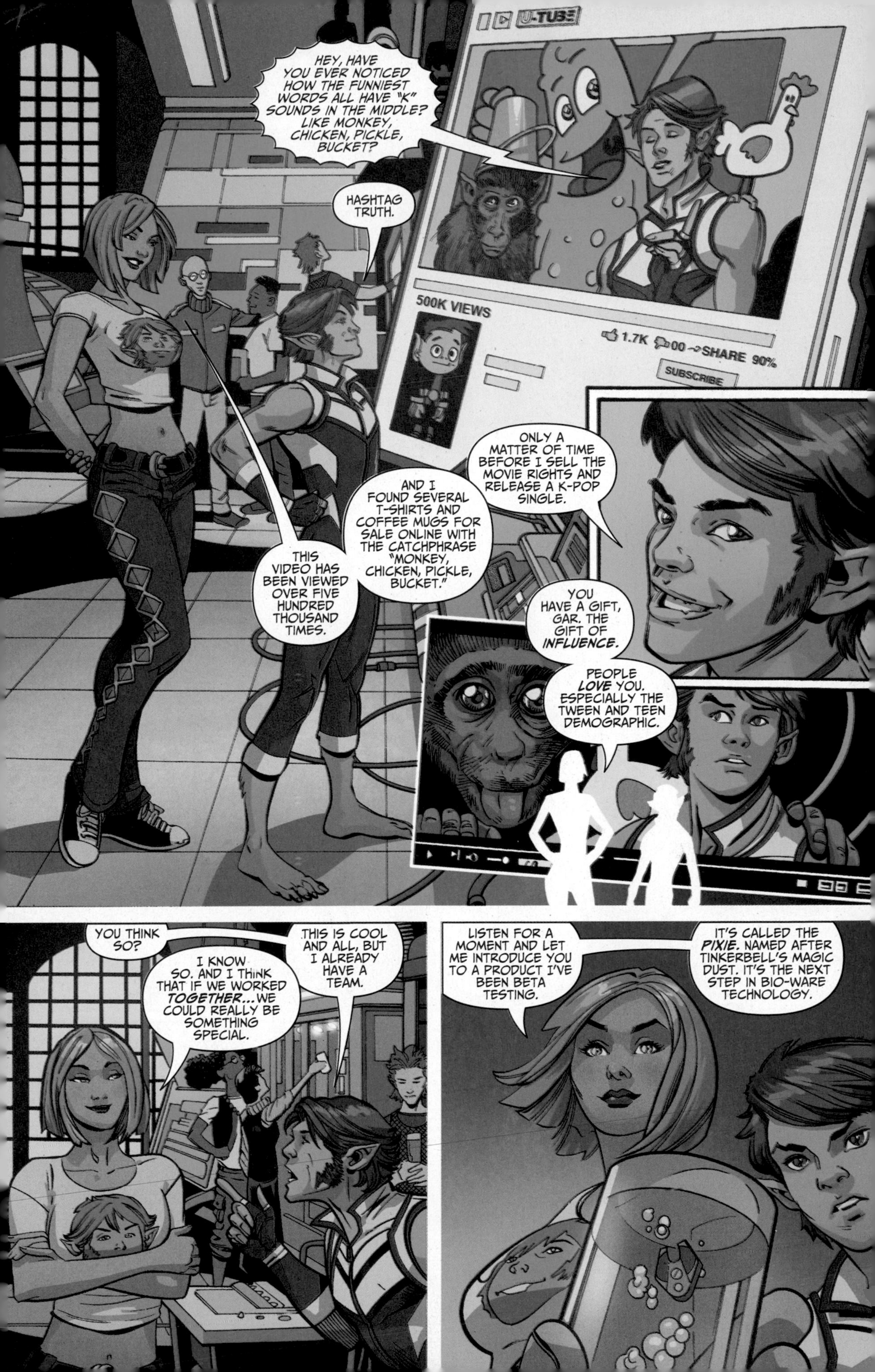
U-TUBE
HEY, HAVE YOU EVER NOTICED HOW THE FUNNIEST WORDS ALL HAVE "K" SOUNDS IN THE MIDDLE? LIKE MONKEY, CHICKEN, PICKLE, BUCKET?
HASHTAG TRUTH.
500K VIEWS
1.7K 00 SHARE 90%
SUBSCRIBE
THIS VIDEO HAS BEEN VIEWED OVER FIVE HUNDRED THOUSAND TIMES.
AND I FOUND SEVERAL T-SHIRTS AND COFFEE MUGS FOR SALE ONLINE WITH THE CATCHPHRASE "MONKEY, CHICKEN, PICKLE, BUCKET."
ONLY A MATTER OF TIME BEFORE I SELL THE MOVIE RIGHTS AND RELEASE A K-POP SINGLE.
YOU HAVE A GIFT, GAR. THE GIFT OF *INFLUENCE.*
PEOPLE *LOVE* YOU. ESPECIALLY THE TWEEN AND TEEN DEMOGRAPHIC.
YOU THINK SO?
I KNOW SO. AND I THINK THAT IF WE WORKED *TOGETHER*... WE COULD REALLY BE SOMETHING SPECIAL.
THIS IS COOL AND ALL, BUT I ALREADY HAVE A TEAM.
LISTEN FOR A MOMENT AND LET ME INTRODUCE YOU TO A PRODUCT I'VE BEEN BETA TESTING.
IT'S CALLED THE *PIXIE.* NAMED AFTER TINKERBELL'S MAGIC DUST. IT'S THE NEXT STEP IN BIO-WARE TECHNOLOGY.

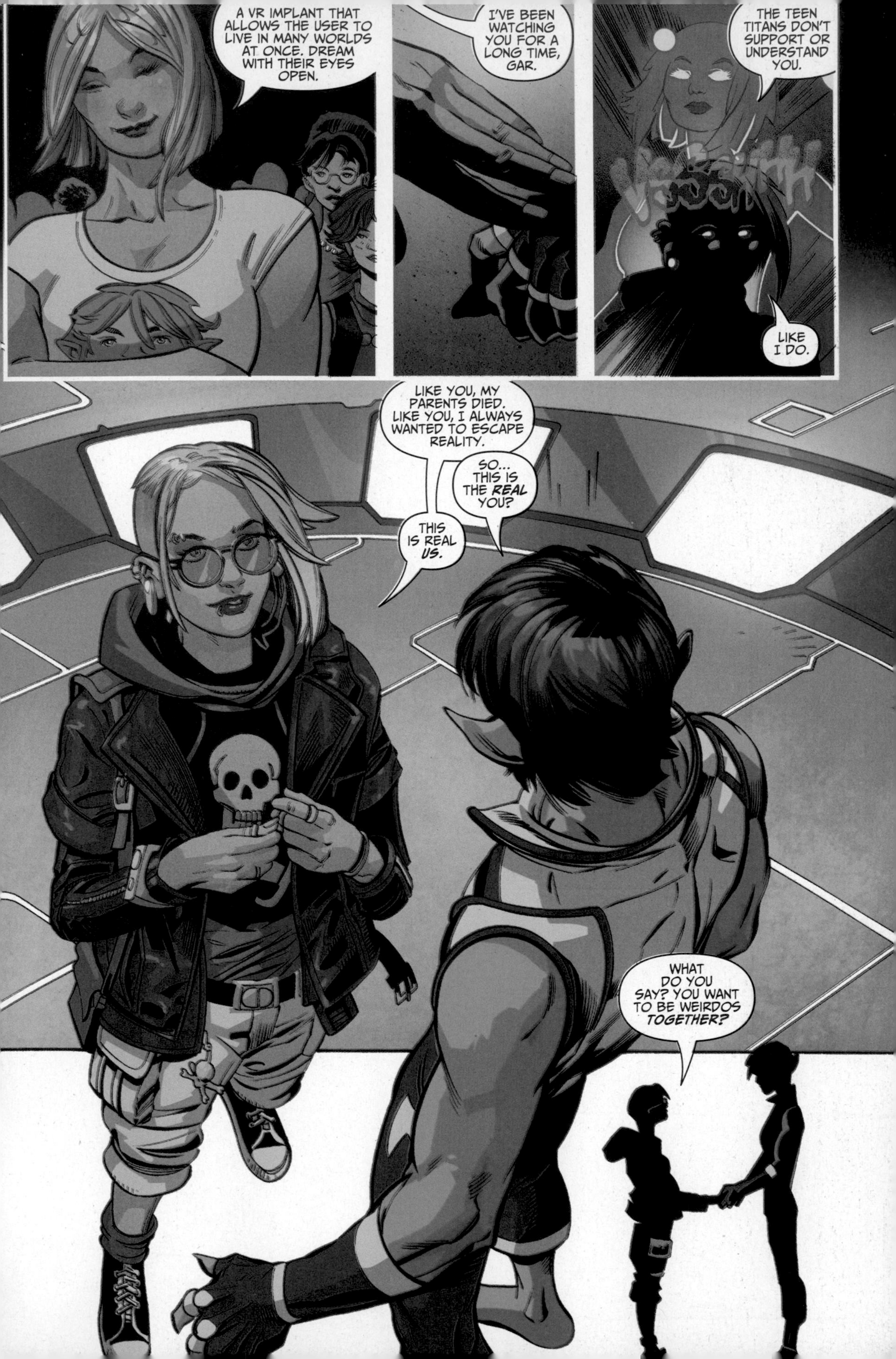
A VR IMPLANT THAT ALLOWS THE USER TO LIVE IN MANY WORLDS AT ONCE. DREAM WITH THEIR EYES OPEN.
I'VE BEEN WATCHING YOU FOR A LONG TIME, GAR.
THE TEEN TITANS DON'T SUPPORT OR UNDERSTAND YOU.
LIKE I DO.
LIKE YOU, MY PARENTS DIED. LIKE YOU, I ALWAYS WANTED TO ESCAPE REALITY.
SO... THIS IS THE *REAL* YOU?
THIS IS REAL *US.*
WHAT DO YOU SAY? YOU WANT TO BE WEIRDOS *TOGETHER?*

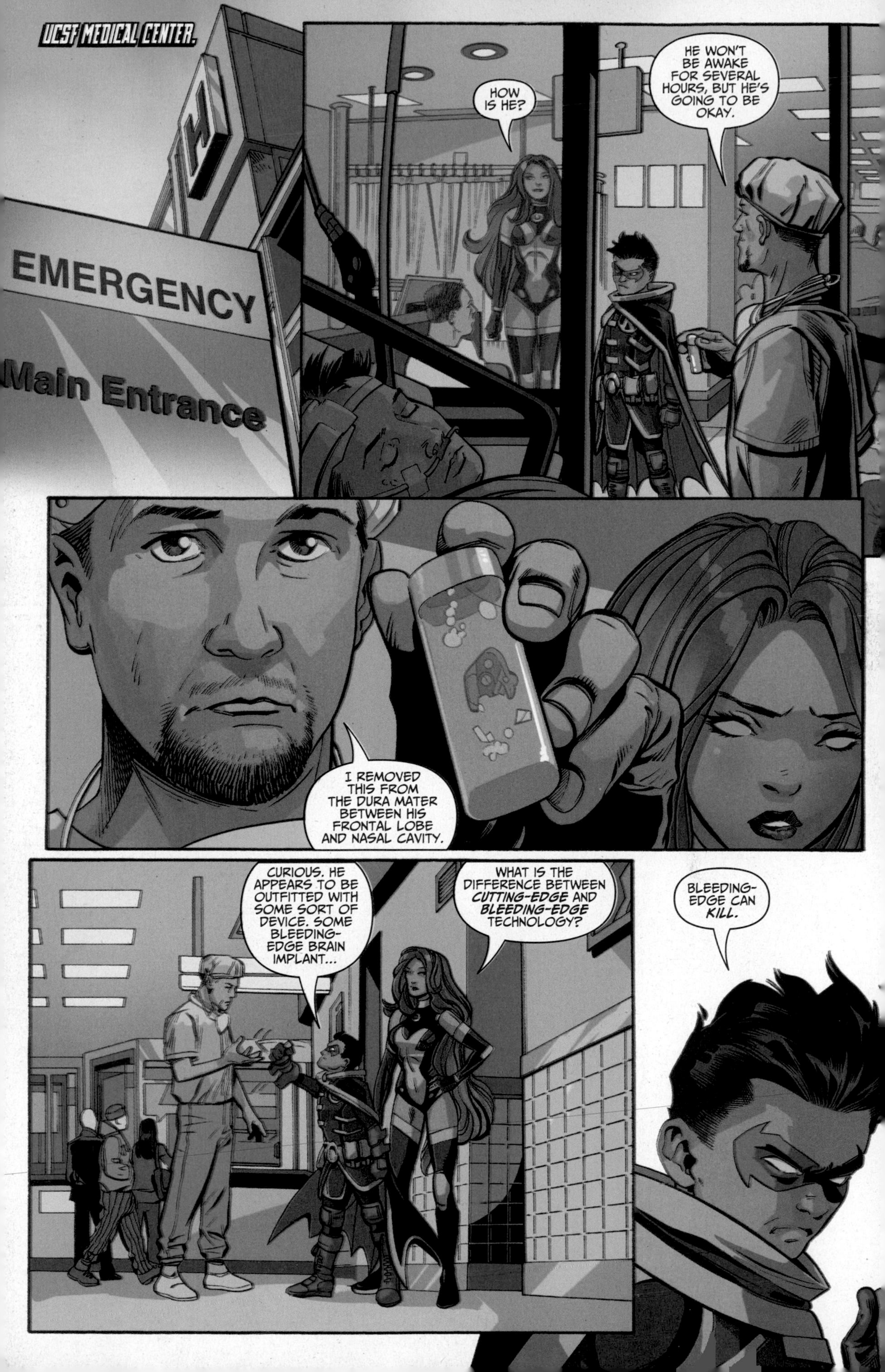
UCSF MEDICAL CENTER.
EMERGENCY
Main Entrance
HOW IS HE?
HE WON'T BE AWAKE FOR SEVERAL HOURS, BUT HE'S GOING TO BE OKAY.
I REMOVED THIS FROM THE DURA MATER BETWEEN HIS FRONTAL LOBE AND NASAL CAVITY.
CURIOUS. HE APPEARS TO BE OUTFITTED WITH SOME SORT OF DEVICE. SOME BLEEDING-EDGE BRAIN IMPLANT...
WHAT IS THE DIFFERENCE BETWEEN *CUTTING-EDGE* AND *BLEEDING-EDGE* TECHNOLOGY?
BLEEDING-EDGE CAN *KILL*.

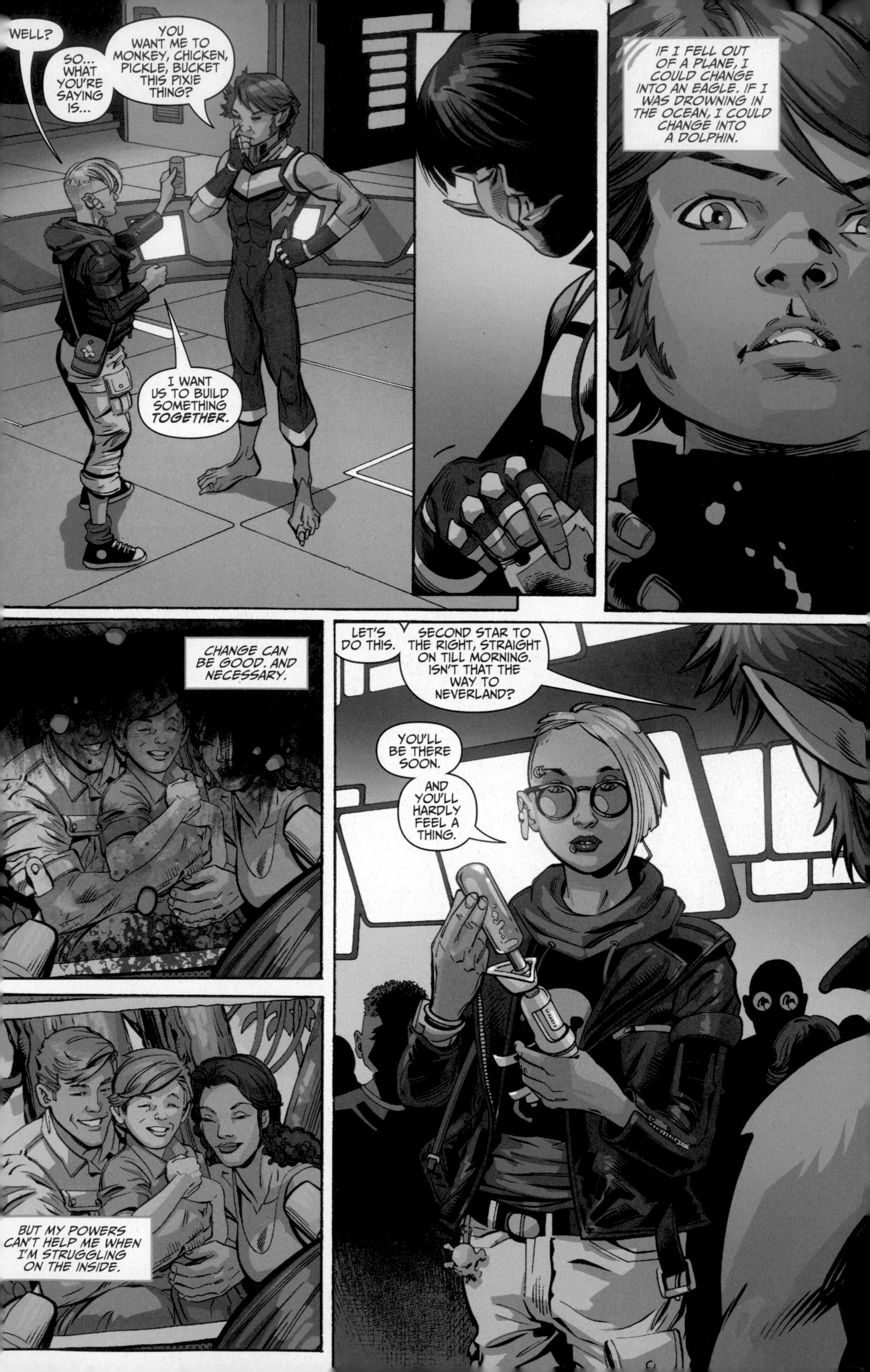
WELL?
SO... WHAT YOU'RE SAYING IS...
YOU WANT ME TO MONKEY, CHICKEN, PICKLE, BUCKET THIS PIXIE THING?
I WANT US TO BUILD SOMETHING *TOGETHER*.
IF I FELL OUT OF A PLANE, I COULD CHANGE INTO AN EAGLE. IF I WAS DROWNING IN THE OCEAN, I COULD CHANGE INTO A DOLPHIN.
CHANGE CAN BE GOOD. AND NECESSARY.
BUT MY POWERS CAN'T HELP ME WHEN I'M STRUGGLING ON THE INSIDE.
LET'S DO THIS.
SECOND STAR TO THE RIGHT, STRAIGHT ON TILL MORNING. ISN'T THAT THE WAY TO NEVERLAND?
YOU'LL BE THERE SOON.
AND YOU'LL HARDLY FEEL A THING.

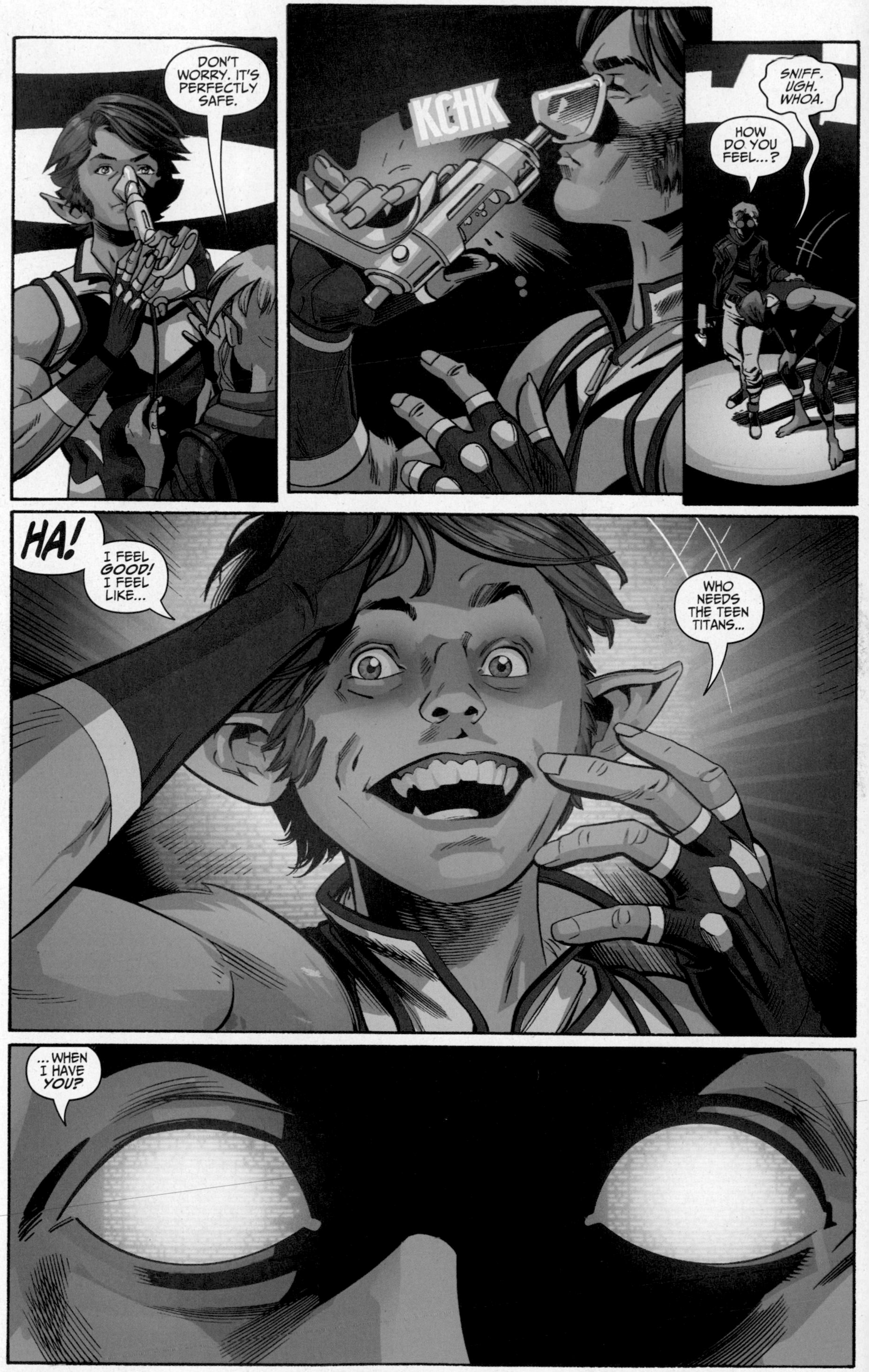
DON'T WORRY. IT'S PERFECTLY SAFE.
KCHK
SNIFF. UGH. WHOA.
HOW DO YOU FEEL...?
HA!
I FEEL GOOD! I FEEL LIKE...
WHO NEEDS THE TEEN TITANS...
...WHEN I HAVE YOU?

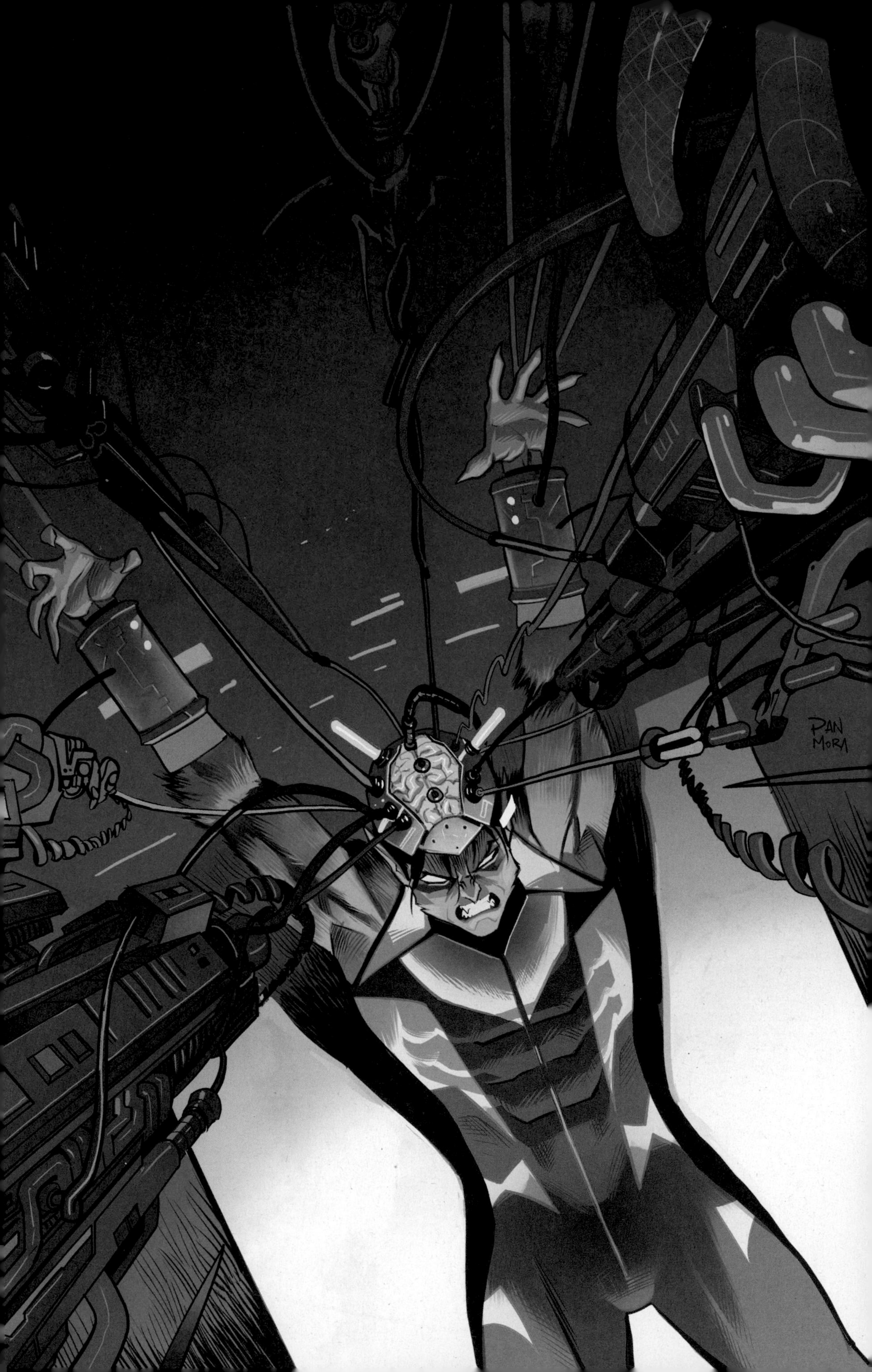
DAN
MORA

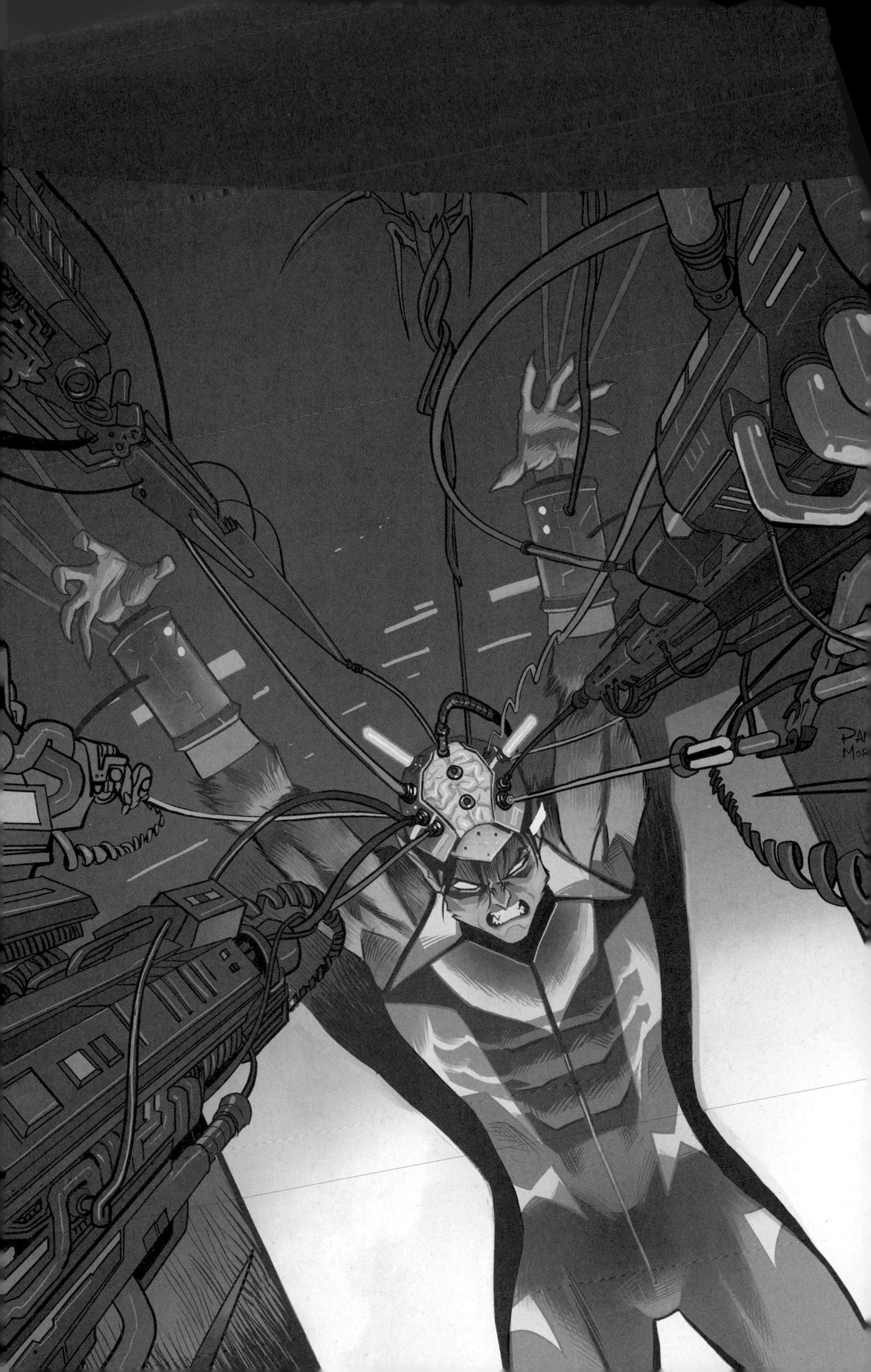

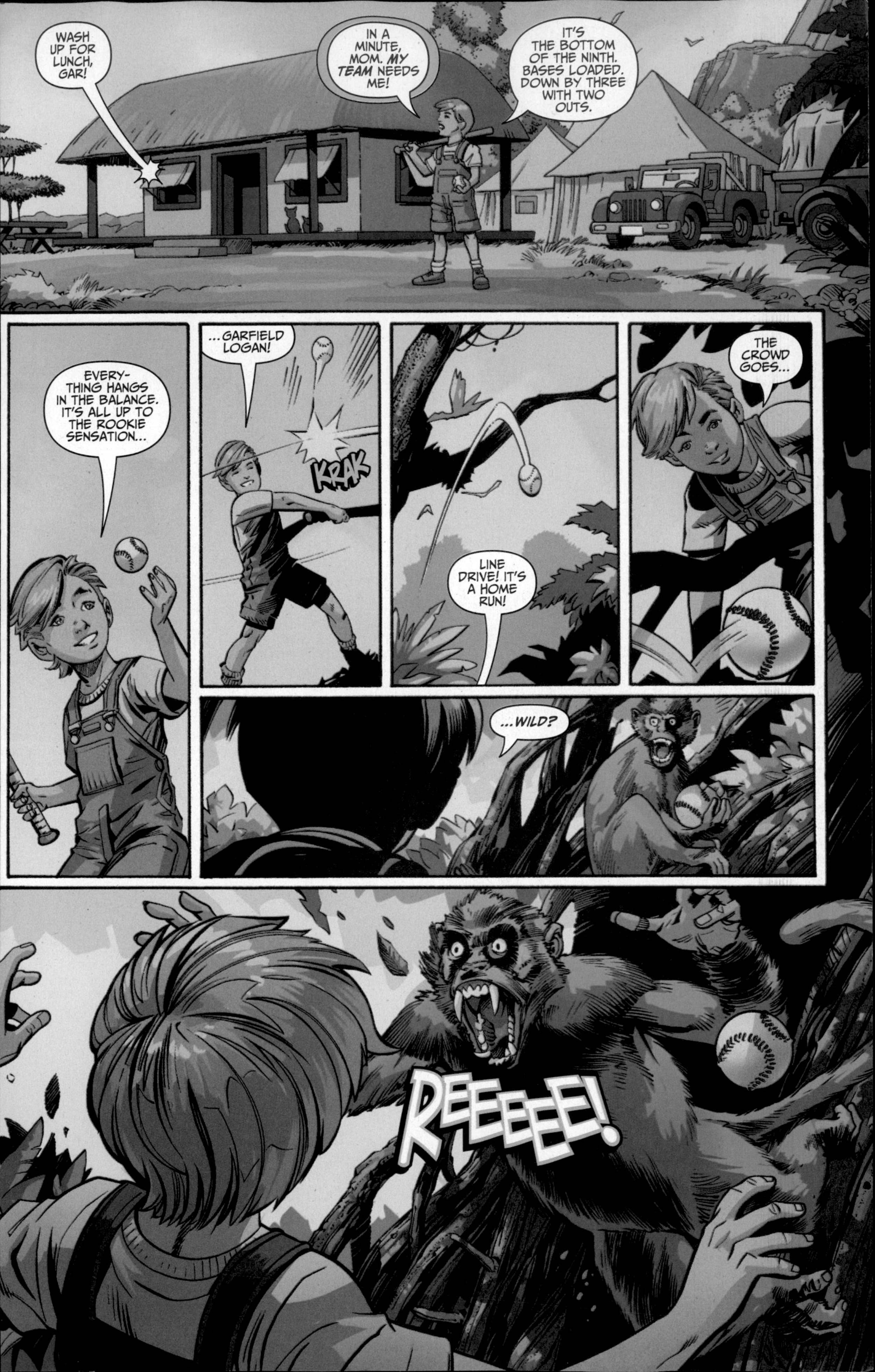
WASH UP FOR LUNCH, GAR!
IN A MINUTE, MOM. MY TEAM NEEDS ME!
IT'S THE BOTTOM OF THE NINTH. BASES LOADED. DOWN BY THREE WITH TWO OUTS.
EVERY-THING HANGS IN THE BALANCE. IT'S ALL UP TO THE ROOKIE SENSATION...
...GARFIELD LOGAN!
KRAK
LINE DRIVE! IT'S A HOME RUN!
THE CROWD GOES...
...WILD?
REEEEEE!

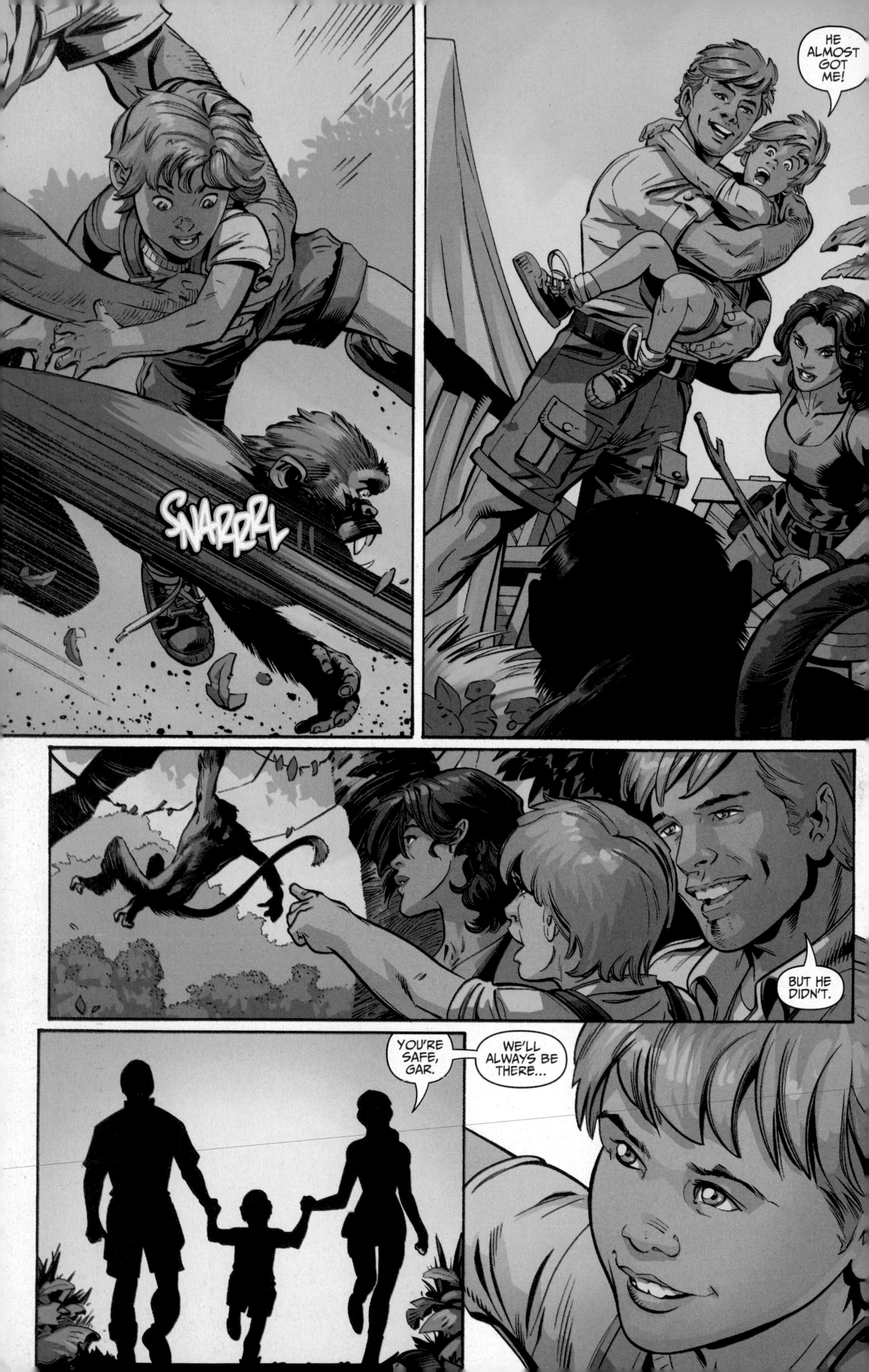
SNARRRL
HE ALMOST GOT ME!
BUT HE DIDN'T.
YOU'RE SAFE, GAR.
WE'LL ALWAYS BE THERE...

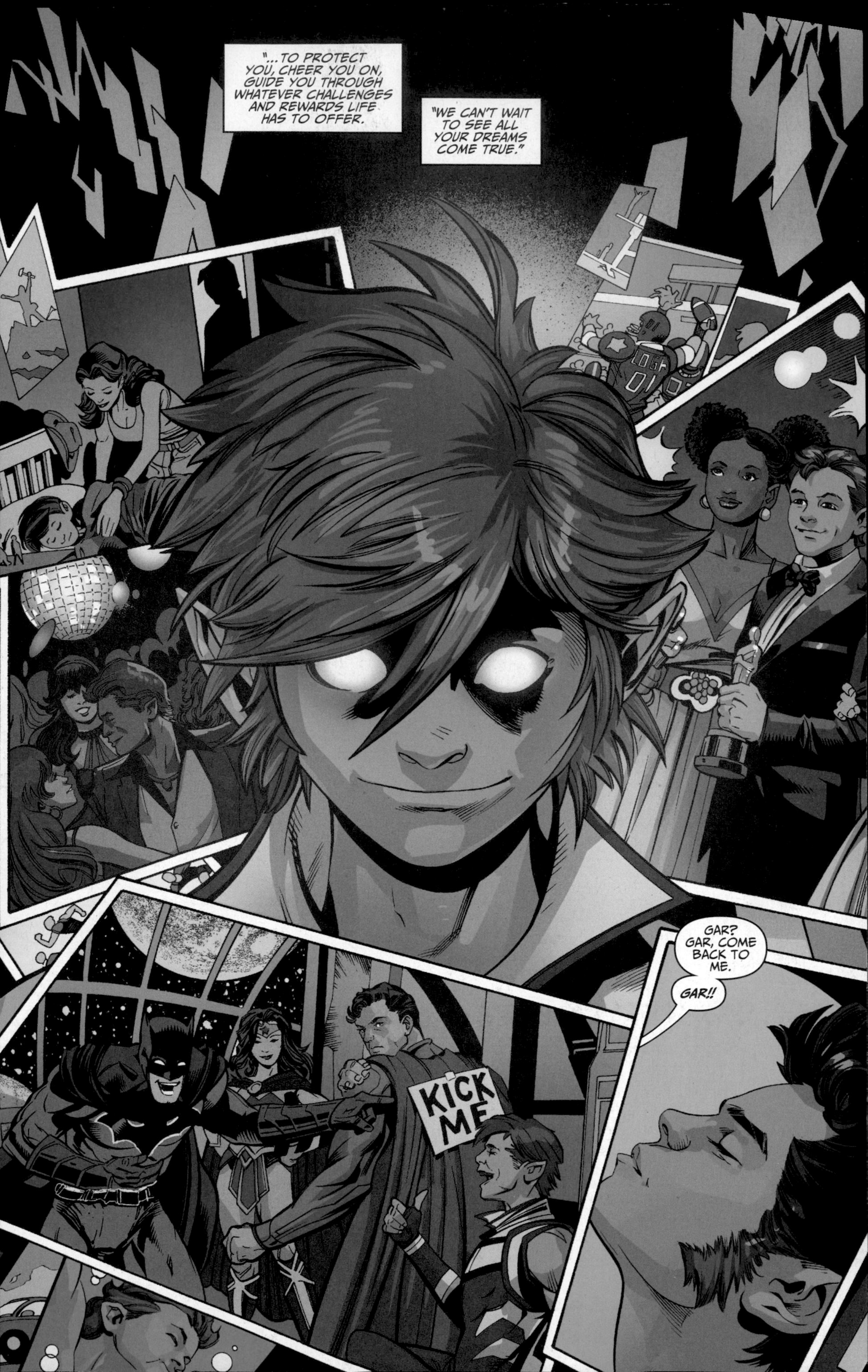
"...TO PROTECT YOU, CHEER YOU ON, GUIDE YOU THROUGH WHATEVER CHALLENGES AND REWARDS LIFE HAS TO OFFER.
"WE CAN'T WAIT TO SEE ALL YOUR DREAMS COME TRUE."
KICK ME
GAR? GAR, COME BACK TO ME.
GAR!!

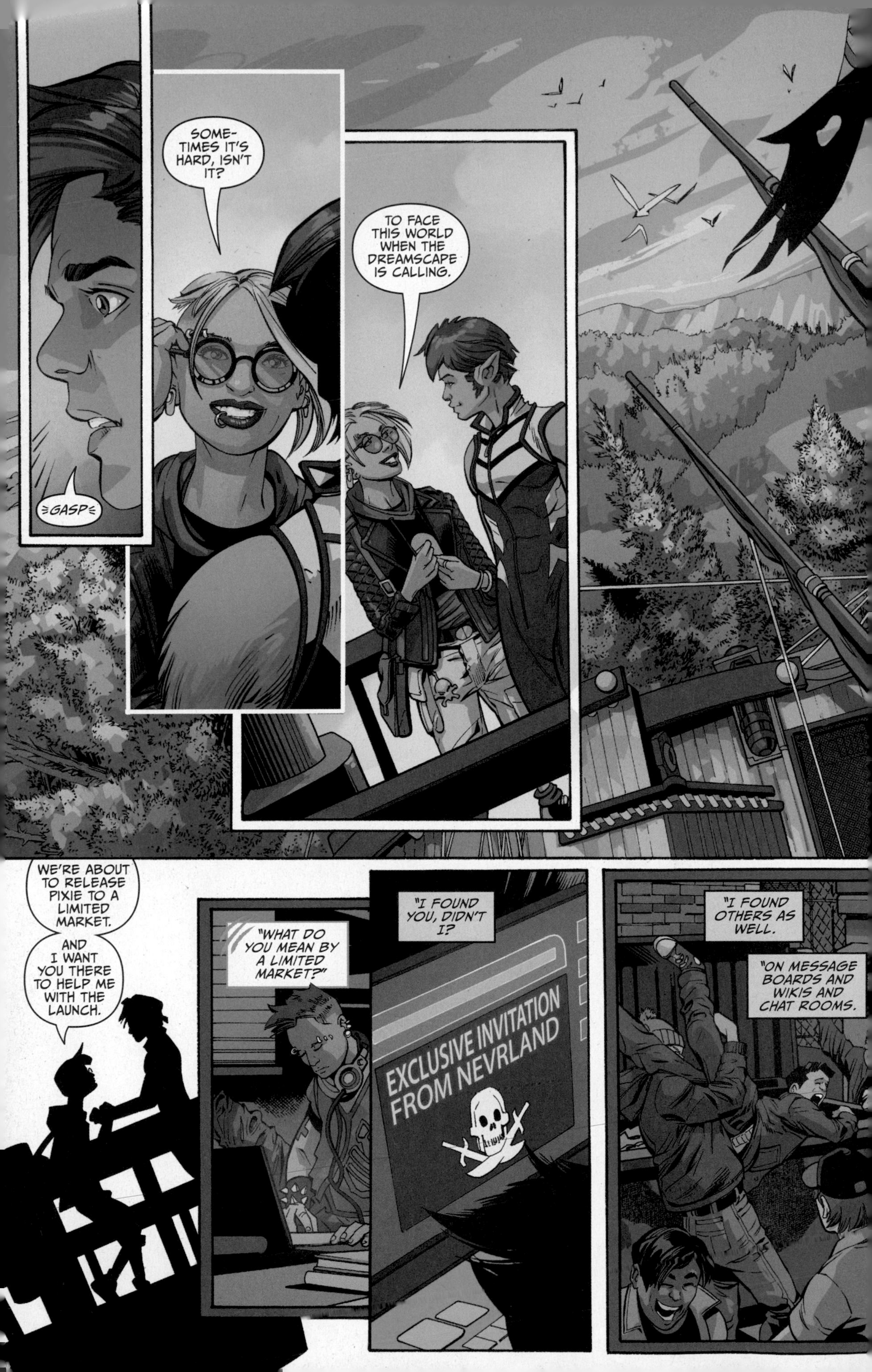
GASP
SOME-TIMES IT'S HARD, ISN'T IT?
TO FACE THIS WORLD WHEN THE DREAMSCAPE IS CALLING.
WE'RE ABOUT TO RELEASE PIXIE TO A LIMITED MARKET.
AND I WANT YOU THERE TO HELP ME WITH THE LAUNCH.
"WHAT DO YOU MEAN BY A LIMITED MARKET?"
"I FOUND YOU, DIDN'T I?
EXCLUSIVE INVITATION FROM NEVRLAND
"I FOUND OTHERS AS WELL.
"ON MESSAGE BOARDS AND WIKIS AND CHAT ROOMS.

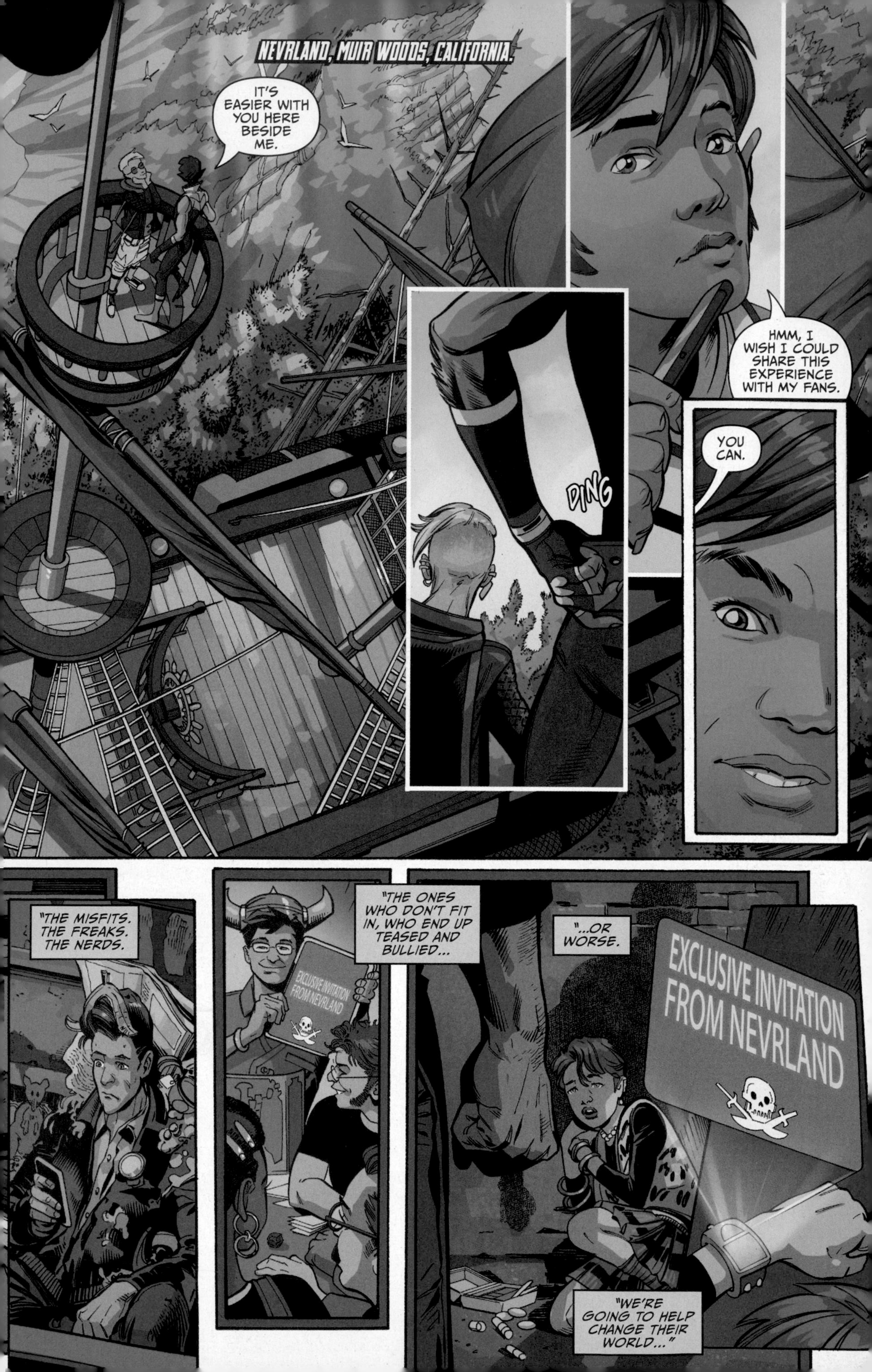
NEVRLAND, MUIR WOODS, CALIFORNIA.
IT'S EASIER WITH YOU HERE BESIDE ME.
HMM, I WISH I COULD SHARE THIS EXPERIENCE WITH MY FANS.
DING
YOU CAN.
"THE MISFITS. THE FREAKS. THE NERDS.
"THE ONES WHO DON'T FIT IN, WHO END UP TEASED AND BULLIED...
EXCLUSIVE INVITATION FROM NEVRLAND
"...OR WORSE.
EXCLUSIVE INVITATION FROM NEVRLAND
"WE'RE GOING TO HELP CHANGE THEIR WORLD..."

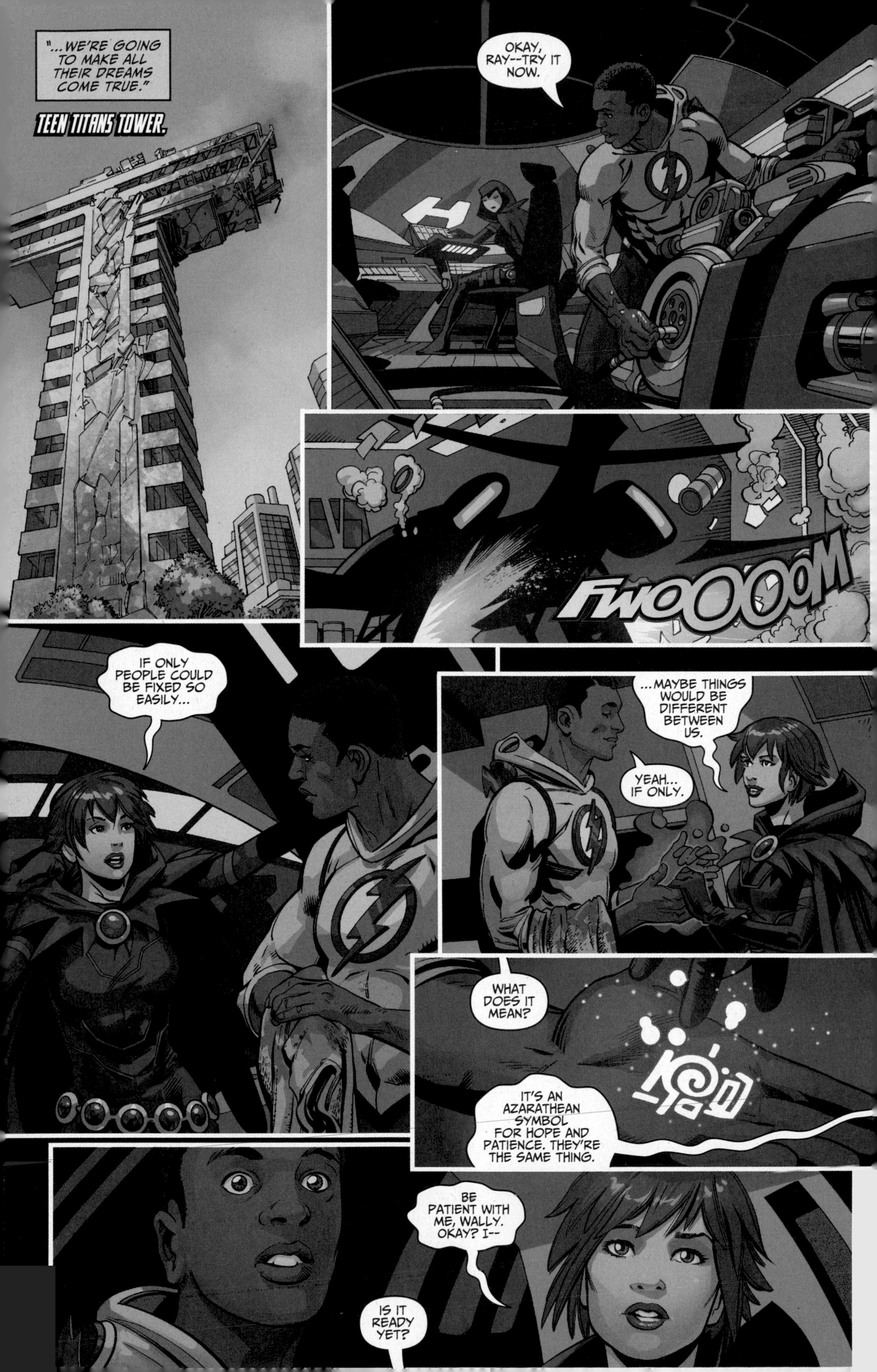
"...WE'RE GOING TO MAKE ALL THEIR DREAMS COME TRUE."
TEEN TITANS TOWER.
OKAY, RAY--TRY IT NOW.
FWOOOOOM
IF ONLY PEOPLE COULD BE FIXED SO EASILY...
...MAYBE THINGS WOULD BE DIFFERENT BETWEEN US.
YEAH... IF ONLY.
WHAT DOES IT MEAN?
IT'S AN AZARATHEAN SYMBOL FOR HOPE AND PATIENCE. THEY'RE THE SAME THING.
BE PATIENT WITH ME, WALLY. OKAY? I--
IS IT READY YET?

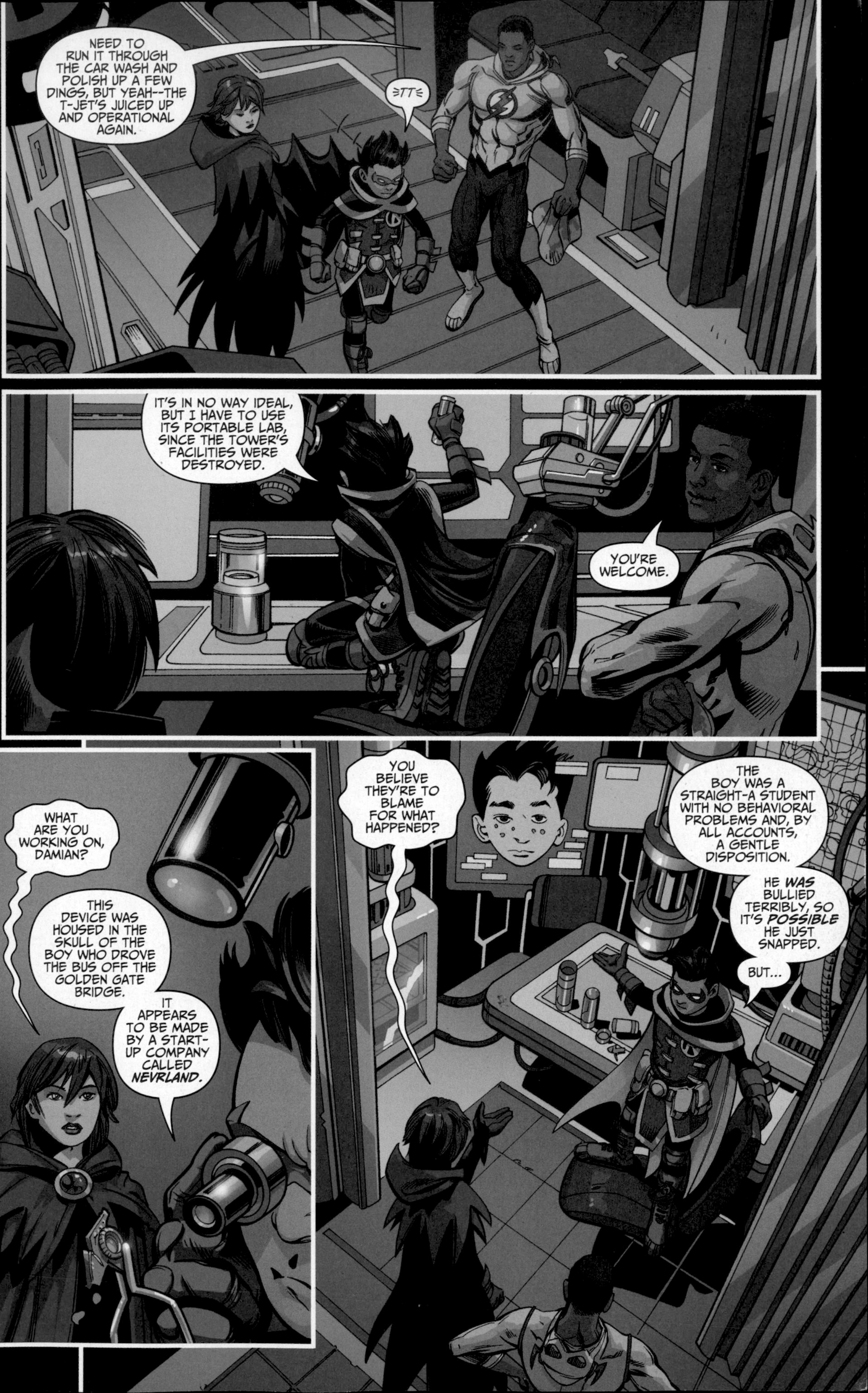
NEED TO RUN IT THROUGH THE CAR WASH AND POLISH UP A FEW DINGS, BUT YEAH--THE T-JET'S JUICED UP AND OPERATIONAL AGAIN.
TT
IT'S IN NO WAY IDEAL, BUT I HAVE TO USE ITS PORTABLE LAB, SINCE THE TOWER'S FACILITIES WERE DESTROYED.
YOU'RE WELCOME.
WHAT ARE YOU WORKING ON, DAMIAN?
THIS DEVICE WAS HOUSED IN THE SKULL OF THE BOY WHO DROVE THE BUS OFF THE GOLDEN GATE BRIDGE.
IT APPEARS TO BE MADE BY A START-UP COMPANY CALLED NEVRLAND.
YOU BELIEVE THEY'RE TO BLAME FOR WHAT HAPPENED?
THE BOY WAS A STRAIGHT-A STUDENT WITH NO BEHAVIORAL PROBLEMS AND, BY ALL ACCOUNTS, A GENTLE DISPOSITION.
HE WAS BULLIED TERRIBLY, SO IT'S POSSIBLE HE JUST SNAPPED.
BUT...

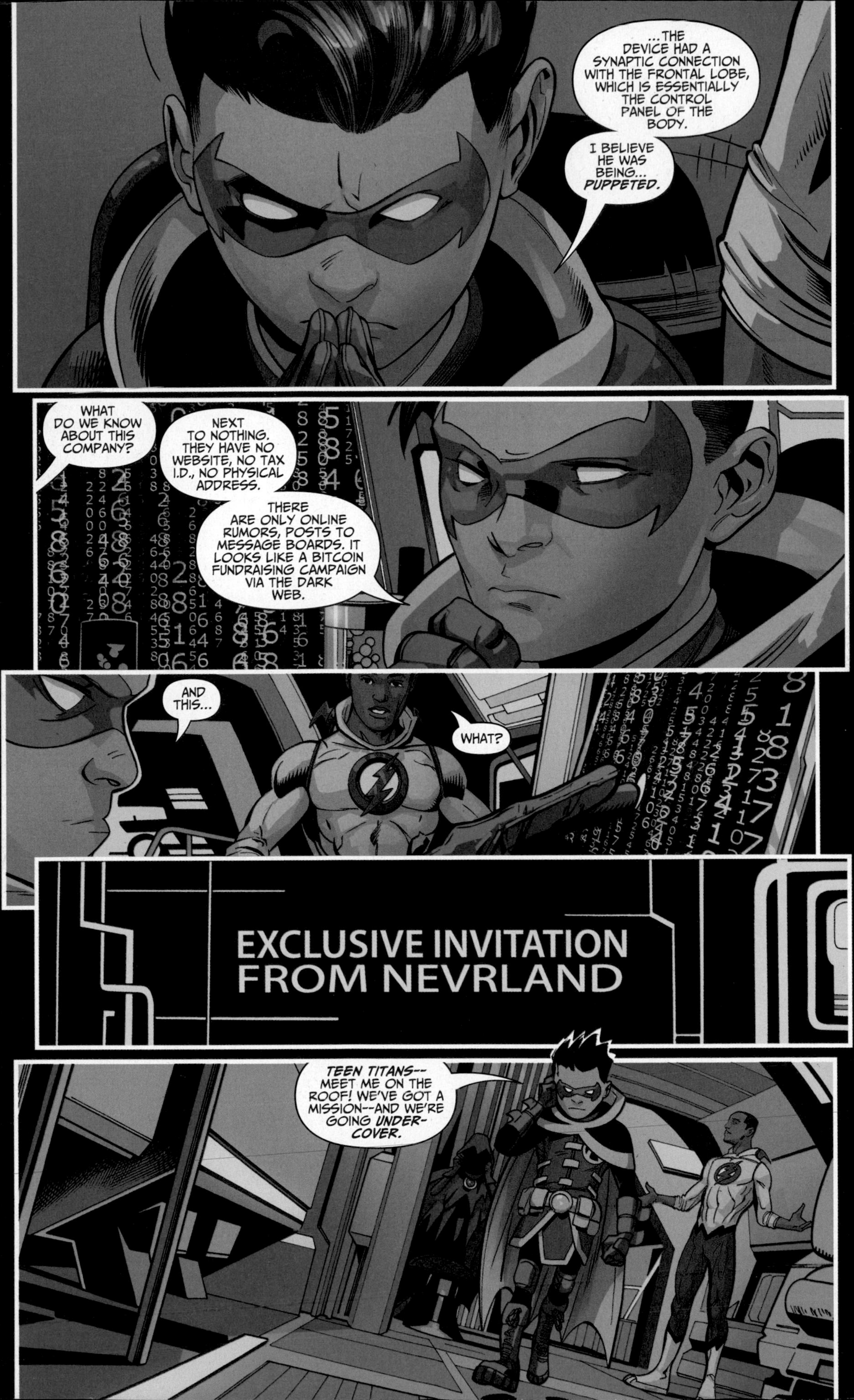

...THE DEVICE HAD A SYNAPTIC CONNECTION WITH THE FRONTAL LOBE, WHICH IS ESSENTIALLY THE CONTROL PANEL OF THE BODY.
I BELIEVE HE WAS BEING... PUPPETED.
WHAT DO WE KNOW ABOUT THIS COMPANY?
NEXT TO NOTHING. THEY HAVE NO WEBSITE, NO TAX I.D., NO PHYSICAL ADDRESS.
THERE ARE ONLY ONLINE RUMORS, POSTS TO MESSAGE BOARDS. IT LOOKS LIKE A BITCOIN FUNDRAISING CAMPAIGN VIA THE DARK WEB.
AND THIS...
WHAT?
EXCLUSIVE INVITATION FROM NEVRLAND
TEEN TITANS--MEET ME ON THE ROOF! WE'VE GOT A MISSION--AND WE'RE GOING UNDERCOVER.

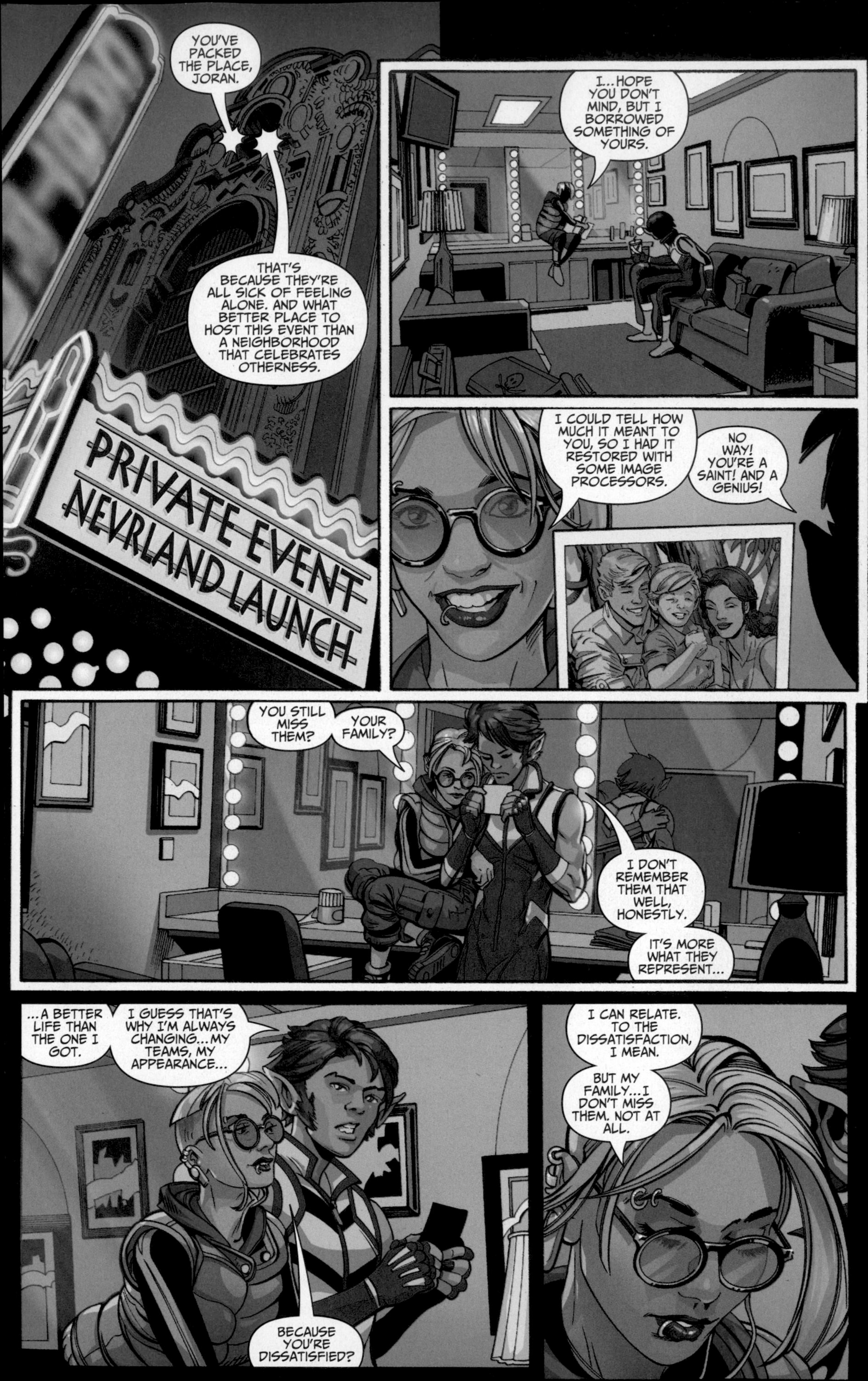
YOU'VE PACKED THE PLACE, JORAN.
THAT'S BECAUSE THEY'RE ALL SICK OF FEELING ALONE. AND WHAT BETTER PLACE TO HOST THIS EVENT THAN A NEIGHBORHOOD THAT CELEBRATES OTHERNESS.
PRIVATE EVENT
NEVRLAND LAUNCH
I...HOPE YOU DON'T MIND, BUT I BORROWED SOMETHING OF YOURS.
I COULD TELL HOW MUCH IT MEANT TO YOU, SO I HAD IT RESTORED WITH SOME IMAGE PROCESSORS.
NO WAY! YOU'RE A SAINT! AND A GENIUS!
YOU STILL MISS THEM?
YOUR FAMILY?
I DON'T REMEMBER THEM THAT WELL, HONESTLY.
IT'S MORE WHAT THEY REPRESENT...
...A BETTER LIFE THAN THE ONE I GOT.
I GUESS THAT'S WHY I'M ALWAYS CHANGING...MY TEAMS, MY APPEARANCE...
BECAUSE YOU'RE DISSATISFIED?
I CAN RELATE. TO THE DISSATISFACTION, I MEAN.
BUT MY FAMILY...I DON'T MISS THEM. NOT AT ALL.

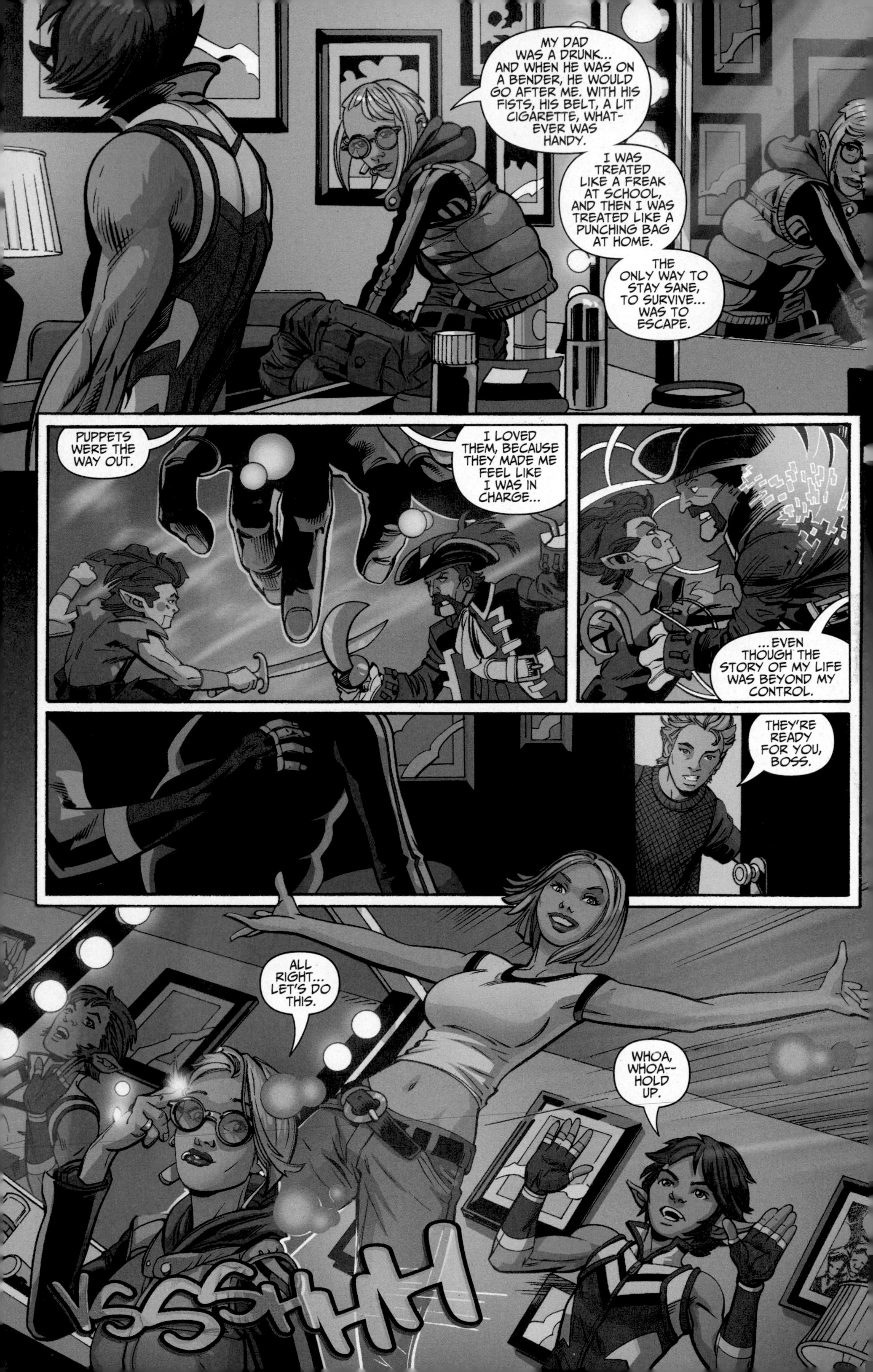
MY DAD WAS A DRUNK... AND WHEN HE WAS ON A BENDER, HE WOULD GO AFTER ME. WITH HIS FISTS, HIS BELT, A LIT CIGARETTE, WHAT-EVER WAS HANDY.
I WAS TREATED LIKE A FREAK AT SCHOOL, AND THEN I WAS TREATED LIKE A PUNCHING BAG AT HOME.
THE ONLY WAY TO STAY SANE, TO SURVIVE... WAS TO ESCAPE.
PUPPETS WERE THE WAY OUT.
I LOVED THEM, BECAUSE THEY MADE ME FEEL LIKE I WAS IN CHARGE...
...EVEN THOUGH THE STORY OF MY LIFE WAS BEYOND MY CONTROL.
THEY'RE READY FOR YOU, BOSS.
ALL RIGHT... LET'S DO THIS.
WHOA, WHOA--HOLD UP.
VSSSHHH

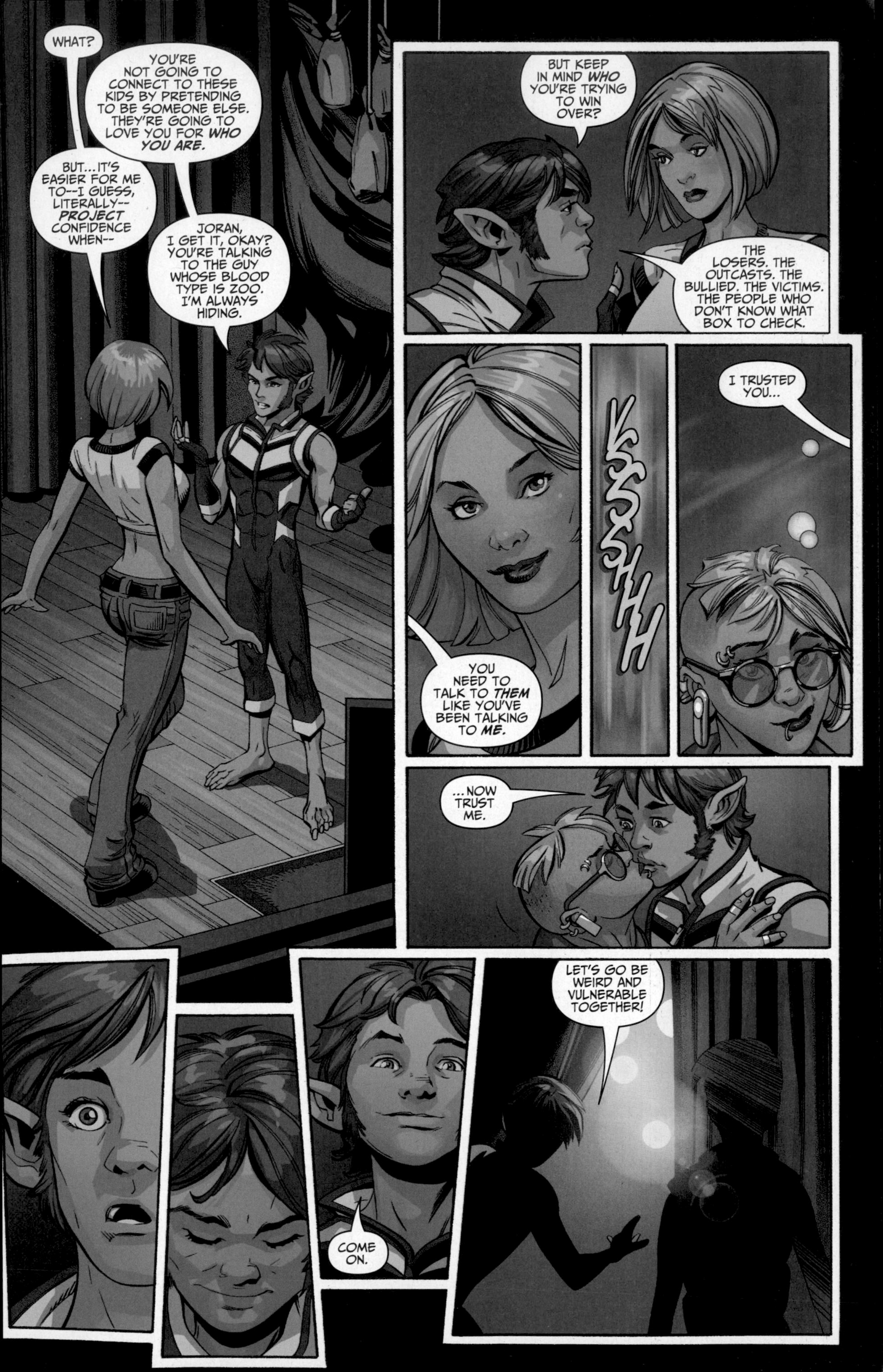
WHAT?
YOU'RE NOT GOING TO CONNECT TO THESE KIDS BY PRETENDING TO BE SOMEONE ELSE. THEY'RE GOING TO LOVE YOU FOR WHO YOU ARE.
BUT...IT'S EASIER FOR ME TO--I GUESS, LITERALLY--PROJECT CONFIDENCE WHEN--
JORAN, I GET IT, OKAY? YOU'RE TALKING TO THE GUY WHOSE BLOOD TYPE IS ZOO. I'M ALWAYS HIDING.
BUT KEEP IN MIND WHO YOU'RE TRYING TO WIN OVER?
THE LOSERS. THE OUTCASTS. THE BULLIED. THE VICTIMS. THE PEOPLE WHO DON'T KNOW WHAT BOX TO CHECK.
YOU NEED TO TALK TO THEM LIKE YOU'VE BEEN TALKING TO ME.
VSSSHHH
I TRUSTED YOU...
...NOW TRUST ME.
COME ON.
LET'S GO BE WEIRD AND VULNERABLE TOGETHER!

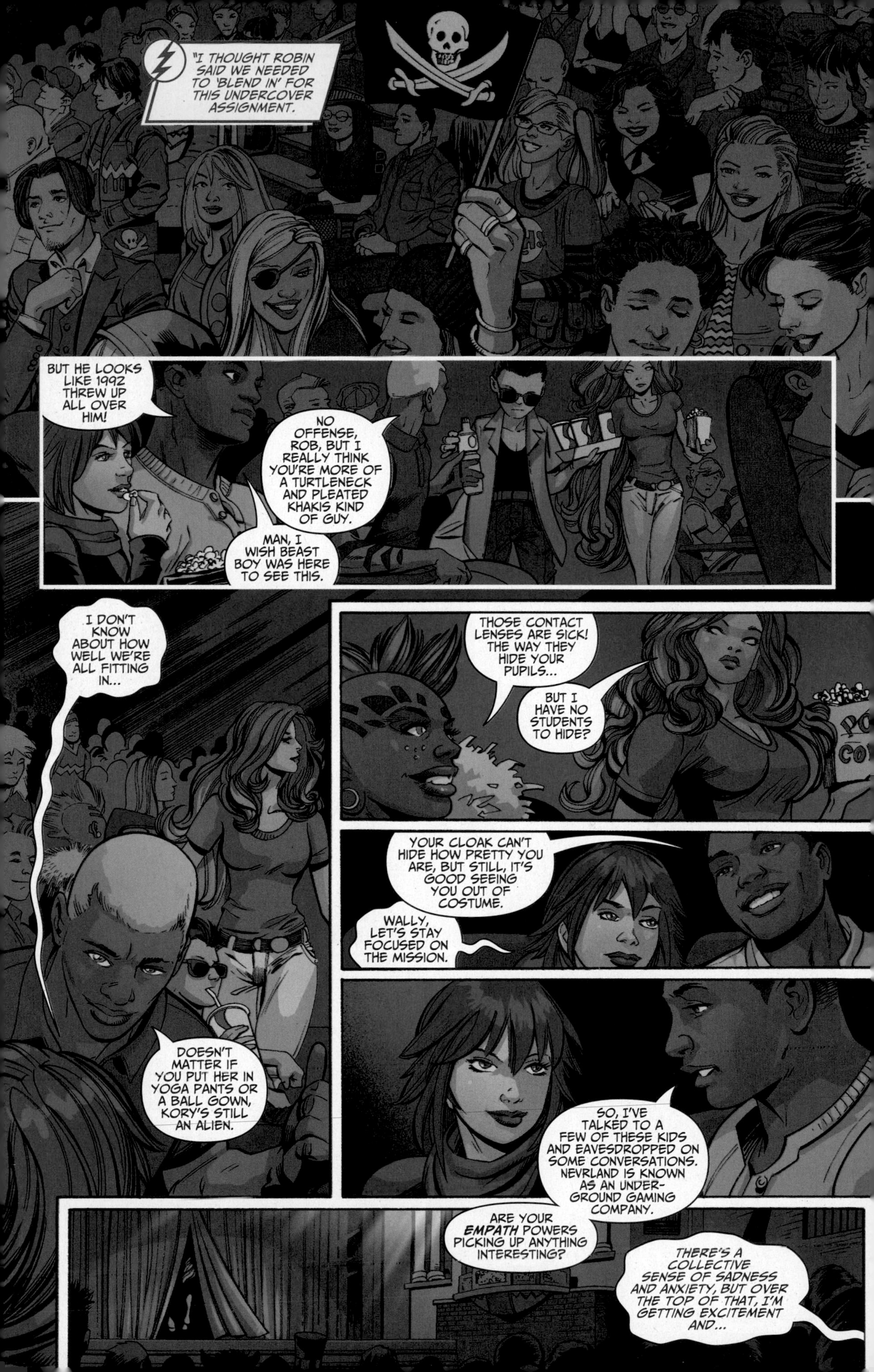

"I THOUGHT ROBIN SAID WE NEEDED TO 'BLEND IN' FOR THIS UNDERCOVER ASSIGNMENT.
BUT HE LOOKS LIKE 1992 THREW UP ALL OVER HIM!
NO OFFENSE, ROB, BUT I REALLY THINK YOU'RE MORE OF A TURTLENECK AND PLEATED KHAKIS KIND OF GUY.
MAN, I WISH BEAST BOY WAS HERE TO SEE THIS.
I DON'T KNOW ABOUT HOW WELL WE'RE ALL FITTING IN...
DOESN'T MATTER IF YOU PUT HER IN YOGA PANTS OR A BALL GOWN, KORY'S STILL AN ALIEN.
THOSE CONTACT LENSES ARE SICK! THE WAY THEY HIDE YOUR PUPILS...
BUT I HAVE NO STUDENTS TO HIDE?
YOUR CLOAK CAN'T HIDE HOW PRETTY YOU ARE, BUT STILL, IT'S GOOD SEEING YOU OUT OF COSTUME.
WALLY, LET'S STAY FOCUSED ON THE MISSION.
SO, I'VE TALKED TO A FEW OF THESE KIDS AND EAVESDROPPED ON SOME CONVERSATIONS. NEVRLAND IS KNOWN AS AN UNDER-GROUND GAMING COMPANY.
ARE YOUR EMPATH POWERS PICKING UP ANYTHING INTERESTING?
THERE'S A COLLECTIVE SENSE OF SADNESS AND ANXIETY, BUT OVER THE TOP OF THAT, I'M GETTING EXCITEMENT AND...

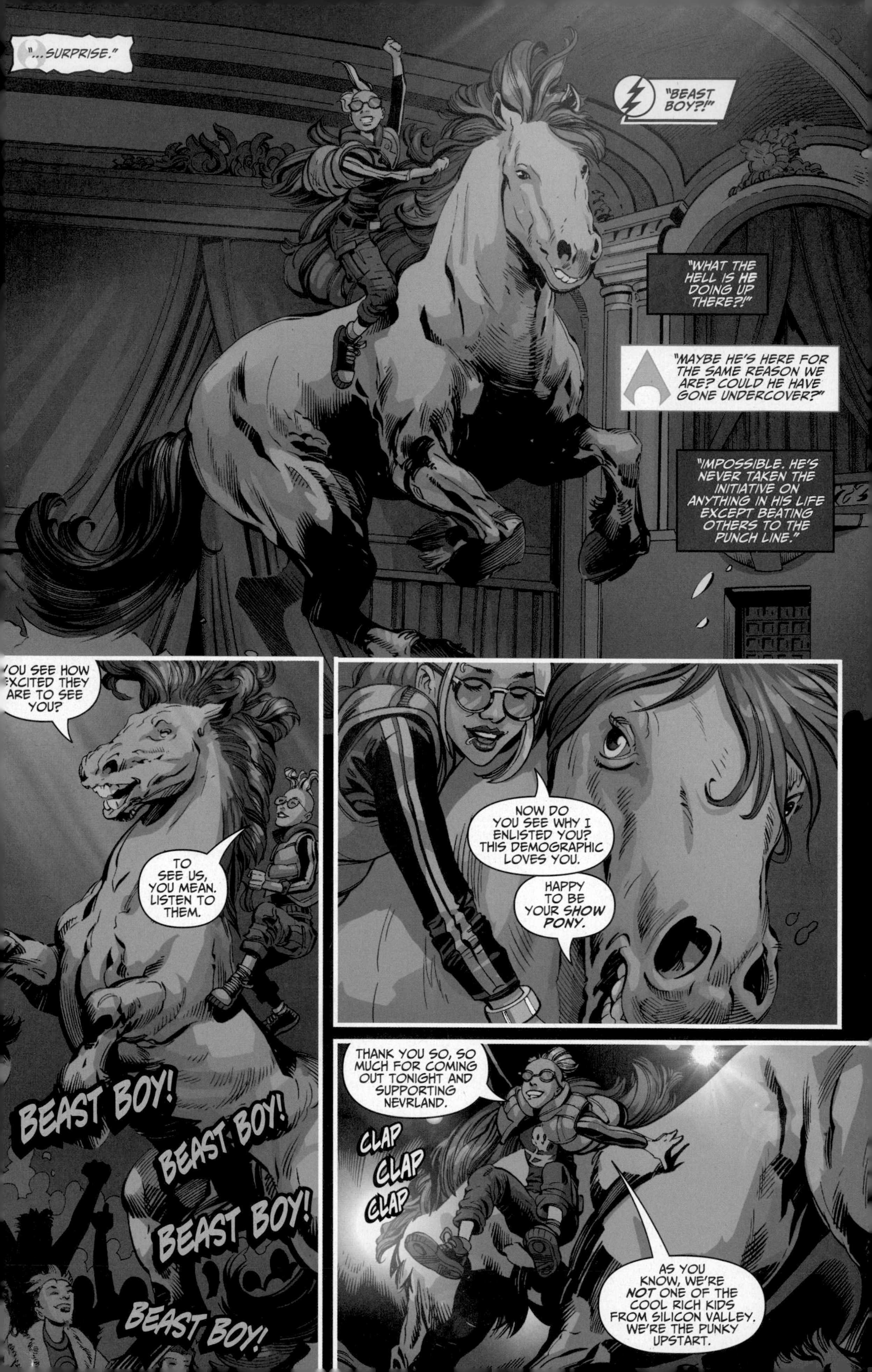
"...SURPRISE."
"BEAST BOY?!"
"WHAT THE HELL IS HE DOING UP THERE?!"
"MAYBE HE'S HERE FOR THE SAME REASON WE ARE? COULD HE HAVE GONE UNDERCOVER?"
"IMPOSSIBLE. HE'S NEVER TAKEN THE INITIATIVE ON ANYTHING IN HIS LIFE EXCEPT BEATING OTHERS TO THE PUNCH LINE."
YOU SEE HOW EXCITED THEY ARE TO SEE YOU?
TO SEE US, YOU MEAN. LISTEN TO THEM.
BEAST BOY!
BEAST BOY!
BEAST BOY!
BEAST BOY!
NOW DO YOU SEE WHY I ENLISTED YOU? THIS DEMOGRAPHIC LOVES YOU.
HAPPY TO BE YOUR SHOW PONY.
THANK YOU SO, SO MUCH FOR COMING OUT TONIGHT AND SUPPORTING NEVRLAND.
CLAP
CLAP
CLAP
AS YOU KNOW, WE'RE NOT ONE OF THE COOL RICH KIDS FROM SILICON VALLEY. WE'RE THE PUNKY UPSTART.

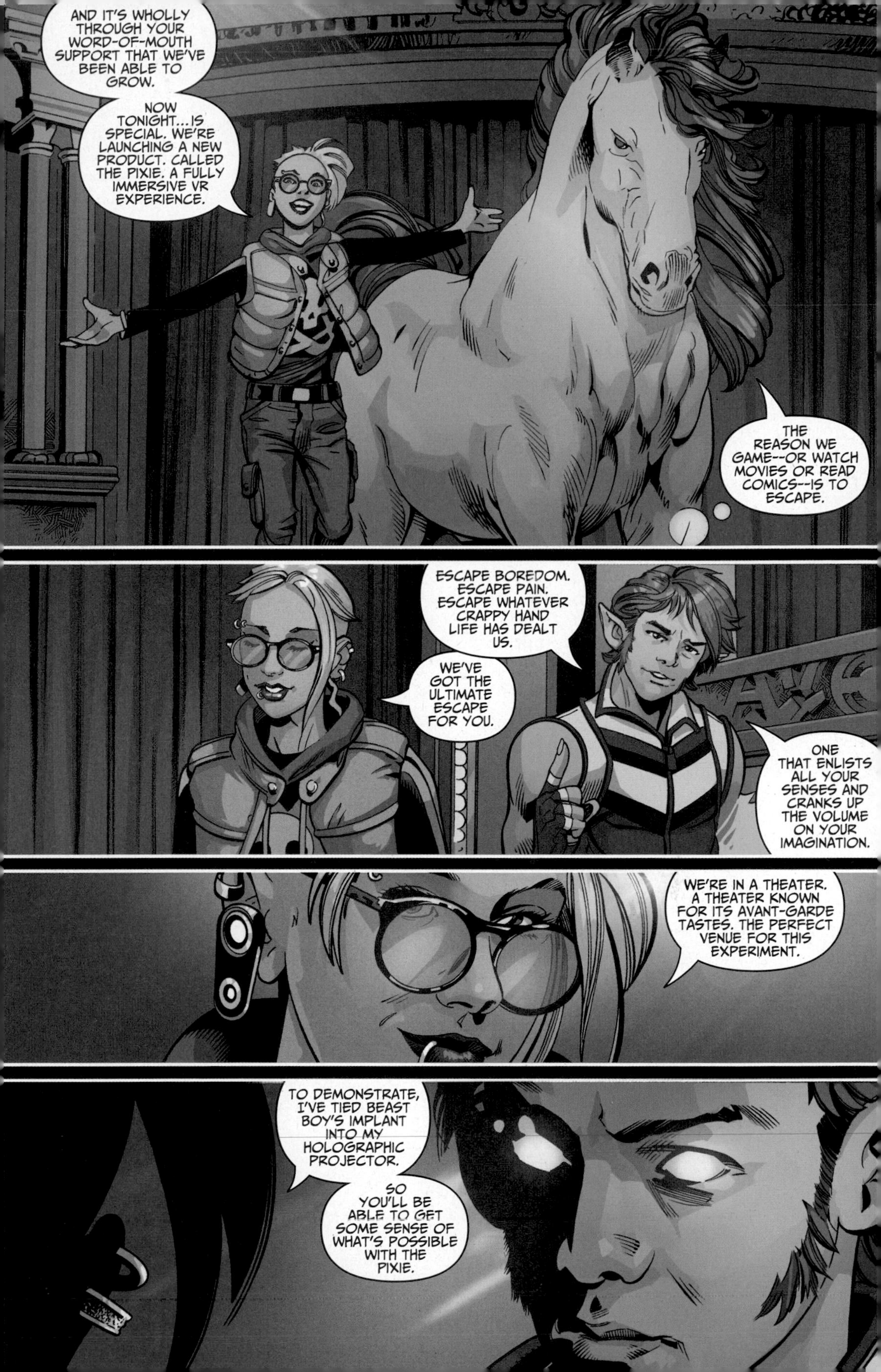
AND IT'S WHOLLY THROUGH YOUR WORD-OF-MOUTH SUPPORT THAT WE'VE BEEN ABLE TO GROW.
NOW TONIGHT...IS SPECIAL. WE'RE LAUNCHING A NEW PRODUCT. CALLED THE PIXIE. A FULLY IMMERSIVE VR EXPERIENCE.
THE REASON WE GAME--OR WATCH MOVIES OR READ COMICS--IS TO ESCAPE.
ESCAPE BOREDOM. ESCAPE PAIN. ESCAPE WHATEVER CRAPPY HAND LIFE HAS DEALT US.
WE'VE GOT THE ULTIMATE ESCAPE FOR YOU.
ONE THAT ENLISTS ALL YOUR SENSES AND CRANKS UP THE VOLUME ON YOUR IMAGINATION.
WE'RE IN A THEATER. A THEATER KNOWN FOR ITS AVANT-GARDE TASTES. THE PERFECT VENUE FOR THIS EXPERIMENT.
TO DEMONSTRATE, I'VE TIED BEAST BOY'S IMPLANT INTO MY HOLOGRAPHIC PROJECTOR.
SO YOU'LL BE ABLE TO GET SOME SENSE OF WHAT'S POSSIBLE WITH THE PIXIE.

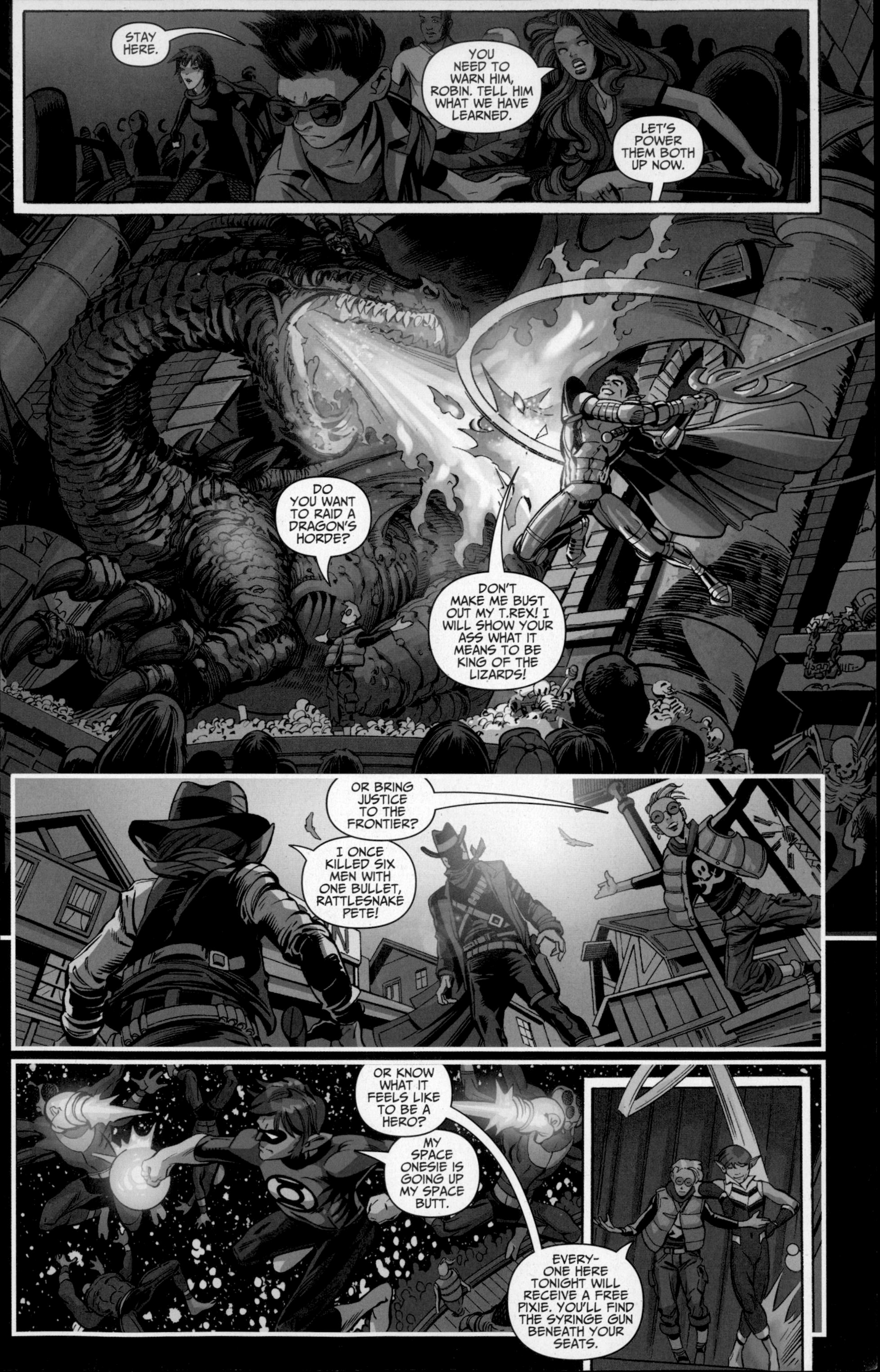
STAY HERE.
YOU NEED TO WARN HIM, ROBIN. TELL HIM WHAT WE HAVE LEARNED.
LET'S POWER THEM BOTH UP NOW.
DO YOU WANT TO RAID A DRAGON'S HORDE?
DON'T MAKE ME BUST OUT MY T.REX! I WILL SHOW YOUR ASS WHAT IT MEANS TO BE KING OF THE LIZARDS!
OR BRING JUSTICE TO THE FRONTIER?
I ONCE KILLED SIX MEN WITH ONE BULLET, RATTLESNAKE PETE!
OR KNOW WHAT IT FEELS LIKE TO BE A HERO?
MY SPACE ONESIE IS GOING UP MY SPACE BUTT.
EVERY-ONE HERE TONIGHT WILL RECEIVE A FREE PIXIE. YOU'LL FIND THE SYRINGE GUN BENEATH YOUR SEATS.

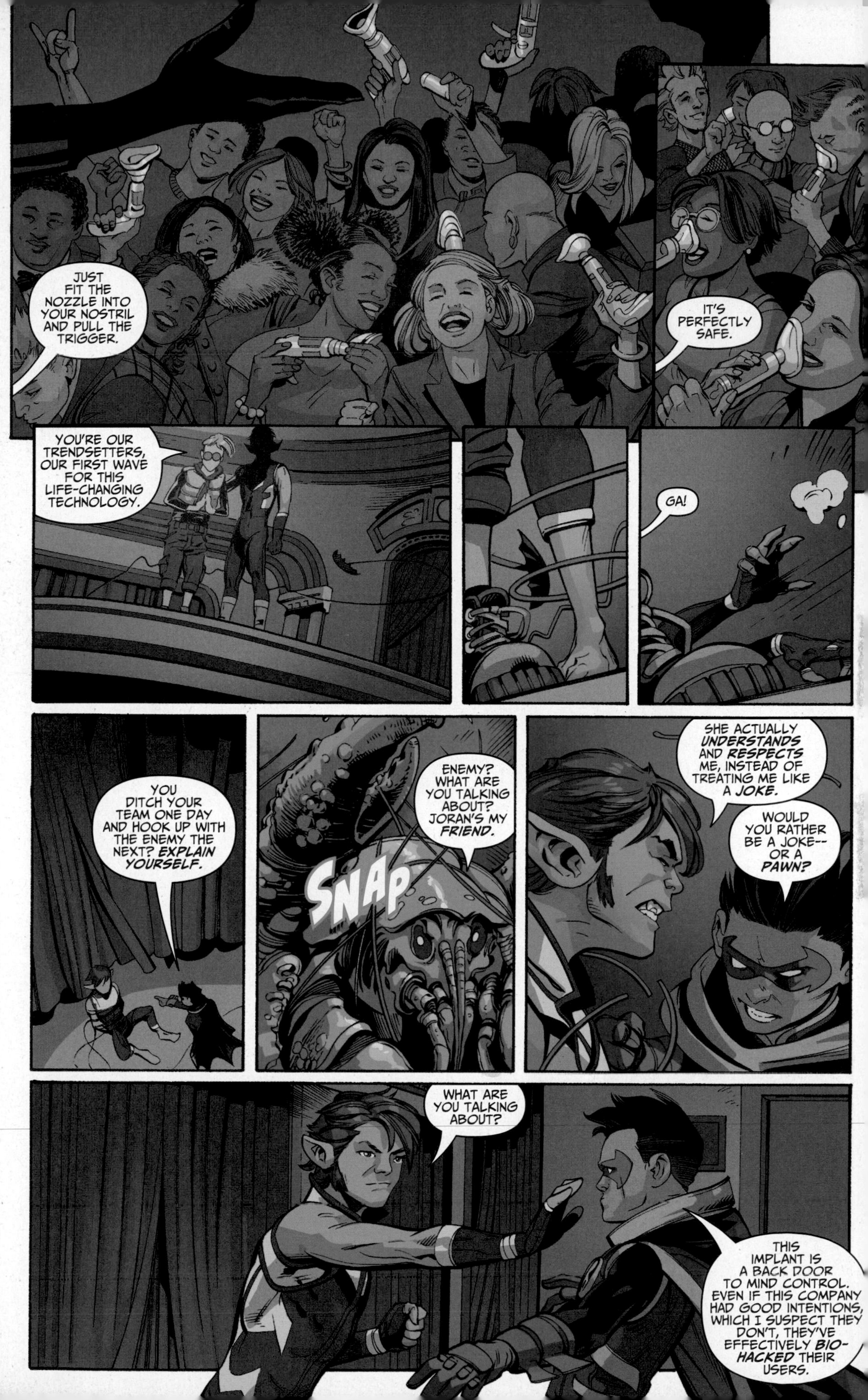
JUST FIT THE NOZZLE INTO YOUR NOSTRIL AND PULL THE TRIGGER.
IT'S PERFECTLY SAFE.
YOU'RE OUR TRENDSETTERS, OUR FIRST WAVE FOR THIS LIFE-CHANGING TECHNOLOGY.
GA!
YOU DITCH YOUR TEAM ONE DAY AND HOOK UP WITH THE ENEMY THE NEXT? EXPLAIN YOURSELF.
ENEMY? WHAT ARE YOU TALKING ABOUT? JORAN'S MY FRIEND.
SNAP
SHE ACTUALLY UNDERSTANDS AND RESPECTS ME, INSTEAD OF TREATING ME LIKE A JOKE.
WOULD YOU RATHER BE A JOKE-- OR A PAWN?
WHAT ARE YOU TALKING ABOUT?
THIS IMPLANT IS A BACK DOOR TO MIND CONTROL. EVEN IF THIS COMPANY HAD GOOD INTENTIONS, WHICH I SUSPECT THEY DON'T, THEY'VE EFFECTIVELY BIO-HACKED THEIR USERS.

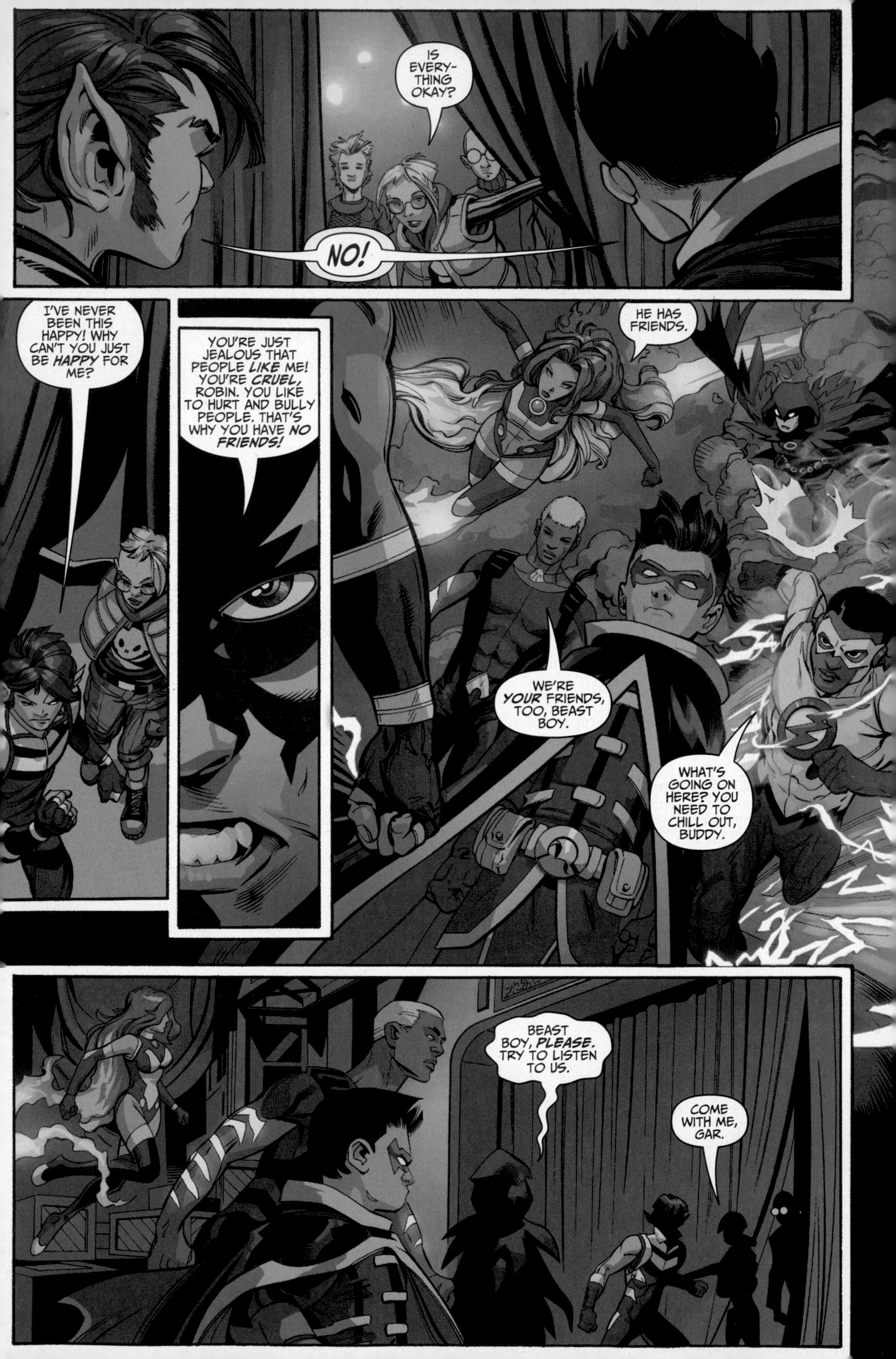
IS EVERY-THING OKAY?
NO!
I'VE NEVER BEEN THIS HAPPY! WHY CAN'T YOU JUST BE HAPPY FOR ME?
YOU'RE JUST JEALOUS THAT PEOPLE LIKE ME! YOU'RE CRUEL, ROBIN. YOU LIKE TO HURT AND BULLY PEOPLE. THAT'S WHY YOU HAVE NO FRIENDS!
HE HAS FRIENDS.
WE'RE YOUR FRIENDS, TOO, BEAST BOY.
WHAT'S GOING ON HERE? YOU NEED TO CHILL OUT, BUDDY.
BEAST BOY, PLEASE. TRY TO LISTEN TO US.
COME WITH ME, GAR.

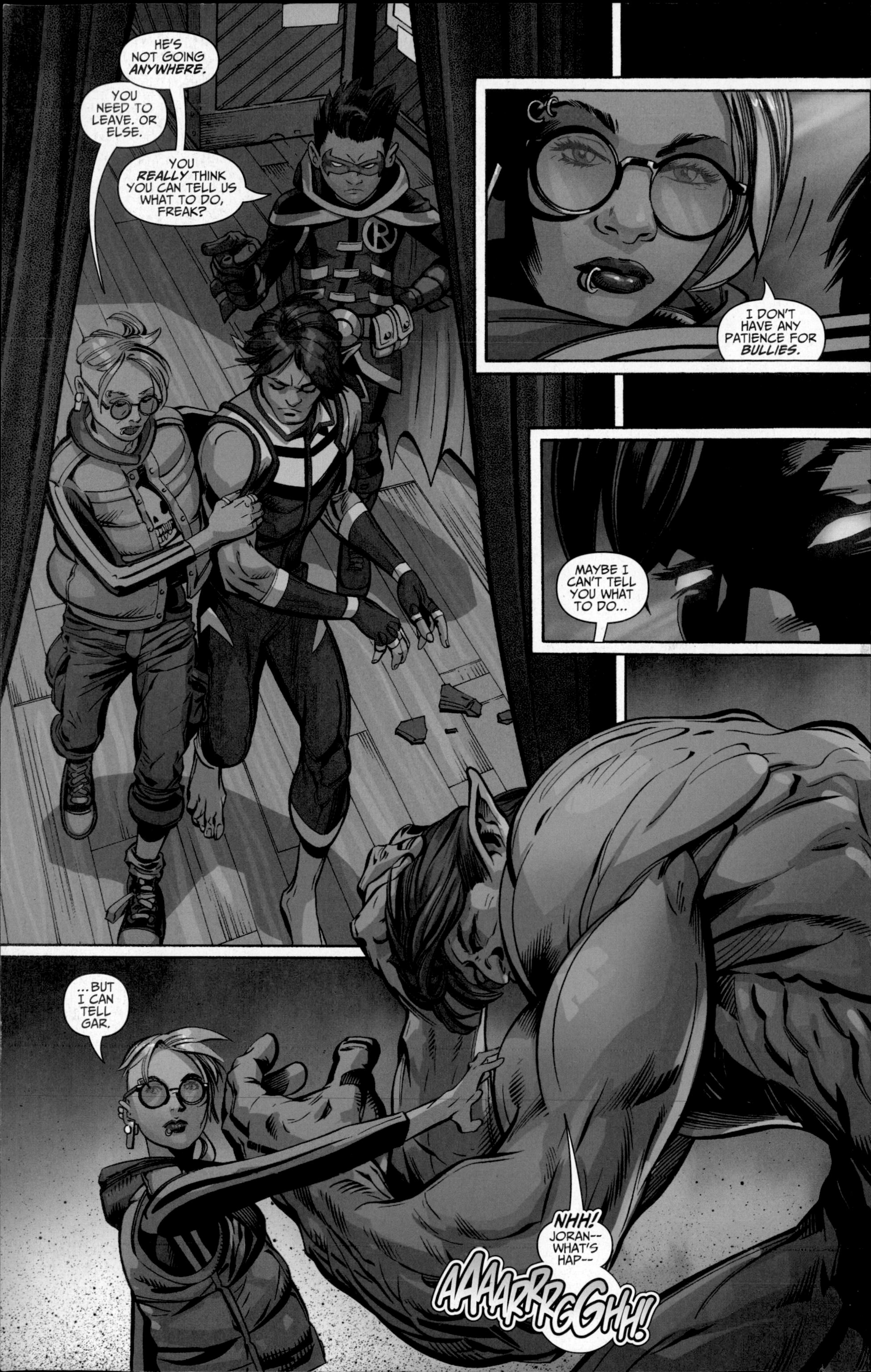
HE'S NOT GOING ANYWHERE.
YOU NEED TO LEAVE. OR ELSE.
YOU REALLY THINK YOU CAN TELL US WHAT TO DO, FREAK?
I DON'T HAVE ANY PATIENCE FOR BULLIES.
MAYBE I CAN'T TELL YOU WHAT TO DO...
...BUT I CAN TELL GAR.
NHH! JORAN-- WHAT'S HAP--
AAAARRRGGHH!

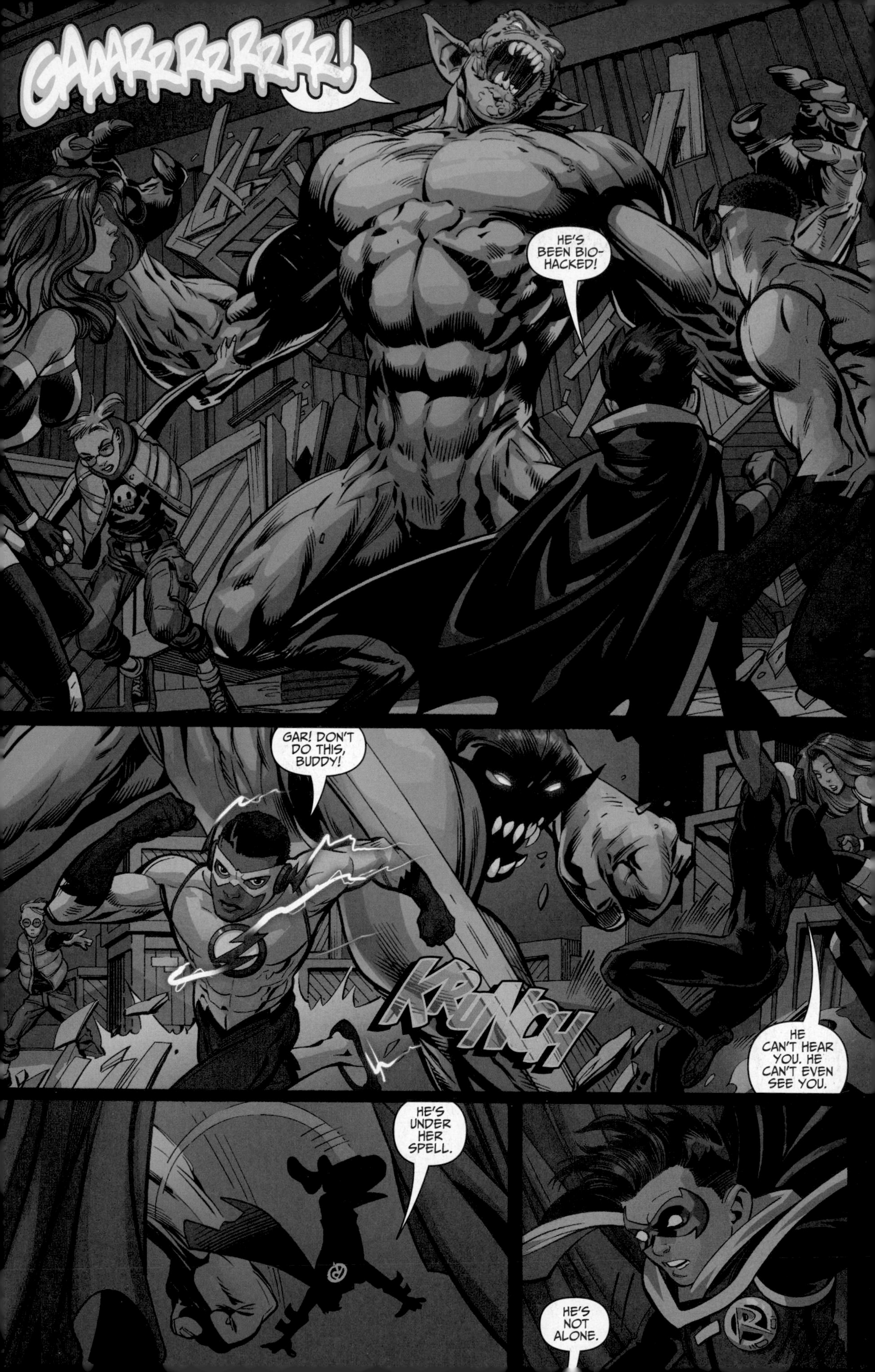
GAAARRRRRRRR!
HE'S BEEN BIO-HACKED!
GAR! DON'T DO THIS, BUDDY!
KRUNCH
HE CAN'T HEAR YOU. HE CAN'T EVEN SEE YOU.
HE'S UNDER HER SPELL.
HE'S NOT ALONE.

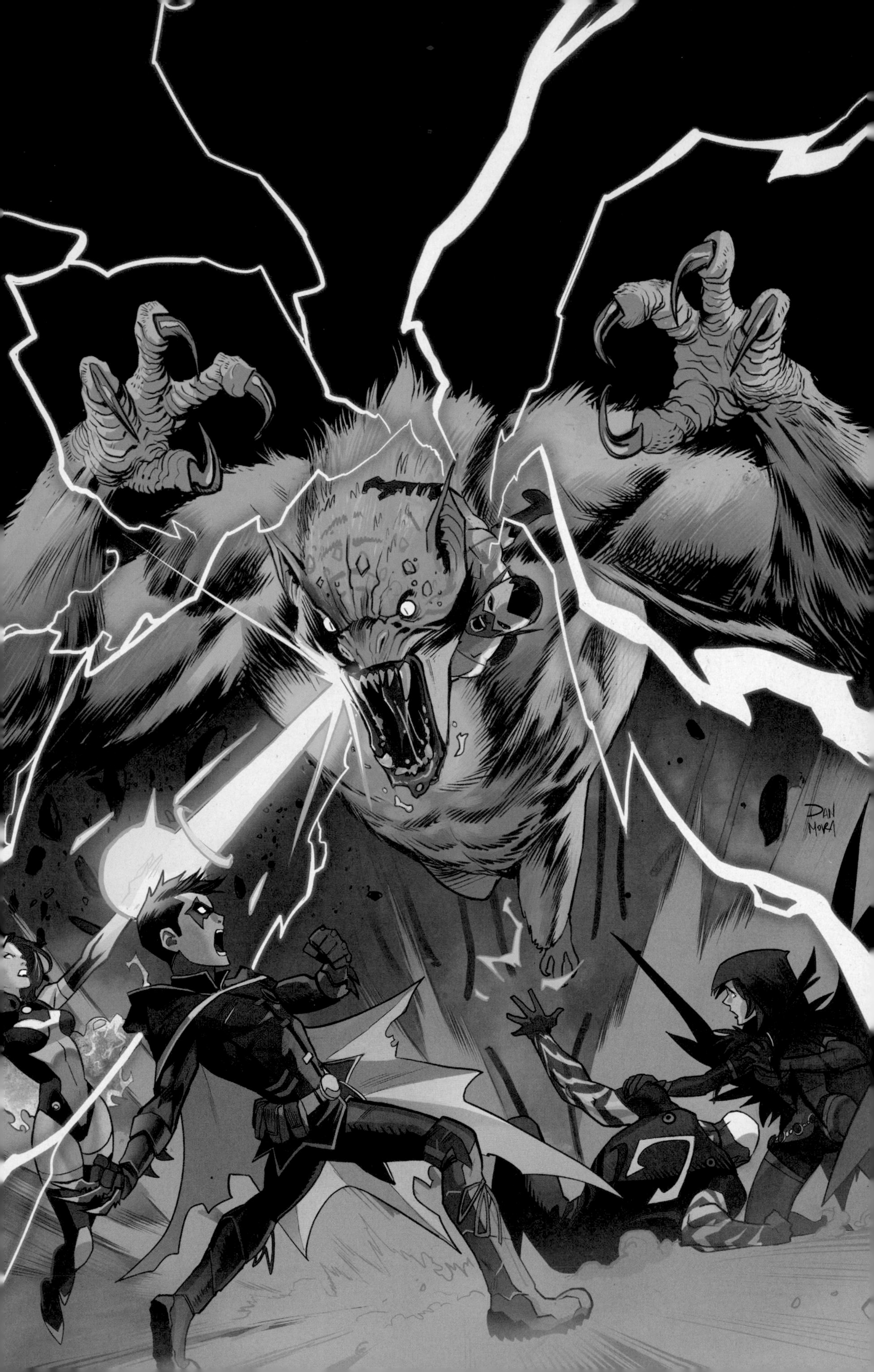
DAN MORA

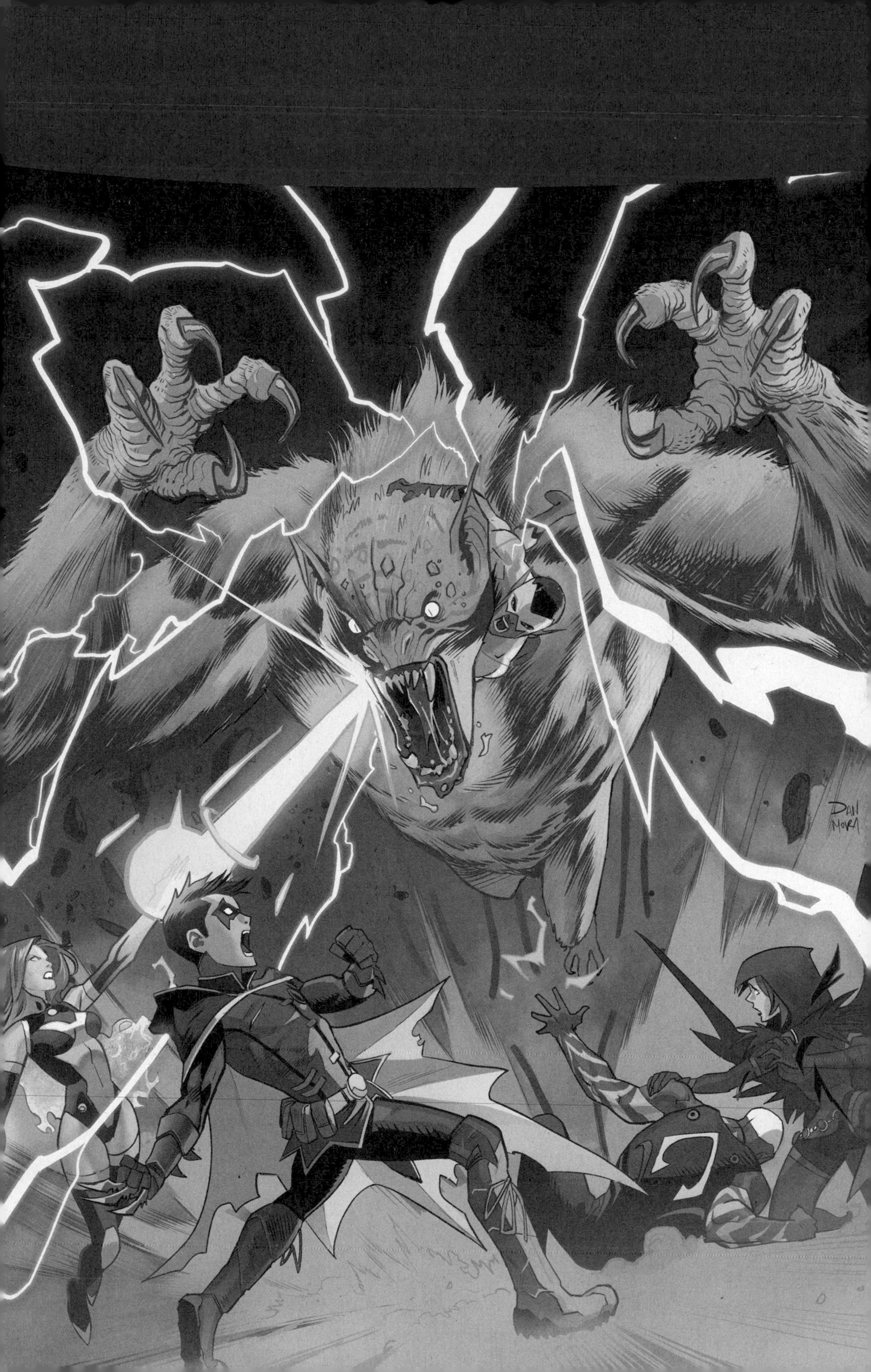
DAN MORA

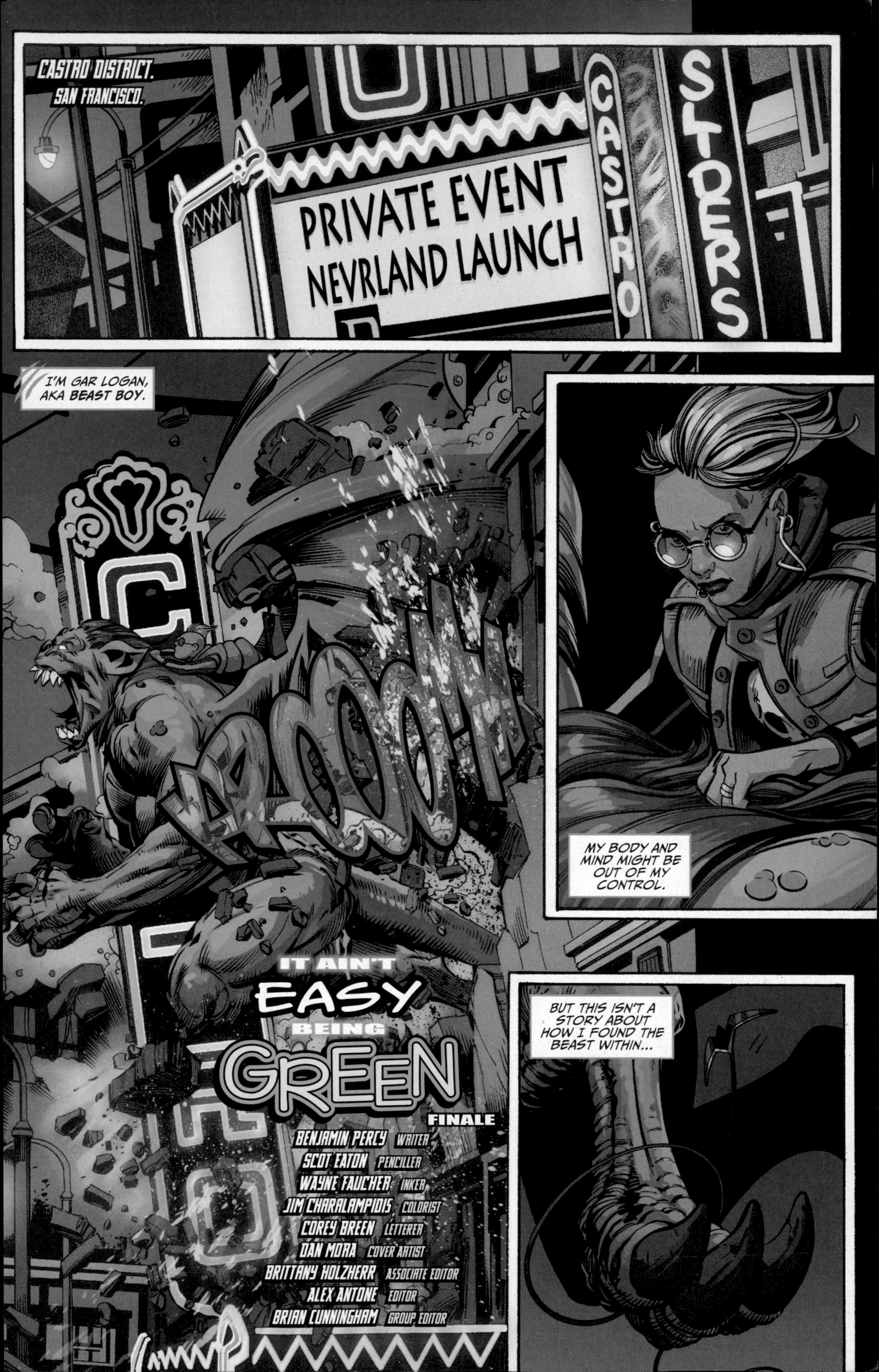
CASTRO DISTRICT. SAN FRANCISCO.
PRIVATE EVENT
NEVRLAND LAUNCH
CASTRO
SISTERS
I'M GAR LOGAN, AKA BEAST BOY.
KRAOOOM
MY BODY AND MIND MIGHT BE OUT OF MY CONTROL.
IT AIN'T EASY BEING GREEN
FINALE
BENJAMIN PERCY WRITER
SCOT EATON PENCILLER
WAYNE FAUCHER INKER
JIM CHARALAMPIDIS COLORIST
COREY BREEN LETTERER
DAN MORA COVER ARTIST
BRITTANY HOLZHERR ASSOCIATE EDITOR
ALEX ANTONE EDITOR
BRIAN CUNNINGHAM GROUP EDITOR
BUT THIS ISN'T A STORY ABOUT HOW I FOUND THE BEAST WITHIN...

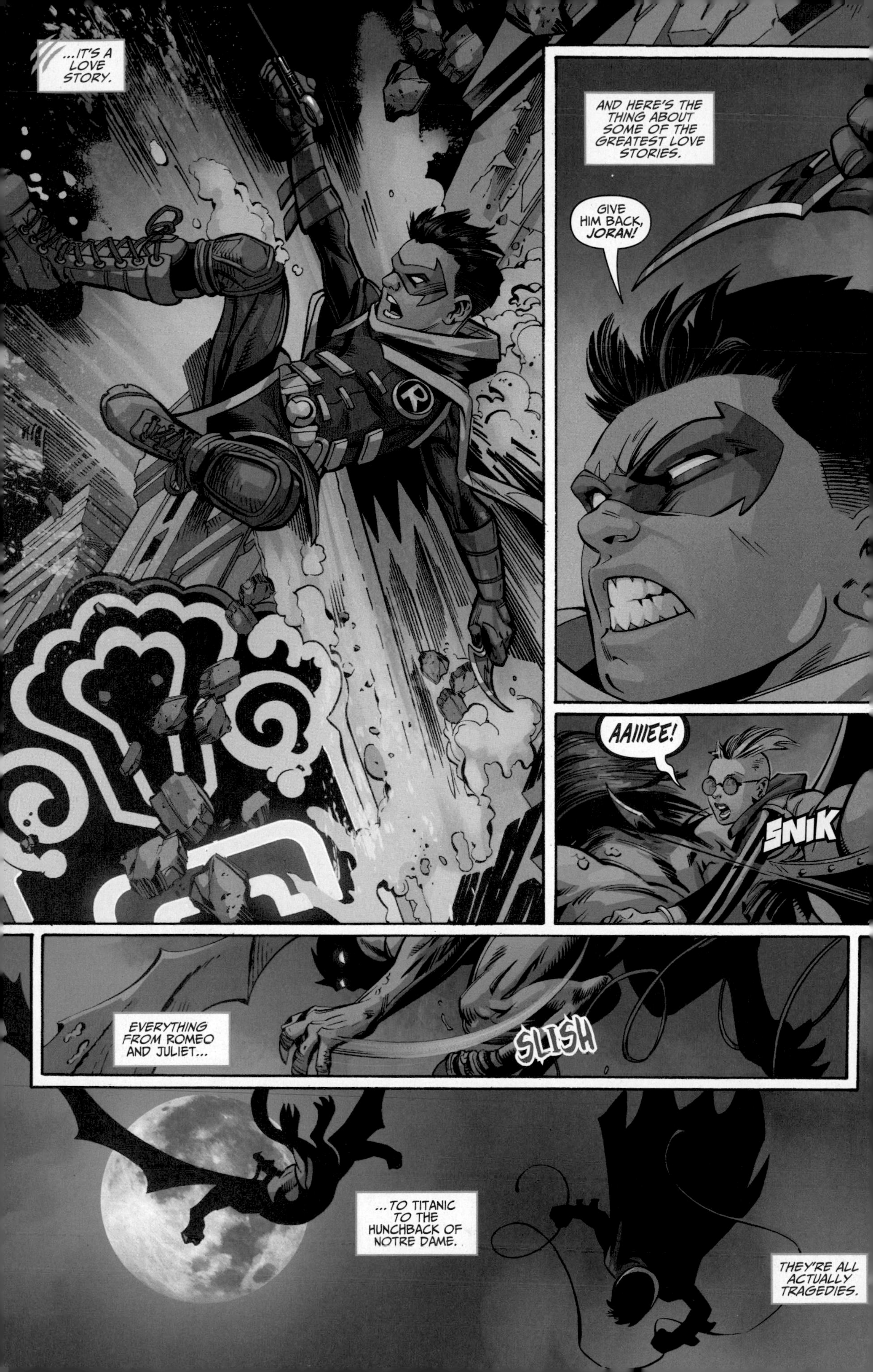
...IT'S A LOVE STORY.
AND HERE'S THE THING ABOUT SOME OF THE GREATEST LOVE STORIES.
GIVE HIM BACK, JORAN!
AAIIIEE!
SNIK
EVERYTHING FROM ROMEO AND JULIET...
SLISH
...TO TITANIC TO THE HUNCHBACK OF NOTRE DAME.
THEY'RE ALL ACTUALLY TRAGEDIES.

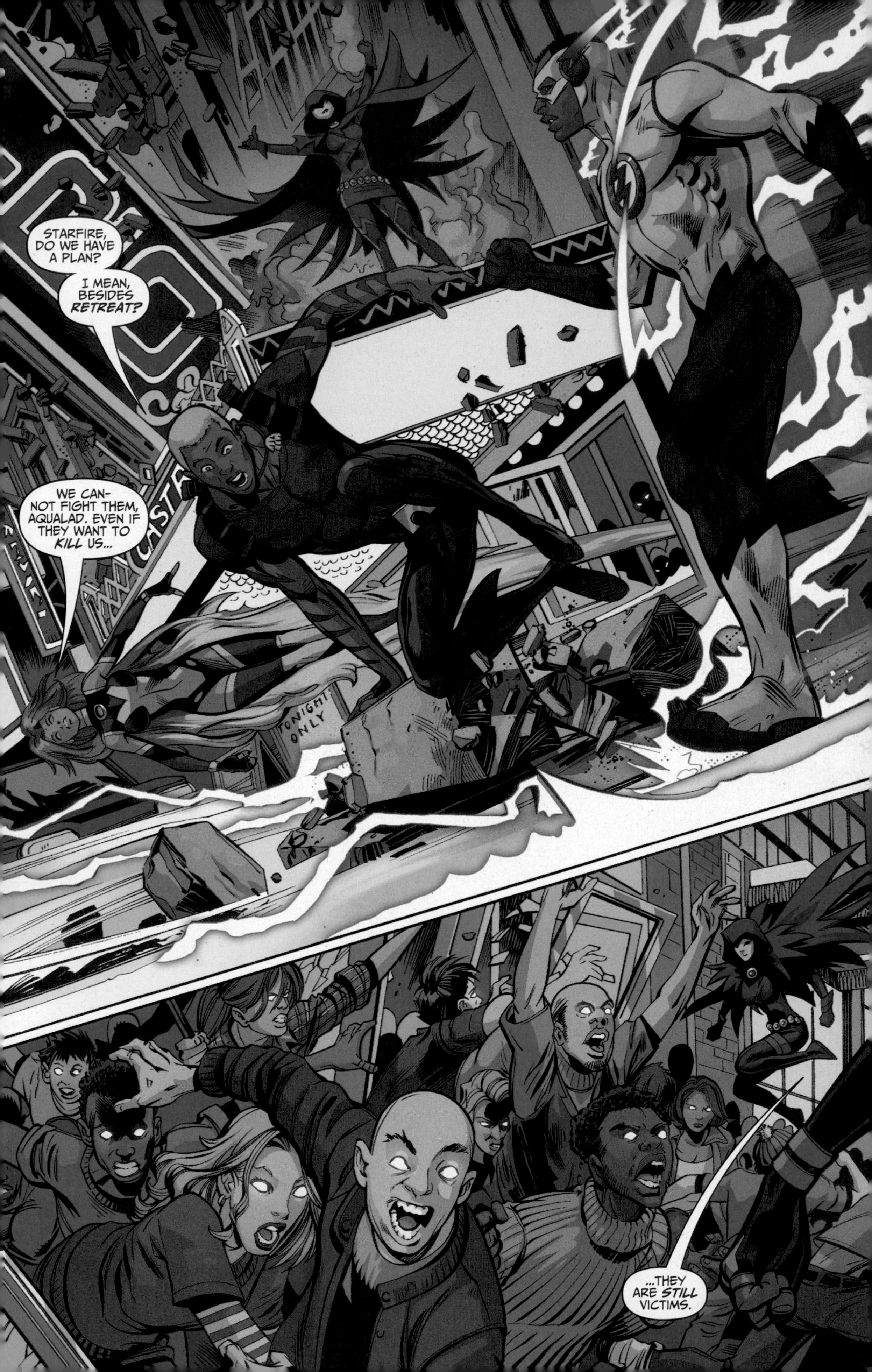
STARFIRE, DO WE HAVE A PLAN?
I MEAN, BESIDES *RETREAT*?
WE CAN-NOT FIGHT THEM, AQUALAD. EVEN IF THEY WANT TO *KILL* US...
TONIGHT ONLY
...THEY ARE *STILL* VICTIMS.

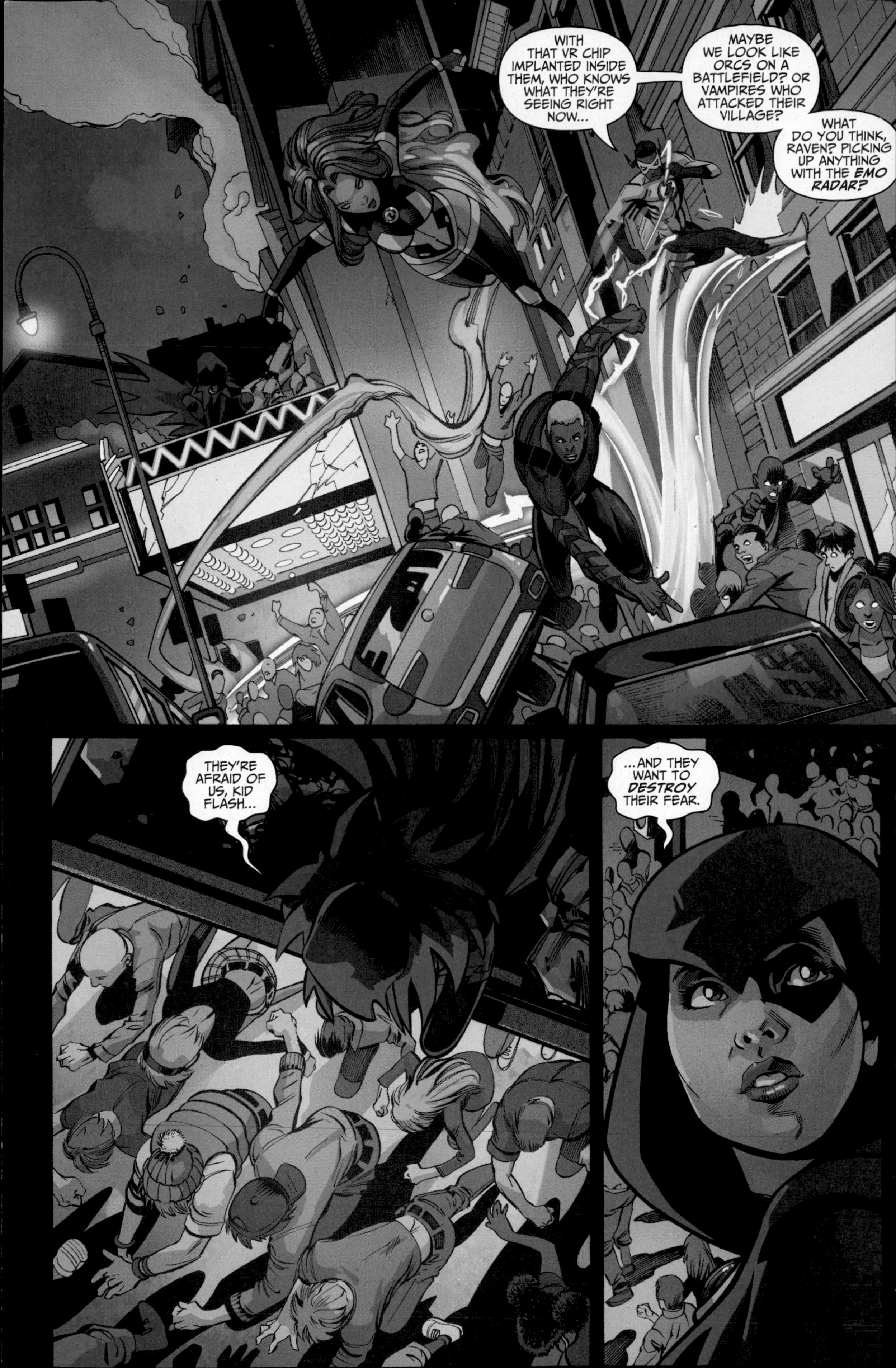
WITH THAT VR CHIP IMPLANTED INSIDE THEM, WHO KNOWS WHAT THEY'RE SEEING RIGHT NOW...
MAYBE WE LOOK LIKE ORCS ON A BATTLEFIELD? OR VAMPIRES WHO ATTACKED THEIR VILLAGE?
WHAT DO YOU THINK, RAVEN? PICKING UP ANYTHING WITH THE EMO RADAR?
THEY'RE AFRAID OF US, KID FLASH...
...AND THEY WANT TO DESTROY THEIR FEAR.

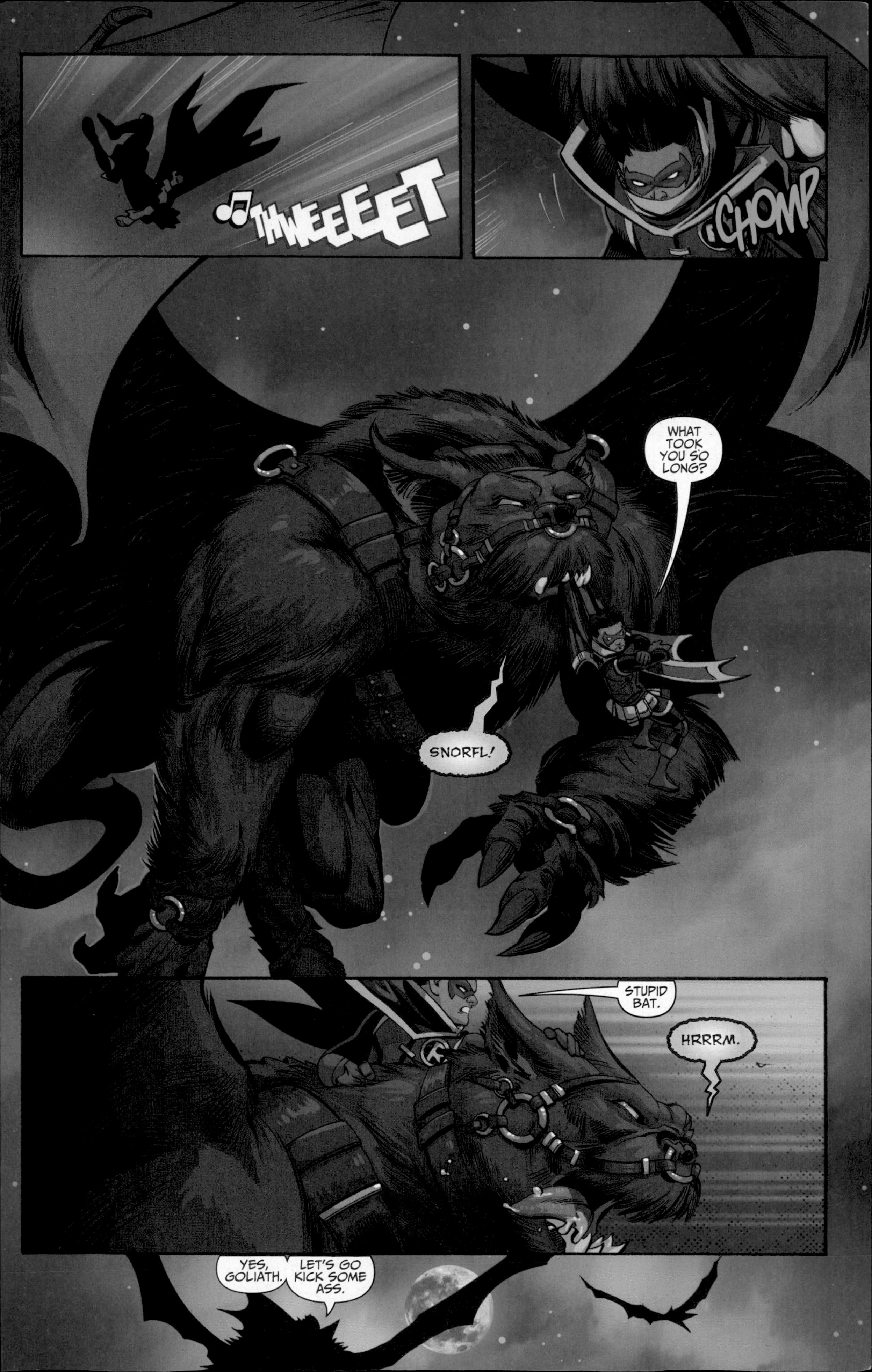
THWEEEET
CHOMP
WHAT TOOK YOU SO LONG?
SNORFL!
STUPID BAT.
HRRRM.
YES, GOLIATH.
LET'S GO KICK SOME ASS.

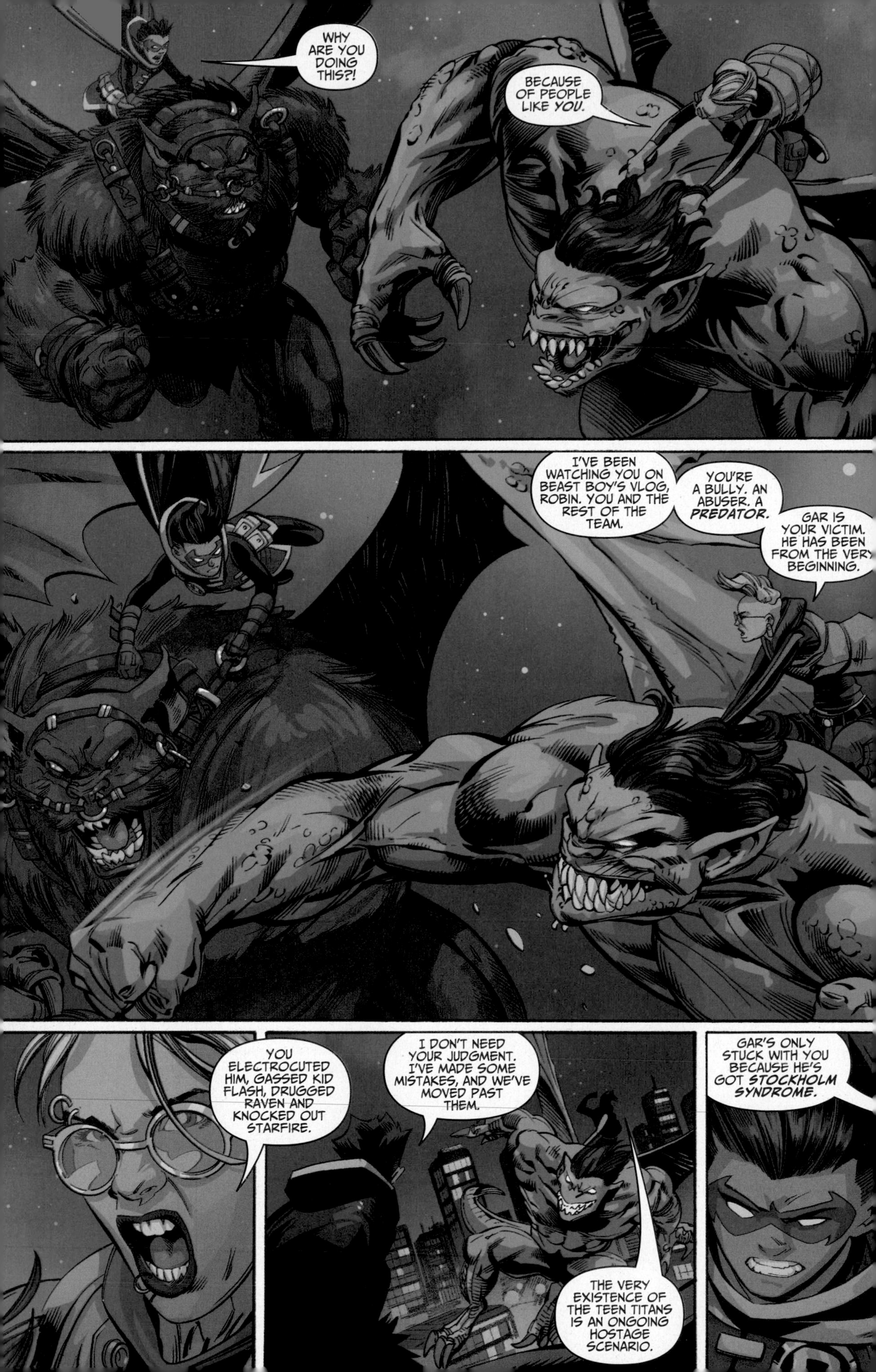
WHY ARE YOU DOING THIS?!
BECAUSE OF PEOPLE LIKE *YOU*.
I'VE BEEN WATCHING YOU ON BEAST BOY'S VLOG, ROBIN. YOU AND THE REST OF THE TEAM.
YOU'RE A BULLY. AN ABUSER. A ***PREDATOR.***
GAR IS YOUR VICTIM. HE HAS BEEN FROM THE VERY BEGINNING.
YOU ELECTROCUTED HIM, GASSED KID FLASH, DRUGGED RAVEN AND KNOCKED OUT STARFIRE.
I DON'T NEED YOUR JUDGMENT. I'VE MADE SOME MISTAKES, AND WE'VE MOVED PAST THEM.
THE VERY EXISTENCE OF THE TEEN TITANS IS AN ONGOING HOSTAGE SCENARIO.
GAR'S ONLY STUCK WITH YOU BECAUSE HE'S GOT ***STOCKHOLM SYNDROME.***

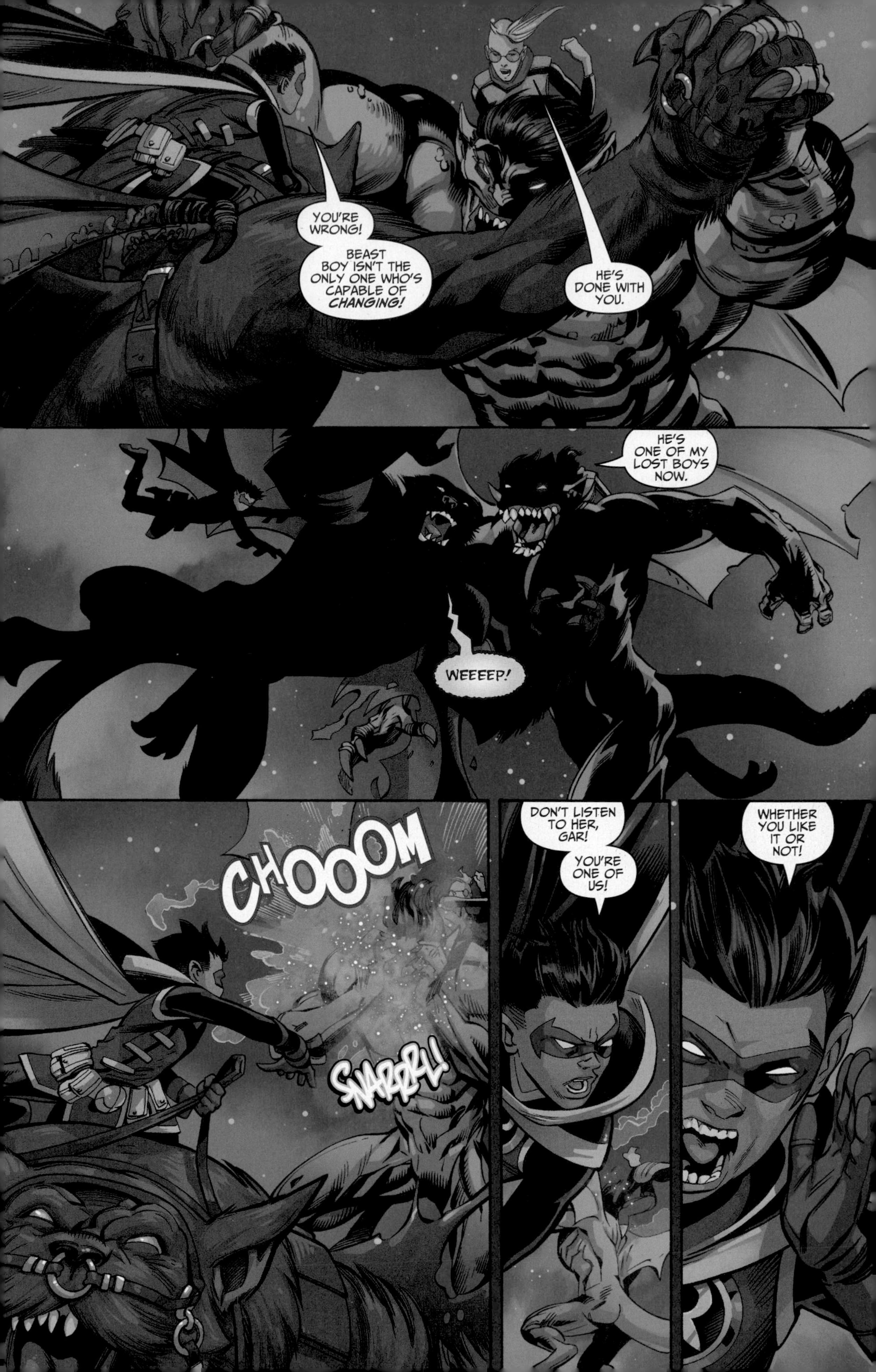
YOU'RE WRONG!
BEAST BOY ISN'T THE ONLY ONE WHO'S CAPABLE OF *CHANGING!*
HE'S DONE WITH YOU.
HE'S ONE OF MY LOST BOYS NOW.
WEEEEP!
CHOOOM
SNARRRL!
DON'T LISTEN TO HER, GAR!
YOU'RE ONE OF US!
WHETHER YOU LIKE IT OR NOT!

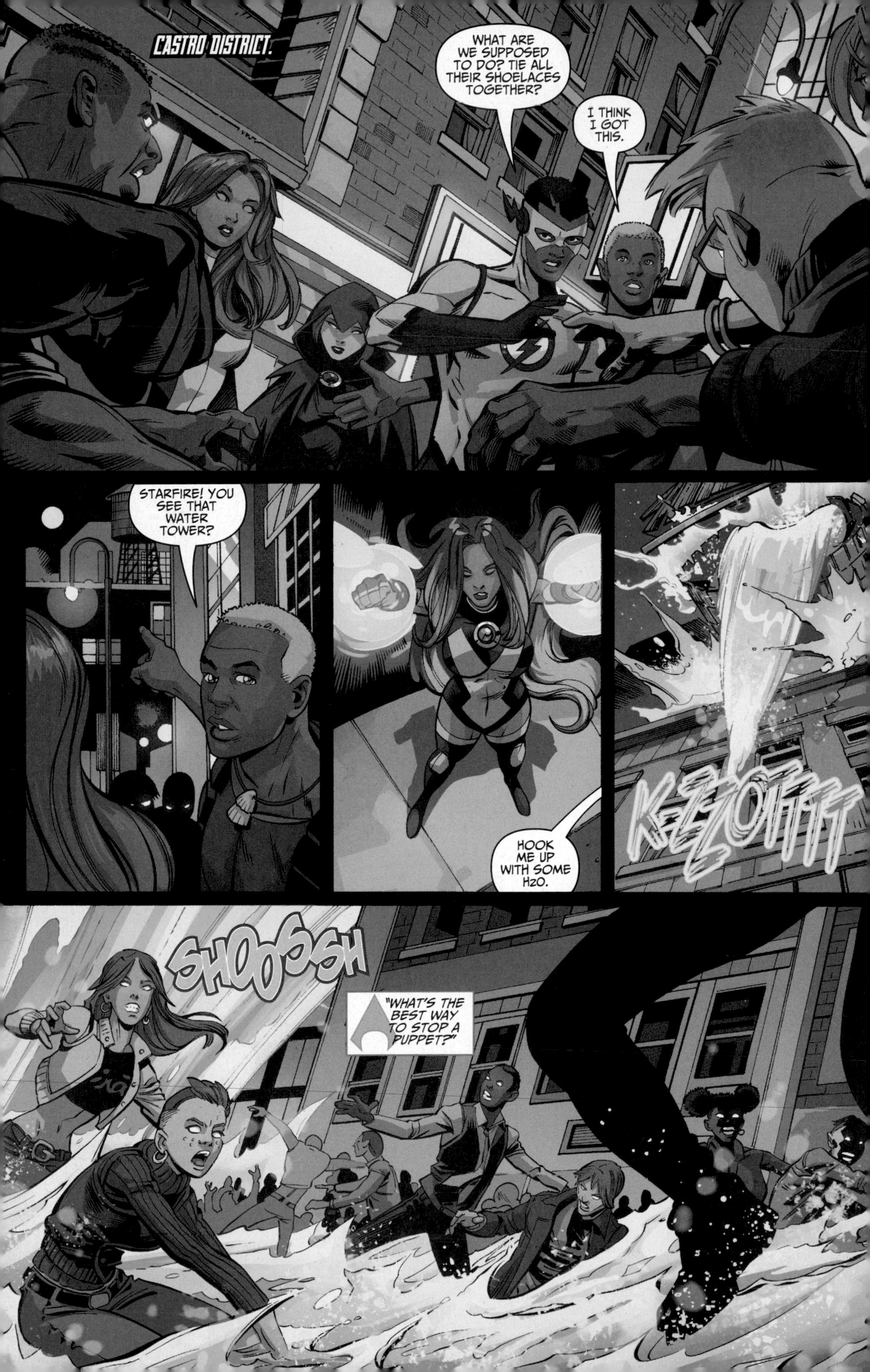
CASTRO DISTRICT.
WHAT ARE WE SUPPOSED TO DO? TIE ALL THEIR SHOELACES TOGETHER?
I THINK I GOT THIS.
STARFIRE! YOU SEE THAT WATER TOWER?
HOOK ME UP WITH SOME H2O.
K-ZZOTTTT
SHOOSSH
"WHAT'S THE BEST WAY TO STOP A PUPPET?"

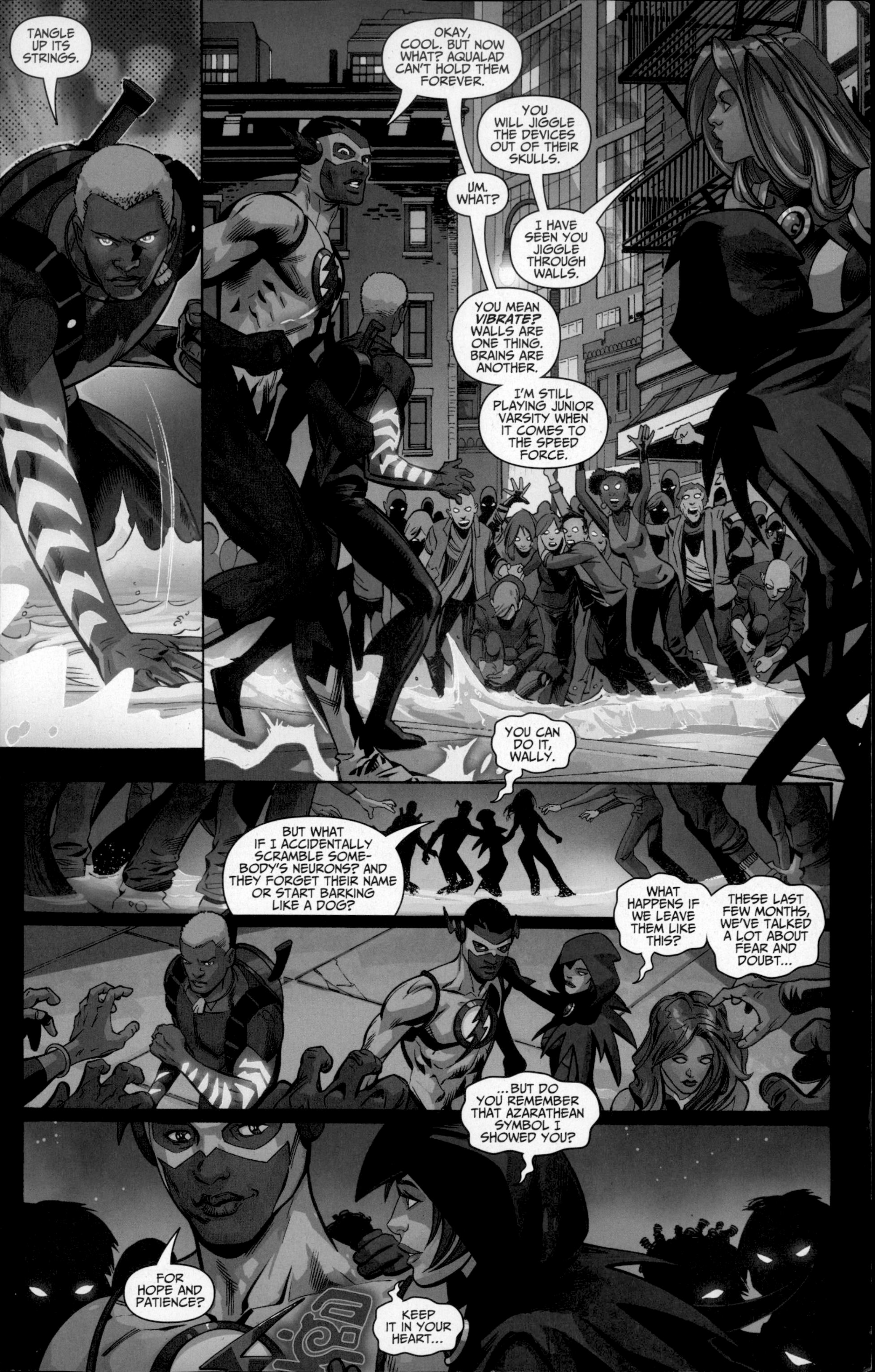
TANGLE UP ITS STRINGS.
OKAY, COOL. BUT NOW WHAT? AQUALAD CAN'T HOLD THEM FOREVER.
YOU WILL JIGGLE THE DEVICES OUT OF THEIR SKULLS.
UM. WHAT?
I HAVE SEEN YOU JIGGLE THROUGH WALLS.
YOU MEAN *VIBRATE?* WALLS ARE ONE THING. BRAINS ARE ANOTHER.
I'M STILL PLAYING JUNIOR VARSITY WHEN IT COMES TO THE SPEED FORCE.
YOU CAN DO IT, WALLY.
BUT WHAT IF I ACCIDENTALLY SCRAMBLE SOME-BODY'S NEURONS? AND THEY FORGET THEIR NAME OR START BARKING LIKE A DOG?
WHAT HAPPENS IF WE LEAVE THEM LIKE THIS?
THESE LAST FEW MONTHS, WE'VE TALKED A LOT ABOUT FEAR AND DOUBT...
...BUT DO YOU REMEMBER THAT AZARATHEAN SYMBOL I SHOWED YOU?
FOR HOPE AND PATIENCE?
KEEP IT IN YOUR HEART...

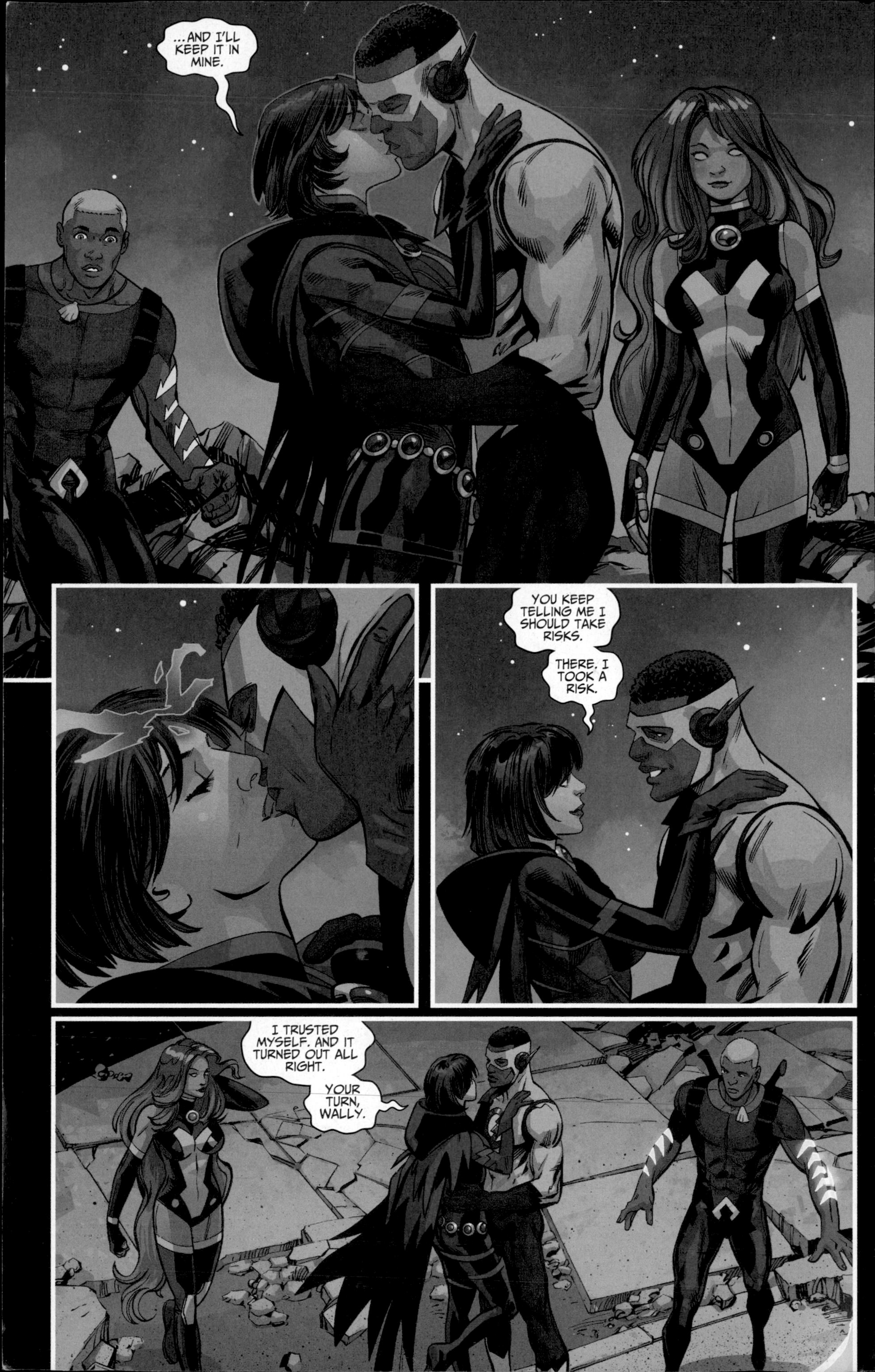
...AND I'LL KEEP IT IN MINE.
YOU KEEP TELLING ME I SHOULD TAKE RISKS.
THERE. I TOOK A RISK.
I TRUSTED MYSELF. AND IT TURNED OUT ALL RIGHT.
YOUR TURN, WALLY.

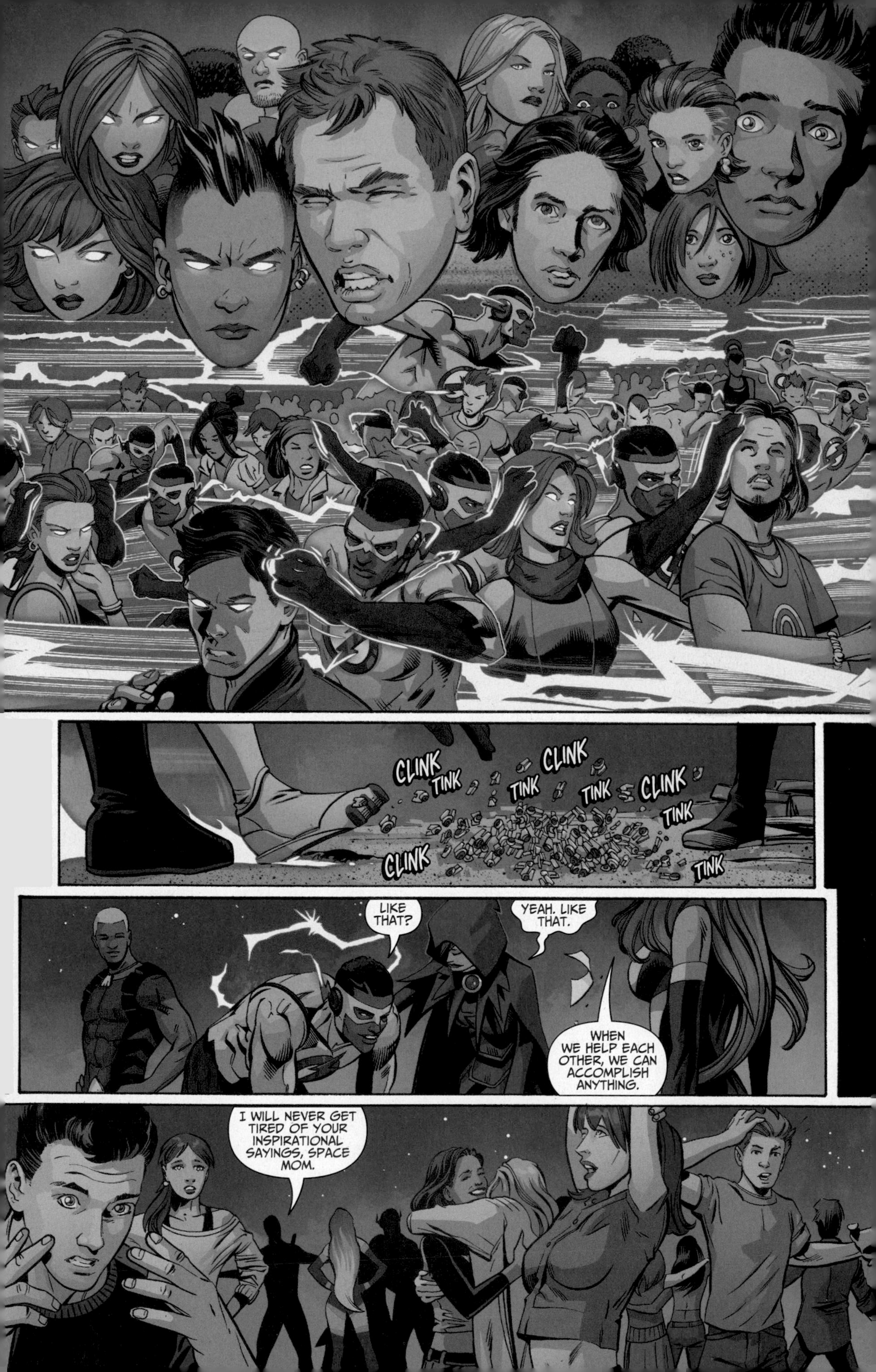
CLINK
TINK
CLINK
TINK
TINK
CLINK
TINK
CLINK
TINK
LIKE THAT?
YEAH. LIKE THAT.
WHEN WE HELP EACH OTHER, WE CAN ACCOMPLISH ANYTHING.
I WILL NEVER GET TIRED OF YOUR INSPIRATIONAL SAYINGS, SPACE MOM.

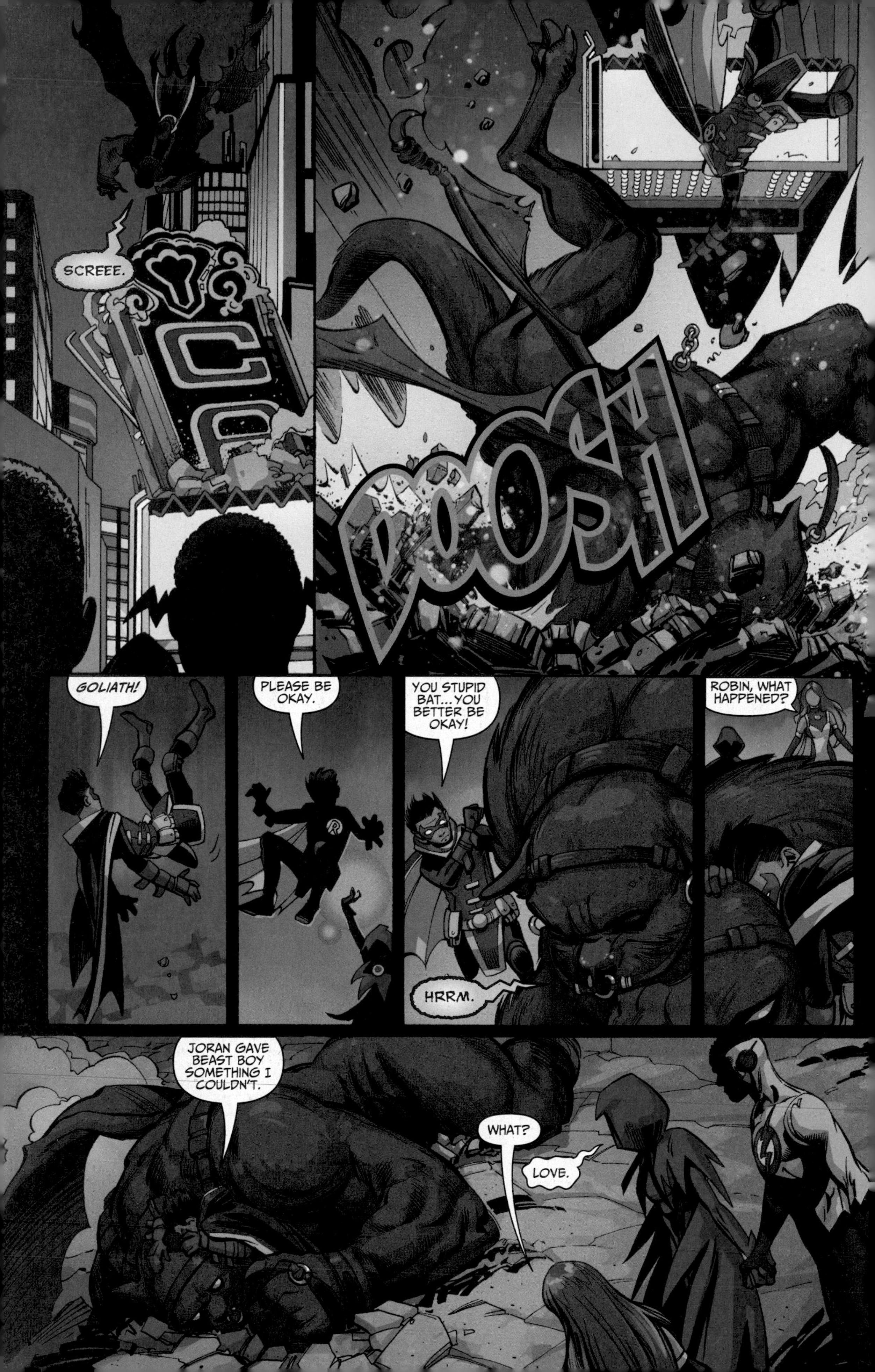
SCREEE.
BOOSH
GOLIATH!
PLEASE BE OKAY.
YOU STUPID BAT... YOU BETTER BE OKAY!
HRRM.
ROBIN, WHAT HAPPENED?
JORAN GAVE BEAST BOY SOMETHING I COULDN'T.
WHAT?
LOVE.

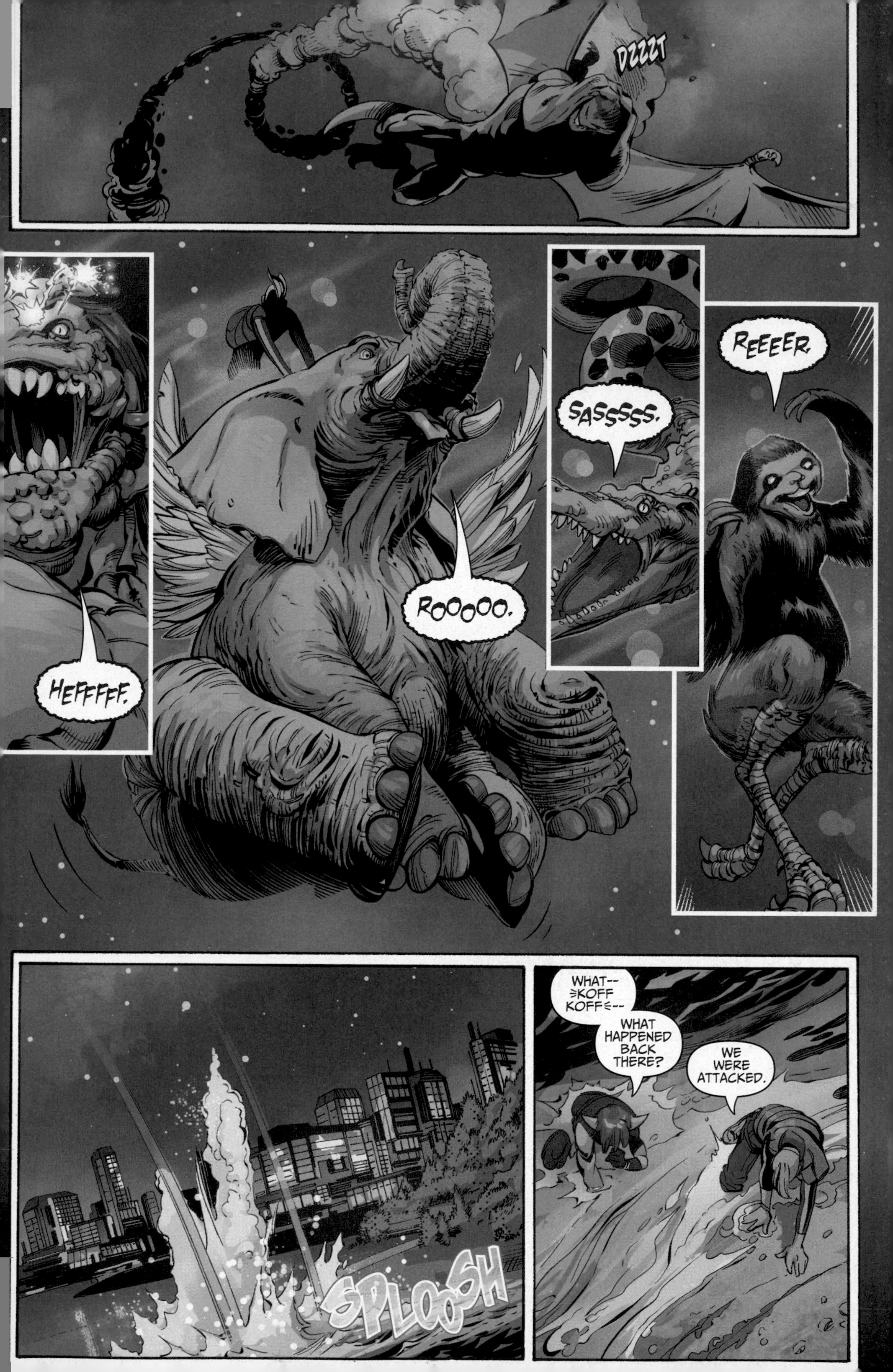
DZZZT
HEFFFFF.
ROOOOO.
SASSSSS.
REEEER.
SPLOOSH
WHAT-- ≡KOFF KOFF≡--
WHAT HAPPENED BACK THERE?
WE WERE ATTACKED.

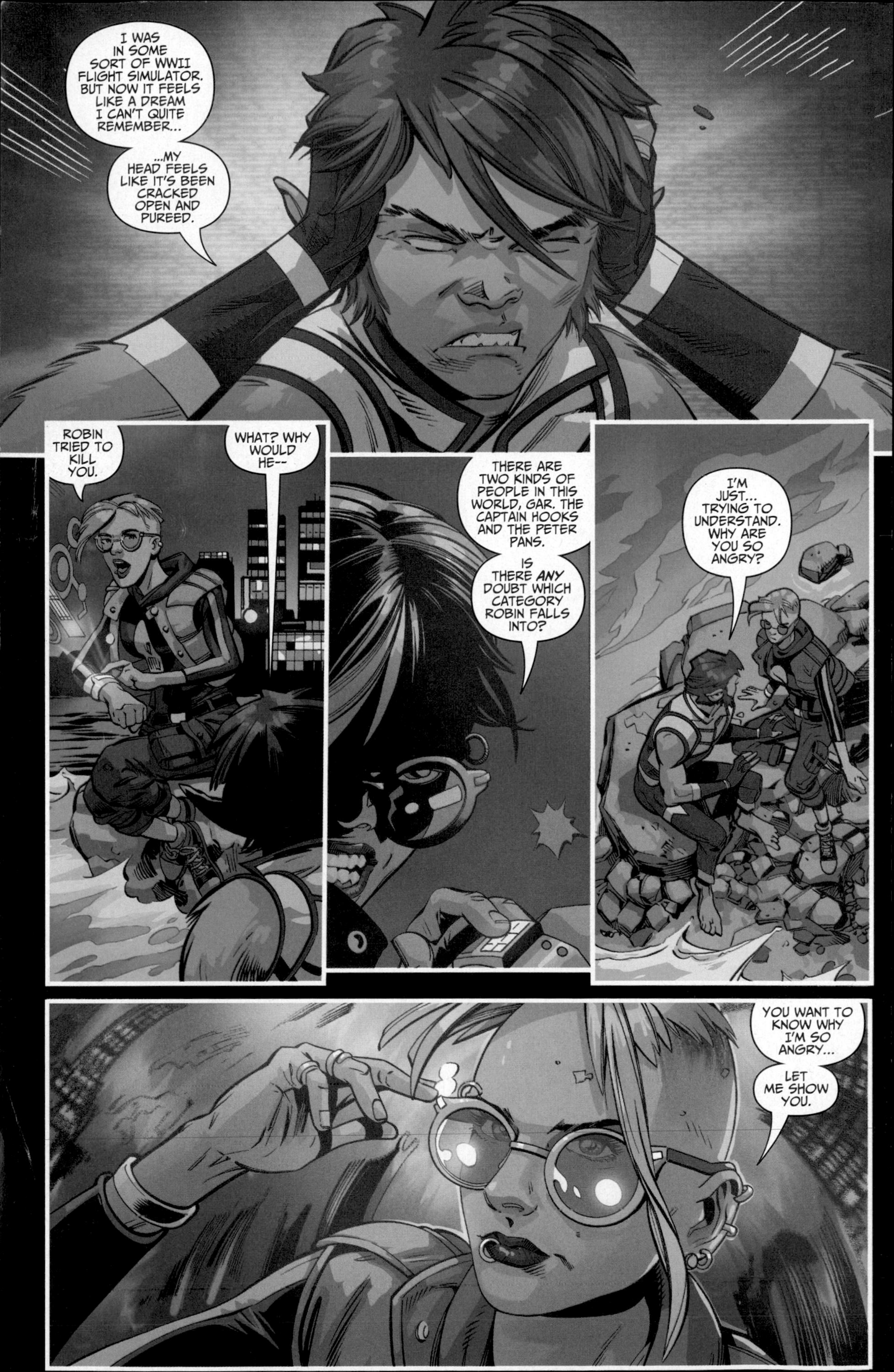
I WAS IN SOME SORT OF WWII FLIGHT SIMULATOR. BUT NOW IT FEELS LIKE A DREAM I CAN'T QUITE REMEMBER...
...MY HEAD FEELS LIKE IT'S BEEN CRACKED OPEN AND PUREED.
ROBIN TRIED TO KILL YOU.
WHAT? WHY WOULD HE--
THERE ARE TWO KINDS OF PEOPLE IN THIS WORLD, GAR. THE CAPTAIN HOOKS AND THE PETER PANS.
IS THERE *ANY* DOUBT WHICH CATEGORY ROBIN FALLS INTO?
I'M JUST... TRYING TO UNDERSTAND. WHY ARE YOU SO ANGRY?
YOU WANT TO KNOW WHY I'M SO ANGRY...
LET ME SHOW YOU.

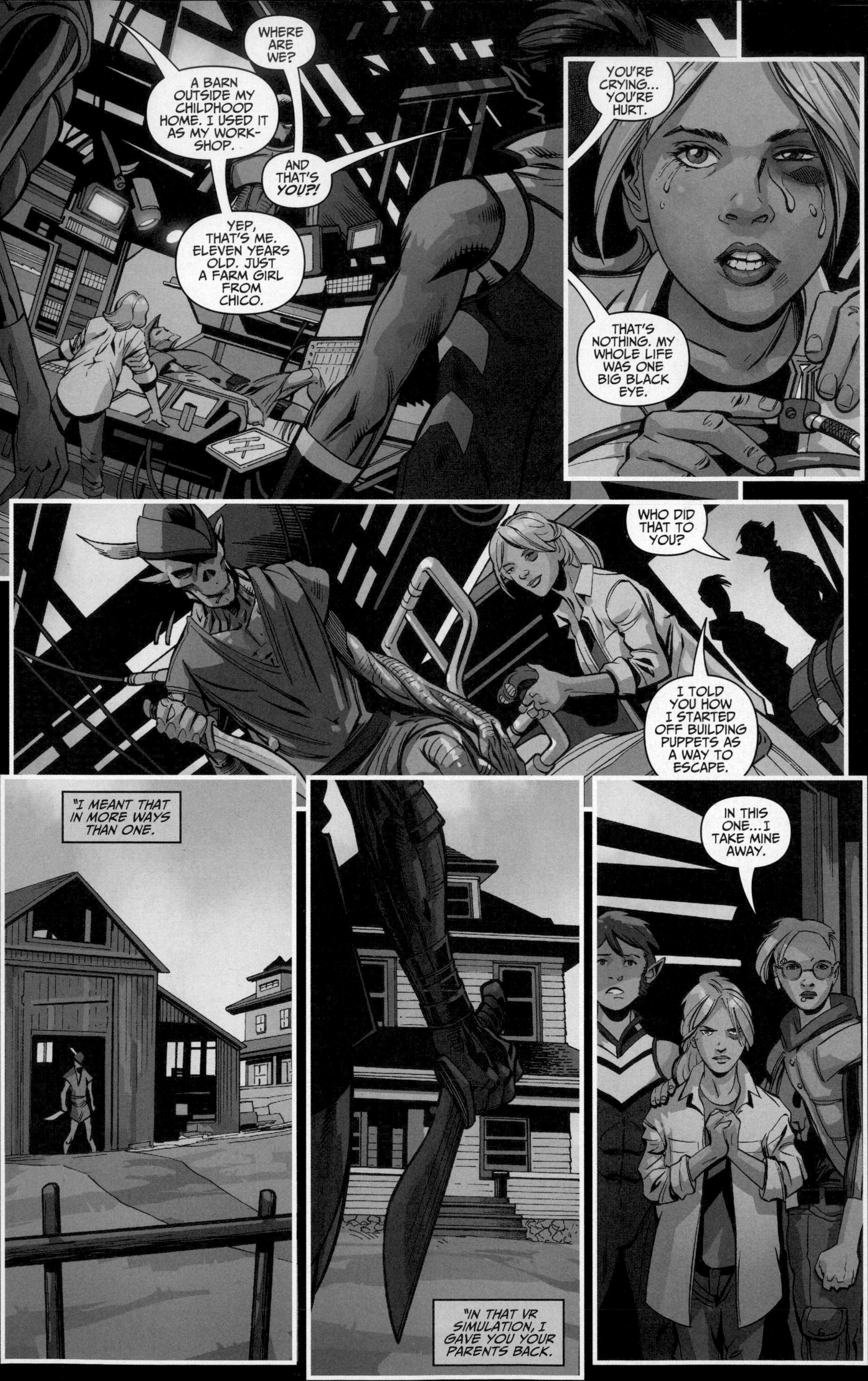
WHERE ARE WE?
A BARN OUTSIDE MY CHILDHOOD HOME. I USED IT AS MY WORK-SHOP.
AND THAT'S *YOU?!*
YEP, THAT'S ME. ELEVEN YEARS OLD. JUST A FARM GIRL FROM CHICO.
YOU'RE CRYING... YOU'RE HURT.
THAT'S NOTHING. MY WHOLE LIFE WAS ONE BIG BLACK EYE.
WHO DID THAT TO YOU?
I TOLD YOU HOW I STARTED OFF BUILDING PUPPETS AS A WAY TO ESCAPE.
"I MEANT THAT IN MORE WAYS THAN ONE.
"IN THAT VR SIMULATION, I GAVE YOU YOUR PARENTS BACK.
IN THIS ONE...I TAKE MINE AWAY.

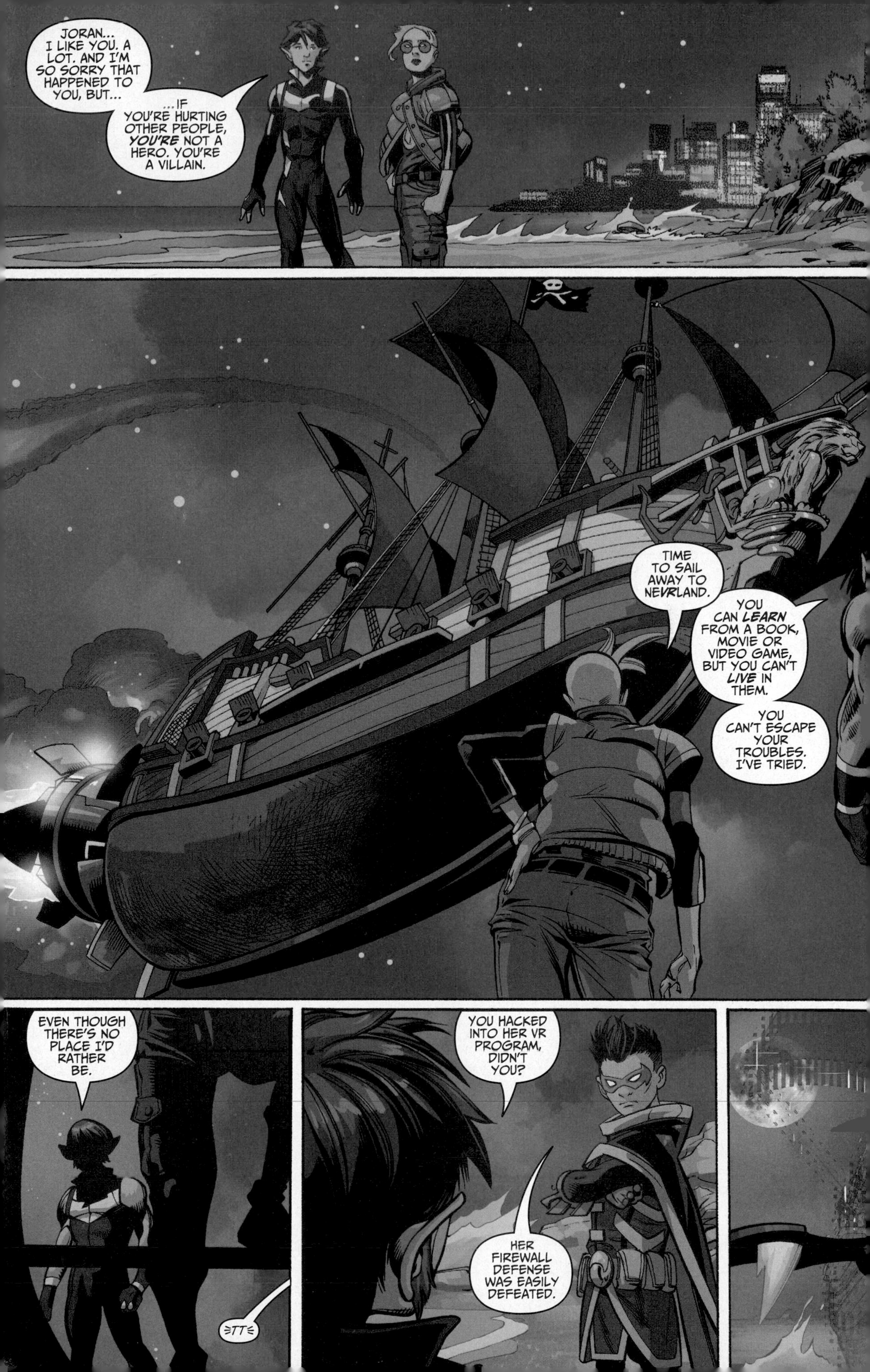
JORAN... I LIKE YOU. A LOT. AND I'M SO SORRY THAT HAPPENED TO YOU, BUT...
...IF YOU'RE HURTING OTHER PEOPLE, ***YOU'RE*** NOT A HERO. YOU'RE A VILLAIN.
TIME TO SAIL AWAY TO NEV**VR**LAND.
YOU CAN ***LEARN*** FROM A BOOK, MOVIE OR VIDEO GAME, BUT YOU CAN'T ***LIVE*** IN THEM.
YOU CAN'T ESCAPE YOUR TROUBLES. I'VE TRIED.
EVEN THOUGH THERE'S NO PLACE I'D RATHER BE.
TT
YOU HACKED INTO HER VR PROGRAM, DIDN'T YOU?
HER FIREWALL DEFENSE WAS EASILY DEFEATED.

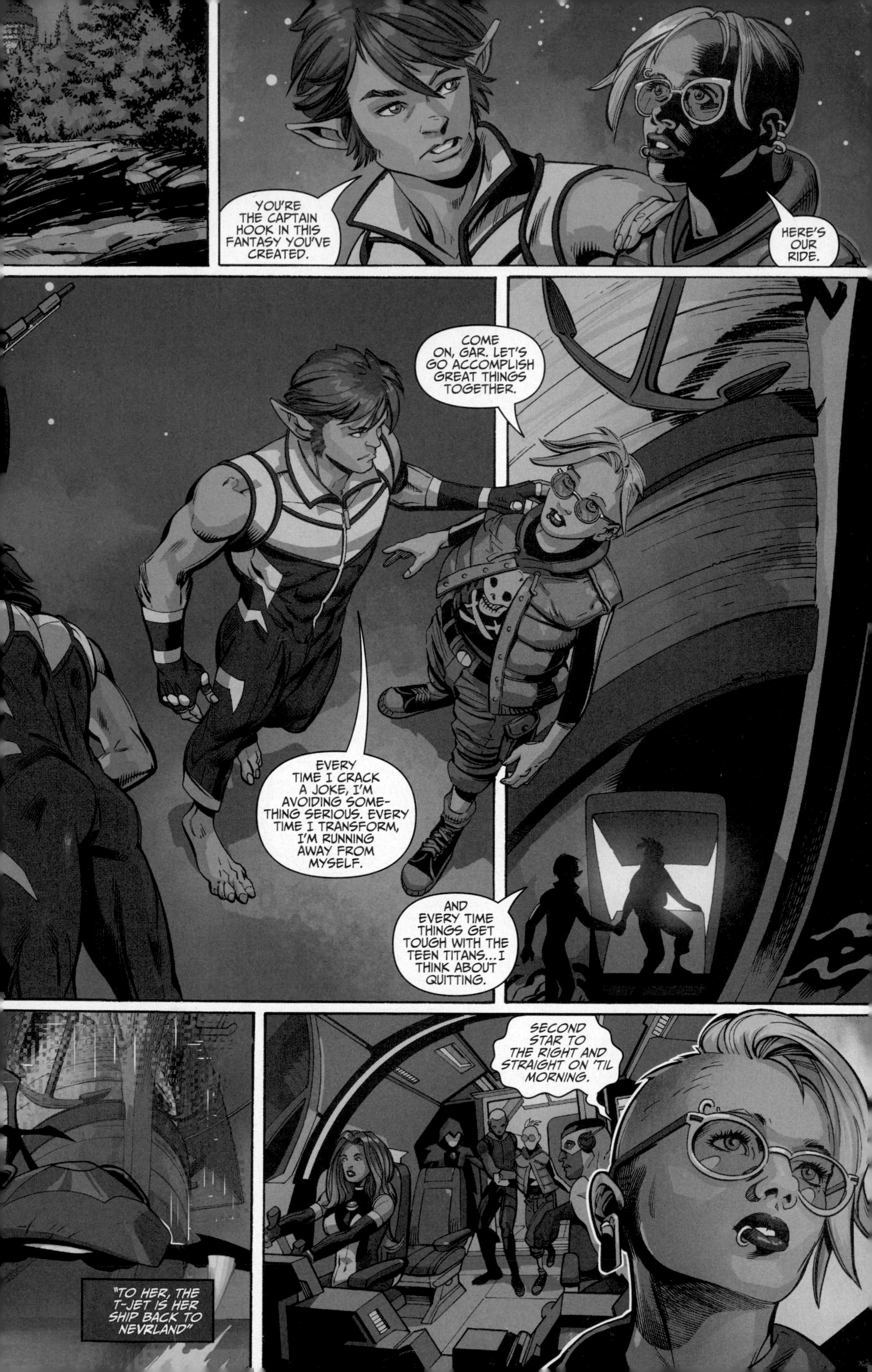
YOU'RE THE CAPTAIN HOOK IN THIS FANTASY YOU'VE CREATED.
HERE'S OUR RIDE.
COME ON, GAR. LET'S GO ACCOMPLISH GREAT THINGS TOGETHER.
EVERY TIME I CRACK A JOKE, I'M AVOIDING SOMETHING SERIOUS. EVERY TIME I TRANSFORM, I'M RUNNING AWAY FROM MYSELF.
AND EVERY TIME THINGS GET TOUGH WITH THE TEEN TITANS... I THINK ABOUT QUITTING.
"TO HER, THE T-JET IS HER SHIP BACK TO NEVRLAND"
SECOND STAR TO THE RIGHT AND STRAIGHT ON 'TIL MORNING.

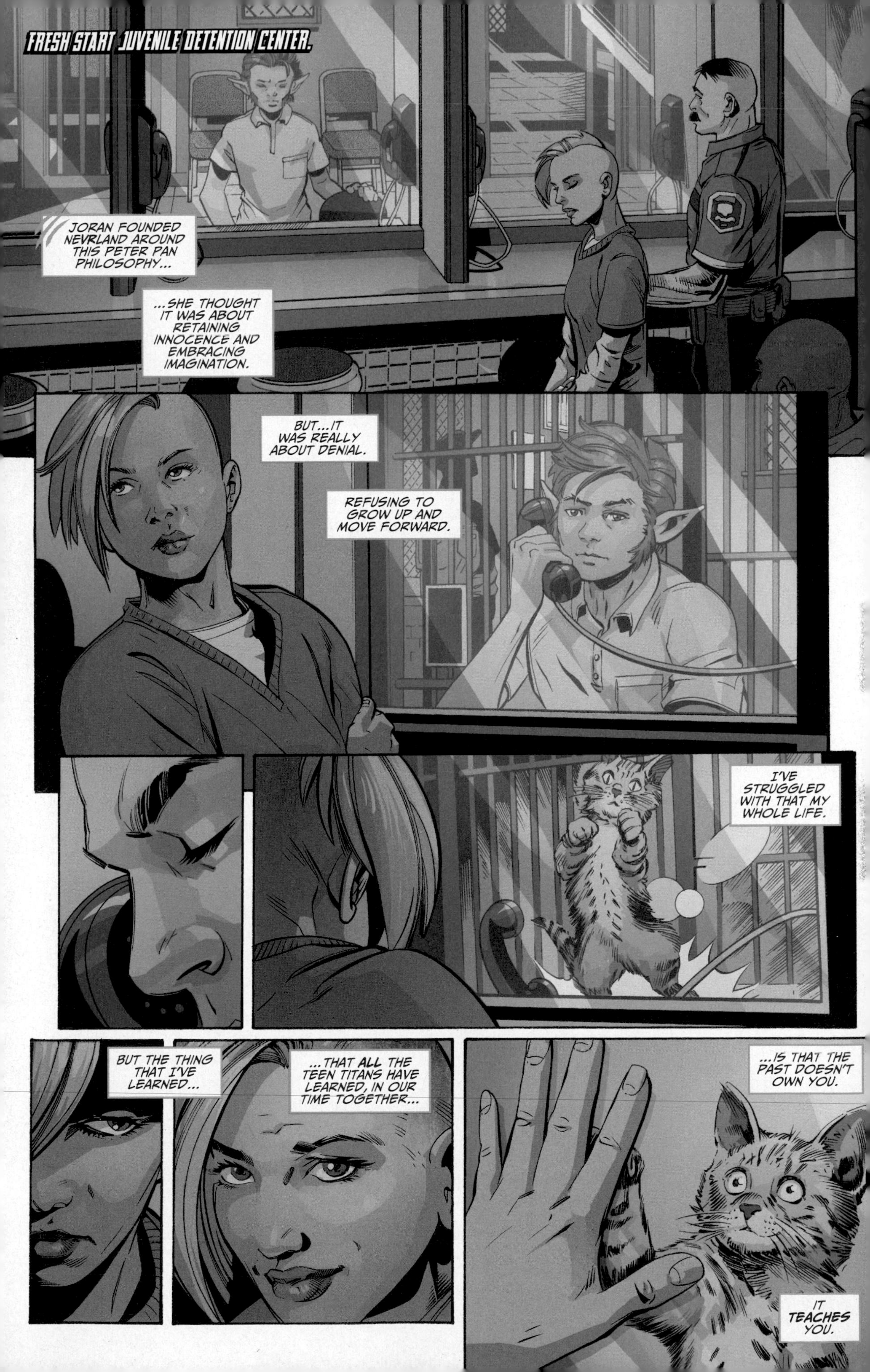
FRESH START JUVENILE DETENTION CENTER.
JORAN FOUNDED NEVRLAND AROUND THIS PETER PAN PHILOSOPHY...
...SHE THOUGHT IT WAS ABOUT RETAINING INNOCENCE AND EMBRACING IMAGINATION.
BUT...IT WAS REALLY ABOUT DENIAL.
REFUSING TO GROW UP AND MOVE FORWARD.
I'VE STRUGGLED WITH THAT MY WHOLE LIFE.
BUT THE THING THAT I'VE LEARNED...
...THAT ALL THE TEEN TITANS HAVE LEARNED, IN OUR TIME TOGETHER...
...IS THAT THE PAST DOESN'T OWN YOU.
IT TEACHES YOU.

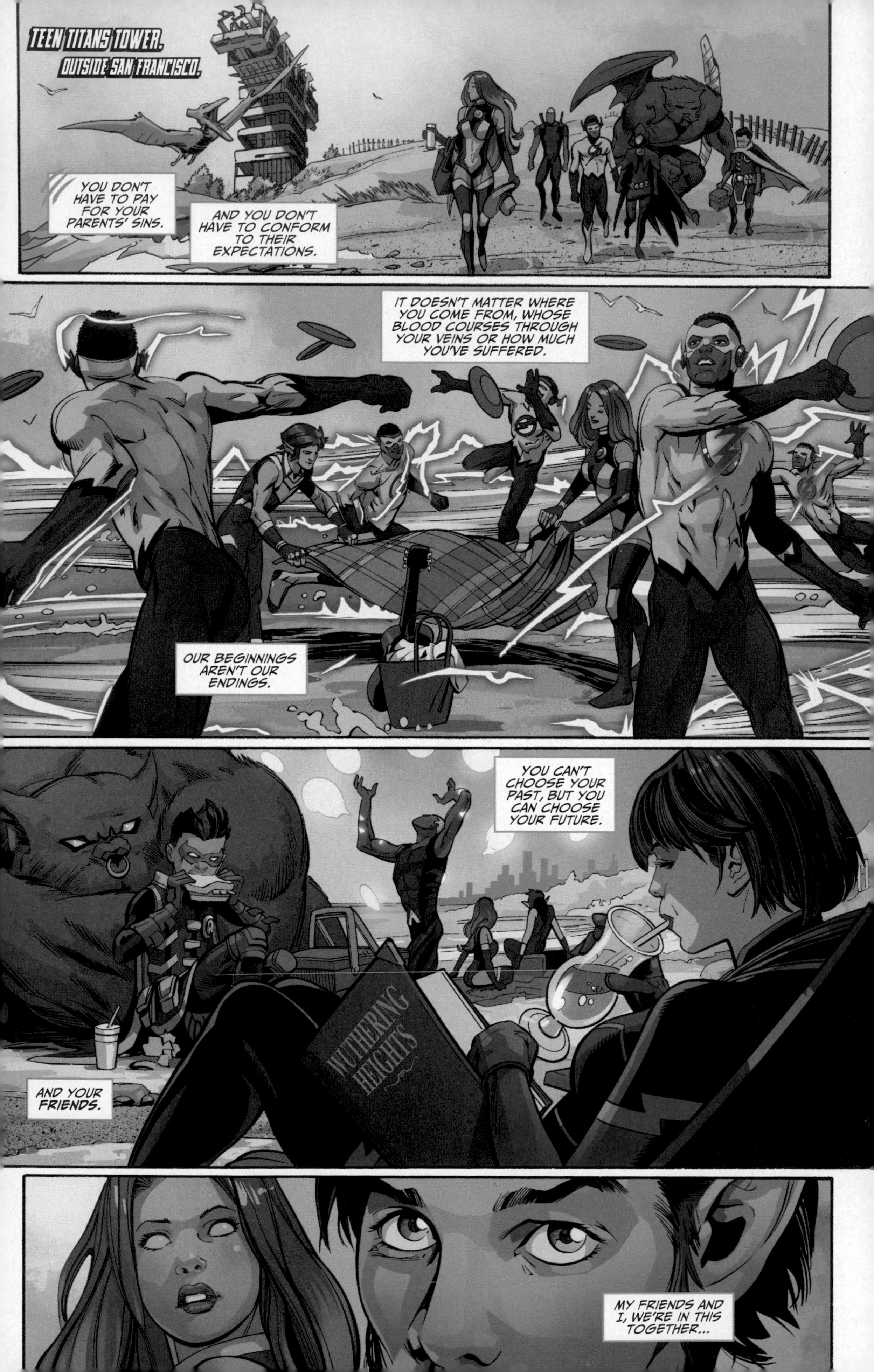
TEEN TITANS TOWER.
OUTSIDE SAN FRANCISCO.
YOU DON'T HAVE TO PAY FOR YOUR PARENTS' SINS.
AND YOU DON'T HAVE TO CONFORM TO THEIR EXPECTATIONS.
IT DOESN'T MATTER WHERE YOU COME FROM, WHOSE BLOOD COURSES THROUGH YOUR VEINS OR HOW MUCH YOU'VE SUFFERED.
OUR BEGINNINGS AREN'T OUR ENDINGS.
YOU CAN'T CHOOSE YOUR PAST, BUT YOU CAN CHOOSE YOUR FUTURE.
AND YOUR FRIENDS.
WUTHERING HEIGHTS
MY FRIENDS AND I, WE'RE IN THIS TOGETHER...

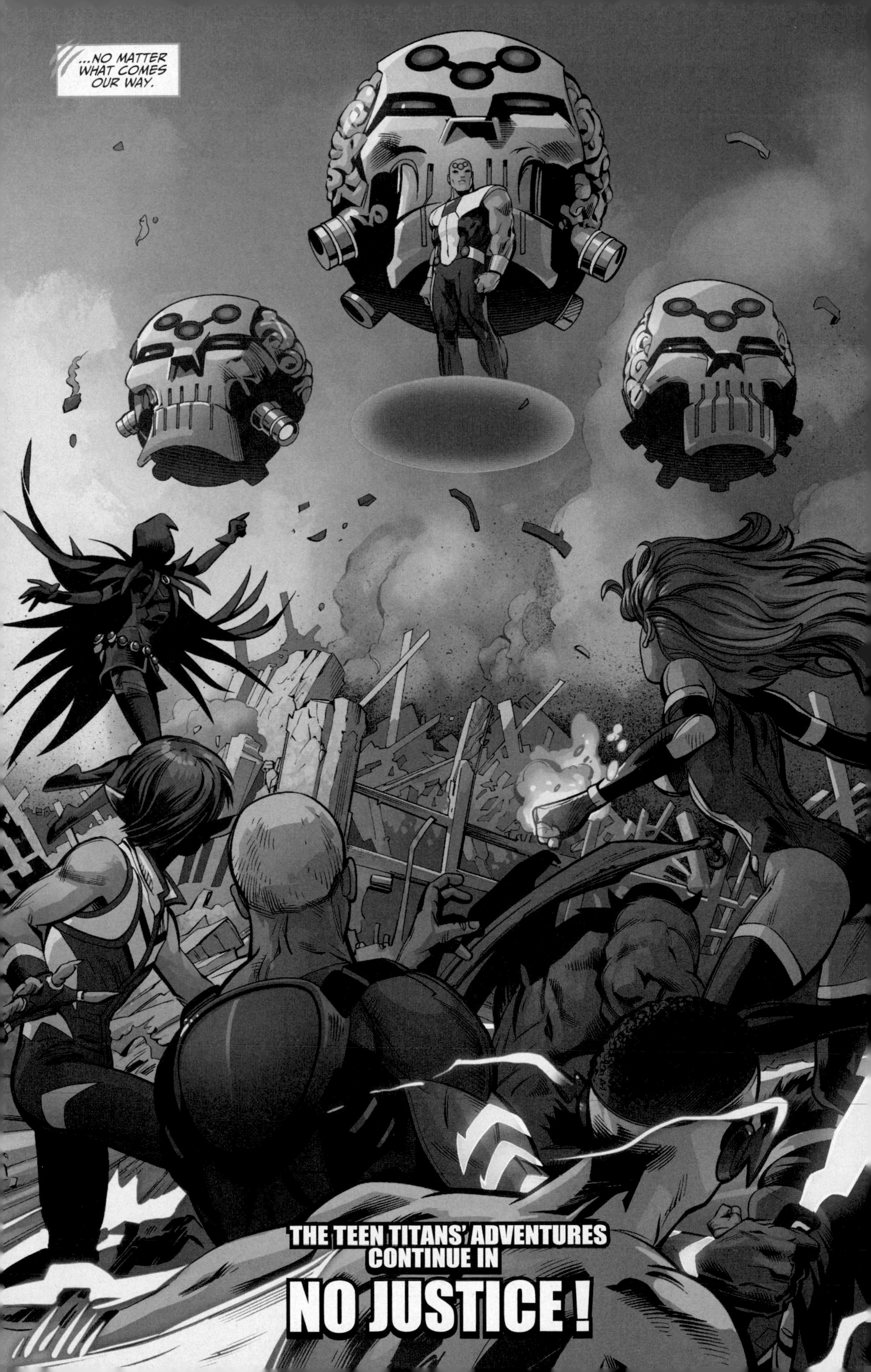
...NO MATTER WHAT COMES OUR WAY.
THE TEEN TITANS' ADVENTURES CONTINUE IN
NO JUSTICE !

TEEN TITANS

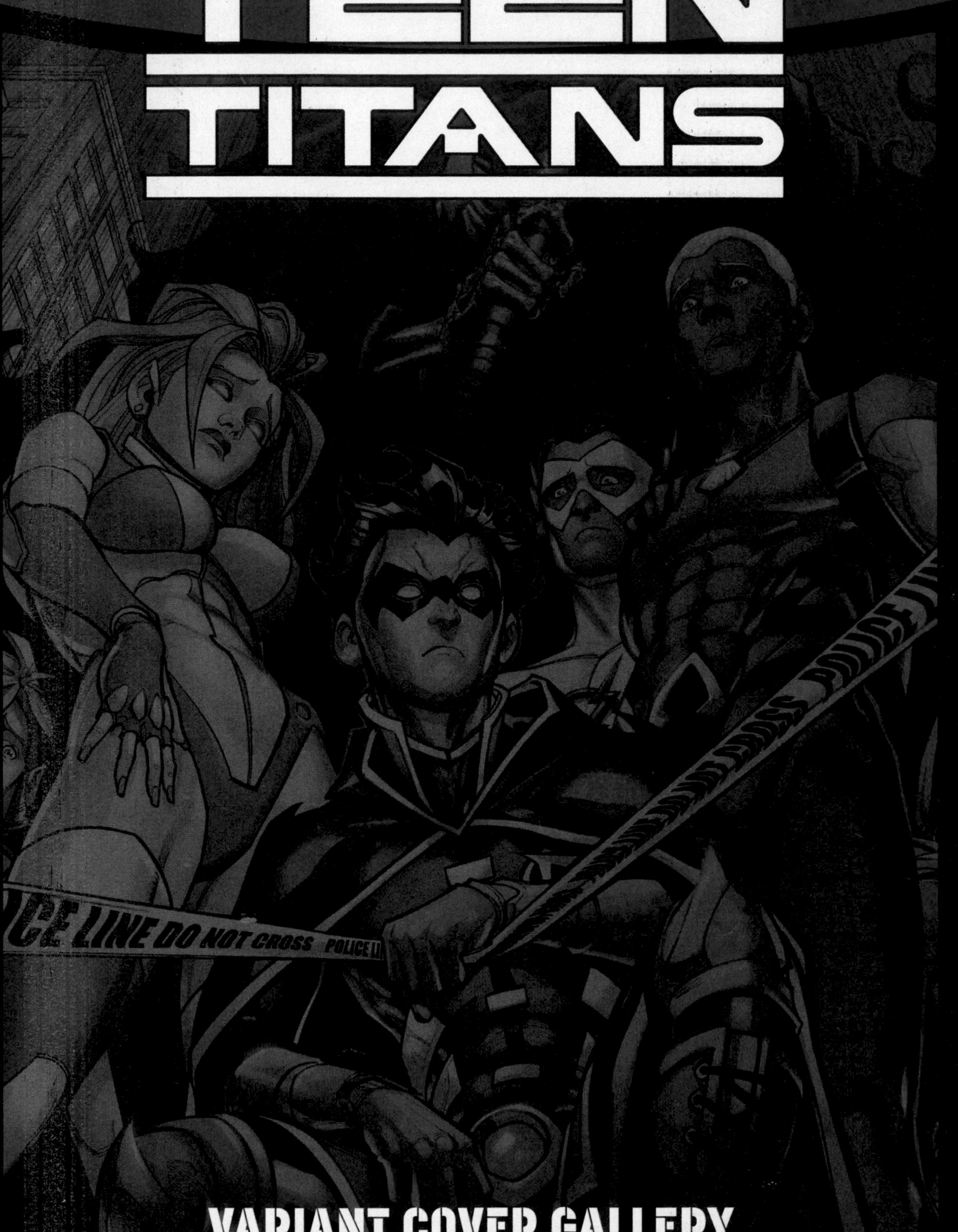
CE LINE DO NOT CROSS POLICE LI

VARIANT COVER GALLERY

TEEN TITANS #13 variant cover
by CHAD HARDIN and ALEX SINCLAIR

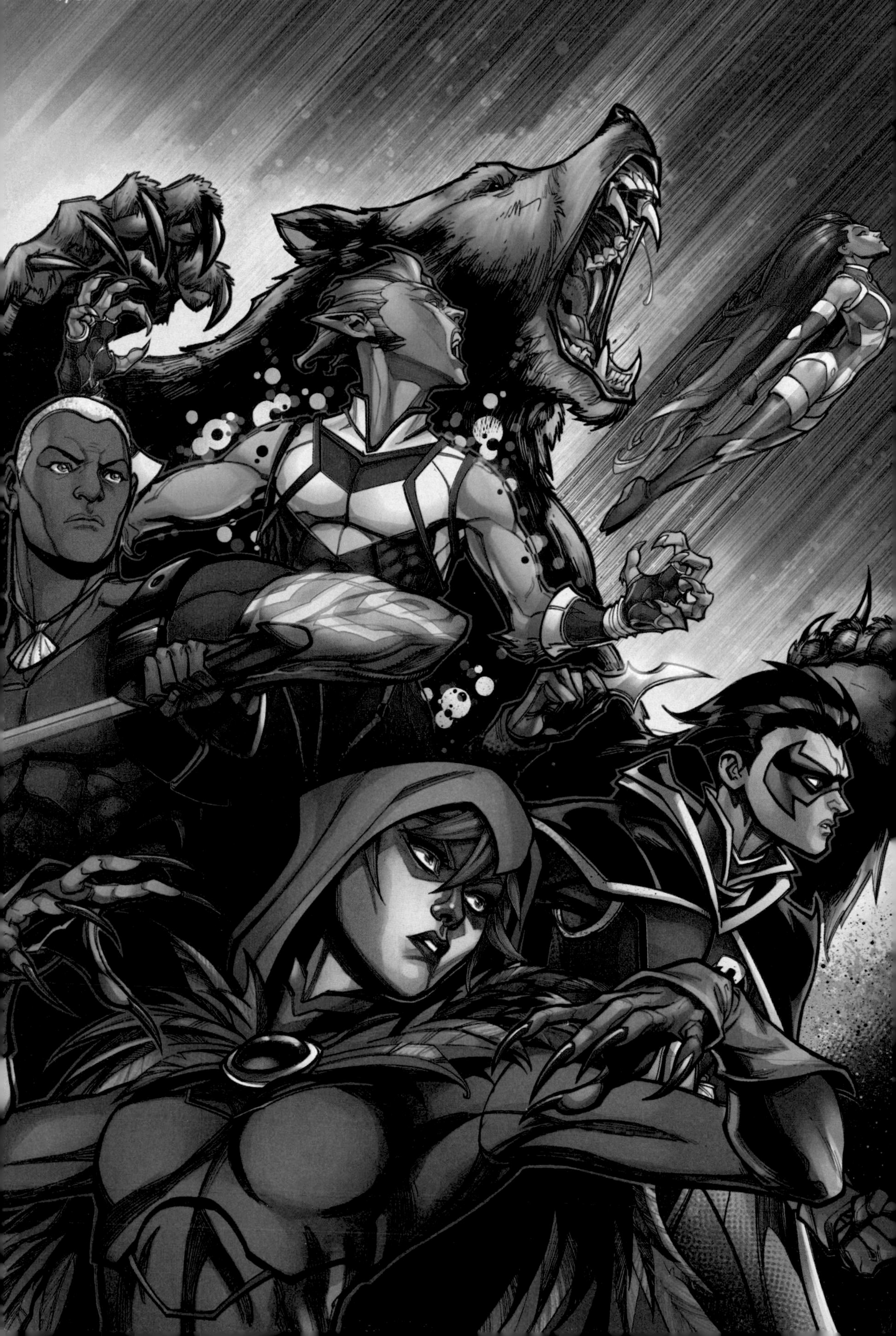

TEEN TITANS #14 variant cover
by CHAD HARDIN and ALEX SINCLAIR

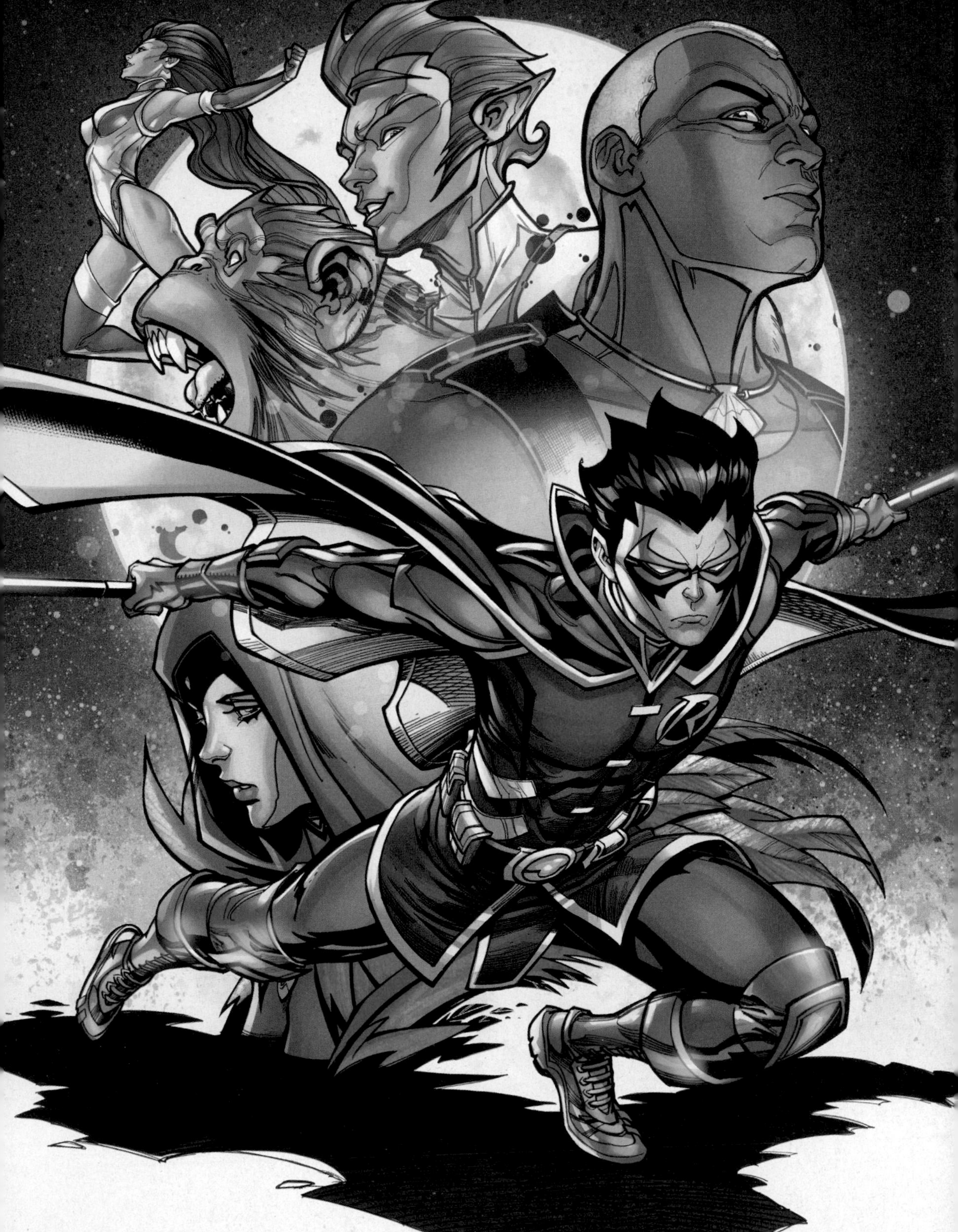

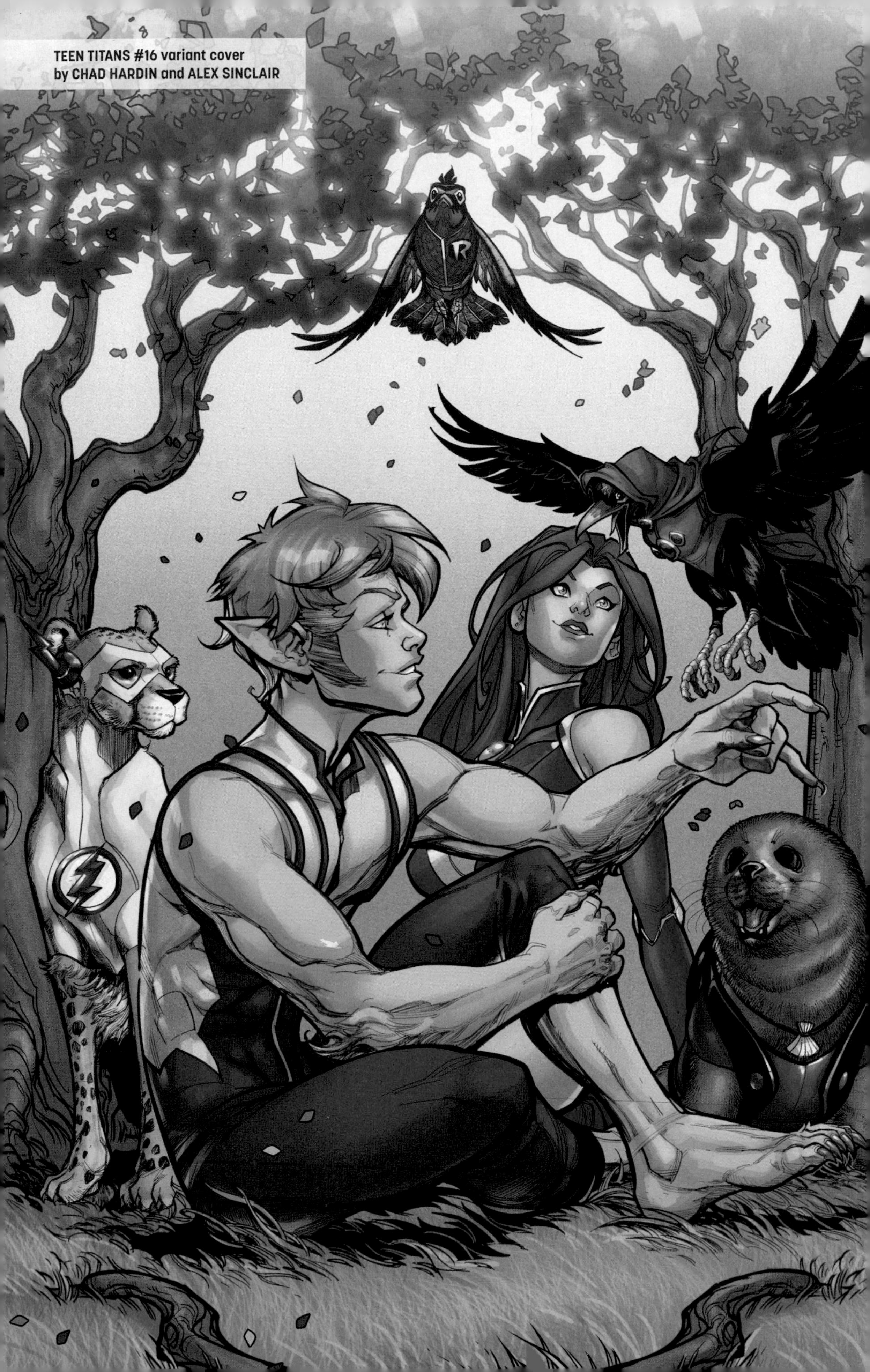
R

TEEN TITANS #16 variant cover
by CHAD HARDIN and ALEX SINCLAIR

TEEN TITANS #17 variant cover
by CHAD HARDIN and ALEX SINCLAIR

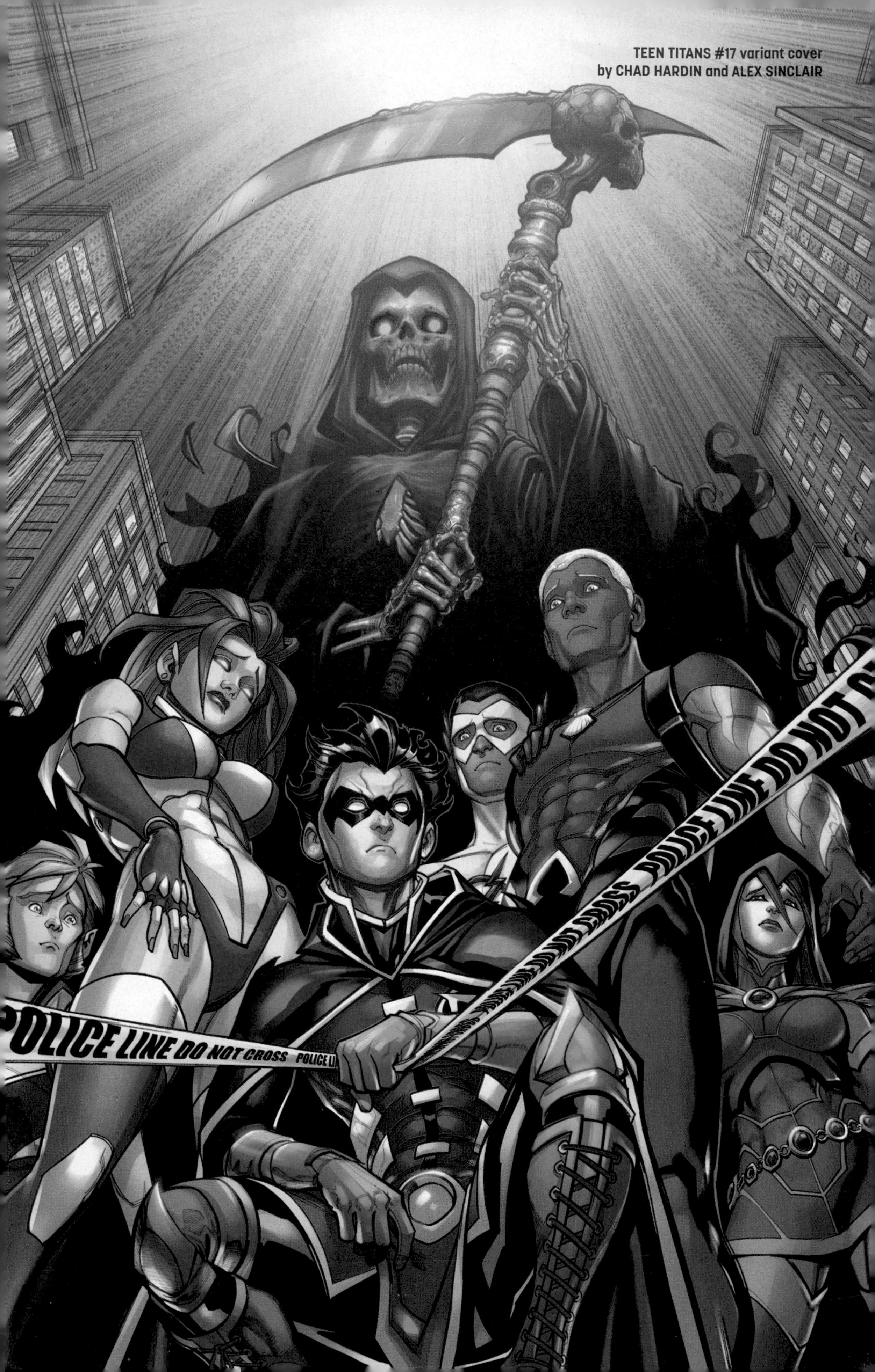
POLICE LINE DO NOT CROSS POLICE LI
POLICE LINE DO NOT CROSS

TEEN TITANS #18 variant cover
by JOËLLE JONES and FCO PLASCENCIA

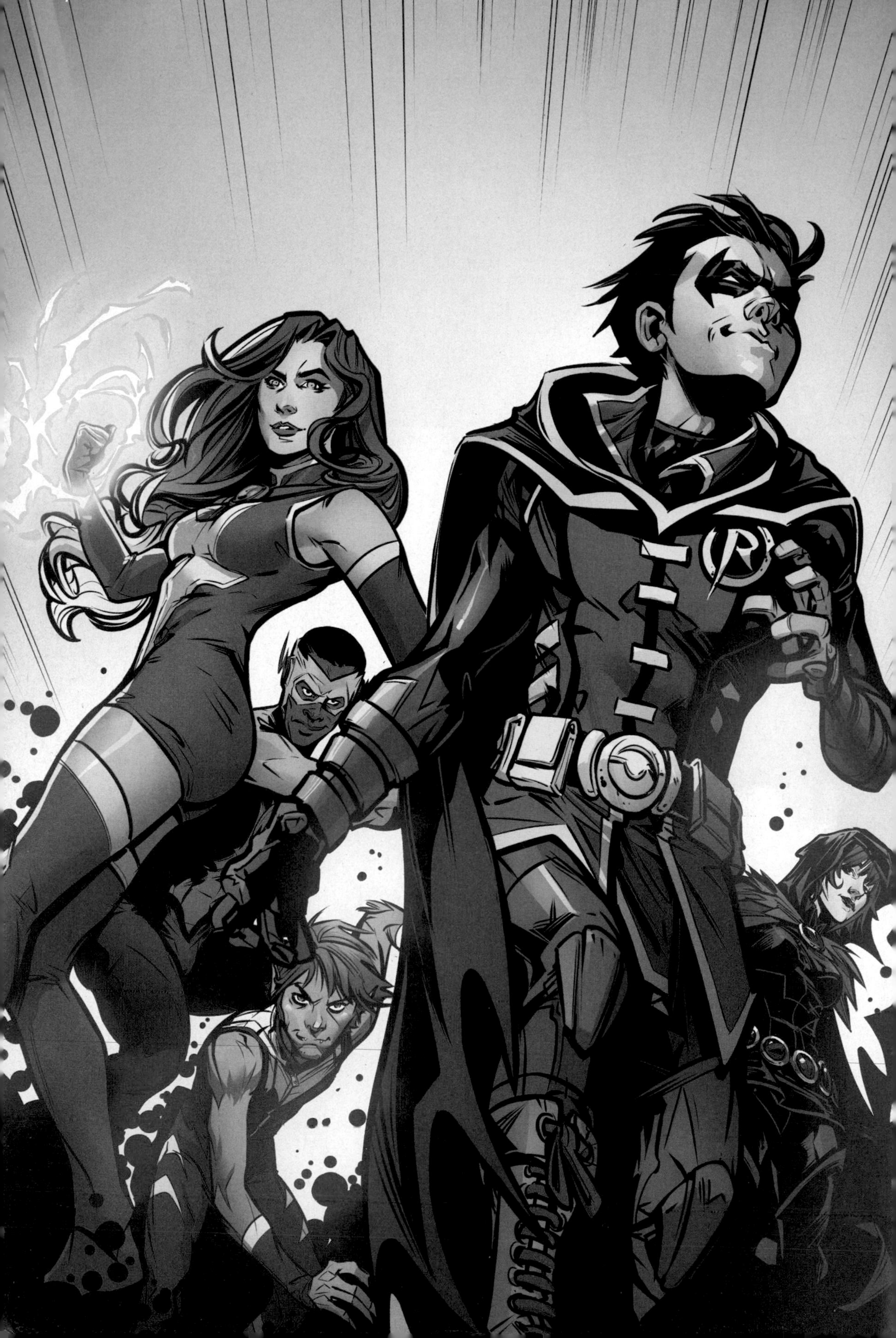

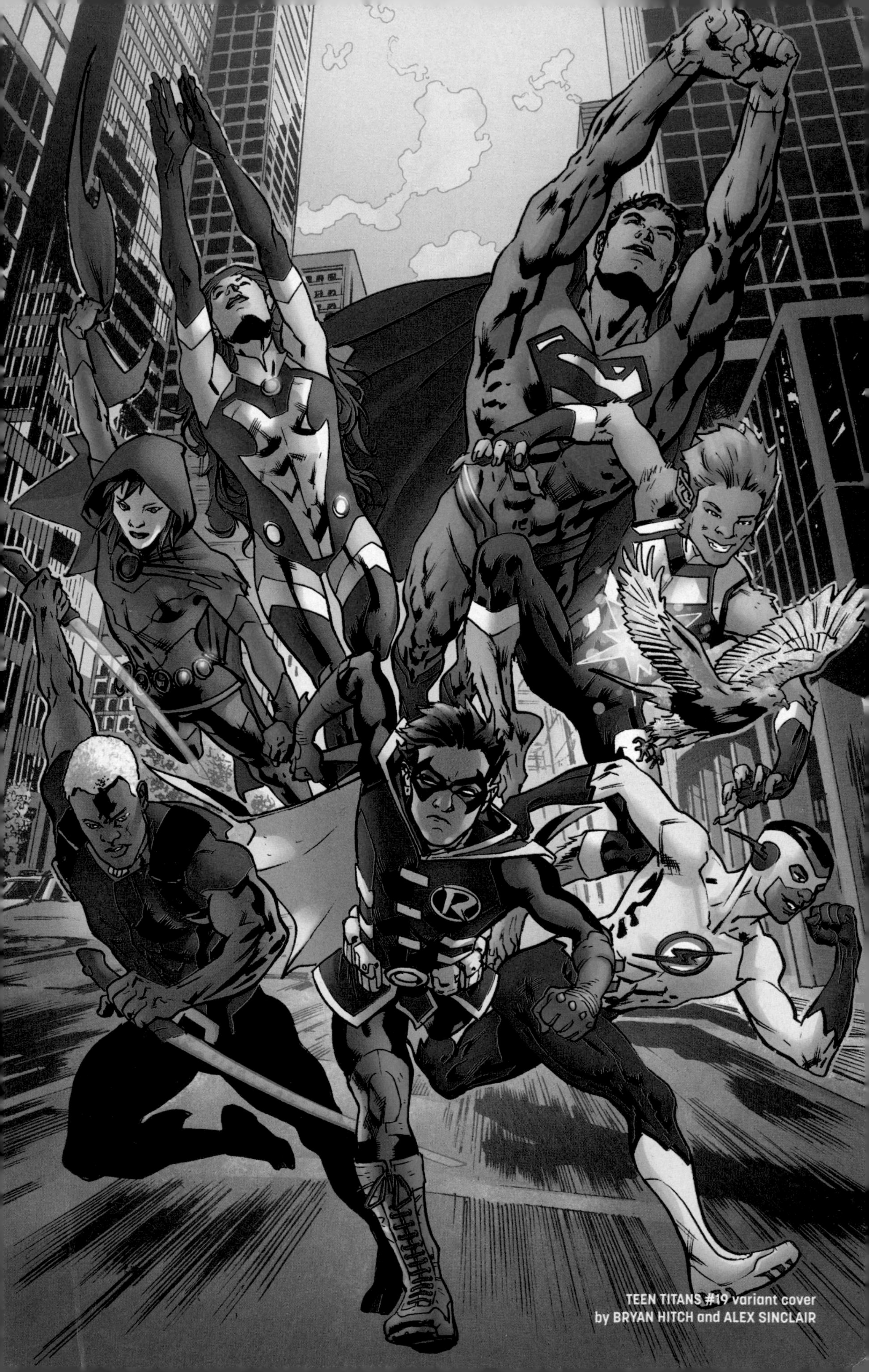

TEEN TITANS #19 variant cover
by BRYAN HITCH and ALEX SINCLAIR

DC UNIVERSE REBIRTH

THE FLASH
VOL. 1: LIGHTNING STRIKES TWICE

JOSHUA WILLIAMSON
with CARMINE DI GIANDOMENICO
and IVAN PLASCENCIA

"Joshua Williamson's writing is on point."
– NERDIST

"Williamson makes [The Flash] as accessible as possible to new readers."
– COMIC BOOK RESOURCES

VOL.1 LIGHTNING STRIKES TWICE
JOSHUA WILLIAMSON ★ CARMINE DI GIANDOMENICO ★ IVAN PLASCENCIA

**JUSTICE LEAGUE VOL. 1:
THE EXTINCTION MACHINES**

**TITANS VOL. 1:
THE RETURN OF WALLY WEST**

**HAL JORDAN AND
THE GREEN LANTERN CORPS VOL. 1:
SINESTRO'S LAW**

Get more DC graphic novels wherever comics and books are sold!

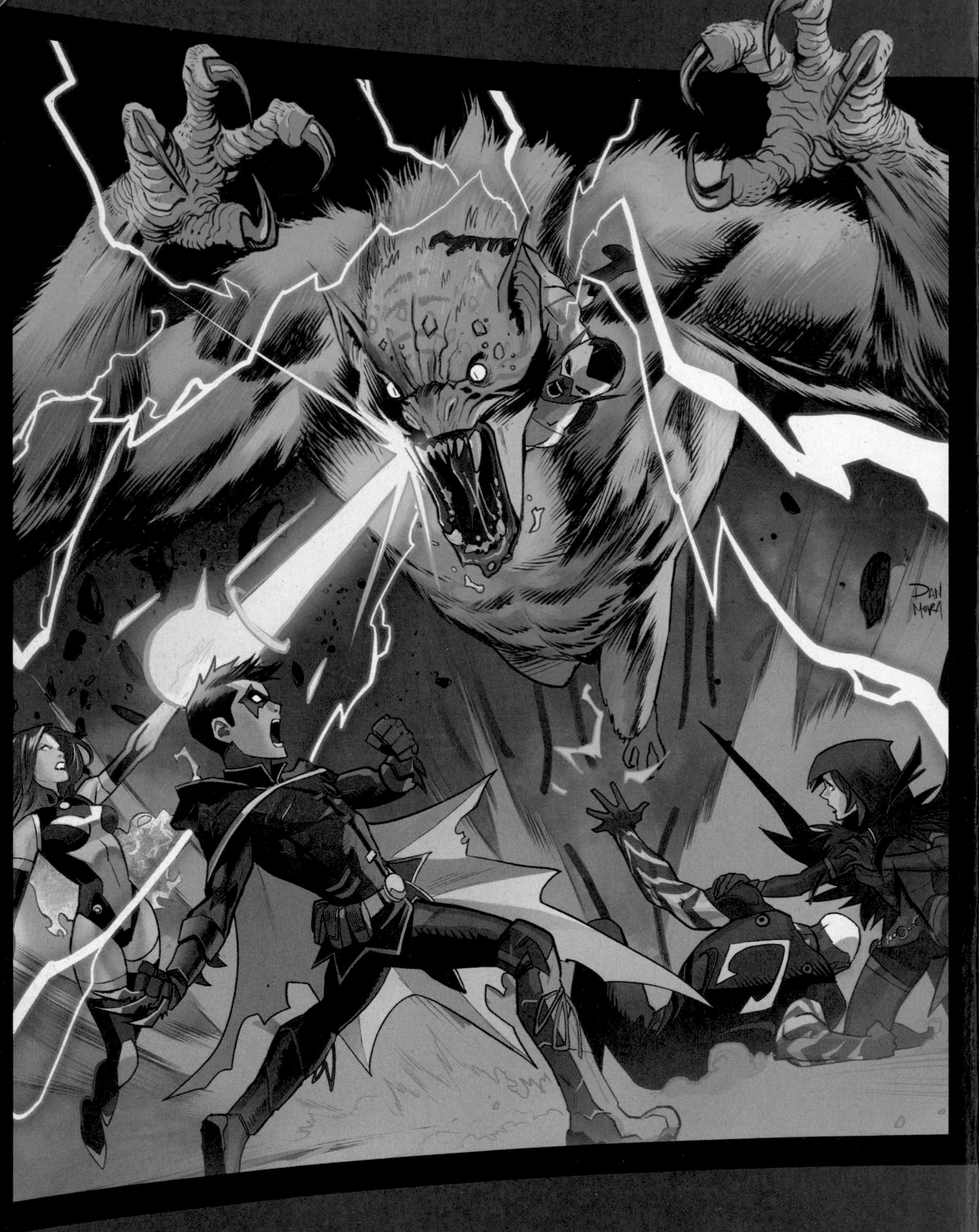
DAN MORA

RECEIVED

NO LONGER
S

D0608294

TY O

RAR

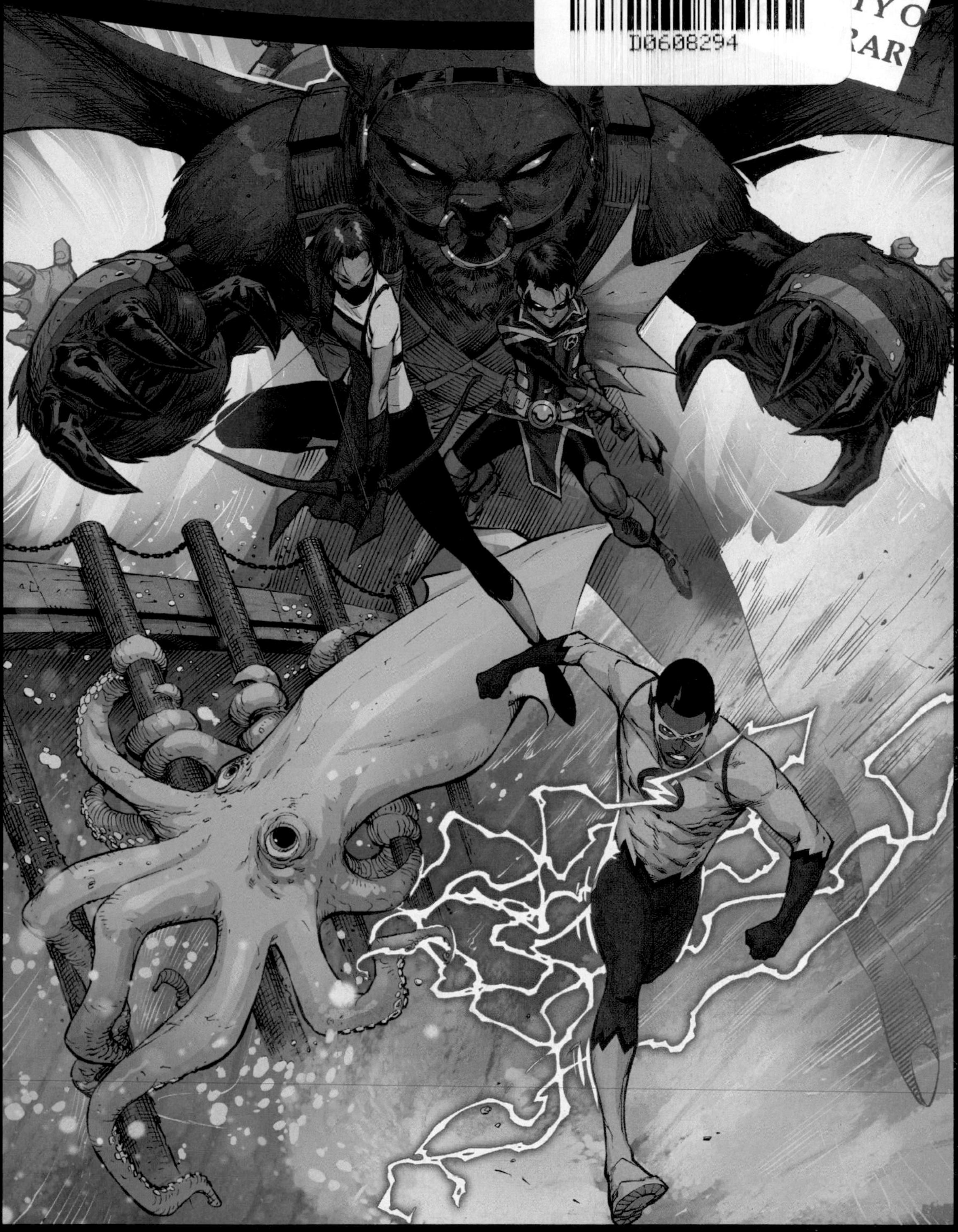

TEEN TITANS

VOL.3 THE RETURN OF KID FLASH